EMPATHY

Development, Training, and Consequences

EMPATHY

Development, Training, and Consequences

Arnold P. Goldstein
Gerald Y. Michaels
Syracuse University

LEA LAWRENCE ERLBAUM ASSOCIATES, PUBLISHERS
1985   Hillsdale, New Jersey   London

Lawrence Erlbaum Associates, Inc., Publishers
365 Broadway
Hillsdale, New Jersey 07642

Library of Congress Cataloging in Publication Data

Goldstein, Arnold P.
  Empathy: development training, and consequences.

  Includes bibliographies and index.
  1. Empathy.   I. Michaels, Gerald Y.   II. Title.
[DNLM: 1. Empathy.   BF 575.E55 G624e]
BF575.E55G65   1985   155.2'32   85-1516
ISBN 0-89859-538-X

Table of Contents

Preface

This book seeks to thoroughly examine and better understand a dimension of interpersonal relations which has often proven elusive, confusing, and quite difficult to operationalize. Empathy has been diversely defined, hard to measure, often resistant to change, yet emerges as a singularly important influence in human interaction. Our lengthy effort to better understand its nature, consequences and alteration has not been an easy journey, and yet has been a rewarding one. This book presents the fruits of that journey, and thus we hope the reader will feel equally rewarded.

The several diverse definitions of empathy are sequentially presented and examined in Chapter one, in an effort to begin this book with a shared understanding of the major historical and contemporary meanings of the construct. We conclude this initial chapter by subscribing ourselves to a particular components definition of empathy, a definition we predict will prove particularly useful in enhancing future understanding, investigation, and application of empathic behavior. This components definition, therefore, substantially influences and shapes much of the content of the rest of the book.

Chapter two thoroughly considers the development of empathy in childhood and adolescence, and does so by comprehensively examining the major relevant theories and their supporting research. The perceptual, affective reverberation and cognitive analysis stages of the empathic process are examined in depth in Chapters three and four, as both diverse and, we believe, novel applications of research domains not obviously relevant to empathy are brought to bear.

Why empathy is a construct of such great and enduring interest in psychology and kindred professions is perhaps made especially clear in the three chapters which then follow, each of which presents and integrates research on the consequences of empathy. In psychotherapy (Chapter five), education (Chapter six) and parenting (Chapter seven), high levels of provider empathy are documented to generally have positive, growth-enhancing consequences. If this broad conclusion is correct, then the enhancement of empathy becomes a valuable social and interpersonal goal. Our final chapter, on empathy training, presents in concrete form the several means by which such empathy training might optimally proceed. Consistent with the view presented throughout this book, that empathy is most usefully understood as a four stage process, this final chapter highlights apparently effective training techniques for each of the separate stages—by this means thus proposing an inclusive training sequence for the reliable enhancement of empathy in human relations.

We indeed hope the reader finds, as we have, that empathy—its understanding and enhancement is an intriguing and valuable pursuit.

Arnold P. Goldstein
Gerald Y. Michaels
Syracuse University

EMPATHY

Development, Training, and Consequences

1 Historical and Contemporary Definitions

The term 'empathy' derives from the Greek word empatheia, which implies an active appreciation of another person's feeling experience.

(Astin, 1967, p. 57)

Lipps [1907] believed that empathy was a form of inner imitation. An observer is stimulated by the sight of an object and responds by imitating the object. The process is automatic and swift, and soon the observer feels himself into the object, loses consciousness of himself, and experiences the object as if his own identity had disappeared and he had become the object himself.

(Katz, 1963, p. 85

Empathy means . . . to glide with one's own feeling into the dynamic structure of an object . . . or even of an animal or a man, and as it were to trace it from within, understanding the formation and motoriality of the object with the perceptions of one's own muscles; it means to 'transpose' oneself over there and in there.

(Buber, 1948, p. 97)

Empathy can be described as a process of 'projection' or 'introjection'; both are metaphors referring to the experience of partial identity between the subject's mental processes and those of another with the resulting insight into the other's mental state and participation in his emotions.

(Koestler, 1949, p. 360)

Empathy will be used . . . to denote the imaginative transposing of oneself into the thinking, feeling and acting of another and so structuring the world as he does.

(Dymond, 1949, p. 127)

1

Empathy is the capacity to take the role of the other and to adopt alternative perspectives vis a vis oneself.

(Mead, 1934, p. 27)

Empathy is the process by which a person momentarily pretends to himself that he is another person, projects himself into the perceptual field of the other person, imaginatively puts himself in the other person's place, in order that he may get an insight into the other person's probable behavior in a given situation.

(Coutu, 1951, p. 18)

Empathy ultimately is vicarious introspection—we introject the other person into ourselves and contemplate him inwardly.

(Katz, 1963, p. 93)

empathy . . . seems the essence of what client-centered therapists have referred to as adopting the patient's frame of reference, or what psychoanalysts have referred to as transient, controlled identifications.

(Bachrach, 1976, p. 35)

the ability to step into another person's shoes and to step back just as easily into one's own shoes again. It is not projection, which implies that the wearer's shoes pinch him and that he wishes someone else in them; it is not identification, which involves stepping into another person's shoes and then being unable or unwilling to get out of them; and it is not sympathy, in which a person stands in his own shoes while observing another person's behavior, and while reacting to him in terms of what he tells you about shoes—if they pinch, one communicates with him, if they are comfortable, one enjoys his comfort with him.

(Blackman, Smith, Brokman, & Stern, 1958, p. 550)

we list four phases in the empathic process, following Theodore Reik's outline . . .

   (1) Identification. Partly through an instinctive, imitative activity and partly through a relaxation of our conscious controls, we allow ourselves to become absorbed in contemplating the other person and his experiences.
   (2) Incorporation. By this term we mean the act of taking the experience of the other person into ourselves. It is hard to distinguish this phase from the initial act of feeling oneself into the other person . . . These are two sides of the same process. When we identify, we project our being into others; when we incorporate, we introject the other person into ourselves.
   (3) Reverberation. What we have taken into ourselves now echos upon some part of our own experience and awakens a new appreciation. . . We allow for an interplay between two sets of experiences, the internalized feelings of others and our own experience and fantasy.
   (4) Detachment. In this pase of empathic understanding, we withdraw from our subjective involvement and use the methods of reason and scrutiny. We break our identification and deliberately move away to gain the social and psychic distance necessary for objective analysis.

(Katz, 1963, p. 41)

the measurement of affective sensitivity or what might be termed generically, empathy. Affective sensitivity is conceptualized as the ability to detect and describe the immediate affective state of another, or in terms of communication theory, the ability to receive and decode affective communications.

(Danish & Kagan, 1971, p. 51)

The way of being with another person which is termed empathic has several facets. It means entering the private perceptual world of the other and becoming thoroughly at home in it. It involves being sensitive, moment to moment, to the changing felt meanings which flow in this other person . . . It involves communicating your sensing of his/her world as you look with fresh and unfrightened eyes.

(Rogers, 1975, p. 4)

Accurate empathy involves more than just the ability of the therapist to sense the client or patient's private world as if it were his own. It also involves more than just his ability to know what the patient means. Accurate empathy involves both the therapist's *sensitivity to current feelings* and his *verbal facility to communicate this understanding* in a language attuned to the client's current feelings. It is not necessary—indeed it would seem undesirable—for the therapist to *share* the client's feelings in any sense that would require him to feel the same emotions. It is instead an appreciation and sensitive awareness of those feelings.

(Truax & Carkhuff, 1967, p. 46)

The first phase of emphatic behavior begins as the worker perceives the various overt behaviors of the client, including his explicit verbal message and its paralinguistic qualities.

In the second phase of empathic behavior, the worker's perception elicits both cognitive and feeling responses in himself . . . In order to achieve high levels of empathy with the client, the worker must allow his initial feeling responses to remain as free as possible from cognitive distortion. Cognitive distortion includes stereotyping, making value judgments, or analyzing perceptions according to a fixed theoretical schema.

In the third phase of empathic behavior, the worker must consciously separate feelings held by himself alone from those sensed and shared with the client. The foregoing . . . empathic behaviors . . . all characterize the worker's receptivity to the client. But accurate reception must be complemented by accurate feedback.

(Keefe, 1976, pp. 11–12)

this model delineated the following empathizer behaviors as the components of empathy: (1) perception of verbal and nonverbal messages from the other person, (2) accurate understanding of the meanings of the other person's messages . . . , (3) experience of one's somatic responses to the messages of the other person while holding complex cognitive elaboration . . . in temporary abeyance, (4) separation of feelings shared with the other person from those held alone, and (5) accurate communication of reactive feelings back to the other person in harmonious understandable verbal and nonverbal messages.

(Keefe, 1979, pp. 30–31)

CONCEPTUAL DEFINITIONS

The concept of empathy has had a long, varied, and at times conflicting definitional history. This pattern has been true both within and between the diverse fields of inquiry in which empathy has been a significant construct, namely aesthetics, sociology, and psychology. We wish in the sections that follow to trace this definitional history and examine its flow and evolving meaning. As we do so, we seek to reduce the substantial levels of conceptual chaos inherent in this history and move toward that comprehensive definition that later chapters of this book—those examining the consequences of empathy in diverse contexts—begin to demonstrate to be a construct valid and heuristically optimal way of defining this elusive and often confusing concept.

In 1897, Lipps introduced the term *Einfühlung* in his writings about aesthetic perception and appreciation. Einfühlung meant "feeling oneself into," in German, and was translated as *empathy* by Tichener in 1910. In examining and contemplating an object (of art, nature, etc.), Lipps believed one projected oneself into the object (e.g., "feeling together with"), established an identification between it and oneself, engaged in a process of inner imitation, and in this manner came more fully to understand and appreciate it. Some years later, Lipps (1926) extended this definitional position to include people and not only objects as the targets of empathic efforts. In doing so, he elaborated further the notion of motor mimicry as the central process constituting Einfühlung. The perceiver engages, he held, in imitating the target object or person by consciously or unconsciously assuming aspects of its posture and, in the case of target persons, taking on certain of his or her physical stances, gestures, or expressions. In this manner, Lipps posited, inner cues are created in the perceiver that lead to a heightened appreciation and understanding of the object/person and, in the case of target persons, a shared feeling experience. Thus, for Lipps, empathy proceeded by means of projection and imitation, could involve both objects or persons as targets, and consisted largely of heightened understanding of the other through cue-produced shared feelings. As noted earlier, much the same focus is explicitly expressed in definitions of empathy put forth somewhat later by Buber (1948) ("to glide with one's own feeling into the dynamic structure of an object") and Koestler (1949) ("the experience of partial identity").

With the work of George Mead (1934), however, the definitional focus of empathy shifted in two important directions. A cognitive component in the form of "an ability to understand" was added to the earlier affective emphasis. And, furthermore, the blending or merging of identities notion yielded to a self-other differentiation in which the empathizer temporarily "took the role of the other" or "put themselves in the other's place" as the heart of the empathic process. As Deutsch and Madle (1975) observe: "Empathy was no longer viewed as purely a perceptual awareness of an individual's affect or sharing of feeling, but rather an ability to understand a person's emotional reactions in consort with the context" (p. 270). The "imaginitive transposing," "momentary pretending," "introjection of the other,'' and ''adopting the other's frame of reference'' described, respectively, in the Dymond (1949), Coutu (1951), Katz (1963), and Bachrach (1976) definitions of empathy provided earlier each fully reflect the role-taking or perspective-taking essence of Mead's (1934) view of the meaning of empathy.

This temporary, momentary, as if, borrowing-in-order-to-understand quality remained a feature of the definition of empathy as its target more fully and explicitly became the ongoing emotional state of the other. In the Reik (see Katz, 1963) definition, for example, note how the Identification, Incorporation, and Reverberation stages of the empathic process combine to provide the empathizer with an extended opportunity to ''try on'' the target person's ongoing emotional experience prior to the Detachment stage, in which the empathizer seeks to gain distance from the other in order to engage in more objective, cognitive analysis. Beyond this joint affective and cognitive focus, the several *affective sensitivity* definitions of empathy—presented earlier in this chapter—that have emerged more recently (Danish & Kagan, 1971; Rogers, 1975; Truax & Carkhuff, 1967) added yet a new component. The act of empathizing, according to each of these definitions, involved not only the ability to sensitively comprehend the other's affective world, but also to accurately and sensitively communicate this understanding to the target other; that is, empathy for these persons involved ''communicating your sensing'' (Rogers, 1975), ''detecting and describing'' (Danish & Kagan, 1971), and ''facility in communicating this [affective] understanding'' (Truax & Carkhuff, 1967).

These affective-cognitive-communicative features of what we view as a comprehensive definition of empathy are reflected most fully in the phase definition of empathy offered by Keefe (1976, 1979) and depicted in Fig. 1.1.

Keefe (1976) suggests that the first phase of the empathic process begins as the worker perceives (c) the feeling state and thoughts of the other (a) by means of the overt behavioral cues displayed by the other (b). In the second phase, the worker's perceptions generate both cognitive and affective responses in himself (d). Here, in a manner consistent with Reik's notion of reverberation, the worker seeks to avoid stereotyping, value judgments, the formulation of hypotheses, or other forms of cognitive analysis. Instead, he or she seeks to hold such cognitive processes in abeyance while allowing and encouraging a largely unfettered, as-if, experiencing of the other's affective world (e). In the next, detachment (Reik, 1949) and decoding (Danish & Kagan, 1971) phase, the worker seeks to distinguish among, sort out and label his or her own feelings and those he or she perceives as being experienced by the other person (f). Finally, as we noted is true for other, more recent definitions of empathy, in Keefe's view the worker communicates accurate feedback to the target person as the final phase of the empathic sequence (g). Keefe (1976) summarizes this sequence:

> The foregoing four empathic behaviors—perceiving accurately the client's gestalt, allowing a direct feeling response to arise, holding qualifying or distorting cognitive processes in abeyance, and separating his own feelings from those shared

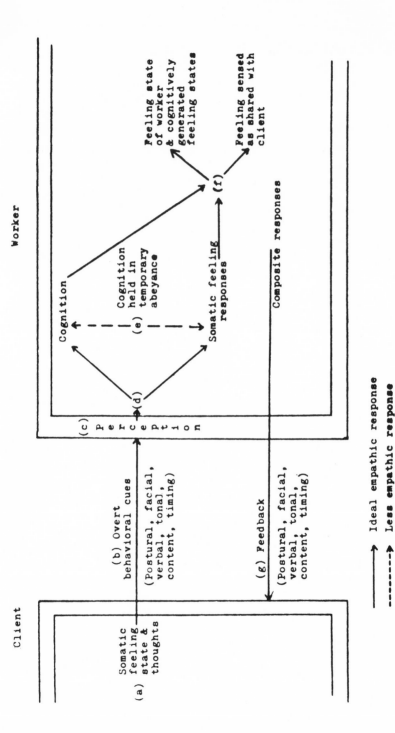

FIG. 1.1. Behaviors comprising empathic skill

with the client—all characterize the worker's receptivity to the client. But accurate reception must be complimented by accurate feedback. (pp. 12–13)

Macarov (1978) observes that empathy has three contemporaneous meanings. Consistent with Keefe and others, our more comprehensive affective-cognitive-communication stance is that empathy is optimally defined by *all three* of these meanings combined:

1. Taking the role of the other, viewing the world as he or she sees it, and experiencing his or her feelings.
2. Being adept at reading nonverbal communication and interpreting the feelings underlying it.
3. Giving off a feeling of caring, or sincerely trying to understand in a nonjudgmental or helping way. (p. 88)

RELATED CONSTRUCTS

Having now traced the definitional history of empathy and defined it in terms of what it is, our understanding of the meaning of empathy will be enhanced further if we differentiate it from what it is not, by examining a number of related constructs with which it often appears to overlap.

Sympathy

Differences between sympathy and empathy exist in terms of their respective contents, their constituent processes, and their interpersonal consequences. Sympathy, as Ehmann (1971) observes, contains major elements of condolence, pity, and/or agreement, none of which characterize empathy. With regard to constituent processes, Buchheimer's (1963) differentiation of sympathy from empathy re-emphasizes the temporary "merging into" stage of the empathic (but not sympathetic) process noted in several earlier definitions. He comments:

When we examine another term in the German language, *Mitfühlung* (sympathy) in relation to *Einfühlung*, we can see the implications of the [empathy] concept clearly. *Mit* in this context must be translated as 'along with' rather than "together with.' A sympathetic person feels *along with* another person but not necessarily *into* a person . . . Empathic behavior implies a convergence . . . Sympathetic behavior implies a parallelism in the behavior of two individuals. (p. 63).

Katz (1963) makes much the same distinction. Empathy, he holds, focuses our attention on the feelings and context of the other person. Sympathy, in contrast, is a heightened attention to one's own feelings and the assumed similarity between such feelings and those of the person who is the stimulus for it.

He states (Katz, 1963): "When we empathize, we lose ourselves in the new identity we have temporarily assumed. When we sympathize, we remain more conscious of our separate identity" (p. 9). The manner in which the two processes may be distinguished in terms of locus of attention, as just noted, has immediate consequences for the information about the other person actually gathered by and available for use by the perceiver. In the case of empathy, the perceiver optimally is sensitive to the full range and depth of the other's affective state or situation and thus may proceed fully through the empathic subprocesses of affective reverberation, cognitive analysis, and accurate feedback. The sympathizer, in contrast, is more preoccupied with his or her own feelings in response to the other and thus is less able to respond to, for, or with the other in a manner sensitive to the other person's actual ongoing emotional world and its context.

Projection

The relationship of empathy and projection, at a conceptual level appears rather straightforward. As Dymond (1950) noted in her early and pioneering work on personality correlates of empathy:

> Projection seems to be an antithetical process to empathy since projection involves the attribution of one's own wishes, attitudes and behavior to some thing, or some one other than the self. If projection is involved, therefore, the thoughts and feelings of the self are attributed to the other rather than [as in empathy] those of the other being experienced. (p. 344)

Although our own thinking is compatible with this early view of Dymond's, a view for which there even is some empirical support (e.g., Norman & Ainsworth, 1954), it becomes clear later in this book that as one moves from conceptual to operational efforts the relationship of empathy and projection is more complex indeed. We leave this further examination of their somewhat tangled meanings to this subsequent presentation.

Identification

According to the American Psychiatric Association (1957), identification has been defined as "a mental mechanism, operating unconsciously, by which an individual endeavors to pattern himself after another" (p. 19) and (by Symonds, 1946) as "the modeling of oneself in thought, feeling or action after another person." (p. 37). Dymond (1950) sought to distinguish this process from empathy by proposing that identification was a special instance of role taking, one that was more lasting, less frequent, and more emotional than empathy. Identification, but not empathy, she held, implied a desire to be like the other individual, to form a strong emotional tie with the other. A similar differentiation between the two concepts based on intensity, depth, permanence, and similar qualities has also been made by Luchins (1957) and Rogers (1949). Further, Greenson (1960), writing from a psychoanalytic perspective, asserts that identification is an unconscious and permanent process whose goal is to overcome anxiety, whereas empathy is preconscious, temporary, and essentially an effort to understand.

Empathy, then, for us is a perceptual-affective-cognitive-communicative process, different in discernable ways from sympathy, projection, and identification. Its historical and current meanings may more fully be explicated by our attention to its operational measurement, to which we now turn.

OPERATIONAL DEFINITIONS

Attempts to adequately measure empathy have, even more than has been true for its conceptual definitions, revealed the wide diversity of meanings attributed to the term. All major modes of psychological measurement have been utilized— physiological (Gellen, 1970; Stotland, 1969; Vanderpool & Barratt, 1970), behavioral (Danish & Kagan, 1971; Guzetta, 1974; Truax & Carkhuff, 1967), self-report (Barrett–Lennerd, 1962; Campbell, Kagan, & Krathwohl, 1971; Hogan, 1969), and projective (Bachrach, 1968; Dymond, 1950; Symonds & Dudek, 1956). These several measurement approaches may conveniently, following Deutsch and Madle (1975), be categorized as of two basic types, predictive and situational.

Prediction tests of empathy, introduced by Dymond in 1949 and actively elaborated by a number of investigators in the period that followed, sought to reflect perspective-taking conceptual definitions of empathy by means of a variety of self- and predictive-of-other ratings on several dimensions, the derived difference scores from which were held to represent empathy. In its earliest and simplest format (Dymond, 1949), ratings were obtained on dimensions such as friendliness, selfishness, humorlessness, shyness, leadership, and security such that: (1) A rates himself (A); (2) A rates B as he (A) sees B; (3) A rates B as he thinks B would rate himself; (4) A rates himself as he thinks B would rate him; (5) B rates himself (B). In this example, one index of A's level of empathy is calculated by determining how closely A's predictions of B's ratings correspond with B's actual ratings. As the development of the predictive measurement of empathy evolved into more complex formats, precedures were put forth to reduce or remove the possible influence upon ratings obtained of processes other than empathy, especially projection and stereotyping (Cottrell, 1950; Hastorf & Bender, 1952; Kerr & Speroff, 1954). In the mid-1950s, however, Cronbach (1955; Gage & Cronbach, 1955) published a methodological critique of this means of empathy measurement from which the approach never recovered. Though initially appealing and quick to gain popularity, the approach was convincingly shown by Cronbach to suffer from telling artifactual contamination and has largely faded from the contemporary research scene.

Situational measures of empathy, more diverse in format and task demands than the predictive, are measures in which affect-laden situations (broadly defined) to which an empathic response would be an appropriate reaction are presented to subjects. Test stimuli used in this manner have included real-life situations (Goldstein, 1982; Stotland & Walsh, 1963) or live actors (Goldstein, 1982; Guzzetta, 1974; Perry, 1970); photographs and line drawings of situations, facial expressions or story sequences (Borke, 1971; Deutsch, 1975; Feshbach & Roe, 1968); audio recordings (Goldstein & Goodhart, 1973; Rothenberg, 1970); and videotaped interaction sequences (Danish & Kagan, 1971; Deutsch, 1974). In contrast to the prediction tests of empathy, which were largely cognitive perspective-taking measures, these several situational measures appear to draw more heavily upon both the affective sensitivity and cognitive analysis components of our earlier stated comprehensive conceptual definition of empathy. As Deutsch and Madle (1975) observe with regard to these approaches:

> Typically, empathy is measured by having the subjects correctly label the contextual stimuli and/or affective response portrayed, or by responding with a statement of action appropriate to [the other] person's affective state, or with a statement reflecting how the subject felt when observing another's affect. (p. 273)

Literally several dozen different—especially situational—measures of empathy have been reported in the research literature. As noted earlier, their nature and diversity not only reflects the conceptual confusion of the concept itself but, in addition, a host of measurement problems. Does the generally low, often zero-order correlation among empathy measures primarily reflect the relationship of different components of a broader construct (Bachrach, 1968; Kurtz & Grummon, 1972), or are response set, test format, and other artifactual influences more responsible? And, if a components perspective is the more appropriate, what are they, how are they optimally weighted, combined, and measured? Is empathy most appropriately considered and measured as a trait likely to be reflected across stimulus situations for a given individual (Hastorf & Bender, 1952), or is situation specificity more likely the case, as Hornblow (1980) and Smither (1977) propose? Would adequacy of measurement be enhanced by pursuing operationally the conceptual suggestion that different *types* of empathy may exist, e.g., additive empathy (Means, 1973), emotional empathy (Mehrabian & Epstein, 1972), primordial empathy (Katz, 1963), genotypic and phenotypic empathy (Hogan, 1975), individual and mass empathy Reik (1949), cognitive, affective, and cognitive/affective empathy (Gladstein, 1977a), postural empathy (Allport, 1937), and what Schelar (1954) has described as compathy, mimpathy, unipathy, and transpathy? With sympathy, projection, and identification having been largely put to rest as possible contaminants, how can empathy measures be refined in order to more adequately reduce the likelihood that still other sister variables, both different from but overlapping with empathy, are not being reflected, e.g., warmth (Rausch & Bordin, 1957), communicated commitment (Kiesler, Mathieu, & Klein, 1967), insight (Murphy, 1932), inference and intuition (Goodyear, 1979), similarity of background (Cowden, 1955; Helfand, 1955), and similarity of experience (Helfand, 1955). And the more traditional psychometric concerns of reliability and validity of the array of available empathy measures, as Deutsch and Madle (1975) cogently explore, are far from exemplary at their current levels. It is clear that many relevant questions remain to be answered before the measurement of empathy can be considered to be psychometrically sound and experimentally fully useful.

SUMMARY

We have sought in this chapter to set the stage for the remainder of this book by defining its central focus, empathy. A series of specific definitions opened the chapter, definitions presented in rough chronological order of what might be termed *conceptual development*. We then traced this development explicitly, moving in effect through the fields of aesthetics, sociology, and then psychology as we shifted from the early (but still useful) motor mimicry definitional perspective of Lipps, through the role-taking emphasis of Mead and others, on to the focus upon affective sensitivity of Rogers and his psychotherapist colleagues, ending with the perceptual-affective-cognitive-communicative definition comprehensively offered by Keefe and strongly subscribed to by us.

Our understanding of empathy, we held, could be deepened further, by separating it conceptually from concepts with which it has often been confused. We sought to do so with regard to sympathy, projection, and identification. Finally, we turned to operational definitions and provided an overview of existing measures and categories of measurement, as well as of the host of yet unanswered questions that must be resolved before the fully adequate measurement of empathy can be possible.

These chapter goals—defining empathy conceptually, separating it clearly from sister constructs, and examining means for refining its measurement—are returned to frequently in the chapters that lie ahead, as we present and evaluate research on the development, training, and consequences of empathy.

2 Development of Empathy

In this chapter we turn from the description of the fully formed adult empathic experience to trace the developmental roots of this multicomponent concept. The overriding theme of our discussion is the existence of individual diversity within the general developmental pattern of empathy growth. We describe both maturational and socialization influences on empathy that can lead to its systematic, stage-like development, and factors that lead to individual and group differences in children's empathic abilities. This kind of approach to studying individual differences within patterns of systematic developmental change is now finding favor in the child area as a whole (Belsky, Spanier, & Rovine, 1983).

Methodological considerations also figure prominently in our discussion. During the course of the approximately 15 years of intensive research into the development of children's empathy, developmental psychologists have addressed many of the conceptual and theoretical issues relevant to empathy outlined in Chapter 1. Theoretical models for children's empathy that contain constructs that could be operationalized and studied empirically have been put forth. The results of early studies are now in and are being used successfully for further theoretical and definitional refinement. Additionally, the focus on understanding how empathy develops across different ages compelled these developmental psychologists to search for a wide variety of behaviors and responses that could be considered indicative of empathy, but which all still fit their particular theoretical model. Finally, knowledge gained about the changing nature of the child's developing cognitive, affective, and communicative capabilities helped greatly in the search to understand qualitative differences in children's empathic experience and to develop indices that could address such differences.

12

We examine the development of empathy from the standpoint of the multi-component approach presented in Chapter 1, focusing first on the two major models of particular salience in developmental psychology research and theory. We then examine the development of the perceptual, affective, cognitive, and communication components individually. Particular attention is given to the affective and cognitive components, because the study of these has been the major focus of developmental researchers. Finally, we review research on the socialization of empathy, and particularly its development in the context of the parent–child relationship.

MULTIDIMENSIONAL VIEWS OF EMPATHIC DEVELOPMENT

After a good deal of controversy about how to define empathy and what processes were central to its operation (e.g., Borke, 1971, 1972; Chandler & Greenspan, 1972), developmental researchers have largely moved to viewing empathy as a multidimensional process, with particular emphasis placed on its cognitive and affective components. There are currently two important multidimensional models of children's empathy, that of Martin Hoffman (1975, 1976, 1977a,b, 1980, 1982) and that of Norma Feshbach (1975, 1978, 1980, 1982a, b, c). These two models are described and then compared to the four-component model of empathy presented in Chapter 1 as a framework for integrating the diverse areas of theory, research, and intervention described in this book.

Hoffman's Model

Martin Hoffman's theoretical model of the development of altruistic motivation focuses on empathy as the major mediator of prosocial behavior and is a model that has proven to be an influential theory of empathy's development. Hoffman (1982) defines empathy as "a vicarious affective response . . . that is more appropriate to someone else's situation that to one's own situation" (p. 281). He stresses at the outset that there need not be an exact match between the observer's and the stimulus person's affect, a point of some contention in the field as a whole. We also see that, whereas cognitive processes play a vital role in defining a child's empathic experience at successive ages, the core of the empathy experience for Hoffman is an affective response, not a cognitive one. The focus of the model is on empathic distress, which Hoffman believes to be central to altruistic behavior. However, Hoffman (1982) does suggest that the model may also be pertinent to the development of empathy for other kinds of feelings.

An important and innovative aspect of the model is its description of the different modes of empathic arousal. Hoffman identifies six different modes through which the vicarious emotional response is aroused. Their use by the child follows more or less a developmental progression, and they differ from one another in such areas as the degree to which the child's perceptual and cognitive processing are involved, the type of environmental stimuli that elicit the response, and the quality and quantity of past experience necessary for empathic arousal to take place.

The first mode is the "reactive newborn cry." Hoffman (1982) cites several studies showing that infants tend to cry when exposed to the sound of another person's cry, including research by Simner (1971) and Sagi and Hoffman (1976). Sagi and Hoffman's research with 1-day-olds not only confirmed the existence of this reactive cry but showed that, rather than being merely imitative vocal responses, these cries were vigorous and of an intensity that made them indistinguishable from the cries of infants who were actually in distress. Hoffman (1982) suggests that the occurrence of this reactive cry may be an innate response, involving a circular reaction whereby the infant, unable to tell the difference between his own and the other's cry, first responds to the stimulus cry as if it were his own and then continues to cry to the sound of what is now truly his own cry. Another possibility is that the stimulus cry may be associated with the infant's own actual past distress, leading to his own crying. Hoffman considers this reactive cry to be a very rudimentary precursor of empathy, because the infants in this study were in fact experiencing distress within themselves in the presence of distress cues from another person. Of course, at this early point in development the infant is not aware of what is happening and cannot differentiate his distress from the other's distress. Yet, this mode of empathic arousal may pave the way for the later development of the full empathic response, because the child comes to expect that he or she will experience distress when this is perceived in another.

The second mode through which the empathic response is evoked is classical conditioning. A precondition for the development of this mode is a rudimentary capacity for perceptual discrimination. Therefore, it is thought to emerge slightly later than the reactive cry. Classical conditioning of empathic distress occurs when the infant observes the distress of someone else and, at the same time, is also experiencing distress. The other's distress cues then become the conditioned stimulus that leads to feelings of distress in himself. To illustrate this, Hoffman (1982) gives the example of an anxious mother whose tension while holding her baby causes the child to become upset. Later, the mother's facial and verbal expressions, which had accompanied her anxiety state, may function as conditioned stimuli that lead to anxiety or distress in the child, even when the child is not actually being held. Through stimulus generalization, similar facial and verbal expressions in others may arouse similar distress in the child. Aronfreed's work (e.g., 1970) has shown existence of classically conditioned affective empathy responses, and Hoffman cites this work as support for the existence of this mode of empathy transmission.

The third mode of empathic distress arousal depends on the child already having accumulated memories of painful and distressful experiences. When the child now observes someone else having discomfort, the observations of the other's distress serve as cues for the elicitation of these memories, and a resultant empathic distress response occurs in the child. Unlike classical conditioning, here it is not necessary that the distress cues from the other and the child's own distress occur at the same time. Hoffman suggests that this is a much more general associative mechanism than the classical conditioning mode, and that it may be the mode for the experience of many types of empathic distress experiences, in adults as well as children.

The fourth mode for empathic distress arousal is motor mimicry. The process occurs when, upon observing the stimulus person's facial signs of distress, the child automatically imitates these emotional expressions by engaging in slight movements in facial expression and posture. These imitative movements then cause inner kinesthetic cues that aid the child in experiencing and understanding this same feeling. The existence of this mode of empathic transmission, as well as its possible innate origins, has been given support recently in an exciting group of infant studies showing successful motor mimicry of facial expressions during the first months of life (Barrera & Maurer, 1981; Field, Woodson, Greenberg, & Cohen, 1982; Nelson, Morse, & Leavitt, 1979; Young–Browne, Rosenfield, & Horowitz, 1977).

The fifth mode of empathic arousal was termed *symbolic association*. Here, rather than directly experiencing distress cues from the stimulus person, the observer is exposed to symbolic cues of distress, such as the label for the emotion or a description of an emotional event that was being experienced by the stimulus person. These symbolic cues then become associated with the child's own experienced distress, as in the third mode. Hoffman believes this mode to be more advanced than the first four modes because it requires that the child understand such symbolic cues.

The first five modes of empathic arousal are automatic. Once the child is able to perceive and discriminate the affective cues (behavioral or symbolic), the vicarious affective response follows. However, the sixth mode, role taking, requires greater cognitive maturation and depends much more on purposive action. Here the child deliberately tries to take the perspective of the stimulus person, i.e., imagines himself as the victim of the perceived distress. Hoffman suggests that taking the role of the other elicits associations with actual events in the child's past in which he or she experienced the same emotion, leading to the experience of this emotion once again in the present. This mode is like previous ones in that a cue from the stimulus person leads to an association with the child's own previously experienced distress. However, in this mode the cues come about through the child forming a mental representation of himself in the victim's situation. Hoffman cites research by Stotland (1969) indicating that a larger amount of affective empathic arousal takes place after the individual imagines how he or she would feel if experiencing the same emotional stimuli as the victim.

It is notable that, although cognitive role taking is seen as important in Hoffman's model, it operates in the service of the affective empathy response, rather than for the purpose of furthering cognitive understanding of the other's emotional experience. Hoffman is not describing an independent cognitive form of empathy.

These six modes might be viewed as channels of information processing utilized by the child in forming a vicarious emotional response to another's feelings. The quality and quantity of the vicarious distress response is shaped by the mode through which emotional cues in the stimulus person are transmitted to the child. Hoffman believes that the reactive cry disappears after infancy, but that the next five modes are still used by adults, with the role-taking mode primarily found during adulthood. Once the child has access to more than one mode of affective arousal, the mode that operates in a particular situation is determined by which cues from the stimulus person are available and salient. For example, if facial cues are readily available, motor mimicry will be the main mode of empathic distress arousal. When several kinds of cues are operative, the transmission of empathic arousal may occur through several modes at once. In this case, the strength of the arousal is usually heightened. However, sometimes the existence of multiple cues may also cause an interference in empathic arousal.

The Role of Cognitive Processes in Hoffman's Model.   Though Hoffman (1982) believes that the vicarious sharing of another's emotional experience is "the essential feature of empathy" (p. 285), it does not, by itself, constitute the entire empathy experience in his model. The model also posits an important role for cognitive processes in the experience of affective empathy. The particular cognitive process that Hoffman's model is concerned with is that of the child's maturing ability to differentiate self from others.

Hoffman (1975, 1977a,b) has outlined the developmental progression through which increasing self–other differentiation qualitatively changes one's level of empathic awareness. The first level of affective empathy occurs during the first year of life when, cognitively, the infant has not yet achieved person permanence and still experiences a fusion of self and other. Empathic distress is experienced globally. The experience is a fusion of unpleasant feelings that result from stimuli that come from the infant's own body, from the other, and from the situation, all at once. According to Hoffman, at this point the infant feels distress but does not know who is having it or from where it comes. The very young child may mistakenly assume that what was causing distress to the stimulus person was occurring to him.

When the child has achieved person permanence, he moves to the second level of empathy that Hoffman called *egocentric empathy*. The child can now distinguish his physical self from the physical other and realizes that, to relieve the stimulus person's distress, this person must be relieved of his (and not the child's own) distress cues. However, at this point the child still does not differentiate self and other sufficiently in the area of inner thoughts and feelings. Hoffman cites the example of a child who, upon seeing another child upset, takes this second child to his mother for comfort, even though the second child's mother is also available. Although the affective response is appropriate, an effective action based on this response is not yet forthcoming.

The next level of empathic experience occurs at age 2 or 3 when the child begins to be able to engage in role taking. Now he can truly understand that the other's feelings may differ from his own and are based on different needs and perspectives. He is also becoming aware that how he perceives things may differ from the perceptions of others. This leads to his becoming more attuned to the cues given by others that pertain to their subjective experiences and feelings. Many research studies, some of which are discussed later, indicate that children by age 3 or 4 can empathize with the feelings of happiness and sadness if the experiences in which these feelings occur are quite simple. Hoffman (1982) maintains that a great leap in empathic potential takes place when the child develops language, because he is now capable of obtaining meaning from symbolic cues of affect, not just behaviorally expressed cues. This allows him to empathize with a greater number of feelings, and eventually with more complex feelings, with multiple feelings, and even with contradictory feelings. We see that the process by which older children become capable of empathizing with such complex feelings and clusters of feelings remains almost unresearched within the developmental literature on empathy.

Another transformation in empathy takes place when the child becomes aware that both he and others exist as continous persons with past histories and future expectations that form a general life situation or condition. Now the child's empathy can extend beyond the immediate distress experience. For example, the observer may watch a terminally ill child playing with toys and experience empathic sadness (Hoffman, 1982). His empathic reactions become influenced by the types of judgments he makes about the other's general life condition (i.e., is the distress long lasting, is this a happy interlude in an otherwise sad existence, etc.). Whereas there is still a vicarious emotional response, the very act of contemplating the stimulus person's general situation creates a certain distancing from the other that will characterize the individual's empathic experience from this time onward.

Hoffman states that the last extention of this level of empathy occurs when the child becomes able to respond empathically to the distress of a group of people (i.e., poor people or oppressed people). It is at this point that the vicariously experienced distress may reflect a high level of empathy and yet not be an exact match of the distress that the stimulus person(s) are experiencing.

Hoffman believes that the empathic distress response for the victim may, as a natural occurrence, be partially transformed into a feeling of concern and compassion for the victim, along with a conscious wish to help the victim. This feeling for the other, which he termed *sympathetic distress,* is thought to be based on real compassion and not simply on the wish to relieve one's own vicariously experienced distress. It represents the link between empathy and altruistic behavior that Hoffman sought. Hoffman believes that sympathetic distress may undergo a developmental sequence that parallels the development of empathic distress, but he acknowledges that there is at present only circumstantial evidence of this.

Feshbach's Three Factor Model of Empathy

The second major developmental model of empathy has been put forth by Norma Feshbach (1975, 1978, 1980, 1982a, b, c). Her's is a "three factor model," containing two distinct cognitive components and an affective component. The first cognitive component is the child's developing ability to discriminate the emotional state of another person. Feshbach believes that early expressions of empathy depend on the child possessing this cognitive skill. To empathize with an emotion such as sadness, the child must be able to identify the emotional cues that distinguish sadness from other feelings and from stimuli representative of a neutral affective state. In her (Feshbach, 1982a) assertion that this "elementary form of social comprehension" (p. 320) is necessary for empathy, Feshbach differs somewhat with Hoffman. In Hoffman's model cognitive factors are thought to mediate and modify a vicarious emotional response already present in the child at or near birth.

The second cognitive component of Feshbach's model is the child's developing ability to assume the perspective and role of the other. To empathize with another person requires that the child be able to cognitively understand the situation from this second person's viewpoint. Again, a comparison of Feshbach's and Hoffman's models indicates that, whereas role taking enters as a cognitive mediator of the affective empathy experience in both models, in Feshbach's model it is considered a separate and necessary component of empathy, whereas for Hoffman role taking is one mode by which the stimulus person's affective experience can be transmitted to the observer. Considerable attention in the developmental literature has been given to the question of what importance role taking development plays in empathy, and a more detailed discussion of this issue follows shortly.

The third component of Feshbach's model is emotional responsiveness. In order to share another's emotional experience, the child must be able to experience the emotion that the other is having. This component is similar conceptually to Hoffman's definition of empathy as a vicarious emotional response. There are some important differences however. One important way in which the Hoffman and Feshbach affective components differ is with respect to the range of empathically aroused emotion each model purports to explain. Feshbach has developed her model in an attempt to investigate children's development of a wide range of empathy experiences. Much conceptual and empirical emphasis has been placed on the different rate of acquisition of empathy for different emotions, as well as on how individual differences among children may influence the rate of acquisition and performance. Hoffman's model was originally developed to explain the role that empathy plays in the development of altruism (Hoffman, 1975). Because he believes that empathic distress is a major motivator of altruism, his model does not focus on other empathically aroused feelings and specifically does not deal with empathically experienced positive affect such as joy or pleasure. Furthermore, Feshbach's model requires that the child's affective response be identical to the stimulus person's before it can be considered empathy, whereas as we noted previously, Hoffman's model only requires that there be a fairly close match between observer and stimulus person.

Feshbach (1978), like Hoffman, does not consider her model of empathy to be a completed theory at this point. Rather, she thinks of it "as a framework from which a detailed theoretical formulation might evolve." The efforts of her research group are presently being directed toward gathering systematic data about empathy's development and function (e.g., as a possible inhibitor of aggression), about methods of assessment, and about strategies for intervention. She expects that each component of empathy will eventually be shown to undergo unique developmental changes, as well as developmental changes that are interactive with changes in the other components.

Comparison to the Keefe Empathy Model.   There are several salient differences between the Hoffman and Feshbach developmental models and Keefe's (1976) model that, in Chapter 1, we proposed as a framework for integrating the diverse directions that empathy research has followed across the various disciplines. First, both Hoffman's and Feshbach's models, although multidimensional, conceptualize empathy as being primarily affective, rather than cognitive. For example, Feshbach (1978) argues that it is just this vicarious emotional reaction that separates empathy from the general area of social cognition and role-taking research. In Keefe's model, cognitive understanding is central to the empathy experience. Cognitive involvement goes beyond affect identification and role taking and includes more complex judgments directed inward toward the observer's own affective reverberation process. Furthermore, the Keefe model presents empathic behavior as a sequential process, moving from stimulus perception, to affective reverberation, to cognitive mediation, and finally to communication. Hoffman's and Feshbach's models do not specify such a sequential process for each individual component of empathy. Hoffman and Feshbach also do not emphasize affective reverberation in their models, and, in general, the conditions that promote such resonance to the perceived feeling have not been investigated in children. Finally, neither Hoffman nor Feshbach include empathic communication as an inherent part of the empathy process. Yet, it is particularly this empathic communication component that has been the focus of the psychotherapy, teaching, and parenting empathy literature. We feel that including a communication component as part of a broader empathy model will help integrate the various strands of empathy research from different disciplines.

In the next sections we turn to an examination of the developmental process in each of the four components of empathy identified in Keefe's model. We begin with the cognitive and affective components, because they receive by far the most attention.

THE COGNITIVE COMPONENT

In the child literature, research on the cognitive component of empathy has been closely tied to broader interest in the development of social perception or social cognition (Feshbach, 1978). This larger field deals with many forms of social understanding in addition to comprehension of how another is feeling. Whereas empathy researchers are concerned specifically with understanding of emotions, it is uncertain whether the cognitive processes involved are essentially similar to those involved in understanding another person's thoughts and intentions, understanding his visual perspective, or understanding his behavior (Shantz, 1983). In her recent review of the social cognition field, Shantz (1983) states that, as yet, the content of perspective-taking tasks has not been shown to have a major influence on performance, or in the intercorrelations between perspective-taking tasks. However, there still remains much to be learned about the nature of the social cognitive processes involved in empathic understanding.

Decentration and Role Taking

Of the many phenomena that have been investigated by social cognitive researchers, the concept of egocentrism has historically played the largest role in both defining the cognitive component of empathy and delineating the research questions that have been asked. Piaget described egocentrism as a state of fusion or undifferentiation between the self and other people. Early infancy is characterized by this. The infant cannot separate self from environment or his wishes from reality. However, in late infancy the young child begins to be aware that objects in his world have a separate existence apart from his experience of them through his senses and are centers of forces that are not dependent on his will. This marks the achievement of a stable physical world that has been separated in time and space from the child's own sensory impressions and motor manipulations. During the toddler and preschool years, egocentrism continues, though there is somewhat less tendency to fuse self and object. The "preoperational" toddler does not understand the difference between the physical and social world. He engages in "animism" and does not understand the separateness of his and others' psychological experiences.

At 6 or 7 years of age, with the advent of "concrete operations," Piaget found there to be a significant lessening of egocentrism. At this point the child is aware that other people do have different thoughts, feelings, and perspectives than his own. His accuracy in identifying these also grows. Piaget believed that conflicts with others (around their wishing something different from what he wishes, for example) play a large role in facilitating the child's perspective-taking ability at this stage (Shantz, 1983). Then, in adolescence, with the advent of formal operations, egocentrism undergoes another significant decline. The adolescent, like the adult, now is capable of recursive thinking (e.g., thinking about thinking about oneself). However, this ability still involves a large amount of viewing reality in terms of the self that does not diminish for several more years (Elkind, 1967; Shantz, 1983).

Perspective-Taking Ability

Although the ability to engage in nonegocentric reasoning has been viewed as an important aspect of cognitive empathy, Shantz (1983) notes that perspective-taking or role-taking ability has been frequently misconstrued as identical to nonegocentrism. She states that nonegocentric functioning is a prerequisite for role taking. After a child comes to recognize that in a particular situation the other thinks and feels differently than himself, role taking is one very important (but not the only) kind of inferential process than can be used to gather information about what the differences between his own and the other's perspectives are. Furthermore, one may have achieved the ability to accomplish self-other differentiation but lack the inferential abilities or knowledge about the other necessary to take his role.

Two models of role-taking development have gained favor in the developmental literature, the model proposed by John Flavell (Flavell, Botkin, Fry, Wright, & Jarvis, 1968) and the model proposed by Robert Selman (1980). Flavell's is an information-processing model. It hypothesizes a series of cognitive acts that need to take place when a child learns to take the role of another:

1. Existence—that there *is* such a thing as "perspective," that is, that what you perceive, think, or feel in any given situation need not coincide with what I perceive, think or feel.

2. Need—that an analysis of the other's perspective is called for in this particular situation, that is, that such an analysis would be a useful means of achieving whatever one's goal is here.

3. Prediction—how actually to carry out this analysis, that is, possession of the abilities needed to discriminate with accuracy whatever the relevant role attributes are.

4. Maintenance—how to maintain in awareness the cognitions yielded by this analysis, assuming them to be in active competition with those which define one's own point of view, during the time in which they are to be applied to the goal behavior.

5. Application—how actually to apply these cognitions to the end at hand, for example, how to translate what one knows about the other's listener role attributes into an effective verbal message. [p. 208]

This sequence can be interpreted both as a developmental model for role-taking ability and as a model of the cognitive process an individual goes through each time that he performs a role-taking act (Shantz, 1983).

Robert Selman's (1980; Selman & Bryne, 1974) model of perspective taking follows more within the Piagetian tradition than does Flavell's. It describes a series of five cognitive advances in the self's understanding and coordination of its own relationship to others. Level 0 is termed *egocentric or undifferentiated perspectives*. Generally occurring between the ages of 3 and 7, the child has awareness that he and others may have different perspectives but he cannot consciously represent two people's perspectives and then decide whether or not they are similar. If, for example, he believes that playing with cars is fun, he expects everyone to feel this way. He attributes his own perspective to everyone who is in the same situation as he. Level 1 is marked by recognition of the basic subjectivity of people. The child now has the ability to comprehend that, when he and another are in the same social situation, their perspectives may either be the same or different depending on the information they have, their motives, and their goals. He also begins to have concern for the other's possibly different subjective state. At Level 2 (usually occurring between 6 and 12 years of age), he recognizes that he himself may be the object of the other's perspective taking, just as he tries to take the role of the other. Thus, this level of perspective taking allows for reciprocity of thought. However, the reciprocity is limited in that it is between the self and one other person. Selman calls this a *second-person perspective*. At Level 3, *third-person or mutual perspectives* becomes possible. Usually between the ages of 9 and 15, the child comes to understand the recursive nature of reciprocal perspectives (e.g., "He feels that I feel that he feels . . ."). He also comes to be able to view himself, the other, and the mutual perspective-taking in an impartial, relatively detached way, as if he were watching two actors playing their roles. Then usually between the ages of 9 and 15, the fourth level labeled *society or in-depth perspective,* is attained. Now the child can consider the perspectives of whole groups of people rather than only of individuals. Perspective taking is viewed as forming a network between people, and the child develops concepts of societal or cultural viewpoints. He also comes to understand that sometimes a group's perspective consists of unverbalized attitudes or values.

We reiterate once again that the concepts of egocentrism and perspective taking have been developed to address social comprehension across several different content areas. From the perspective of our model of empathy, it is specifically perspective taking in the affective realm that is related to the cognitive component of empathy, and we now turn directly to this field of theory and research.

In the early 1970s a debate emerged among empathy researchers focusing on the question of whether children who were still mainly egocentric, as Piaget defined this, were capable of understanding another's feelings. Helen Borke (1971) started off the debate with the publication of a study in which children as young as 3 years old showed awareness of other people's feelings. In the empathy task they successfully performed, the children were presented with affect-arousing stories illustrating fear, anger, happiness, or sadness. Each story (e.g., losing a toy, having a favorite snack) is accompanied by a picture illustrating the story situation, but leaving out the face of the main character. The children are then asked what the story character feels and answer by selecting one of four stylized drawings of faces showing fear, anger, happiness, or sadness. Happy or sad stories were identified more often than anger and fear stories by preschool, as well as first-grade subjects. Borke argued that her findings challenged Piaget's conclusion that children under age 7 are primarily egocentric and unable to take the perspective of another.

A short time later however, Michael Chandler and Stephen Greenspan (1972) published a study in which they argued against Borke's contention that children of preschool age actually engaged in true empathic behavior. In their own investigation they studied children of ages 6 to 12 and found that, although children could successfully identify another person's affect on a procedure that was similar to Borke's, the youngest children were not able to successfully perform a role-taking task that required them to differentiate their own perspective from that of an uninformed bystander. On this task they tended to confuse their own perspective with the bystander's and to attribute information to the bystander that was only available to themselves. Chandler and Greenspan speculated that Borke's subjects probably were making their correct identifications of the other's feelings through either a process of projection or a process of stereotyped knowledge. In the case of projection, children sometimes make correct responses by attributing their own feelings to the story character when there happens to be a correspondence between the two. In the case of stereotype accuracy, the children are basing their responses on knowledge they had of how other children, in general, behave in situations that were like that of the story. Chandler and Greenspan (1972) argued that "given the rather stereotypic character of the thematic materials provided, egocentric and nonegocentric subjects could be expected to perform in an almost identical fashion" (p. 105). This criticism is quite similar to Chronbach's (1958) critique of R.F. Dymond's (1949, 1950, Dymond, Hughes, & Raabe, 1952) original predictive empathy measures with adults. In response, a number of investigators attempted to develop story–picture measures that utilize situations where the character's emotion is incongruous with the story situation, so that responses based on projection of how the subject would feel in the situation would now yield an incorrect response (Burns & Cavey, 1957; Iannotti, 1975). However, other investigators have criticized these revised instruments for changing the complexity of the task. Feshbach (1978) remarked that such procedures are more appropriate for studying children's understanding of incongruent stimuli and other cognitive dilemmas. Hoffman (1977b) noted that young children are often confused cognitively by contradictory person and situation cues. An alternative approach that would also control for projection was suggested by Feshbach (1978). This suggestion calls for the use of a set of experimental stimuli in which more than one type of feeling can justifiably be expected to result from the situational context of the story. Another approach, used in a study by Rothenberg (1970), is to use situations and characters who are in adult emotionally arousing situations that are unfamiliar to children.

In the same journal issue in which Chandler and Greenspan's article appeared, Borke (1972) herself presented a rebuttal to the criticism that young children cannot have cognitive empathic skills. She stated that, whereas young children may use projection or stereotyped knowledge to attempt to understand another's feelings, this does not take away from the fact that they do appear capable of making a judgment that the person has thoughts and feelings that are different from their own. She argued that this constitutes a preliminary form of empathy that admittedly is less developed than the level of empathy described by Piaget as the ability to put oneself in the place of another's experience and view the world through that person's eyes. She (Borke, 1972) then argued very persuasively:

> As long as children under 7 years of age are perceived as egocentric, there is no need to emphasize an understanding of the other's viewpoint as part of the socialization process. If we accept as valid the evidence that empathic awareness develops very early, we might begin to consider seriously ways of behaving empathically toward young children and encouraging their attempts to behave empathically toward others. (p. 109).

It has been this viewpoint that has characterized the research effort into the development of children's cognitive empathy over the dozen years since these words were written.

Our own position is that both nonegocentrism as Piaget used the term and role taking or perspective taking as Shantz (1983) distinguished this are very important cognitive processes that influence quantitatively and qualitatively how a child will comprehend another person's emotional experience. However, just as nonegocentrism does not, by itself, determine role-taking ability, nonegocentrism and role-taking ability are not the only cognitive processes that influence empathy. In fact we see later in this book that even the processes that Chandler and Greenspan argued indicated an absence of empathy: Projection and stereotyping, if followed by an awareness of how one's judgments are being formed, can be very useful in understanding the other's emotions. For example, psychotherapists are trained to utilize these processes as conscious techniques for generating hypotheses about their clients in the therapy situation. We now turn to an examination of some recent findings concerning the development of role-taking abilities in the emotional realm. Following this, we review several studies that have identified important nonrole-taking cognitive processes involved in the understanding of emotions.

Affective Role Taking

A study by Gove and Keating (1979) sheds some light on what the earliest manifestations of role taking for emotions may be like. In their study, children of two age groups, one averaging 3 years 10 months and the other 5 years 2 months, were presented with two types of stories. In one type, two child protagonists expressed different feelings as a result of events for which the emotionally relevant cues were available in the situation (e.g., one child is happy when winning a game, whereas another child, who loses, is unhappy). In the second type of story, different feelings are again expressed by the two protagonists, but now, in order to identify the emotions correctly, the subject is required to consider the story character's subjective state as well as situational cues (e.g., when given an identical-appearing dog, one story character reacts with happiness whereas the other story character reacts with fear). The children's task was to both discriminate and explain the differing feelings of each of the story characters. Gove and Keating hypothesized that correct explanations for the situational-inference stories would be significantly easier than for the psychological-inference stories for all subjects. Furthermore, they expected subjects' response patterns to be hierarchically ordered, with correct responses on the psychological-inference stories only occurring when the situational inference stories had been mastered. The findings supported these predictions, leading the authors to speculate that, in terms of developmental progression, emotions are first considered to be a part of the situation itself, with role taking, at this early point, consisting of simply reading off the affective aspect of the event. The child need only understand that different people may have differing emotional responses to the same situation. Later on, when children understand that feelings are psychological events or processes, they become focused more on the internal state of the particular stimulus person, and role taking becomes the traditional perspective taking described in the developmental research.

In another study Kathryn Urburg and Edward Docherty (1976) attempted to clarify the nature of the stage-like developments in role taking that were posited by such investigators as Flavell and Selman. The fact that they were specifically concerned with role taking in the affective realm makes their work directly relevant to the concerns of this chapter.

The authors first point out that it is necessary to consider the distinction between structure and content when analyzing what aspects of role-taking ability are needed to successfully complete a particular role-taking task. The structure of the task consists of the cognitive operations necessary to perform it. Two examples are the number of dimensions or aspects of a problem that have to be considered, and whether these aspects are considered in sequence or must be simultaneously coordinated. The content of a role-taking task consists of the particular concepts that the operations work on to produce a solution to the task. When a child is asked to infer another child's feelings, he must have already developed for himself the concept of the emotion that he is being asked to judge and must have already gained some knowledge of the kinds of situations that might produce this emotion in another person. Referring back to the debate about whether stereotype knowledge should be distinguished from role taking, Urburg and Docherty (1976) suggest that stereotype knowledge can be one important way to learn role taking. They write: "role-taking can be represented as a continuum ranging from shared cultural stereotypes at one end to sophisticated knowledge of the unique ways events affect individuals at the other" (p. 199). They then suggest that all role-taking tasks can be ordered along a continuum of difficulty of its structural and content components.

Their own investigation focused on development of a child's abilities in the structural domain. They first constructed a series of new role-taking tasks that differed in the complexity of the structural component, whereas all utilized the same affective content. The content domain was kept at a very simple level so that it would not cause difficulty even for the least advanced subjects.

The first task, which was based on Borke's (1971) work, involved a judgment of another's feelings based on commonly known cultural knowledge. The second task required subjects to make two different stereotypic inferences about two story characters, but the inferences could be made sequentially. The third task, which was modeled after Burns and Cavey's (1957) work, also required two different inferences, but only one was stereotypic. The other required that the subject take into account information unique to the individual in the story. The fourth task, which was developed newly for this research, required simultaneous consideration of conflicting roles. Here, too, however, the content remained simple and stereotypic. Finally, the fifth task required not only consideration of simultaneous conflicting roles but added the aspect of the redintegrative nature of the story. Analyzing the performance of a group of 3-, 4-, and 5-year-olds on these tasks, Urburg and Docherty found evidence of the following levels of role taking for emotions:

Level 0: These subjects did not pass any of the tests. They had a median age of 3 years 5 months.

Level 1: Sequential decentration.   These subjects can infer another individual's viewpoint if it can be done by sequentially focusing on different aspects of the situation. The median age for successful performance at this level was 4 years 5 months.

Level 2: Simultaneous decentration: These subjects are able to infer another viewpoint even when it requires simultaneous consideration of two aspects of the situation. The median age was 5 years 4 months for children who could successfully perform at this level.

In contrast to the traditional view that role-taking stages were universal, the authors (Urburg & Docherty, 1976) argue that any developmental sequence depends on the particular structure and content of the tasks:

> We would suggest, then, that it is possible to define close to an infinite number of developmental sequences of role-taking skills. This suggestion implies that looking for *the* sequence of development of these skills is futile. Rather than considering role-taking as a global, unidimensional ability, the variables that are known or hypothesized to affect the role-taking process should be examined to determine the developmental course of each as well as the interactions between them. (p. 203).

This viewpoint adds further complexity to the already very complicated problem of understanding the development of empathy's cognitive component, for not only is role taking not the sole cognitive process involved in empathy, but role taking is itself a process composed of numerous separately interacting abilities. In line with this belief, a redefining of the cognitive component of empathy along the lines suggested by Greenspan, Barenboim and Chandler's (1976) working definition seems appropriate: "empathic skill is defined as the ability to consider and integrate all available relevant information relating to the affect state of the target character" (p. 82).

Given the complexity of the cognitive processes that are being identified as involved in empathy, nearly all the assessment procedures that have been developed to measure the cognitive component have been overly simplistic, being unable to distinguish which cognitive and inferential processes have been used in arriving at a correct response. In part this has been due to past tendency to oversimplify conceptually the cognitive aspects of empathy, as we have just seen. The task of developing more appropriate measures will not be an easy one, however, because even with a broader and more complex view of the cognitive component, it will be very difficult to create assessment procedures that, on the one hand, take into account the complexities and, on the other hand, are designed so that young children can perform the required assessment tasks. In developing new instruments that are sensitive to the complexities of the cognitive processes involved in empathy, researchers should keep in mind two cautions voiced by Norma Feshbach (1978): (1) that children's response systems are not highly differentiated and (2) that young children's verbal repertoires may not be sufficiently elaborated to convey their apperceptions and experiences. A great deal of creativity in the devising of such measures will be necessary.

Non Role-Taking Abilities Involved in Cognitive Empathy

Karniol (1982) has developed an information-processing model of prosocial behavior in which empathic-like behaviors are dependent on cognitive processes that do not involve role taking. This is described as an illustration of how nonrole-taking cognitive skills can aid in the child's ability to consider and integrate information relating to the affective state of another.

Karniol believes that an important aspect of prosocial behavior is need awareness, i.e., becoming aware that the other person is in distress and has the need for help. Rather than explaining need awareness as the result of the child's role-taking activities, she suggests that it is based on the child's understanding of the other's overall situation. This, in turn, occurs when information retrieval processes are initiated within the observing child by situational stimuli, as part of the child's processing of these stimuli. Karniol (1982) states:

> We are suggesting, then, that need awareness is reached through the accessing of stored situational information which provides an interpretational context for the sequence of actions and goals in the situation. Thus, need awareness is not dependent on imaginative attempts to understand what the other is thinking, feeling, or experiencing. We 'simply know' that help is needed because of previously stored information that is accessed by exposure to the relevant scene. We do not need to put ourselves into the other's place, try to understand what he or she feels, and then conclude that help is needed. (p. 260)

Not only does Karinol argue that role taking is not essential for altruistic behavior, but she suggests that "need concern," which seems similar to our description of affective empathy, may not be either. Karinol states that, whereas concern may sometimes be a part of the behavioral sequence of helping, coming to the assistance of another may also occur out of the individual's motivation to maintain the self-schema. Markus (1977) defines the self-schema as a "cognitive generalization about the self, derived from past experience, that organizes and guides the processing of self-related information" (p. 64). In this case, the self-schema would include being kind or helpful. This schema becomes activated by the processing of relevant situational information (e.g., "this is an occasion for helping someone") and results in the retrieval of appropriate scripts from the person's past experience (e.g., "I helped the lady with the parcels last week"). Once past scripts are activated, they become the basis of the present action, which should be consistent with the activated self-schema. Individual differences in helping reflect the fact that people differ in the labels they use for both their self and the situations in which they find themselves.

There is some empirical confirmation for the importance of need awareness in children's naturally occurring prosocial bebaviors. Eisenberg–Berg and Neal (1979) interviewed nursery school children in their classrooms and on the playground immediately after they had been observed performing a prosocial act. The children were asked why they had acted in that particular way. Tied for the most frequently given reason for sharing, helping, or comforting another child was "needs of others orientation or needs-oriented reasoning" in which the child referred to the other's physical or psychological needs as a justification for the prosocial behavior (e.g., "he's hungry.").

Children's Understanding of the Cognitive
Empathy Process

So far we have focused on cognitive processes involved directly in the comprehension of another's emotional state. It may be useful, however, to broaden the scope of our discussion of the cognitive component of empathy to include children's cognitions about their own empathic responses. How a child understands his affective and cognitive empathic responses may have much to do with the way that empathy mediates social behavior.

A recent study done by Hughes, Tingle, and Sawin (1981) is one of the few to address the relationship between cognitive empathy and reasoning about that empathy. These authors used an interview technique as the basis of their research. Employing interviews in child empathy research has sometimes been criticized, because the interveiw is open to response variations based on children's verbal abilities. These authors chose this approach anyway because interview techniques had proven useful in describing the developmental course of other cognitive processes related to the specific processes they were studying. However, knowing the criticisms of the interview method, they attempted to develop rating scales for the interview in which scores would not depend on verbal fluency.

Forty-eight kindergarten and second-grade boys and girls were the subjects in the study. To measure empathy, they used two happy and two sad stories from Feshbach and Roe's (1968) Affective Matching Test that was originally developed to measure affective empathy and is described in more detail in the next section. The stories are accompanied by a series of slides. For example, in one of the happy stories, a child is initally portrayed waking up and realizing that today is his or her birthday, then shown greeting friends who are coming to the birthday party, then shown at the party with friends gathered around a birthday cake and presents.

Each subject participated in two sessions, 1 week apart. One session focused on the child's comprehension of the story child's affect (called "Other session"), whereas the second session focused on the subject's own reaction to the story children's affect (called "Self-session"). One happy and one sad story scenario was seen at each session. In the "Other Interview" the subjects were asked questions such as "How does the child in the story feel," "What makes the child feel this way," "Why does that make the child feel this way," and "How can you tell that the child in the story feels this way"?. Questions in the "Self Interview" included "How do you feel," "What makes you feel this way," and "Why does that make you feel this way"?

The results of their study showed a number of consistent developmental trends in children's cognitive empathy as well as in their understanding of their own emotional responses in these empathy situations. First, with respect to cognitive empathy itself, between the ages of 5 and 8 years of age the children showed increased awareness of the other person's emotional state. They also become progressively more aware of the personal and psychological characteristics of others that may be influencing their emotional reactions. Thus, younger subjects tended to understand the other's feelings mainly from situational cues and from the most salient causal events, whereas older children were more likely to focus on the person and give inferences about possible psychological reasons why the story character felt a particular emotion. These developmental trends appear to parallel developmental changes in social perception generally, where research has shown that young children perceive others in terms of observable behaviors and surface characteristics, whereas older children are more oriented to general traits and internal dispositions (e.g., Lively & Bromley, 1973).

The children's understanding of their own emotional responses in these empathy situations also changed with age. In general, older children showed a better understanding of their reactions to affect than did the younger children. Although nearly all the children reported feeling happy in response to the happy stories and sad in response to the sad stories (i.e., they reported affective empathy reactions), older subjects were more likely to use cognitive role taking in their responses (i.e., when asked how they felt they gave evidence of placing themselves cognitively in the position of the story character). The older children also had better understanding of what caused their feelings, being more likely to report affective empathy (e.g., ''Because he's sad.'') or role taking (e.g., ''I'd be sad if . . .'') as the reason. Younger children tended more to give egocentric reasons for why they felt a particular way in reaction to the stimulus stories (e.g., ''that I lost my dog.''). Although the older children still had little knowledge of the empathic process within themselves, they were more likely to see the link between their own feelings and the story child's feelings. The older children also were more likely to cite internal psychological reasons as the cause of their own emotional reactions (''because I feel like someone loves and likes me.'') rather than external, situational events, which were characteristic of the younger children.

Older children also seemed to spontaneously engage in role taking. They attempted to put themselves in the other's place, both in terms of their own emotional reactions and in their explanations for the causes of their empathic reactions. Spontaneous use of role taking in understanding another's feelings may be an important step in the development of cognitive empathy and certainly enhances the likelihood that empathic capacity will be translated into action.

An additional finding of this study also has interesting implications for future research. Children were found to be more able to comprehend the story character's feelings after first introspecting about their own feelings. The authors suggested that such self-observations may not be egocentric but may aid the empathic response. Citing work by Youniss (1975), they suggest that children may naturally reflect on their own thoughts and feelings as part of their attempt to understand the thoughts and feelings of others. We address this point again in the psychotherapy chapter where we see that reflecting on one's own affective reac-

tion in order to better understand a client's problems is an important psychotherapeutic skill. The precursors of this skill apparently appear in the elementary
school years.

New Directions

Most of the time, when a feeling is expressed, it is not as qualitatively "pure" as
is the case with the emotions children have been asked about in empathy research. Several feelings occur simultaneously in the person with whom we are
attempting to empathize. A person's feelings also may be contradictory or ambivalent. Often, "beneath" the surface feeling lies a second feeling that is not
being openly expressed, but which may have even more significance than the
manifest feeling. Whereas discriminating these more complex affective situations is not possible in early childhood, sometime during middle childhood or
adolescence the individual becomes better able to decipher complex feelings and
patterns of feelings. The development of the higher level cognitive empathy
skills required to do this is a fertile ground for future research. As we discuss in a
later chapter, understanding the development of such higher forms of cognitive
empathy may be important for the selection of people for professional training in
psychotherapy, education, or other professions that call for advanced interpersonal sensitivity.

Person versus Situation Cues   We close this section with some further
thoughts about the present state of the situation versus person controversy in
cognitive empathy research. Until recently, judging another person's feelings
through the use of situational cues was tied closely to notions that the individual
was using projection, stereotyped knowledge, or previous experience with the
situation as the basis of his response. Although this certainly happens, the evidence we have presented indicates that this is not always the case. The use of
situational cues may actually be part of a sophisticated cognitive empathic response. Thus, whereas it is relatively easy to devise a situation, like the sad boy
at a birthday party, in which the stimulus character's affect will be missed by
someone who uses situational cues alone, it is also evident that, if the situation
contains some clues about why this child might be sad (such as a broken toy
mentioned in the story or shown in the background of the picture), then a focus
on the situational cues may actually help in the understanding of the other's
emotions. Furthermore, mistakes can occur if the child becomes over reliant on
person cues, just as they can with over reliance on situation cues. An example of
this would be the case where an individual is crying out of happiness at receiving
a beautiful gift. Other times, a neutral face may hide an emotion from the
observer that could have been available had situation cues been the object of
scrutiny. On the other hand, facial, postural, tonal, and other cues available from
the person may at times provide nuances of feeling that are unavailable from the

situation. It would seem, then, that person cues and situational cues, if used together, may help us comprehend the more complex feelings that we have discussed here.

In a recent study, Reichenbach and Masters (1983) performed two experiments in which preschool and third-grade children were required to make judgments of happy, sad, angry, and neutral emotions of other children on the basis of: (1) facial cues presented in slides of children's faces, (2) contextual cues based on story vignettes describing the stimulus child in an emotionally arousing situation, or (3) both types of cues. The results showed that, for both age groups, the contextual cues produced greater accuracy in affect identification than did the facial cues. Interestingly, in the condition where the children were presented with inconsistent facial and contextual cues together, the younger children relied more on facial cues whereas the older children relied more on contextual cues. The authors suggest that this age difference may reflect either the older children's understanding of the operation of "display rules" that regulate the way people allow themselves to openly show emotions or that older children are more aware of the greater potential information available from contextual versus facial cues. It should be noted that, although facial expressions are certainly a type of person cue, the source of information is very much on the "surface" for the child to see and does not involve the complex judgments of the other's underlying emotional state that Gove and Keating (1979) found required higher role-taking skills. In the future, researchers will need to identify and distinguish between the different kinds of person and situation cues that are used by children of different ages in the formation of emotional judgments.

If researchers accept the importance of both situation and person cues in cognitive empathy, a new conceptualization of what is meant by a higher level cognitive empathy response suggests itself. Individuals with high cognitive empathy may be especially aware that people sometimes feel in incongruous ways, i.e., in ways that most other people and oneself might not feel if in the same situation. Then, if there is evidence that the stimulus person is having such an incongrous feeling, the highly empathic person would begin to search for cues in both the person and the situation that would tell him about the other's emotional experience. The search may ultimately lead him to posit that there are ambivalent or underlying feelings involved in the incongruent emotional response, and if this were the case his empathic response would be toward the ambivalence and the underlying feelings. This process is not inherently different from what a psychotherapist goes through when confronted by a woman who is smiling as she talks about her husband's death. The therapist does not immediately conclude that the woman is either happy or sad but becomes attentive to what he knows is a complex set of feelings that he will have to decipher.

If situational cues are to be given an important role in children's comprehension of other's emotional experiences, we need to begin to develop research methodologies that can examine how children perceive and integrate emotionally relevant information from the environment. An approach used by Ross Buck (1975) in a study of nonverbal communication of affect in children, though it did not measure empathically produced emotion, may provide a useful methodological direction. In this study, observers were required to observe a stimulus child's facial expressions and make judgments about which of several emotionally arousing slides the child was viewing. Although the observers were adults, a similar approach might be used with children. Child subjects could first be shown a close-up view of a stimulus person expressing some feeling (live, on a slide, or on a videotape) and then be asked to choose which of a variety of possible situations might have produced this emotional response. The situations likewise could be presented in any of a variety of modalities (e.g., story, picture, videotape) and could be varied along a number of dimensions in order to elucidate what determines children's ability to integrate situational and person emotional stimuli at different ages.

AFFECTIVE COMPONENT

Carolyn Shantz (1983) described the affective component of empathy as "the emotional response of the self to, or with, the other's affect" (p. 517). Most investigators require that the child's vicarious feeling be identical to the stimulus person's feeling for it to qualify as affective empathy. However, some researchers also consider similar nonidentical emotional responses by the child to be empathy. For Hoffman (1977a) it is important that "(a) affect is aroused in the observer and (b) that quality and direction of the affect correspond sufficiently to that experienced by the model to warrant calling it a vicarious response" (p. 191).

How does the affective component of empathy develop? Aronfreed (1968) has formulated a conditioning theory. As children learn that other peoples' distress often is followed by their own distress (e.g., when mother is upset she cannot attend to the child's needs), they develop an emotional distress reaction to the distress cues emitted by others. In time they come to experience this vicarious emotional arousal even in situations where there is no reason to anticipate that the other's distress will lead to direct negative consequences for themselves. Aronfreed also related this form of empathic arousal to altruistic behavior. Because the empathic distress response is aversive, activity to help the other is undertaken to reduce the empathic distress that the child experiences. The altruistic act, if it is successful in reducing the other's distress, is reinforced by the cessation of the child's own empathic distress response. Aronfreed (1970) describes a study (Aronfreed & Paskal, 1968) that showed that empathic pleasure as well as empathic distress could be conditoned in children. However, whereas these investigators were successful in demonstrating that both classical and operant conditioning may play a role in the formation of a vicarious emotional response, the qualitative aspects of the empathic reaction were not being studied and developmental psychologists have generally turned their attention to models of affective empathy that posit a more maturationally based process.

In the discussion to follow, research findings are grouped by the type of measure used to assess children's affective empathy. At this early stage of empathy research, the findings on the development of empathy's affective component are still inextricably tied to the kind of measurement approach used. Until more research has been conducted using multiple measures that focus on different modalities (e.g., physiological measures, facial expressions, and self-reports), we are not able to tease out differences in affective sensitivity across the different modalities, from method variance that may be related to problems in reliability, subject demand characteristics, or other factors.

Results with Picture–Story and Videotape Self-Report Measures

The most widely used measure of affective empathy in children has been the Feshbach and Roe (1968) Affective Situation Test for Empathy (FASTE). This measure was an improvement on earlier picture–story instruments because it used pictures (slides) instead of cartoon stick figures and because it used a series of these slides forming a vignette, rather than a single picture, as, for example, Borke's (1971) picture–story measure employs. Both visual and auditory information about the affect situation were presented. The slide sequences showed 6- to-7 year-old children in situations that had previously been identified by both adults (parents and psychologists) and other children as reflecting the feelings of happiness, sadness, fear, and anger. Each of the four emotions was represented by two slide vignettes (consisting of three slides each). Duplicate vignettes were created with either a boy or a girl as the central character. The themes of the happiness vignettes were a birthday party and winning a television contest; the themes for the sadness vignettes were a lost dog and experiencing social rejection. The theme of the fear vignettes were a lost child and a scary dog, and the themes of the anger vignettes were a toy being taken and a false accusation being made. The stories that accompanied each vignette were matched for number of words and avoided the inclusion of any affective labels. After watching the vignettes, which were introduced as stories about other children the same age, the subjects were asked, ''How do you feel?'' and ''Tell me how do you feel?'' The subjects' verbal reports were used as the measure of empathy, and a correct response was one in which the feeling that had been reported matched the feeling of the stimulus vignette. A total empathy score was recorded based on the number of correct responses given across the different affective situations.

Studies with the FASTE have shown that performance increases consistently between the ages of 4 and 8. For example, Fay (1970) found higher empathy in 8-year-old boys and girls than in 6-year-olds and Kuchenbecker, Feshbach, and Pletcher (1974) found a significant relationship between empathy scores and age in a sample of kindergarten, first-, and second-grade children. However, between the ages of 8 and 10 the scores stop increasing. Feshbach (1978) attributes this to a probable ceiling effect, because the content of the FASTE was originally designed for use with 4-to-8 year-old children.

A number of criticisms have been raised concerning possible problems with picture–story techniques to measure empathy. One problem concerns the demand characteristics inherent in any self-report measure in which an adult is continuously asking a child how he or she feels. This may undermine the validity of the FASTE and similar measures (Lennon, Eisenberg, & Carroll, 1983). There is also some evidence that sex of the examiner may interact with sex of the child in influencing the child's responses to such measures (Lennon et al., 1983). Furthermore, although the FASTE was designed to measure affective empathy, all self-report measures of affective empathy necessarily include cognitive and communication components in that the child is required to indicate what he is feeling. If the child experiences an emotional response to the stimulus person's feeling but cannot label this feeling accurately or can't communicate it to the experimenter, he will appear to have missed the particular test item. Finally, as we discuss later, the child's self-reported emotional reaction may be influenced by such cognitive factors as his or her expectations and values about experiencing and expressing feelings, and his reasoning about such feelings.

Feshbach and her colleagues have recently developed several new empathy measures that they hoped could alleviate some of these problems. The most sophisticated of these is the Feshbach and Powell Audiovisual Test for Empathy (Feshbach, 1982b). An audiovisual format was selected in order to more closely duplicate real-life emotion-arousing situations. Also, a more sophisticated scoring system was adopted than had been used in the FASTE. It is described later. The new measure consists of a series of videotaped stories showing children in common situations related to the experience of five emotions: pride, happiness, anger, fear, and sadness. Two separate videotaped stories were developed for a particular affect, each lasting about 2 minutes. Because sex differences were a major focus of the planned research, a separate set of of videotapes were developed for males (with a male as the central character) and for females (with a female central character). The story situations are related by the visual context of the videotapes as well as by a narration describing the situation and by a dialogue between the actors. Children can be administered the test individually or in a small group. The children are asked to state verbally after each presentation of a videotape how they felt and how much they felt that way on a scale of 1 to 9. The videotapes are presented in counterbalanced order with respect to emotion and a task designed to guard against emotional overlap between the stories is presented between videotapes.

The two different scoring approaches that have been developed appear to tap different aspects of empathy. In both procedures, the degree to which the subjects' self-reported emotional response matches the emotional experience by the child in the videotaped story is examined. One approach uses a matching procedure that allows for a determination of the degree of emotional match between the subjects' responses and the emotion depicted in the stimulus character. The empathy score represents the distance between the subject's reported affect and the actual affect. The distance is calculated based on a two-dimensional space formed by two orthogonal factors of hedonic tone or valence and physiological activity level. The second scoring procedure utilizes the intensity scores given by the children to their self-reported emotions. The test was administered to a different sample of children and the proportion of subjects who reported a particular emotion to each videotape was measured. These proportions were then assigned as weights to the feelings reported by the subjects in the study and were multiplied by the intensity ratings that the child gave on the self-rating scale for each videotape.

Sex Differences in Emotional Empathy. Research with the new videotape measure sheds new light on two important issues: (1) sex differences in the development of affective empathy and (2) the role that empathy plays in children's prosocial development. As in previous studies, girls tend to be somewhat more empathic than boys, with this sex difference showing up mainly on the happiness and pride videotapes. However, some of the most interesting findings centered on the different social behavior and cognitive factors that appeared to mediate empathy in boys and girls. Using the first method of scoring empathy, which measured affective match without taking into account intensity of feelings, it was found that, for boys, empathy was strongly related to cognitive competence (i.e., vocabulary, reading skills, comprehension, spacial perspective taking, fantasy elaboration, and the recognition of changes in feelings of others). This measure of empathy was also related to low aggression in boys. In girls, however, empathy was found to be related to positive self-concept and prosocial behavior, as well as negatively related to antisocial behavior. These findings were consistent across the different kinds of affects tested.

With the use of the second scoring system, which did take into account intensity, an even more complex set of findings emerged. For girls, the findings are very similar to those with the first empathy scoring. Empathy was found to be positively related to positive self-concept, prosocial behavior, and social understanding. Empathy was also negatively related to aggression and antisocial behavior in girls. However, for boys a complicated pattern emerges in which empathy is influenced by the interaction of type of affect (e.g., dysphoric vs. euphoric) and the intensity of the reported affective arousal. Boys who had strong dysphoric feelings when they viewed the stimulus film in which a child character has experienced a dysphoric emotion (i.e., sadness, fear, or anger) were more likely to engage in helping behaviors and to perceive themselves as being helpful. They were also lower on aggressiveness, when this was rated by teachers and peers, and they appeared to be more sensitive to other peoples' motives. However, boys who reported intense euphoric emotions when they saw the videotapes of a child experiencing happiness or pride tended to see themselves and be seen by their peers as aggressive. They were also seen by their teachers as antisocial. These children also were lower in rated prosocial behavior, had poorer self-concept, and experienced higher anxiety over aggression. Thus, for boys, emotional empathy for euphoric affect appears to be associated with negative behavioral attributes.

Feshbach (1982b) suggests the following possible explanation for these findings. Experiencing another person in distress may be quite upsetting for the child who is observing and may motivate the child to take action to attempt to alleviate the other person's felt distress. This motivational sequence may serve to control the child's own empathically produced distress feelings that, if not controlled, would seek release through impulsive behavior, sometimes including aggression. On the other hand, empathic experience of euphoric emotion would not have these motivating consequences and therefore would not be expected to lead to the child needing to exercise self-control against impulsively releasing his emotions. The kinds of emotional release that could follow might include boisterousness, hyperactivity, and aggressiveness. Thus, rather than promote prosocial behavior, this kind of empathy may further aggressive and antisocial behavior. Presumably, such antisocial impulsive expression of emotion is less controlled in boys than in girls. In discussing these findings, Feshbach (1980) hypothesizes that empathy appears to be a more convoluted process for boys than girls. Whereas girls benefit from direct socialization to become sensitive to others' feelings (see later), boys must rely on either having attained higher cognitive maturation or experiencing a more intense dysphoric emotional response. Even when the experienced empathy is the same, boys appear to have a more difficult time translating their empathic reaction into socially approved behavioral responses.

Feshbach's explanation appears to make the assumption that uncontrolled euphoric emotional expressions on the part of children who are experiencing euphoric empathy are likely to be antisocial, rather than prosocial. Even if this proves to be true generally, it need not always be the case. One might expect that sometimes children would want to share the happiness that they are experiencing empathically. Moreover, this would serve to further the duration of one's own empathically produced euphoric experience and therefore be rewarding. Certainly, during adulthood, the opportunity to experience vicarious emotional happiness when things go right is one of the important reasons that an individual decides to make a career in the helping professions, and this may also play an important role in parents' and teachers' empathy. An important task for future research is to examine the processes by which the empathic experience is channeled into behavioral expression, in order to determine the critical mediators of whether the response will be prosocial or antisocial.

Feshbach (1978) writes that tests of emotional empathy should be developed for use by older children. She suggests that the 10- to -12-year-old-age range may be particularly interesting, because it is during this period that important changes in role taking and referential communication skills are believed to take place (Chandler & Greenspan, 1972; Feffer & Gourevitch, 1960). A widening of her research group's focus to include the adolescent years would help forge a link to the current research on adult empathy, where similar videotape methodologies are also being developed.

Finally, we note that, whereas sex differences have been repeatedly obtained in tests of affective empathy, this does not appear to be as consistently the case for the cognitive component of empathy. For example, Hoffman (1977a) reviewed the literature on sex differences in recognition of affect and cognitive role taking and concluded that there were no apparent sex differences. This highlights the distinction between the two components and raises the further question of how cognitive and affective empathy are related. We return to this later.

Paper and Pencil Measures

A new paper and pencil test of affective empathy has been developed by Brenda Bryant (1982). It was modeled after the Mehrabian and Epstein (1972) adult empathy scale, with many of the original adult items reworded in order to be appropriate for use with children. The answer format was also changed from a Likert-type 9-point scale to a simple yes–no response. The new scale was administered to a sample of first-, fourth-, and seventh-grade boys and girls. Thus, it is one of the few published affective empathy studies that includes adolescents. An analysis of the empathy scores produced by the different groups showed that seventh-grade boys and girls scored higher than did first- and fourth-grade children, whereas the first and fourth graders did not differ in affective empathy as measured by this instrument. Girls scored higher in empathy than boys.

An interesting extension of the age- and sex-difference finding was provided by an analysis of empathy scores on same versus cross-sex stimuli. The instrument included some items twice, with the only difference being the substitution of a male or female stimulus character (e.g., ''I get upset when I see a boy being hurt'' or ''I get upset when I see a girl being hurt''). Bryant found a fourth-grade-''cootie'' effect in which fourth graders showed significantly lower empathy toward cross-sex stimulus figures than either first or seventh graders, and, in fact, this was the lowest condition for both boys and girls. If these findings are replicated with longitudinal data, they may indicate that affective empathy for the opposite sex develops along a curvilinear path.

Different results for same-sex stimulus persons also emerged for boys and girls. Whereas girls increased their empathy scores with age when confronted with female stimulus figures in the test items, boys decreased in their empathy for the same sex, to the point where the girls had higher empathy for males than the boys did at seventh grade. Bryant suggests that males in early adolescence tend to shun the idea of showing emotional reactions to other males. She believes that the basis of this affective taboo is these boys' fears regarding sexual identity and social ostracism.

Another study with older adolescents using the original Mehrabian and Epstein measure was performed by Nancy Eisenberg–Berg and Paul Mussen (1978). The subjects in the study were ninth-, eleventh-, and twelfth-grade boys and girls. Subjects' empathy scores were unrelated to grade level at these ages. However, empathy was found to be significantly related to level of prosocial moral reasoning (ranging from immature hedonistic to higher level reasoning based on internalized values) for both boys and girls. Empathy was also found to be related to helping (volunteering to perform a dull experiment for no pay) for boys.

The paper and pencil measures of affective empathy have several problems. Hoffman (1977a) argued that the Mehrabian and Epstein measure contains some items that are not indicators of empathy. Also, experiencing empathic feelings may be confounded with a subject's willingness to report that he or she has experienced these emotions (though Bryant was able to show that scores on her empathy measure were uncorrelated with a measure of social desirability). Furthermore, in both the original Mehrabian and Epstein measure and the modified measure for children, subjects are required to reflect on their empathic response, rather than reporting a present feeling directly (e.g., checking ''yes'' to the item ''Seeing a girl who is crying makes me feel like crying'' is not equivalent to a statement that, at this moment, the child feels like crying).

Nonverbal Measures of Affective Empathy

A number of nonverbal indices have been proposed as measures of affective empathy in children, though their actual use in research has up to now been primarily with adults. Martin Hoffman (1977a) reveiwed and critiqued the possible use in the child area of two physiological measures: an increase in skin conductance and an increase in heart rate. These measures have the advantage of being a more direct idex of an affective response than either the picture–story, audiovisual, or paper and pencil tests discussed earlier. They also avoid the demand characteristics inherent in the other measures. On the other hand, there are important problems. Physiological measures are hard to use unobtrusively and children may react negatively, or with anxiety, thus interfering with any attempt to assess empathy. Secondly, it is difficult to determine whether the subject's emotional response is identical or highly similar to the emotion being experienced by the stimulus person. For example both anger and fear can lead to increased heart rate, and, whereas an increase in skin conductance may usually be the result of an empathic reaction, such an increase may also occur for a number of other reasons including: (1) as the result of a startle reaction to the stimulus person's body movements; (2) as a direct reaction to the noxious stimuli that are being observed; or (3) out of fear that the plight of the stimulus person might befall oneself (Hoffman, 1977a). Researchers have sometimes attempted to control for the uncertainty of the type of emotion being experienced by including self-report measures asking the subject to state what emotion he is feeling and toward whom it is being directed. In some studies the stimulus person's movements have been controlled to limit the possibility of a startle response. Subjects have also sometimes been told directly that they would not receive similar noxious stimuli, in order to control for fear responses. Despite these limitations, Hoffman concludes that the available evidence suggests that the physiological measures do assess empathy most of the time, and he holds some hope for their usefulness in the child domain. One technique that he suggests might be especially appropriate for work with children is the technique for obtaining telemetered heart rate data. This could be done in a relatively nonobtrusive manner, and it is one of the few methods that is appropriate for studying empathy at different ages.

Facial and Gestural Measures

Very recently, researchers have begun to explore the possible use of facial and gestural measures of children's affective empathy. This approach has been spurred on, in part, by the problems with self-report and physiological measures. However, their use has also been advanced by the finding that facial and gestural empathy measures do seem to predict children's altruistic behavior. The hypothesized relationship between empathy and altruism has been the focus of much of the child empathy research. Yet, studies using the FASTE or other self-report measures have generally found either limited support, or no support, for this major hypothesized role of empathy (e.g., Eisenberg–Berg & Lennon, 1980; Fay, 1970; Underwood & Moore, 1982). Because of the close theoretical link between empathy and altruism, the findings of empirical relationships between altruistic behavior and facial and gestural empathy measures give important support for their validity.

There are additional reasons why the use of facial expressions in child empathy research appears to be so promising. First of all, there is convincing evidence from recent research that trained raters can make reliable discriminations of emotions from children's and from infants' facial behavior, even when the observer is unaware of the situation that has elicited the child's emotional reaction (Hiatt, Campos, & Emde, 1979; Izard, Huebner, Risser, McGinnes, & Dougherty, 1980). Detailed studies of infants' facial movements are being conducted (Izard, 1979; Oster & Ekman, 1978), and coding schemes are being developed that should greatly aid the accuracy with which facial emotions can be measured (Lamb & Campos, 1982).

Thus, researchers in Caroll Izard's laboratory are finding that, at birth, infants are able to display facial configurations indicative of interest and disgust (as well as precursors of social smile and the feelings of sadness and surprise). By 4–6 weeks they exhibit the social smile; by 3–4 months, the emotions of anger, surprise, and sadness; by 5–7 months, fear; by 6–8 months, shame, shyness, and self-awareness; and by the second year of life, contempt and guilt. Izard believes that the sequence with which these emotions develop corresponds to survival needs and the infant's maturing abilities at various ages. For example, the disgust expression that is present in the first few days of life is thought to aid in the rejection of distasteful substances from the mouth, whereas the social smile helps insure a strong parental bond and positive interaction with caregivers. The infants' emotions are spontaneous reactions to specific situations, and it is only as they mature that they begin to control their expressions. Izard believes that these emotional states are related to different states of the brain, and that the different emotions are loosely linked (i.e., with considerable flexibility) to specific behavioral expressions. In the section on the perceptual component, we discuss research showing that not only are infants capable of expressing emotions, but they apparently can distinguish adult facial expressions and mimic these facial expressions as early as 36 hours after birth, suggesting an innate ability in this area.

A study by Lennon, Eisenberg, and Carroll (1983) is instructive in this regard not only because it measures facial and gestural empathy directly in children, but because these nonverbal measures are related to the FASTE and to measures of children's altruism. The study also makes an important distinction between facial and gestural "state empathy" and facial and gestural "trait empathy" that needs to be considered seriously, not only by the child empathy researchers, but by investigators in other areas of empathy research as well. State empathy, as defined here, refers to the occurrence of an empathic response in a particular situation for a particular person. Trait empathy, on the other hand, refers to a general tendency to empathize and can be operationalized as a high level of measured empathy across at least two situations.

The authors (Lennon et al., 1983) based their measures of facial and gestural empathy on children's responses to two videotapes showing children in an emotionally arousing situation. The situation in one of the two tapes was described as follows:

> In this film, two preschoolers (a boy and a girl) demonstrated activities they engage in during a typical day at preschool while verbally interacting with an off-camera male narrator. The narrator asked the children questions about their activities (e.g., playing with blocks or on a slide), as well as about other activities they like to do while at preschool.
>
> Next the children began to play on a large, hollow, concrete pipe. The narrator warned the children to be careful because they might fall and hurt themselves. Immediately following the warning, the children gave a cry of distress, and the camera was focused on the children as they lay on the ground emitting vocal and gestural cues of distress. An adult female appeared and asked both children what happened. She examined the children, announced that their arms were hurt, and went for help. The camera remained focused on the children until the end of the film. (p. 4)

At one session the children, who were preschoolers between the ages of 4 years 2 months and 5 years 7 months, were administered the FASTE and one of the two empathy tapes, as well as a donation task involving the voluntary contribution of stickers to children who were in the hospital. At the second session the second empathy tape was administered, followed by a Comforting Task. For this comforting assessment, the subjects were told that the videotape they had seen was real and that the children who were hurt were now home in bed. They were offered the opportunity either to make cut-out forms for a favorite game of these children (who were too hurt to make the forms themselves) or to play with toys. In the period between the two sessions, a public donation task, also involving contributing stickers to children in the hospital, was administered.

The following measures of facial-gestural empathy were scored: (1) latency from the presentation of the distress stimuli to the subjects' facial response; (2) intensity of the child's negative facial expressions on a 5-point scale; (3) intensity of the child's gestural reactions, including turning the head and covering the face with hands, also on a 5-point scale.

The results of the study showed that facial and gestural empathy scores increased with age in this group of preschool children. The results also showed significant correlations between the facial intensity, gestural intensity, and low latency responses. Furthermore, these investigators found considerable stability and consistency in the children's facial-gestural empathy responses across assessments, suggesting that such measures are reliable indicators of preschoolers' affective empathy.

The attention given to the distinction between state and trait empathy produced some very interesting findings with the facial/gestural empathy measures. Boy's facial/gestural empathy was found to be related to prosocial behavior when the object of empathy and the object of prosocial behavior were the same (i.e., state empathy). In other words, they were likely to seek to help a person whose situation had directly aroused their empathic distress. There was no relationship between empathy and helping when the person to be helped was someone other than the person whom the child subject observed in the distressful situation. In contrast, girls' facial/gestural empathic responses were related to helping behavior only when the recipient of their empathy was not the same as the recipient of their helping. The authors speculated that state empathy is more closely related to boys' prosocial behavior than is the general trait of empathy, whereas for girls, the opposite is true. It should be noted that this finding fits well with Feshbach's belief that, for boys, a strong motivation to reduce one's own empathic distress may serve to channel into prosocial activities what might otherwise become an impulsive release of the emotional arousal through nonadaptive, and perhaps, aggressive behaviors.

Observational Measures

Observational measures of children's empathic behavior in naturalistic situations may provide still another method of measuring the affective component of empathy. In such studies, children are watched for their responses to others when an emotionally arousing situation has occurred. However, one of the difficulties in the use of such behavioral measures is to distinguish indicators of affective empathy from indicators of empathy's other components. It is also hard to distinguish between an empathic response in an affectively charged situation and an altruistic response that may or may not be accompanied by empathy.

Summary of Developmental Trends in Affective Empathy

Because of the evidence that all measures of affective empathy are not measuring the same thing, it is difficult to accurately determine the developmental progression of this component of empathy (Hoffman, 1977b). As we have seen, data based on self-report measures such as the FASTE indicate that affective empathy appears to increase between the preschool years and 8 years of age. Based on paper and pencil measures it also appears that adolescents experience greater affective empathy than do younger children. However, the evidence for age-related increases in affective empathy using nonself-report measures is more equivocal. It should be noted that Hoffman's model of empathy does not necessarily predict increases in vicarious emotional response with age, but rather that the child's original empathic response will be mediated by increasingly complex cognitive processes as he grows older. On the other hand, Hoffman (1977c) does not rule out the possibility that affective empathy can increase with age and suggests that there may, in fact, be such an increase, but that it could be counteracted by the child's acquisition of "display rules" that lead him to mask or neutralize the felt emotion.

Relationship of Cognitive and Affective Empathy

Because of the distinction made within the developmental research about whether empathy is primarily cognitive or primarily affective, researchers have typically chosen measures for their studies that represented one, but not the other, of these two points of view. With the more recent multidimensional view of empathy as a process containing both cognitive and affective components, the question of how the two components are related has come to replace the question of which approach, the cognitive or affective, is *the* correct one. This is a complicated question because, as we have seen, both components undergo developmental changes, and, therefore, the way these components interact may be different at different ages.

Feshbach and Roe's (1968) study with the FASTE utilized both a self-report affective empathy measure focusing on how the subjects felt in the presence of the test stimuli and a self-report social comprehension measure in which the children were required to identify the feeling being expressed by the central figure in the story sequence. The children scored considerably higher on affect labeling than on affective empathy. Furthermore, in the study conducted by Kuchenbecker, Feshbach, & Pletcher (1974), the affective and cognitive empathy measures were found to be differentially sensitive to modality variations— i.e., whether the stimuli were presented auditorally only, visually only, or in both modes. These investigators found that social comprehension scores were highest under the visual modality, whereas the audiovisual modality resulted in the highest affective empathy scores. Furthermore, although sex of the experimenter was unrelated to social comprehension scores, the highest affective empathy scores occurred in the presence of a female experimenter. Finally, as noted earlier, sex differences have more often been found with measures of affective empathy than with measures of cognitive empathy.

Findings such as these led Feshbach (1978) to conclude that the cognitive and affective empathic processes represent distinct components. Because cognitive scores were higher than affective scores and because the developmental progression of both appeared to be similar to the developmental shifts noted in cognitive abilities at these ages, Feshbach also suggested that social comprehension may be a necessary prerequisite for affective empathy. However, there is reason to question this hypothesized progression from cognitive to affective empathic experience. As pointed out earlier, the Feshbach affective empathy measures require the subjects to give a verbal report and presumably to make some cognitive judgment about their feeling state, so that a certain level of cognitive ability would have to be in place for the subjects to successfully complete the affective empathy items. Hoffman's theoretical model of empathy presents a different viewpoint, in that vicarious emotional arousal is thought to be present in early infancy. Then, as the child's cognitive abilities begin to mature, the expression of empathy changes as a function of the way cognition mediates the original affective response. However, whatever the developmental sequence, in general researchers are moving to a position that both affective and cognitive components of empathy develop much earlier in childhood than was previously thought to be the case.

A problem with forming any conclusions at this point about the extent of the relationship between affective and cognitive empathy is that, within the affective component, the relationship between alternative methods of assessment has not been demonstrated. For example, the Lennon et al. study we described earlier generally found no relationship between a facial-gestural measure of affective empathy and FASTE scores. Furthermore, measures of accuracy of facial expressions and skin conductance may sometimes be negatively related (Hoffman, 1977b). Conclusions about the relationship of various components of empathy must await further specification of the type of processes being tapped by the various empathy measures in use.

Whereas the results discussed here point to the distinctiveness of the affective and cognitive components, researchers have not yet studied the more interesting question of how these components interact, i.e., the ways that the child's cognitive empathic processes work on his vicarious emotional experiences and vice versa. Specifically, in the theoretical model of empathy presented in Chapter 1, an affective reverberation phase is posited. This is essentially a period during which the observer lets himself experience and resonate with the other's emotions and then brings to bear his own cognitive processes to understand the feeling that now exists within himself, as well as in the other, and in the situation. The process that the observer undergoes, then, may involve using his own affective receptivity as a kind of emotional "sounding board" that, when actively reverberating, can be "worked on" by cognitive processes searching to understand the feeling. The individual can then move back and forth between attending to external stimuli and attending to internal stimuli as he seeks to both experience and understand the other's feelings. This process of alternating one's focus outward and inward has not yet been investigated developmentally, and the factors that contribute to flexibility in this need to be explored.

COMMUNICATION COMPONENT

Whereas communication of nonemotional role taking has received some attention in the developmental literature (e.g., Flavell et al., 1968; Fry, 1966), how a child verbalizes his understanding of, or affective response to, another's feelings has not been a focus of investigation. In developing research instruments to measure children's empathy, researchers have usually tried to make the child's task of communicating the vicarious affect, or understanding the affect, as easy as possible. In some tasks, this has involved allowing the young child to indicate the feeling nonverbally (e.g., pointing to a sad or happy face). This failure to study the development of empathic communication represents an important lack of integration between the child and the adult research on empathy, because in the latter the communication component has been a major focus of study (e.g., in psychotherapy).

There may be a number of reasons for the lack of attention to children's communicative empathy. The developmental literature has traditionally seen the young child as egocentric and dependent. Communicative expression of empathic internal responses in a way that would be experienced as understanding, accepting, and supportive by the person undergoing the emotional distress was not thought to occur until much later, especially in naturalistic situations.

Secondly, and somewhat paradoxically, the lack of attention may have been due to the large amount of attention given to the development of altruism, helping, and other forms of prosocial behavior. Internal empathic responses were identified early on as playing an important role as a mediator of altruistic behavior, and this provoked numerous studies examining the relationship between the two. When behavioral measures of prosocial behavior were used in these studies, they were seen as indicators of altruism, not empathy, and there was little attention given to behaviors that were direct expressions of empathy whereas not necessarily being accompanied by overt helping.

Once more, this is not the state of affairs in the adult literature on empathy where, for example, a psychotherapist may be observed communicating accurate empathy to a client without actually intervening directly to alleviate the cause of the client's distress. Similarly, a good parent or teacher will sometimes refrain from intervening to end a child's unhappiness or frustration if some benefit will come from the child's learning to handle the problem himself. Yet, the same parent or teacher may indicate verbally his or her understanding of, and sensitivity to, the child's feelings in this problem situation. In the developmental literature, empathic communication and altruistic behavior have never really been separated conceptually. However, because the concept of empathy has been used to indicate affective and cognitive responses to both negative and positive affect, we need to determine not only what empathic communication would be like in the presence of a person who is distressed and needs our help, but also what empathic communication would be like in the presence of vicariously experienced euphoric emotion.

Once we have specified a communication dimension in children's empathy, we can seek to identify a developmental progression in the child's ability to verbalize acceptance and understanding of another's feelings. Both maturational and socialization processes may be involved, and these may best be addressed from a life-span developmental perspective. For example, we have indicated earlier that very little research attention has been given to developments in empathy during adolescence. However, it is possible that during this period, which has traditionally been seen as a time of self-preoccupation (Elkind, 1967), the individual may also for the first time become capable of the kind of empathic communication that has been the focus of the adult literature.

Early Precursors of Empathic Communication. A very few studies have investigated the earliest developments in children's ability to communicate empathically. Some of the research that focuses on the development of altruism and prosocial behavior touches on empathy indirectly. For example, Zahn–Waxler and Radke–Yarrow (1982) used ratings made by carefully trained mothers to identify 10 categories of young children's prosocial intervention when confronted with another person in distress. Several categories appear to represent empathic verbal communcation. Eighty-seven percentage of the children between 62 weeks and 134 weeks expressed some form of verbal sympathy, reassurance, or concern. ("That's okay, Mary, you're all right, you'll be all right [with concerned expression]" (p. 123). This same percentage also engaged in self-referential communications, i.e., their words contained comparisons of self and other in circumstances of distress ("Home vistors' 'injured' foot: Subject says, Ow, and rubs his own ankle: Kiss it, and makes kissing noises in visitor's direction").

These responses were conceptualized by the investigators within the general framework of children's prosocial interventions in the face of witnessed distress. The earliest prosocial interventions, present in all children by about 1 year of age, consisted of positive physical contact with the distressed other, such as touching or patting. Although this form of interaction remained important, prosocial interventions became more specific and more diverse by the end of the second year and now included the two "empathy" categories just mentioned.

A study by Strayer (1980) also investigated empathy through the use of behavioral measures, but the behaviors observed were conceptualized as empathic motivation, rather than empathic communication. Naturalistic assessments were made of 14 preschoolers during free play periods at their day care center for 2 hours, twice a week, over an 8-week period. Based on an event sampling procedure, the frequency of empathic behavioral interactions was recorded. Empathic interactions were defined as the presence of a prosocial response to a peer's display of one of four categories of affect, namely happy, sad, angry, or hurt. When an affective display occurred, the child displaying it was identified and neighboring children were observed for their responses. Specific responses that were scored as empathic were participation in the affect displayed, comforting, help giving, and giving reinforcing comments. The observers also noted whether the empathic response occurred spontaneously or only after a request for a reaction by the child displaying the emotion. The results showed that children gave an empathic response 39% of the time. They gave the most empathic responses to displays of happy emotions and the least to displays of anger. The majority of these empathic responses were given without a request for intervention by the person experiencing the feeling. Furthermore, different affect displays tended to elicit different kinds of empathic behavior. Direct participation in the affect of the stimulus person was highest for displays of happy feelings. Behavioral responses included smiles and laughter or verbal reinforcement such as "that's a good one." Sad displays most often elicited responses to share an activity or toy. Displays of anger were most often reacted to by the child subjects with verbal or physical acknowledgment of the expressed anger, and displays of hurt feelings by the peer were most often met by questions such as "You OK?" It should be noted that, whereas Strayer conceptualized these responses as "empathic," they are really quite similar to the behavioral responses that Zahn–Waxler and Radke–Yarrow called prosocial behavior, and that only a minority of these responses would constitute what we might call true communicative empathy.

School Age

A study with first-, third-, and fifth-grade children by Kallman and Stollak (1974), although still not focusing on communicative empathy directly, comes closer to the examination of verbalizations like those we consider in Chapter 6. These authors examined children's verbal responses and parents' written responses to children in "need-arousing situations." Such situations usually involve some kind of affective reaction by the child who is in need. Because overtly need-arousing situations occur relatively infrequently, Stollak (1973) developed a projective instrument called the Sensitivity to Children Questionnaire (STC) to measure how individuals would respond to hypothetical need-arousing situations. The STC contains a series of three different types of vignettes: those in which the problem that produces a need centers on the child, those in which the problem centers on the adult, and those in which the problem centers equally on the adult and child. An example of a child-centered problem is the following vignette: "Your child has just come home from school; silent, sad-faced, and dragging his/her feet. You can tell by his/her manner that something unpleasant has happened to him/her." The subject is asked how he or she would respond. Whereas Stollak's research with this measure usually focused on the parent's or adult's response, in this particular study the children were also asked to indicate how they would like their parents to respond to them if they found themselves in the hypothetical situations. Kallman and Stollak then scored the parent's as well as the children's responses on a variety of "ineffective" and "effective" response categories. Examples of ineffective communications were "ordering, directing, commanding," "preaching, moralizing, exhorting," and "interpreting, analyzing, diagnosing." Examples of effective communications were "reflection of the child's feelings, needs, or wishes," "statement of acceptance of the validity of the child's feelings, needs, and wishes," "a statement of the adult's own feelings," "providing alternate routes of expression of the child's feelings—in the present," and "providing alternate routes of expression of the child's feelings—in the future."

Raters were able to reliably code the child's wishes for parental responses along this rating system. Though the results showed that the use of the effective categories by children was very small across these age groups, the scoring of children's direct empathic communications with these categories was successful. Further studies might increase the likelihood of finding more examples of empathic communication in an older sample. However, the finding that parents used more ineffective than effective responses to the STC items suggests that even in adulthood, high-level empathic communication may occur infrequently in problem situations. To rectify this, it may be necessary to develop intervention strategies that will train both adults and children in empathic communication skills.

An exploratory intervention study done with a small number of 10-year-old children by Vogelsong (1974) provides some interesting preliminary findings regarding the feasibility of giving training to elemantary schoolchildren in the same kinds of empathic communication skills that have been addressed in adult training programs. Training was conducted once a week for 10 weeks during a 45-minute "activities period" at the end of a regular school day. Half the children were assigned to the skill training group where they met with an adult trainer, whereas the other half, who formed the control group, spent this time in another classroom doing craft projects assigned to them by their teachers. During the first 2 weeks, the intervention focused on nonverbal ways of recognizing and showing emotions. Children were asked to both portray and identify others' facial expressions of feelings such as happy, hurt, surprised, afraid, etc. During the second 2 weeks, training focused on the importance of showing empathic acceptance to others. The following description of the training procedures for weeks three and four was provided by the author (Vogelsong, 1974):

> Their task was first to identify the feelings he [the trainer] expressed and then state those feelings in a declarative sentence. For example, the trainer may say, I hope it doesn't snow today. I haven't put the winter tires on my car yet, and I don't want to have a wreck.' The child's response is 'You are afraid it might snow and you will smash up your car.' Various possible accepting or feeling identification responses were discussed after each series of statements the trainer made. By the end of the second week of this stage of training each child had practiced making several responses to the trainer's statements. The trainer modeled appropriate statements when the children had difficulty making responses, and verbally reinforced each child for what he or she did well. (p. 274)

During the fifth and sixth weeks, practice opportunities were provided on a variety of topics. Children worked in pairs to both discuss with, and respond empathically to, the other's statements on such topics as "what I would change if I were principal" or "my favorite pet," while the trainer gave verbal reinforcement and helped shape the empathic responses. Such practice continued in the seventh and eighth weeks when, in addition, the children discussed in a group how it felt to know that they were understood by another person. Finally, in the ninth and tenth weeks, practice continued, and, in addition, toward the end of the class period the child was asked to state how he or she felt at the moment.

Guerney's (1977) Acceptance of the Other Scale was used to assess empathy at both a pre and posttraining session. This is an 8-point scale that measures the communicator's ability to verbalize acceptance and encourage the other to pursue his thoughts and feelings. The scale also assesses the communicator's sensitivity to the other's feelings, needs, and motivations as communicated through his words and manners. Thus, arguing and accusing responses are scored lowest, normal social responses receive a middle score, and communication of acceptance of deeper feelings is scored at the highest level.

The results indicated that the skills-training children improved more in empathic acceptance than did the control children, and that, in fact, the only change took place in the skills-training group. These results are encouraging but should be treated as tentative, because the control group did not also experience a focused program that was different from their regular school routine. Furthermore, generalization of the increased empathic communication was not investigated. It should be noted that more sophisticated empathy-training projects have been developed for children in which many more controls were instituted, (e.g., Feshbach, 1981), but these did not specifically attempt to train the communication component of empathy.

Adolescence

Haynes and Avery (1979) developed a communications skills-training program for adolescents that provided 16 hours of training in the skills of self-disclosure and empathy. Self-disclosure was defined as "the process whereby individuals allow themselves to be known to another through open, honest expression of feelings, thoughts, and ideas." Empathy was defined cognitively and communicatively as "the ability to recognize and understand another person's perceptions and feelings, and to accurately convey that understanding through an accepting response" (p. 527). Twenty-five male and female students made up the training group whereas 23 students served as a control group. The training program was conducted during the students' English class period over a span of 4 weeks. During the training period, the control group was involved in its regular English class.

The training program used a structured educational approach and included both didactic and experiential training. Each session had as its goal to provide trainees with relevant conceptual knowledge and behavioral practice of self-disclosure and empathy skills. The level of empathy and self-disclosure was assessed in two ways: First, the students participated in a 20-minute audiotaped interview in which they were required to discuss with a peer "things I like and dislike about members of my same sex" and "things I like and dislike about members of the opposite sex." Each student alternated between discussing his or her own feelings for 10 minutes and listening to the other person's feelings for 10 minutes. The second assessment procedure used a written format. The subjects were required to read 12 paragraphs describing situations involving a parent, peer, or dating partner and tell how they would respond, writing the actual words they would say. The audiotapes and written responses were both scored according to Guerney's Self-Feeling Awareness Scale (Guerney, 1977) and Acceptance of Other Scale (Guerney, 1977). The audiotaped interviews were used to assess behavioral skills, whereas the written responses were used to assess subjects' ability to generalize their skills to other situations involving significant others.

The results showed that the experimental group significantly increased its level of both self-disclosure and empathy relative to the controls. This was true both for the behavioral measure and for the written vignette items. An interesting finding regarding sex differences also occurred. At the pretest females were higher in self-disclosure, supporting the view that females are socialized to be more expressive than males. However, by the posttest, there were no sex differences, indiciating that, with training, the sex differences appear to diminish, if not disappear altogether.

Although this intervention study does not directly examine naturally developing communication abilities during the adolescent years, the authors suggest that adolescence may be an important period for the development of communicative empathy skills. It is during these years that the individual first begins to take responsibility for developing significant interpersonal relationships. Many adolescents express anxiety over the development of heterosexual relationships (Glass, Gottman, & Shmurak, 1976), which appears to be related to expectations that personal skill deficits, such as inability to initiate or carry on conversations, will lead to negative outcomes (Curran, Gilbert, & Little, 1976). At this "taking off point" for future relationship building, the authors believe that the development of communicative empathy skills may be especially crucial. They suggest that future research should attempt to develop behavioral measures that can assess empathic communication nonobtrusively in a variety of situations with a variety of significant others.

Children's attitudes toward, and expectancies about, communicating empathically is another area for future research attention. For example, Saarni (1979) asked children in first, third, and fifth grades about when they would expect to hide their feelings from others, when they would try to hide their real feelings by substituting another affective expressive behavior, and when they would allow their feelings to be openly expressed. Older children were more likely than younger children to expect that affective behavior would be regulated. All children reported occasions of hiding and dissimulation of their emotional experiences, and the older children gave more subtle and numerous explanations for when and why to do this. In another study, Saarni (1983) found that parental attitudes about emotional expression were related to their children's expectations in this regard. She suggests that in emotional socialization others' expectations may be very influential and should be seen as possibly independent of children's behavior being shaped by observing adult models who regulate emotional expression. This line of research may also provide important information about the socialization of empathic communication ability.

THE PERCEPTUAL COMPONENT

In our components model of empathy, the first step in the individual's experience of another's feelings is perceptual, i.e., the observer must attend to and "take in" the postural, facial, verbal, tonal, content, and timing cues that the target person is expressing so that these cues can be further "worked on" by the individual's affective and cognitive processes. Yet, until very recently, the process by which perception of emotions is linked to subsequent stages of empathic processing has received very little attention in the developmental literature.

Discrimination and Imitation of Emotions During the Neonatal Period. One exciting area of research focuses on the apparent ability of very young infants to discriminate and also imitate facial expressions. A recent study by Field, Woodson, Greenberg, and Cohen (1982) is illustrative. It used a habituation paradigm to show that neonates (average age 36 hours) discriminated happy, sad, and surprised facial expressions being expressed by an adult. In the habituation paradigm, the time the infant spent visually fixated on the adult's expression decreased across trials with the same facial expression and increased between the late trials with one expression and the early trials of a new expression. The visual habituation and dishabituation of the facial stimuli suggest that these very young infants can discriminate these three basic facial expressions.

Furthermore, the authors found different visual fixation patterns for the different emotions. The infants fixated more on the model's mouth region during the happy and sad emotion trials than during the surprised emotion trials. Alternating between fixating on the mouth and the eye region occurred more frequently for the surprise expression. These differences in fixation fit well with the fact that happy and sad expressions in the adult model were actually characterized mainly by mouth positions (widening of the lips in the happy face; tightening and protruding of the lips in the sad face), whereas surprise was actually characterized by widening of both eyes and mouth in these adults. The different fixation patterns indicate that the neonates were able to distinguish the distinctive features of the happy, sad, and surprised facial expressions modeled by the adult.

Even more relevant to understanding the earliest phases in the interaction between affect perception and experience was the finding that the neonates also appeared to imitate the facial expressions of the adults. Thus, infants engaged in significantly more eye and mouth widening when exposed to a surprise face, significantly more lip widening when exposed to a happy face, and significantly more tight-protruding lips and furrowed brow when exposed to sad facial expressions. Because the greatest amount of imitation occurred during middle trials, these responses do not appear to be due to general arousal, on the one hand, or fixed action tendencies, on the other hand. Instead, the authors (Field et al., 1982) favor an explanation that attributes to the infants, "an innate ability to compare the sensory information of a visually perceived expression [as evidenced in this study by their ability to discriminate the facial expressions] with the proprioceptive feedback of the movements involved in matching that expression [as manifested by their differential responses to the facial expression]" (p. 181). This explanation is consistent with Hoffman's position that motor mimicry is a major, early mode by which the other's feelings get transferred to the observer.

Perception of emotions in early infancy precedes the development of social perception processes that are currently being studied in great detail by developmental psychologists. Much can be learned about the development of perception of emotion from research in the area of person perception generally. For example, the general finding that younger children tend to focus on surface and behavioral characteristics when formulating their perceptions of other's characteristics, whereas older children tend to focus more on the other's traits and other internal characteristics (e.g., Shantz, 1983) should have implications for the way in which a child perceives emotions in others. The Hughes, Tingle, and Sawin (1981) study described earlier, in which younger children between ages of 5 and 8 attended more to situational cues for emotion, whereas older children in this age range based their judgments of emotions more on their perceptions of the other's personal and psychological characteristics, points in the direction we are suggesting. The study by Kuchenbecker, Feshbach, and Pletcher (1974), which found that children's affective and cognitive empathy abilities depended on the modality by which the emotional cues were presented, also points to a potentially productive area for research.

THE SOCIALIZATION OF EMPATHY

The evidence that both the affective and cognitive components of empathy involve naturally unfolding maturational processes does not rule out the role of socialization factors in empathy's development. In the review to follow, both theoretical writing and research on the socialization process are intertwined in an attempt to present a preliminary picture of how social and environmental forces influence the development of empathy. Where applicable, we distinguish between the socialization of empathy's various components (i.e., perceptual, cognitive, affective, communication). However, this is not always possible as researchers have been somewhat slower in coming to a multidimensional view of the socialization of empathy than they have in bringing a multidimensional perspective to the study of maturational processes in empathy.

Socialization for Emotions

Whereas we reviewed evidence that affective empathy occurs fairly automatically and may be present from birth, Aronfreed's research showed that a vicarious emotional response to another's affect can also be acquired through conditioning, which requires personal experience with the emotion in question. Hoffman (1982) suggests that kinds of socialization techniques that encourage children to experience a variety of types and intensities of feeling will increase the child's capacity to empathize. Whereas Hoffman mainly focuses on affective empathy, it seems reasonable that socialization experiences that result in the building of a broad emotional repertorie in the child should also lead to increases in cognitive empathy and perhaps in empathy's other components as well. For example, experience with a wide variety of emotions and the situations in which these occur should aid in the cognitive search to understand another person's emotional experience, and empathic communication should be aided by personally gained knowledge of what kinds of verbal responses were helpful to oneself. On the other hand, we would expect that preventing the child from experiencing a wide range of emotions (for example, by protecting the child from all kinds of negative feelings) would interfere with the development of a child's empathic capacity. Hoffman (1982) states that an exception to this general hypothesis may occur when the intensity of the emotion the child experiences is too high. Extremely distressful or unhappy emotional experiences may lead to a variety of defense mechanisms that, once in place, may lower the child's ability to empathize with this kind of emotion.

Relevant to the issue of providing the child with opportunities to experience a wide range of emotions is the important research on socialization for emotions now being done with infants. Recently, Malatesta, working at Carol Izard's Human Emotions Laboratory (Trotter, 1983), has shown that mothers appear to shift their modeling and shaping of an infant's emotions as the child begins to grow older. Originally, mothers seem to model and encourage a wide range of emotional expression in the infant, including both positive emotions such as happiness, joy, and surprise, and negative emotions such as anger, sadness, and concern, which are usually modeled playfully for the child. As the infants grow older, mothers appear to move away from the negative expressions. Malatesta has also found that emotional modeling is different for boys and girls, with mothers more restrictive in the range of feelings they encourage in young boys than in young girls. She suggests that young boys tend to be more irritable than girls, and that mothers' greater frequency of smiling at them may help keep them happy. Furthermore, mothers may learn that too wide a range of expressed emotions may overexcite the more emotionally reactive boys. If girls are exposed early to a wide range of emotions, this may be an early influence on their development of greater emotional expression, generally, and on their ability to experience and express empathy more specifically. Extrapolating from her observations of mother–child interaction, she estimated that between 3 to 6 months, which is the period of the highest mother–child face to face play, there occur approximately 32,000 examples of maternal facial emotional expression. This would indicate that parental socialization is a major force in emotional development during infancy.

Of course, researchers need to examine more closely the relationship between socialization for emotions, generally, and socialization for empathy. One might think of the emotional repertoire that a child possesses as a prerequisite for empathic responses, which then requires the further ability and willingness to perceive, experience, comprehend, and communicate these emotions when exposed to another person's feelings.

Socializing the Child to Attend to Others

Parental discipline techniques that cause the child to focus attention on the internal emotional experiences of other people may also enhance the develop-

ment of affective empathy. Of particular salience may be those discipline encounters between parent and child where the child has actually been the cause of
another person's distress. These encounters can serve as a natural occasion for
the child learning (1) that others have feelings, (2) that it is important to attend to
the other's feelings, and (3) that his own behavior may influence the other's
feelings. Hoffman (1970) termed discipline techniques in which a parent makes
the child focus on the pain or hurt that he caused, (e.g., "you made Susie feel
sad") or which encourage the child to imagine that he was in the place of the
person who was hurt (e.g., "think how you would feel if he did that to you")
inductive discipline techniques. Inductive discipline has been shown to be related
to altruistic responding by children (Hoffman, 1970; Zahn–Waxler, Radke–
Yarrow, & King, 1979), and the mediator of this relationship may very well be
an increased tendency to engage in affective empathy.

Providing the child with numerous opportunities to engage in perspective
taking may enhance the development of cognitive role-taking ability. By practicing role taking, the child is practicing paying attention to others' viewpoints and
using his maturing cognitive abilities to search for situational and person cues
that will help him understand what the other is feeling. However, Hoffman
(1982) argues that all role-taking experience does not enhance empathy equally.
He cites preliminary evidence that role-taking practice in prosocial situations is
effective, whereas role-taking practice in competitive situations may not lead to
increased empathy.

The use of social learning principles such as reinforcement and modeling may
also lead to increased empathy in children. The support for this view is mainly
indirect. Although there have been few studies of reinforcement and modeling of
empathy, there have been numerous studies of the relationship between altruism
or others forms of prosocial behavior and these social learning variables. As we
discussed in the section on empathic communication, prosocial behavior measures have often included verbal and nonverbal behaviors that can be considered
forms of empathic responding. Thus, when a child is reinforced for verbalizing
sympathetic feelings to a person who is in distress, this should lead to a future
tendency to make empathic rather than nonempathic attributions about the cause
of other people's unhappy experiences (Hoffman, 1982).

Grusec's (1982) review of socialization processes in the development of altruism includes a number of techniques that may also increase empathy. She
divides the salient socialization processes into those administered after the occurrence of the desired prosocial behavior (reinforcement, attribution of characteristics), those that follow lack of the desired behavior (punishment, reasoning,
moral exhortation, direct instruction, and forced appropriate behavior), and those
procedures that occur independently of the child's prosocial behavior, but which
later facilitate concern for others (including training affective empathy and training perspective taking). One of the most interesting of these techniques is that of
verbally attributing prosocial characteristics to the child, because this seems to

work through altering the child's self-concept and appears to generalize more to other situations than does reinforcement.

Grusec (1982) utilized a technique of training mothers to record the altruistic behaviors of their children (giving, sharing, helping, cooperating, protecting, encouraging, making restitution, comforting, showing affection, concern, or consideration) over a period of 4 weeks. Although the results of her study are more applicable to altruism research than to the development of empathy, one interesting finding was that parents tended not to make much use of training in role playing or perspective taking to teach children to respond altruistically. This led Grusec to speculate that training in role playing and perspective taking may be done more naturally in a formal setting such as a school. On the other hand, we see in Chapter 7 that parents can be trained to educate their children in role taking. We have also speculated that inductive discipline functions as one type of role-taking instruction frequently undertaken by parents. With respect to parental modeling of empathic behavior, the most salient occasion for modeling may be the parent's interaction with the child himself. Not only will the child have the opportunity to observe the behavior being modeled, but he will also directly experience the beneficial effects of being responded to empathically. Because the child in need or in distress may not be able to attend fully to the type of parental response that elicits feeling cared about, the parent may have to accompany this modeling with appropriate instruction and reflection on the process that took place.

Feshbach (1975) studied white, middle-class children age 6 to 8 years whose mothers and fathers each completed a set of Childrearing Practices Q Sort Items, which covered general attitudes toward children and specific parenting practices concerning areas such as handling aggression, independence, discipline, independence, affiliation, and emotional expressiveness. A factor analysis of the items yielded 12 factors, which were used to construct discrete subscales of parenting involvement. Mothers and fathers parenting practices were related to boys' and girls' empathy scores as measured by the FASTE.

The results showed a striking difference in the role that the mother–child relationship plays in the development of boys' and girls' empathic abilities. Girls' empathy was related to a positive mother–daughter relationship and to maternal tolerance and permissiveness. Empathy was negatively related to maternal conflict, maternal rejection, and excessive maternal control and punitiveness. On the other hand, fathers' childrearing practices and attitudes were not significantly related to the development of empathy in girls.

Parental childrearing practices had little relationship to the development of empathy in boys. No significant findings were obtained for mothers and sons, whereas the only significant finding for fathers and sons was a negative relationship between the extent to which the father fostered competitive behavior in their sons' and boys' empathy. Feshbach (1982b) suggests that these sex-difference findings are consistent with a psychodynamic theoretical position in which mothers and daughters are thought to have a unique and particularly close relationship. The maternal behaviors that lead to higher empathy in girls are similar to the behaviors that lead to prosocial behavior and a positive self-concept in girls.

Feshbach (1982b) suggests that empathy in boys is more closely linked to the development of a variety of cognitive skills than it is to affectively oriented socialization experiences: ''It is as though empathy in girls develops through identification, normative role adaptations and positive child-rearing experiences, whereas the routes to empathy in boys are as numerous as the diverse manifestations of empathy for this sex. Another way of phrasing the sex difference is that empathy is ego—or role—syntonic for girls and less so for boys'' (p.332). She suggests, as Hoffman also does, that the combination of social understanding and the dysphoric empathic arousal that generally occurs when the boy comprehends another person in distress leads to helping and altruism. If the boy has himself experienced a similar distressful situation, there is a stronger likelihood of empathic arousal and a stronger likelihood that he will act to attempt to relieve the other's distress. In line with the sex-difference findings discussed earlier, Feshbach also suggests that for some boys socialization experiences that promote excessive euphoric empathic arousal may lead to a reduction of altruism, because these experiences may sometimes result in a heightening of egocentrism and a lowering of impulse controls.

It should be noted that a minimal level of parental acceptance and positive affective involvement is probably a necessary condition for the development of empathy in boys as well as girls. In the cases of severe parental neglect or abuse, the mediator of this may be the child's low level of general adjustment. Thus, Straker and Jacobson (1981) found physically abused boys and girls between 5 and 10 years of age to be lower in empathy, measured with the FASTE, than a carefully matched (including IQ) sample of nonabused children. The abused children were also found to be significantly more emotinally maladjusted. These results are notable because abused children might be expected to be highly motivated to develop their empathic abilities in order to potect themselves from potentially abusive situations. With somewhat less, though still highly problematic parent pathology, this may in fact be the case. In a very recent study, Zahn–Waxler, Cummings, McKnew, and Radke–Yarrow (1984) found that children of manic-depressive parents sometimes showed heightened distress and preoccupation with the suffering of other people, especially adults. They were likely to become fixated or rivited in their attention to distress, finding it harder to turn away from their perceptions of suffering to re-engage themselves in normal activities.

A study by Barnett, King, Howard, and Dino (1980) sheds some light on the complexity of the hypothesized role of parental acceptance and empathy in the development of children's empathy. These authors found that the salient pattern of parental socialization was a particularly sex-stereotyped distribution of mother–father empathy. The investigators used the FASTE to assess affective empathy in a group of 5-year-old boys and girls from a middle-class Kansas community. Parents' empathy was measured by the Mehrabian and Epstein (1972) measure, as well as by an interview question about how frequently the parent engaged in interactions focusing on the feelings of another. The results showed significant findings for girls, but not for boys, with higher scoring girls coming from homes where the mother was markedly more empathic than the father. Father's empathy was actually found to be negatively related to empathy in these girls. The authors suggest that, in the situation where the mother is more empathic than the father, girls may come to view empathic behavior as gender appropriate, thereby enhancing the degree to which it is internalized by girls. These authors' failure to find a relationship between parental socialization and affective empathy in boys is consistent with other studies.

Power Assertion and Punishment

Hoffman and Saltzstein's (1967) and Feshbach's (1975) research supports the contention that power-assertive discipline by the mother may impede the development of affective empathy. However, the relationship between the use of power assertion and punishment by parents and inhibition of empathy development may not be a simple causal one. Roe (1980) suggested that such factors as the relative power status of each parent, the type and degree of power assertion used, and the quality of the parent–child relationship may mediate the relationship between this type of parenting behavior and empathy. This belief led her to conduct a series of cross-cultural studies in settings with different childrearing attitudes and behaviors. Her earlier findings with Greek children (Roe, 1976, 1977) showed that Greek children had lower empathy scores than their American counterparts, perhaps because of the higher use of power assertion by Greek parents. These earlier studies, however, had not gathered specific information on the disciplinary techniques of individual children's families. Returning again to the Greek Island where she had previously studied empathy, Roe used an interview format to measure "caring." Forty-two 9- and 10-year-old children responded to the question "Why do you think children should not be mean and hurt others?" Other questions focused on the children's fear of physical punishment from mother and father, on the amount of spanking received from each parent, fear of either parent, and father's time spent away from home for long periods. Results showed that these boys' and girls' caring scores were negatively related to their fear of physical punishment from both parents, but especially from their fathers. Boys and girls who were low in caring also reported that they were spanked more often by their fathers than their mothers, and that they feared their fathers more than their mothers. Finally, children whose fathers were away most of the year had higher empathy scores.

Roe interprets these findings in light of the relatively distant relationship Greek children have with their fathers and the positive relationship they have with their mothers. She suggests that when punishment is given by a parent with whom the child already has a close, affectionate relationship, it may not be very inhibiting of the child's development of empathy. This reinterpretation of the hypothesized role that parental punishment and power assertion play in the inhibition of empathy will need to be further investigated with more established empathy measures and more direct measures of parent–child interaction. The relationship between empathy and absence from the home of the parent who was felt to be more fear inducing also needs further examination. Roe suggests two alternative explanations: that greater empathy is directly attributable to a reduction of fear or that a relatively greater amount of time is spent with a role model who is empathic.

Socialization of Empathy in Adolescence

There has been very little research on socialization of empathy during adolescence, an area that needs more attention if we are going to achieve the goal of linking developmental and adult empathy research. In one study, Bull (1980) administered a self-report empathy measure and collected empathy ratings by parents and best friends of a group of 15- and 19-year-olds. Scores on the empathy measures were related to the adolescents' perceptions of the quality of their interactions with their best friends. Results showed that for males acceptance by best friends, autonomy granted by best friends, and consistency of limits set by mothers were postively related to empathy. For females, acceptance by best friends was positively related to empathy, whereas control by fathers was negatively related to empathy.

Although the relationships found between empathy and peer interaction point to the need to study the role of peer socialization, the author's conclusion that best friends are a major source of socialization for empathy seems premature. For example, the treatment an adolescent receives from his best friend may be influenced by his already-existing level of empathy. Furthermore, the influence of the peer group may not be as much through direct socialization as through a norm it sets concerning the appropriateness of, or expectation for, empathic behavior among its members.

Socialization for Sex Differences in Empathy

Differences in the socialization of boys and girls may partially account for the reported sex differences in empathy. As part of sex-role socialization, girls in our society are taught to be more sensitive to interpersonal cues and to value more relating expressively to others. A special role is also given to the importance of empathy in the mother–child relationship. Females are socialized from childhood to show caring and concern for the emotional state of babies and young children. They are expected to develop personal attitudes and traits that will allow them to do this well.

A theoretical analysis of empathy in object relational terms provided by Jordan (1983) offers interesting areas for further study of differential socialization for males and females. Jordan begins by suggesting that the factors that inhibit the development and utilization of empathy by males and females may be different.

> Males tend to have more difficulty with the essential and necessary surrender to affect and momentary joining with the other, as it implies for them passivity, loss of objectivity, and loss of control. This may lead to widespread constriction of empathic responsiveness in men. Problems of empathy in females, however, typically involve difficulty reinstating a sense of self and cognitively structuring the experience. (p. 3)

She then examines the role of differential socialization patterns on these separate difficulties of males and females. Females in our society typically are socialized for characteristics most adaptive to the mothering and nurturing role, which relies on a careful tuning to the subtle and unarticulated internal states of the infant. To enhance this ability, young girls are encouraged to attend to others' emotional states through maintaining close proximity to others. Girls are also encouraged to express feelings that are nonagressive and prosocial (i.e., empathic), and they are taught to develop their ability to perceive how others are reacting to themselves.

Boys, on the other hand, are socialized to become competitors in a largely alienated work world. Here, a large amount of empathy is seen as unadaptive. Instead, young boys are taught to strive toward "mastery" of tasks and to hold in emotions, especially the kind that suggest interpersonal needs, fear, or inability to be self-reliant.

Jordan then speculates that interacting with these general socialization patterns are unique characteristics of the mother–daughter relationship and mother–son relationship that further the differences in the quality of the female and male child's empathic experience. Because mothers identify more with their daughters, they may feel more comfortable encouraging a girl to feel closely attached to them at an emotional level. For the boy, on the other hand, the process of looking to the mother for "mirroring" and conforming becomes questionable as both he and his mother recognize his differentness. A lower degree of emotional attachment to, and identification with, the mother ensues that may lead to the boy's lowered sense of being in contact with and understanding another person in a directly emotional way.

Society also encourages mothers to raise boys not like them, but like their fathers, which generally implies teaching them the pattern of affective control described previously. Fathers may pursue this even more strongly, encouraging their son's to suppress emotional sensitivity and expression and to accept male standards of toughness and invulnerability, traits that emphasize a disconnectedness from others generally, and from others' feelings specifically. Furthermore, because fathers typically spend much less time than mothers with their families, as the boy switches identification from mother to father the new identification is likely to be more general, more abstract, more role defined, and less affectively specific than is the case for girls' identification with their mothers. Jordan believes that this type of idetification also leads to lowered interpersonal involvement and to lowered capacity to engage in affective empathy.

Although the occurrence of these complex and highly interactive processes remains speculative, to the extent that they can be operationalized they present some very interesting directions for future research. An important issue pertaining to Jordan's theoretical ideas, as well as to the socialization of empathy generally, is what impact the trend toward increasing equalization of male and female roles in our society will have on the way socialization and maturational processes interact in the development of children's empathy.

CONCLUSION

It is quite unlikely that people who have not developed normal empathic abilities during childhood and adolescence will be able to later develop either the minimal empathy skills necessary for normal adult social relations or the advanced empathy skills needed by therapists, educators, and successful parents. It is also probably safe to say that not even intensive instruction or intervention will make up entirely for such early deficits and that, to be successful, training in empathy during adulthood probably must build on a set of naturally developing abilities that begin in childhood and that continue to emerge across the life-span. Such a life-span developmental perspective provides an important context for the chapters on empathy in psychotherapy, education, and parenting that now follow.

3 Perceptual and Affective Reverberation Components

Mark R. Davis
Syracuse University

As detailed in earlier chapters, the perceptual and affective reverberation phases of the empathic process describe how we gather data about the affective state of a person, and, having gathered that data, how we assimilate it into a distinguishable affective production within ourselves. "Reverberation" is given by one desk dictionary as "the persistance of a sound after its source has stopped, caused by multiple reflections of the sound within a closed space." The popular use of the term *vibrations* to refer to emotional states speaks to the aptness of this physical analogy. *Affective reverberation, then, most simply describes the production, tuning, and maintenance of an affective state within ourselves that is a faithful reproduction of that initially presented to us by another person.* We are striving therefore, in this analogy, for a process of "high fidelity."

Several sources of contamination of this process may be described. Simply not wanting to feel what the other person is feeling would suffice to motivate terminating the process. This disinclination to reverberate may be conscious or unconscious and result from numerous motivations. We may be absorbed in our own emotions and simply not want to relinquish them, or we may dislike or fear a person and prefer to keep this attitude toward them foremost in our minds. Conscious or unconscious discomfort, unwillingness, or inability to experience certain emotions can also impair our ability to reverberate.

To some extent, the preceding outcomes represent disenablings of a reverberatory response that are carried out within a basically intact psychological structure. Poor reverberatory processing can also occur because of some biological or social impairment of the personality structure itself. For example, a developmentally disabled or severely isolated individual cannot be expected to have developed sufficient ability to differentiate between or generate increasingly subtle shadings of affect. Individuals whose emotional experience has primarily included such affects as simple happiness, sadness, anger, or fear cannot be expected to accurately resonate to more subtle affects such as wistfulness, regret, and the like. The perceptual aberrations occurring in psychotic states also represent disturbances in reverberatory functioning that may be secondary to some profound deficit in the biological and psychological structure of the individual. Methods of training affective reverberation, as well as those directed toward other stages of the empathic process, must therefore consider the etiology and locus of the deficits occurring in any given individual before they can expect much success.

MOTOR MIMICRY

An analysis of several methods that purport to enhance the affective reverberation component of empathic ability must begin with an appraisal of the concept of motor mimicry. The role of motor mimicry in empathy has a long history and continues to receive popular currency. This position may be concisely stated: The adoption by an observer of the postural positions, tensions, or movements exhibited by another creates an internal, referent sensibility of the other's feeling state within the observer. With few exceptions, this position has remained largely anecdotal and uninformed by empirical investigation. However, in conjunction with the model described in this chapter, it has substantial heuristic value for evaluating current training practices relevant to the affective reverberation phase of empathy.

Motor imitation was mentioned as an important component of the "sympathetic emotions" as early as Baldwin's (1895) description, where he noted that:

> Emotion, we have seen to be, largely, in its gualitative marks, a revival product, a clustering, so to speak, of organic and muscular reverberations about relived elements of content . . . . The sight of the expression of emotion in another stimulates similar [motor] attitudes directly in us, and this in turn is felt as the state which usually accompanies such a reaction. (pp. 333–334)

As described in Chapter 1, Lipps (1926) specifically stated that motor mimicry was the essential component in Einfuhlung whereby the perceiver generates internal cues similar to those experienced by the other. Although George Mead (1934) extended and refined the definitional focus of empathy, he also underscored the importance of motor mimicry in the communicational interchange. This position was also adopted and extended by Buber (1948) and Katz (1963) in their descriptions of the empathic process; each author expressed his belief that assuming the "motoriality" of the other would cause distinct perceptual cues to arise from the observer's own muscles.

The psychologist McDougall, writing in 1908, noted that spectators at a sporting event tended to adopt the positions and postural tensions of players, especially during critical moments, and Fromm–Reichmann (1950) reported that adopting the postures and tensions exhibited by her clients enabled her to gain understanding of their emotional states and feelings. This view has been adopted by Hammer (1977), who recommends that testers assume the positions exhibited by the characters produced in self-drawings, and Gombrich (1972) has described motor mimicry as an important component in the perception of art.

Although technically difficult, the motor mimicry concept should not be impossible to experimentally assess. As a first approximation, occurrences of shared posture and movement between interactants should bear some orderly relation to the degree of empathy or mutual affective understanding occurring in the relationship. Almost all such tests have assessed motor mimicry by noting the appearance of congruent or mirrored body postures. Congruence here refers to the degree of similarity with which two or more interactants maintain the positions of their legs, arms, torso, or head. The criteria for scoring congruence in studies of this phenomenon have varied widely, ranging from no explicit criteria (Scheflen, 1964), to independent coding of arm and leg positions in accord with a predetermined coding scheme allowing as many as 12 different positions for each arm (LaFrance & Ickes, 1981). Beyond demonstrating a correlation between mimicry and empathy, a strict experimental test of this model must provide evidence that motor mimicry is an active and integral component rather than a mere epiphenomenon of empathy.

In what amount to observational descriptive studies, Scheflen (1964) reported the occurrence of congruent body postures between participants in a series of filmed individual and group psychotherapy sessions. Although noting that congruent postures often typified those group members who shared a common ideological position, Scheflen (1964) observed that "Even in cases where opposing or alternate issues have not yet been formulated, one can notice that often one postural set is maintained by those on one side of the table, another by those on the opposite side of the table" (p. 328). Thus, it is not clear whether empathy, rapport, or even agreement is necessarily signaled by postural congruence. Expressing reservations about the concept, Scheflen noted a phenomenon of dissociation, in which marked postural congruence occurred simultaneously with clear "signals of alienation." One can imagine a great deal of postural congruence occurring between fighters or arguing lovers, yet this is clearly a result of common moods and expressive postures and not necessarily a leader–follower mimicry or the empathic sharing of feelings.

Charny (1966) analyzed a motion picture film of a half-hour psychotherapy session photographed at 24 frames per second using specific operational criteria for postural congruence. After identifying periods of congruence and noncongruence, he submitted the verbal statements made in each period to a content analysis and noted that:

the vocal correlates of congruent posture were significantly different from those correlated with noncongruent posture: they were consistently positive, interpersonal, specific, and bound to the therapeutic situation, whereas those occurring with noncongruent configurations were more self-oriented, negational, and nonspecific, and tended to be self-contradictory and nonreferenced. (p. 305)

Charny concluded that these congruent postural configurations (which increased over the course of the session) were behavioral indicators of rapport or relatedness. Following Charny, most experimental investigations of postural congruence have concerned themselves with the relationship between congruence and rapport. Whereas rapport refers to a somewhat different and less inclusive process than empathy, it remains concerned with the positive sharing of similar feelings and is in this respect similar to affective reverberation. The studies considered in the following sections, although addressing rapport, remain relevant to the analysis of motor mimicry in affective reverberation.

LaFrance and Broadbent (1976) made in-class observations of the number of students simultaneously mirroring or congruent with the body and arm postures of the teacher and found that frequency of mirroring but not congruence was significantly correlated with student's ratings of their rapport and involvement in the class.[1] The frequency of incongruent postures was negatively correlated with these same ratings. In a subsequent study, LaFrance (1979) obtained ratings of teacher–student mirroring of torso and arm positions made every 5 minutes from hour-long video recordings of 13 different classes. As before, written ratings were solicited from the students as to various aspects of class rapport. LaFrance obtained high interrater reliability for coding the presence of mirroring, and, as in the previous study, student ratings of involvement and rapport were significantly correlated with the amount of posture sharing observed in the classroom. Using the same procedure in the same classes 5 weeks later, LaFrance attempted an analysis of causality using the cross-lag panel technique described by Kenney (1973, 1975). The positive correlation between posture mirroring and rapport held up across time. Although the results indicated that the relationship between the two variables was probably not due to an undetected third variable, the difference between the component correlations was not large enough to warrant an inference about the direction of causality. These data have been discussed in detail by LaFrance (1982).

In two studies, Dabbs (1969) investigated the effects of deliberately mimicking the posture of another person. In a taped interview setting, a confederate was instructed to copy the movements of one of two subjects who thought they were interviewing the confederate for a sales position. The experiment was conducted with both subjects simultaneously interviewing the confederate. Although the

---

[1]If person A's left arm and person B's right arm are similarly raised, mirroring is scored. Congruence would be scored if person B's left arm was raised.

mimicked subjects consistently rated themselves as "identifying" with the confederate and responded more favorably to him on several measures, these results may easily be attributable to some other factor, because the confederate was aware of the hypothesis under investigation and may have altered patterns of eye contact and intonation when addressing the mimicked interviewer. In a second study, using confederates who were unaware of the hypothesis under investigation, pairs of subjects were asked to discuss a topical question and form impressions of each other. The experiment also included an analysis of the effects of similarity between the two subjects, as assessed by the degree of similarity with which they had individually rated themselves on a number of personality traits. In half of the pairs, one subject was enlisted as the confederate and given instructions to mimick his partner during the discussion. In the second condition, confederates were instructed to adopt postures that were dissimilar to those of the other subject. Results indicated a main effect for mimicry only on the subject's belief that the confederate would be more likely to impress people. An analysis of the degree of similarity based on the subject's self-ratings revealed an interaction between the degree of similarity and the effects of mimicry. Specifically, subjects who were similar to the confederate rated the confederate significantly higher on several measures of liking when they had been mimicked by the confederate, but this effect of mimicry was not observed when the subject and confederate were dissimilar (a problem with Dabb's study is that the personality self-ratings used to assess similarity were collected *after* the discussion.) This study suggested that, whereas motor mimicry could play an important role in forming interpersonal impressions, the effects of mimicry were dependent on the degree of similarity between the two interactants.

In a related study of rapport and mimicry, Trout and Rosenfeld (1980) collected ratings of rapport from 60 students viewing a series of short film sequences of posed psychotherapy vignettes in which congruence and body lean were independently varied. Results indicated that both forward lean and congruence produced higher ratings of rapport by the viewers. However, the largest mean effect on rapport ratings observed for congruence within lean conditions was .5 on a 9-point scale, raising the issue of clinical versus statistical significance in large samples. Forward lean resulted in a mean increase of 2.5 points relative to the no-lean condition. On the other hand, LaFrance and Ickes (1981) have provided evidence that posture mirroring between subjects meeting for the first time in a waiting room was not only unrelated to rapport but was positively correlated with subject's subsequent ratings of self-consciousness and their perception of the encounter as forced, awkward, and strained. This result is reminiscent of the dissociation between congruence and empathy previously described by Scheflen (1964) and raises the following important point about attempts to train people to be more empathic.

For a long time, clinical lore had it that a listener displayed empathy by leaning forward in his chair (Haase & Tepper, 1972), periodically nodding his head and making some verbal acknowledgment such as "uh-huh" or "hmmm." Raymond Birdwhistell is credited with observing that psychotherapy interns given such instructions were in many cases nodding their heads in time with their own anxiety, rather than anything the client may have been doing! One has only to observe trainees distractedly bobbing their heads up and down, murmuring ill-timed um–hmms, and pulling their hair to understand how a client, faced with such a disconnected facsimile of empathic attention, might comment that the therapist appears to be a machine. The point here is that empathy is a complex, multicomponent process that cannot be readily captured or overtly expressed by simply adopting a few nonverbal tricks. LaFrance and Ickes' recent data suggest that a similar sort of maneuver, consciously mirroring posture as in the Dabbs study, might easily produce the opposite of the desired effect. Gimmicky approaches to rapport or empathy, such as using a person's name as many times as possible in a conversation, tend to backfire and leave the vague impression that the person before us may be just a little too slick for their own good. This distinction between genuine empathy and mere appearances of empathy is highlighted by the series of studies inspired by Condon and Ogston's (1966) observation of microsynchrony.

Condon and Ogston made sound films shot at 45 frames per second of people conversing and analyzed them on a frame by frame basis for correlations or patterns between minute body movements and the utterances of the speaker, as well as correlations between movements of the speaker and the listener. These authors described a form of patterning wherein the *timing* of movement changes occurring in different body parts was highly synchronous; that is, a number of body areas would initiate or change direction of movement within one picture frame, sustain those movements over a number of frames, and then abruptly terminate motion or change direction, again within the space of one frame. This coinvolvement of numerous body parts led Condon and Ogston to describe them as "process units." A process unit could be composed of different combinations of body parts at different times, and it was not required that the component parts move in the same direction, only that the boundaries of the movements (initiation, termination, or direction change) occurred at the same point in time (one film frame). The authors concluded from visual inspection of the data that process unit boundaries were also time locked with changes in the phonetic articulations of the speaker, who appeared to be "dancing" in time with his own speech (self-synchrony).

Comparing tables that indicated the frame by frame changes for these process units for both people, Condon and Ogston (1966) reported "a startling and relatively continuous harmony between the body motion configurational change patterns between speaker and listener" (p. 330). More specifically, they observed that the movement boundaries of both people occurred within the same frame of film. A similar analysis was applied to a schizophrenic patient talking with his therapist. Most noticeably, much of the patient's body was held rigidly "frozen" (his paralanguage was also monotonous), whereas those portions of his body that did move were generally dissynchronous with other body parts. However, the patient was in interactional synchrony with the therapist with those portions of his body that were themselves synchronous. These observations of dissynchrony in schizophrenia were replicated and extended by Condon and Brosin (1969).

Although Condon and Ogston neither collected measures of rapport nor addressed the issue, their early study was subsequently described by both Scheflen (1972, p. 53) and Morris (1977, p. 85) as support for their assertions that synchrony typically occurs betwen individuals in "good rapport." Davis (1973) has described several film clips from Condon's files that do appear to indicate a relationship between rapport and microsynchrony. Although these case studies are suggestive, no empirical research has been reported to date specifically addressing this issue. Kendon (1970) attempted a similar frame by frame analysis of a filmed group discussion shot at 24 frames per second. It is difficult to draw conclusions from this study about the relation of congruence or synchrony to empathy, because no formal attempt was made to assess the extent of shared feelings in the group. Kendon specifically described both periods of synchrony and nonsynchrony, although it is difficult to judge from his report whether anything else about the interaction (agreement or rapport) had necessarily changed. This work did suggest several important aspects of relatedness however, in that it identified specific gestures used to signal turns at speech (notably, microsynchrony similar to that observed by Condon did occur just before a listener broke in). Kendon likened this to a musician moving in time just before reentering a symphony and speculated that synchrony reflected the degree of attentiveness or "presence" in the situation. Support for this interpretation is lent by Condon's (1968 cited by Davis, 1972) observations of a mother interacting with her twin daughters, one of whom was schizophrenic. Although the mother showed synchrony with the normal daughter, she exhibited no synchrony with the schizophrenic daughter and would abruptly change her posture when this daughter adopted a posture similar to hers.

Of primary interst in the Condon and Ogston study is the fact that microsynchrony was observed at all. For movement synchrony to occur within 1/48th of a second (the time of one picture frame) suggests that the listener perceives and responds to some aspect of the speaker within approximately 20 milliseconds! Keele (1973, p. 76) relates an experiment conducted by Sports Illustrated on the reaction time of Muhammed Ali in responding to a light (190 millisec), and the time needed to throw a punch (40 millisec). First of all, these times are much slower than those in the Condon and Ogston study. Secondly, Keele points out that, given Ali's reaction times, once a punch is thrown by an opponent it is way too late to respond. Keele interprets successful boxing as depending on a boxer's ability to perceive and use redundancy (recurring patterns of activity) to anticipate and avoid a punch. Kendon (1970) also has attributed microsynchrony to anticipation by the listener of what the speaker is going to say and draws upon Neisser's (1967) work in linguistic speech perception to support this. The answer to the following question is important. Does Condon and Ogston's interactional synchrony result from interactants being attuned to the same cultural pattern of articulatory phrasing, or is the actual sound or movements of the speaker causing, or "driving," a synchronous response in the listener? The latter interpretation seems somewhat plausible in light of Condon and Sander's (1974) observation that 1- and 2-day-old neonates synchronize their movements with the speech patterns of an adult (although these patterns were not elicited by isolated clicking sounds), and Condon and Ogston's (1967) demonstration of synchrony between a human and a chimpanzee. Condon (1982) has drawn on physiological data indicating that motor responses mediated by brainstem pathways can follow an auditory input by as little as 10 millisec (Davis, 1973) and has demonstrated startle responses in children consistently occurring within as little as 50 millisec after a loud noise. If microsynchrony is in fact an empathy- or attention-related phenomenon mediated by basal brain structures, the comparatively sluggish simple reaction time of Muhammed Ali suggests that, unlike the empathy "gimmicks" described earlier, microsynchrony is either "something you got or something you don't," and there is no way that one can deliberately "do" it.

Tantalizing as these concepts may be, microsynchrony has not received consistent empirical support. McDowall (1978a) shot a six-person group conversation from a bird's eye view at 24 frames per second and reported that interrater reliabilities for coding the occurrence of movement boundaries was poor. Following Condon and Ogston, movement boundaries were specified as an initiation, a termination, or a change of direction of movement. McDowall adopted a criterion that the presence of a movement boundary would be scored if it occurred within three consecutive frames of film. Adopting this larger time window resulted in acceptable interrater reliabilities (McDowall, 1978b). McDowall also cautioned that, when two people are moving for whatever reason, some base rate frequency of occurrence of synchronous movement boundaries must be expected to occur by chance. The frequency with which observed synchronies occur must be compared to this statistical base rate before one can confidently state that synchrony as a significant interpersonal process is happening. Despite the more lenient time frame, McDowall observed no significant presence of synchrony beyond that which would be expected to occur by chance. This was true regardless of whether the interactants were friends, lovers, or strangers, which presumably should have been related to rapport or empathy. McDowall also reported that there was no significant increase in synchrony occurring prior to taking turns at speaking, failing to replicate Kendon's (1970) finding that synchrony seemed to play a role in taking turns at speech.

Gatewood and Rosenwein (1981) have pointed out disparities between McDowall's and Condon's scoring procedures that seriously question the comparability of their results. Specifically, McDowall's (1978b) raters initiated their search for movement boundaries while running the film at 24 frames per second. If a boundary was observed the film was then run slowly back and forth, usually at a speed of one frame per second. This is in sharp contrast to Condon, who employed a hand-turned projector (Condon, 1970) and examined individual frames for longer periods of time. Gatewood and Rosenwein also fault Mc-Dowall for failing to employ the concept of "process unit" described previously. McDowall assigns equal weight to movement boundaries occurring in single body parts, despite the fact that Condon had described redundancy, or multiple body parts simultaneously changing inertial state as the criterion for coding a process unit. The occurrence of a single body-part change in one person while the other interactant displayed no change would be scored as a discrepancy by McDowall, whereas Condon would score that frame as indicating concordance between the interactants. Alternatively, Gatewood and Rosenwein have pointed out that Condon has not specified exactly *how many* body-part boundaries constitute a process unit. A detailed critique of this work may also be found in Rosenfeld (1981).

Condon has interpreted microsynchrony as being mediated by auditory signals and demonstrated (Condon & Sander, 1974) that neonates show synchrony with the phonetic patterns of tape-recorded speech. However, this does not rule out visual information as a relevant channel, because if visual and auditory signals were both capable of mediating synchrony, elimination of one channel should not impair the phenomenon. Interviews with professional and avocational dancers suggest a possibly similar form of synchrony (Levi, 1975). What these dancers describe is something that occasionally occurs during improvisational duets, where the two dancers come to feel that they "are moving each other," that there is no distinguishable sense of leader and follower, but a highly connected sense of moving simultaneously through each moment. Of course, the dancer in the middle of the dance may simply have altered perceptions, a possibility whose verification must come from deliberate, rigorously informed studies such as those attempted by Condon and McDowall.

In summary, the phenomenon of postural synchrony as described earlier by Scheflen (1964) does appear to occur in some regular fashion. Independent work by Charny (1966), LaFrance (1979; LaFrance & Broadbent, 1976), Trout and Rosenfeld (1980), and Dabbs (1969) suggests that it is somewhat related to feelings of rapport or "presence," but LaFrance and Ickes' (1981) recent finding and Scheflen's observations of dissociation point out that mirroring or synchrony are subordinate aspects of empathy or relatedness and may occur even when some other signal is clearly describing the interaction as a hostile or unpleasant one. Clearly, simple recommendations to mirror the posture of a client are missing some other component(s) that inhere in the processes of rapport or empathy. However, the available data are not antagonistic to the possibility that conscious or unconscious motor mimicry can contribute to knowledge of the affective state of another.

William James' Theory of Emotion

At this point a key assumption of the motor mimicry hypothesis should be examined. The theorists discussed at the outset of this chapter made explicit statements that motor mimicry was a contributory component that actively provided information about the affective state of another person. But, with the possible exception of Dabb's study, the research described previously is incapable of distinguishing what role motor mimicry plays in the empathic process. The question hinges on whether the occurrence of similar motor behavior is an active cue-producing component in the empathic process, or whether it is only a reflection or expression of the process having already occurred. Do we both smile to one another because we are empathic, or are we empathic *because* we smile? The psychologically conversant reader will notice the similarity of this question to that often posed for purposes of introducing students to the James–Lange versus Cannon–Bard controversy: Do we run because we are afraid, or are we afraid because we run?

In 1884, William James formulated a modest idea about the nature of emotional experience. Felt emotion, James argued, was the result of neural activity transmitted from the body to the brain. Stimuli that elicit excitement or rage each had their effect on the body's nervous system, and this effect was transmitted back to the brain as the conscious experience of emotion. The notion caused a scientific uproar then and continues to spawn brisk position papers today. The motor mimicry hypothesis, and many of the affective reverberation training methods considered later in this chapter, require more or less explicit acceptance of James' theory regarding the basis of emotional experience for their justification.

It is interesting to note that acceptance of both James' theory and the majority of these training methods continues to exist largely beyond the pale of orthodox psychology. With several recent exceptions, the contributory role of somatic sensation in emotional perception has largely appeared in popular works but received relatively little mention in psychology's empirical literature. Although the development of allied methods for training affective reverberation has been accomplished largely apart from orthodox psychology, this has not prevented their adoption by growing numbers of people interested in finding new ways to understand and expand their affective experience (Ferguson, 1980). This neglect by the scientific community seems in part due to the disrepute with which James' theory has been regarded, with the result that therapeutic methods embracing its dictums have largely been relegated to the backwaters of traditional clinical training and practice. Accordingly, portions of this chapter are concerned with examinations of both the research findings and methodologies relevant to the various theoretical points raised by James' model. Whereas such detailed consideration is in some cases a departure from the purely descriptive function of this chapter, it is essential to a critical evaluation of both the model and the training methods based on its tenets.

The physiologist Walter Cannon (1927, 1929) emerged as the main opponent to James' theory and argued in part that the Autonomic Nervous System (ANS) was not well supplied with sensory receptors, had too slow a response time to account for the immediacy of felt emotion, and was in any case incapable of different patterns of arousal that, according to James, must of necessity underly the different patterns of experienced emotion. These criticisms continue to appear in introductory textbooks as evidence against James' theory, thereby committing the same error that much of the discussion of this topic has over the years; the assumption that James was referring only to the Autonomic Nervous System. Actually, James had specifically included changes occurring in the muscular system, whereas Lange (1922) primarily advanced the ANS as the mediating system.[2]

Although Darwin had advanced the idea in 1872, until recently, relatively little discussion has focused on the network of muscles, nerves, and connective tissue comprising the musculoskeletal system as a possible mediator for James' theory of emotion (Gellhorn, 1964; Izard, 1971, 1977; Tomkins, 1962, 1963). Such a formulation avoids the major criticisms originally advanced by Cannon: Response times of this system are faster than the ANS, and the muscles of the face alone are capable of an extraordinary range of configurations corresponding to different emotional experiences.

Despite the musculoskeletal reformulation, the response latency criticism raised by Cannon continues to receive currency and is worthy of closer examination. Although providing numerous lines of evidence supporting the notion that affective responses precede cognitive analysis or even conscious recognition of a situation, Zajonc (1980) rejected the Jamesian formulation and explicitly stated that "interoceptive processes and motor memories are slower than the affective responses they are presumed to activate" (p. 168). Although it is unclear exactly what is meant by "motor memories" in this context, the thrust of Zajonc's assertion is similar to the argument previously raised by Cannon. In this view, the time required by the nervous system to produce motor responses and receive the sensory information generated by this activity is longer than the time required to perceive an emotional reaction. If emotional feelings occur before internal physiological changes are perceived, then the sensory impressions arising from this physiological activity could not account for the immediate experience of

---

[2]This is not to say that Cannon was right. Early work by Wolf and Wolff (1947) and Ax (1953) demonstrated different autonomic response patterns for different emotions. Recent investigators (e.g., Ekman, Levenson, & Friesen, 1983; Schwartz, Weinberger, & Singer, 1981) have clearly identified differential response patterns for a variety of emotions. Although Schachter and Singer (1962) demonstrated a role of both cognition and physiological activity in emotion and suggested that the former effects exerted greater influence over the latter, Marshall and Zimbardo (1979) and Maslach (1979) could not replicate this finding and indicated that physiological arousal exerted a primary influence on the nature of felt emotion. For a reveiw of the issues surrounding the ANS as a mediator of emotion and an appraisal of the other points raised by Cannon, see Schachter (1975).

emotion as James had argued they did. A comparison of reaction times for affective judgments and of those for activation and interoceptive feedback of motor responses can partially address Zajonc's assertion.

Although providing no evidence to directly support his statement, Zajonc does refer to studies by Paivio (1978), who assessed reaction times for making pleasantness judgments of simultaneously presented pictures or word pairs. Although this rendering of a pleasantness judgment does not necessarily involve mobilization of a full-blown affective response and may therefore have occurred more quickly, the fastest reaction times (which occurred for pictures) averaged 800 milliseconds. Unfortunately, the applicability of Paivio's measure for an analysis of the onset time of emotional experience is somewhat confounded by the fact that Paivio measured choice reaction times, which are always longer than simple reaction-time tasks (involving no choice between alternatives) and thus cannot adequately assess the true onset latency of affective responses apart from time necessary to make a choice. The decrement in response speed attributable to choice rather than simple reaction times in this task is difficult to estimate, because it is not clear whether judgments of the two pictures and generation of an incipient response are performed in series or parallel fashion.

What can be said of the speed with which motor and interoceptive processes occur? The response latency for onset of muscle activity in simple reaction-time tasks is approximately 160 millisec (Botwinick & Thompson, 1966), and Condon (1982) has observed startle responses occurring within 50 milliseconds. When added to the time necessary for transmission of sensory impulses back to the brain, this provides an estimate of the response latency with which interoceptive systems are capable of responding and providing information about the body's activity. Franzen and Offenloch (1969) observed onset latencies of 30 milliseconds at low stimulus intensities for the first positive wave of the cortical evoked potential following vibrotactile stimulation of the finger. However, a clear interpretation of this data is also problematic, because it is difficult to determine which of the several peak responses observed in evoked potential recordings actually correspond to conscious perception of the stimulus. Even accepting a more conservative measure than the first positive peak, these observations, in combination with those of Botwinick and Thompson, indicate that motor and interoceptive processes are capable of faster responding than are the processes involved in forming and indicating an affective preference. Whereas this arithmetic is hardly conclusive evidence, Zajonc's (1980) assertion that musculoskeletal mechanisms are too slow to account for the immediacy of affective experience requires further substantiation in order to be accepted.

The Facial Feedback Hypothesis

For many investigators, studies of facial expressiveness have played an important role in research efforts to assess James' theory. An examination of this research indicates some of the difficulties involved in testing the theory: Whereas James' position has generally been supported (and by extension, training methods derived from it), several counterinstances complicate the picture. As indicated earlier, the main controversy revolves around whether the facial muscles serve only an expressive function or whether sensory impressions from facial activity also play an active role in the perceived experience of emotion. The latter position has been adopted (with various qualifications) by Izard (1971, 1977) and Tomkins (1962, 1963).

Laird (1974) attempted an experimental investigation of the role of facial activity on perceived emotion by having male subjects adopt smiling or frowning expressions while rating affectively charged pictures. Sensitive to the observation provided by Schacter and Singer (1962) that subjects would attribute the physiological sensations of an experimentally induced body change to the experiment and not to their own emotional reactions, Laird constructed an elaborate procedure designed to make subjects think they were participating in a study measuring facial muscle activity during perception. This included placing recording electrodes on the subject's faces and asking them to contract certain muscles to facilitate the recording process. The contracted muscles were, of course, those involved in smiling or frowing. Laird further dropped subjects from the study who on posttest questioning suspected that they had been deliberatly asked to adopt smiles or frowns, or who reported an awareness of a relationship between their expressions and their feelings, thus eliminating data attributable to subject's cognitions about what their emotions "should" be. Subjects maintained the required expression while watching pictures of children playing or of Klu Klux Klan members and subsequently rated their emotional experience during the pictures. Although type of picture exerted significant effects on the subject's ratings, an effect of facial expression within each picture was observed, such that subjects rated themselves as more elated when they were in a smile expression and more aggressive when they were in a frown expression. In a second study, Laird asked subjects to rate the humorousness of cartoons as well as their own emotional state. He again observed significant effects of subjects' facial expressions on both the humorousness of the cartoons and ratings of their own emotional state, supporting the hypothesis that the act of smiling itself enhances feelings of happiness. Although employing less stringent controls for demand characteristics and the attributions made by their subjects, Zuckerman, Klorman, Larrance, and Spiegel (1981) also obtained differences in autonomic activity and subjective ratings of affective experience and intensity when subjects were requested to exaggerate or suppress their facial responsiveness to pleasant and unpleasant film scenes.

Lanzetta, Cartwright–Smith, and Kleck (1976) requested subjects to suppress or exaggerate their facial responses to a series of electric shocks of varying intensity. Comparison of subjects' ratings of the shock strengths revealed that posing the reception of no shock resulted in lower verbal ratings of shock strength as well as lower levels of skin conductance in the periods immediately following shock presentation. Consistent with Laird's findings. Lanzetta et al. interpreted their data as supporting Darwin's contention that the free expression of an emotion intensifies it, whereas the repression of expressiveness curtails emotional intensity. Kraut (1982) also observed similar changes for ratings of pleasant and disgusting odors when subjects posed pleased or disgusted facial expressions following presentation of the odor. In a further study, McCaul, Holmes, and Solomon (1982) found that expressions of happiness lowered the perceived intensity of soft and loud noises but did not observe this effect on a second trial with the same subjects. Additionally, a posed fear expression did not result in higher ratings of noise intensity relative to nonposed expressions. This latter finding failed to support the observations of Lanzetta et al. and Kraut, possibly because fear is an expression relatively unrelated to perception of a noise the subject knows is coming.

Tourangeau and Ellsworth (1979) collected affect self-ratings, heart rate, and electrodermal activity from subjects viewing sad, fearful, and neutral films under conditions of posed sad, fearful, or neutral facial expressions. Tourangeau and Ellsworth utilized the same cover story employed by Laird (1974) (electrode placement and facial expressions adopted to ''facilitate recording'') and included a posed nonaffective expression as a control for the effort involved in posing a facial expression per se. Whereas type of film exerted a significant effect on self-report of emotion and physiological activity, the posed facial expressions produced no reliable effect on either variable. Moreover, the neutral posed expression produced approximately similar increases in electrodermal and cardiac activity as the sad and fearful expressions, leading Tourangeau and Ellsworth to argue that the attempt to pose any expression at all may have been responsible for Lanzetta et al.'s results. However, Ekman, Levenson, and Friesen (1983) observed no effect of this control procedure on autonomic activity when it was held by the subject for 10 seconds, a time more comparable to the expression durations occurring in Lanzetta et al.'s study, suggesting that effort per se did not account for their results. The discrepancy between this and Tourangeau and Ellsworth's study is probably attributable to the fact that Tourangeau and Ellsworth required subjects to hold the facial poses for 2 minutes, thereby requiring more effort on the part of their subjects. Although Laird's results for angry and happy expressions and those of Zuckerman et al. supported the facial feedback hypothesis, Tourangeau and Ellsworth failed to support the hypothesis for sad and fearful expressions. Criticisms of the long duration of poses and several other aspects of Tourangeau and Ellsworth's study may be found in Hager and Ekman (1981), Izard (1981), and Tomkins (1981), as well as a rebuttal by Ellsworth and Tourangeau (1981). At issue in these discussions was the unfeasibility of maintaining a single expression for 2 minutes, the ability of Tourangeau and Ellsworth's instructions to actually produce valid analogs of emotional expressions, inherent differences in posed and spontaneous expressions (cf. Rinn, 1984), and the inability of a single manipulation of facial activity to disconfirm hypotheses based on a broad range of internal sensory feedback and cognitive factors.

In summary and review of the facial feedback hypothesis, it is necessary to consider the work of Buck (1979, 1980), who has taken issue with the hypothesis on the basis of his observations of both ANS and facial muscle activity in subjects presented with emotional stimuli. If James' theory is correct, argues Buck (1979, p. 61), subjects who show greater facial expressiveness should experience more emotion, which should itself be reflected in increased activity of the sympathetic nervous system. Contrary to this expectation, numerous studies (see Buck, 1979, 1980 for a review) have demonstrated that subjects who showed more clear facial expressiveness when exposed to affectively loaded pictures exhibited *lower* levels of electrodermal activity than did less expressive subjects.

It should be emphasized that these studies involved intersubject correlations assessing relative differences *between* subjects. Buck (1980) has distinguished "strong" and "weak" versions of the facial feedback hypothesis corresponding to between-subjects and within-subjects experimental designs. The former states that if subject A's expressiveness is greater than subject B's, his emotional response (autonomic physiological activity) will be correspondingly greater. The "weak" version suggests only that the relationship between these two variables will be correlated *within* an individual subject. Buck's studies therefore address themselves to the strong version and are not capable of disconfirming the within-subject version (in fact, Buck, Miller, and Caul, 1974, examined the relationship between expressiveness and electrodermal activity within individual subjects and found a small but significant correlation between the two measures). It is important to remember that the application of James' theory being developed here is predominantly concerned with the relation between physiological activity and affective perception within a given individual. Although the factors that may underlie the failure to observe this relationship across subjects suggest several possibilities for the study of individual differences in emotional expressiveness, they are not germane to our concern with training affective reverberation. The training methods with which we are concerned are exclusively directed to changes occurring *within* the individual, and as will be shown, to enhancing his or her awareness of those changes.

Non Facial Feedback Sources

The obvious relevance of facial activity to emotion has resulted in an emphasis on analysis of expressiveness in these muscles. However, as described next, numerous other musculoskeletal sources exist that are capable of mediating and reflecting affective experience. Additionally, those aspects of James' theory considered thus far represent situations where the sensory information from somatic activity may arguably represent innate or unconditioned emotional responses. For example, children who have been blind from birth exhibit typical smiling responses when happy (Goodenough, 1932), and monkeys raised in isolation show fear when confronted with photographs of an adult monkey in a threatening posture (Sackett, 1966). Although such innate emotional responses are important to this discussion, a deeper understanding of the affective life of the individual must also consider the role of learning experiences. It should be noted that James' theory is not limited to such innate mind–body relationships. Individual differences in emotional functioning acquired through early learning experiences are equally capable of mediation by somatoskeletal mechanisms. In this regard, Hefferline (1958; Hefferline & Bruno, 1971) has presented evidence indicating that sensory impressions from muscles can become associated with unpleasant environmental experiences. When subsequently activated, these sensory impressions themselves were capable of motivating avoidance of the unpleasant situation. These results suggest that individual emotional experiences can become coded in unique patterns of muscular activity, and that these patterns should be considered in the application of training methods.

A further study by Hefferline and Perera (1963) points out the relevance of such learned patterns of muscular activity for the accurate perception of external situations. Hefferline and Perera made electronic recordings of very small muscle twitches that were imperceptible to their subjects. The subjects were then instructed to press a response key whenever they heard a faint tone and were given a monetary reward each time they correctly detected the tone. What the subjects did not know was that the tone was presented only when a muscle twitch occurred. Hefferline and Perera then progressively lowered the intensity of the tone until it no longer could be heard. However, the subjects continued to press the key after each muscle twitch despite the fact that they were not consciously aware of the twitch. Of particular interest was the fact that these subjects also reported hearing the tone, even though it was absent!

Hefferline's studies suggest an important implication for the accurate perception of another's affective display, in that his subjects were capable of "perceiving" physical events that were not there if those events had been previously associated with aspects of the subjects own sensory or motor activity. Similarly, we should expect that one reason people may perceive emotions that aren't there in others is because these emotions have been associated in the observer's previous experience with some aspect of the affective display that actually is present in another person. For example, an individual who has been consistently exposed to hostile, deprecating laughter will come to perceive laughter in a different way than the person not exposed to such a history. Attempts to affectively reverberate with a person who is laughing will be distorted to the extent that the observer projectively "hears" or "sees" hostile overtones in the other person's laughter that are not there. Besides a purely cognitive interpretation, Hefferline's data and James' model indicate that this distortion can reside in the observer's activation of motor and sensory impulses associated with his or her previous reactions to laughter and hostility.

In a fascinating series of studies, Bull (1951/1968, 1962) reported that hypnotized subjects consistently adopted appropriate postures when given suggestions to experience certain emotions. In a subsequent study, when subjects were given instructions only to adopt these postures, this manipulation proved consistently effective in inducing the experience of the attendant emotion, even though emotional references were carefully omitted from the instructions. Finally, Bull again had subjects adopt an affect-specific posture and instructed them to maintain it throughout the session. She then asked them to experience an emotion contrary to that associated with the ''locked-in'' posture. Subjects were unable to feel the suggested emotion as long as they maintained the conflicting posture. Those subjects who were able to experience the emotion were only able to do so by relinquishing the locked-in posture and adopting the affect-appropriate one. Although they may have been susceptible to experimenter bias, these observations are in clear conformance with those that would be predicted by James' theory.

Finally, Hohmann (1966) conducted an analysis of the emotional experiences of a group of 25 paraplegics and quadriplegics with complete lesions of the spinal cord. Hohmann divided his subjects into five groups based on the location of the spinal lesion. Patients in group five, with lesions in the sacral area at the base of the spine, had the majority of their ANS and sensory innervation intact. Patients in group one, with lesions in the cervical segments at the top of the spine, experienced almost total disconnection of the ANS, and sensory loss below the neck. The five groups therefore represented a continuum of autonomic innervation and somatic sensation.

Proceeding with a structured interview, subjects were asked to compare the intensity of their emotions in response to similar incidents occurring before and after the injury. Hohmann coded these descriptions into a change score representing the extent of gain or loss of emotional feelings and observed a striking relationship between the level of spinal injury and the loss of emotional intensity. Patients with high cervical lesions exhibited the greatest decrease in intensity, and those with low sacral injuries the least, with the intermediate groups falling on an ordered continuum in between. The same relationship held for sexual excitement and grief.

Although Hohmann's data make a strong case, it should be noted that a strict or exclusive acceptance of James' theory is not critical for the process of affective reverberation as understood here. Certainly, affective reactions have many components, and it need not be accepted that perception of somatic changes is the only relevant dimension or even the first element to occur in affective perception. It is sufficient to recognize that somatosensory information contributes an important measure of the fullness or flavor of affective experience. The studies just reveiwed provide fairly consistent support for James' theory and suggest that motor mimicry is not merely a reflection of the first stages of empathic processing. *Perception* of another's affective state may in many cases be accomplished by simple recognition of familiar nonverbal features and need not involve motor mimicry. We do not ourselves need to smile in order to perceive that someone is happy. However, it appears that motor mimicry can play a role in perceiving the affective experience of another when their nonverbal display is unique in our experience or not easily associated with previously recognized affects.

Reverberation, the step from perceiving an affect in another to creating it within ourselves would, in light of the preceding data, appear to rely more extensively on some form of motor mimicry. If we ourselves are to be happy, some form of smiling appears to be indicated. It should be noted that studies employing electrical recording of activity in facial muscles (cf. Fridlund & Izard, 1983) or microanalysis of facial behavior (Haggard & Isaacs, 1966) have revealed minute patterns of affectively relevant facial activity that were in some cases undetectable by visual observation (Schwartz, Fair, Salt, Mandel, & Klerman! 1976). These results indicate that the process of motor mimicry need not necessarily involve gross or clearly observable postural or facial changes on the part of the observer. The adoption, even minutely, of similar movements, postures, or expressions should, the observer willing, lead to affectively toned kinesthetic and proprioceptive sensations within the observer that mirror or reproduce those of the person being observed. This entails an important first step in the reverberatory phase, and successful affective reverberation correspondingly entails the observer's openess to and accurate perception of the sensory impressions produced by this activity.

Impairment of these steps in reverberatory functioning could stem simply from the observer's unwillingness or inability to produce similar motor activity. Conversely, impairment could arise from inability either to accurately perceive the attendant sensations or to discriminate those sensations and motor events actually occurring in the other person from those that are idiosyncratic to the observer's own learning history. As Hefferline's data suggest, this latter confusion can pose a problem, particularly for the observer who is unaware of prior associations between motor responses and external events, or for whom the sensory impressions of such activity are not clearly established in consciousness. The requirement for accurate sensory perception of internal states necessarily becomes an important consideration in the analysis of affective reverberation, and it is to this issue that we now turn attention.

Wilhelm Reich and Character Analysis

Here we consider the clinical and experimental evidence for the psychological relevance of individual differences in the processing of internal sensory experience. If we (1) admit of a concept of repression, (2) have established that emotions are at least partially represented by somatic feeling states, and (3) believe that emotions are susceptible of repression or distortion, then we should expect to find diminished or distorted patterns of somatic awareness that vary with the defensive style and personality structure of the individual. It also follows that impairments in affective reverberation would correspond to these distorted patterns of somatic sensation. Such an analysis provides an inroad to the understanding of individual differences in perceptual and affective reverberatory capability, as well as a point of departure for evaluating those training methods attempting to enhance this aspect of reverberatory function.

Aspects of this theory have been nowhere described as completely as in the work of Wilhelm Reich (1933/1949) and his students (e.g., Baker, 1967; Lowen, 1958, 1967, 1975). Although this work is detailed and complex, four main themes may be extracted for our purposes. Primary among these is the observation that body areas and their associated sensations are focal points of developmental psychosexual stages and emotional expression. Besides the psychosexual developmental phases advanced by Freud, psychologically relevant body areas other than oral, anal, and genital erogenous zones include those involved in any expressive activity and those associated with anxiety reactions or anticipation of punishment. Reich's second contribution included detailed descriptions of patterns of chronically maintained muscular tension (which Reich termed armor), that varied systematically with the character structure and psychological conflicts of the individual. Thus, a chronically clenched jaw belied poorly resolved impulses to bite or cry out, and perpetually hunched or ''hung up'' shoulders could reflect the fearful and constant anticipation of punishment descending from above. Third, and pivotal to this discussion, was the observation that *chronic muscle tension served to diminish and distort sensory awareness of the tense body area.* For example, tension in the pelvic area would block sexual sensations. This provided a mechanism supporting repression, and through which anxiety-laden or forbidden feelings, memories, and actions could be kept at bay.

The picture emerging here is that the modulation of sensory information arising from various body sites plays a critical role in the defensive functions of the personality. In this view, distortions of sensory processing correspondingly impair awareness of one's own affective reactions, and this effect extends to the awareness of similar affects occurring in others. Although it is a commonplace observation that empathic sensitivity is impaired in highly conflicted or neurotic persons, Reich provided a mechanism that explicitly described a way in which this may occur. This model further indicated that specific areas of psychological conflict would be related to disturbances in the sensory perception of specific body areas, and these in turn should be related to specific disturbances in affective reverberation. By focusing attention on the location and patterns of muscular armor, the model also suggested a means for diagnosing the content area to which the conflict was related, as in the preceding example of sexual feelings and pelvic tension.

Finally, Reichian and neo-Reichian therapists developed procedures designed to release the muscular tension, with the intent of restoring feeling and mobility to the area, bringing repressed material to the surface, and restoring expressiveness. These procedures included directly massaging the muscles or requiring patients to engage in repeated expressive activity such as kicking, hitting, or biting. In light of the role of somatosensory awareness in the affective reverberatory stage described previously, the procedures developed by Reich should be considered as candidates for inclusion in the group of training methods that may enhance affective reverberation.

Reich was a practicing analyst at the time *Character Analysis* was published (1933) and had earlier served as director of the Vienna Psychoanalytic Technical Seminar. These concepts had been employed to some extent by Ferenczi (1930), were applied by analysts such as Braatöy (1954) and Deutsch (1952), and found their way in diluted form into the formulations of Harry Stack Sullivan (1945), Anna Freud (1936/1966), and Erik Erikson (1950). Whereas psychoanalysis has traditionally posed a vexation for those committed to experimental, objective validation of theory (Luborsky & Spence, 1978) (and Reich himself has posed a vexation for psychoanalysis), this has not prevented these concepts from being employed in various popular ''body therapies'' that continue to exist outside the realm of psychological orthodoxy. However, the four tenets described previously are not impossible of objective validation, and, for the time being, it is largely upon such validation that the potential effectiveness of Reich's and other body therapies as affective reverberation training methods must be assessed. The experimental evidence relative to Reich's propositions puts descriptive muscle on the bones of theory, provides a mechanism underlying impaired affective reverberation, and describes specific individual variations in the nature of this impairment. This research is considered in the following paragraphs.

With regard to the first proposition that body sensations exert affectively and psychologically relevant influences, Fisher (1966, 1970) has completed numerous studies indicating that relatively stable individual patterns of allocation of awareness to specific body areas are related to defensive style, fantasy content, projective themes, and the nature of core conflicts. Many of these studies were correlational in nature and employed several measures of body image, including a two-alternative forced-choice questionaire consisting of pairs of body parts, with the subject requested to indicate which area was most clear in awareness at that moment. However, employing sensory awareness as in independent variable by stimulating sites such as the back of the body with a mechanical vibrator, Fisher was subsequently able to influence selective memory for words associated with dirt themes (1968), tachistoscopic recognition of homosexual stimuli, and paranoid or power content on the Thematic Apperception Test (1972).

Having demonstrated that manipulations of the sensory prominence of specific body sites could exert significant effects on the perception of psychologically related themes, the question arises as to whether manipulation of psychological themes could influence the sensory prominence of related body areas. Following on earlier observations that high awareness of the ocular region was correlated with oral incorporative themes, Fisher (1980) produced increases in eye irritation and discomfort in subjects with past histories of somatization in this area by playing tape-recorded descriptions of consuming a meal. Noting a previously observed relationship between mouth awareness and hostility themes, Fisher also demonstrated an increase in mouth sensations following presentation of tape-recorded hostile themes. Neither of these effects could be produced with tape recordings of neutral themes. Fisher's work has provided consistent evidence that alterations in the degree of sensory awareness of specific body areas play an important regulatory role in the processing of affective material uniquely related to the different body sites.

Reich's second proposition stated that patterns of chronic tension vary with the psychological disposition of the individual. This hypothesis has important implications for diagnostic procedures and, together with Reich's third hypothesis that chronic tension impairs sensory functioning, provides the cornerstone for the present model of disturbed affective reverberation as well as several of the training methods that attempt to improve it. The second hypothesis regarding tension patterns has been investigated with several techniques, including an objective measure of muscular activity, electromyography (EMG), recorded from a variety of body sites. Besides identifying unique profiles of movement patterns (Fisch, Frey, & Hirsbrunner, 1983; Sloman, Berridge, Homatidis, Hunter, & Duck, 1982) in depressed patients, numerous investigations have demonstrated greater overall levels of EMG activity in this population (Rimon, Stenback, & Huhmar, 1966; Whatmore, 1966; Whatmore & Ellis, 1959, 1962), which precedes the onset of depressive episodes and remits as the depression lifts. A more clinically accessible, yet reliable, technique for assessing residual tension, the "spring reflex" has been described by von Baeyer and Wyant (1982), who successfully differentiated those chronic-pain patients with elevated Hysteria, Hypochondriasis, and Depression scales on the MMPI. Plutchik, Wasserman, and Mayer (1975) assessed muscle tension by systematic observations of flexibility and movement patterns and found these functions to be significantly impaired in several psychiatric populations. Goldstein (1964) and Plutchik (1954) have reviewed studies indicating consistently high muscle tension in psychotic and neurotic groups.

Whereas the findings of overall increases in muscle tension in a variety of psychopathologic conditions are partially supportive of Reich's formulations, they are unable to shed light on the specific hypothesis that localized patterns of tension are related to particular psychodynamic conflicts or character formations. Shipman, Oken, Goldstein, Grinker, and Heath (1964) made simultaneous recordings from seven muscle sites in a group of 15 psychiatric inpatients, 11 of whom were diagnosed as neurotic depressives. Recordings were made over 3 separate days: During day 1, interview and experimental procedures were (successfully) designed to arouse as much affect in the patients as possible by administering an unexplained, impersonal procedure while reviewing and dwelling on the major emotional crises of the patient's lives. Day 2 consisted of an interview during which patients were encouraged to review instances in which they had controlled their emotions and were admonished to "get control of yourself" and "hold on to your feelings" during the interview. A third day consisted of neutral conversation and a period of rest. Additionally, a battery of questionaire and projective tests was administered, and observer ratings of affect and self-control were obtained.

Interestingly, no effects on EMG activity were observed as a result of the different interview conditions, although higher tension levels occurred during interviews than were observed during a period of resting alone. Of those results emerging from a truly heroic statistical analysis (over 1000 correlations were computed), few clear patterns occurred. Those relationships that did appear were somewhat perplexing: Patients who showed lower levels of depression and anxiety during the interviews tended to have higher levels of EMG activity compared to baseline in biceps (depression) and frontalis and quadriceps (anxiety). Shipman et al. interpreted their results as indicating that high overall tension occurred in the more emotionally stable, least anxious patients with a capacity for self-control and a sense of personal limits. One of Shipman's coauthors (Goldstein, 1972, p. 350) has speculated that these unexpected results stemmed partially from the fact that all subjects were selected from a psychiatric population with intense depression and acute illness and were therefore not directly comparable with studies investigating differences between patient and normal populations. Although this explanation is not entirely convincing, it is supported by the consistent observations of increased tension levels in patients relative to normal populations. However, it remains difficult to reconcile Shipman et al.'s finding that, *within* a psychiatric population, higher tension levels were present in those patients with the least symptomatology.

Although Shipman et al. employed measures that reflected personality organization, no attempt was made to study the relation between muscle tension and content-specific psychodynamic themes as they occurred in the course of the interviews. Shagass and Malmo (1954) recorded EMG activity from five sites in three patients during psychiatric interview and noted that increased forearm tension was associated with hostility themes in all three patients, whereas increased leg tension occurred during sexual themes in the two women. In one patient followed longitudinally over 9 days, high tension levels were associated with depression and negatively related to cheerfulness as assessed by ward nurses. Clinical improvement was reflected by decreased muscle tension. A similar relationship between tension in biceps during hostility themes and leg tension concurrent with sexual content was observed in a subsequent case study by Malmo, Smith, and Kohlmeyer (1956).

An important caveat is in order with respect to studies employing electromyography as a measure of tension levels, particularly in populations where high tension levels are suspected. Lowen (1975) has observed that chronic tension may be maintained in the absence of descending neural influences, and a similar phenomenon has been reported by Whatmore and Kohli (1974). Sustained contraction of muscle depletes energy reserves stored in creatinine phosphate that are required to lengthen or relax a muscle fiber as well as contract it. At an advanced stage of the process, the muscle may remain contracted in spite of greatly reduced or altogether absent muscle action potentials (Woodbury, Gordon, & Conrad, 1965) and hence be unestimable by EMG recording methods. This effect has been demonstrated in laboratory preparations and human subjects (cf. Whatmore & Kohli, 1974, p. 85).

A second mechanism whereby muscle tension may go undetected by electrical recording techniques has been described by Rolf (1977). In this model, structural changes following sustained periods of muscular contraction and immobility occur in the fascial tissue that surrounds and connects muscle fibers. Eventually, the normally elastic fascial tissue becomes hardened and inflexible, actually binding the muscle into a relatively immobile state regardless of the electrical activity of the muscle itself (Woo, Matthews, Akeson, Amiel, & Convery, 1975). Given these physiological snakes in the grass, a skeptical attitude should be retained toward accepting "objective" electrical recordings as final evidence of the presence or absence of tension. Systematic observations of flexibility and movement such as Plutchik et al.'s (1975) accordingly become an important assessment procedure, as do the trained eyes and hands of the clinician or practitioner.

A sober review of the evidence presented thus far relative to the relation between localized muscular activity and content-specific conflicts or character styles leaves a suggestive, though not compelling, impression of the veracity of the theory that tension patterns faithfully reflect psychological states. The point need not be labored for our conception of affective reverberation in empathy. The observations made by Reich and numerous others (cf. Christiansen, 1963; North, 1975; Wallbott, 1982) concerning individual tendencies to display habitual postures and movement styles reflecting various attitudes, feeling states, or images they wish to project is sufficient. Bull's data and a moment's reflection should make this clear; each of us has had experience with individuals who typically appear belligerent and angry, depressed, or timid and afraid. Rolf (1977) in particular has elaborated the effects that habitual posture exerts on corresponding adjustments throughout the body. The presence of a fixed, unyielding posture must of necessity entail chronic contractions that eventually become self-sustaining, curtailing potential for expressing the full range of affectively relevant experience. Hefferline (1958) states:

> Should this be the predicament of a sizable portion of the adult population, it would
> not be surprising to find well-nigh universal complaints of aches, pains, cramps,

tension, and "run-down feelings," or that Edmund Jacobsen should have had a best-seller on his hands when he wrote *You Must Relax.* (p. 746)

To this point, we have described the role proposed for motor mimicry in producing internal sensations similar to those of the person being observed. Examination of William James' theory and the work of Fisher supported the important role played by these sensations in conveying affective and psychologically relevant information and suggested that profiles of relative awareness of different body sites correspond to personality differences. Having considered the numerous observations of increased muscular tension in persons experiencing psychological difficulty and the less frequent observations that the location of such tension corresponds to specific emotional states or psychological themes, we come to the linking hypothesis of sensory impairment. If Reich's hypothesis that muscular tension inhibits sensory perception is correct, this supplies a mechanism through which impairments in affective reverberation may be understood and treated. Lowen's (1965) description is representative of this position:

> Self awareness means an awareness of the body . . . . In the unaware person there are areas of the body that lack sensation and are, therfore, missing from consciousness . . . . The loss of self awareness is caused by chronic muscle tension. (pp. 15–16)

This proposition has been taken as an article of faith by most of the developers and devotees of the affective reverberation training methods considered later in this chapter but continues to remain elusive of strong experimental validation. Besides evaluating the ramifications of the model of affective reverberation developed here, the validity of this hypothesis is critical for assessing the viability of Reich's and other method's practice of directly intervening at the level of the musculature itself. It is unfortunate that so important a question has yet to be subjected to a highly satisfactory experimental test. The assessment of sensory awareness of tension in muscle groups poses several methodological difficulties that have not been entirely overcome to date. These difficulties are briefly mentioned as the various experimental investigations are now considered.

Does Tension Impair Perception?

Besides the continued clinical observations issuing from neo-Reichian therapists, recent observations stemming from biofeedback applications have suggested that muscle tension impairs awareness of the tense body area. In a series of experiments with tension headache patients, Budzynski, Stoyva, and Adler (1970) utilized a biofeedback-assisted relaxation procedure for muscles of the neck and forehead and reported that those subjects who were able to reduce their pain became "more aware of rising muscle tension (and became able to) abort slight to moderate intensity headaches by relaxing in situations where they felt themselves growing tense" (p. 208). Prompted by these findings and their own observations that "patients with chronic neck and shoulder muscle pain [tension related] seemed to be unusually unable to estimate tension levels" (p. 28), Fowler and Kraft (1974) made EMG recordings from the trapezious muscle, whereas patients who had been referred for pain conditions caused by chronic tension filled out the MMPI. At 5-minute intervals, subjects estimated their tension level at that moment on a scale from 1 to 10. These estimates were correlated with actual EMG activity and results were compared with a group of normals given the same task. Although the patients' averaged estimates of their own tension levels were higher than those of the controls, both groups showed a random correlation between tension estimates and actual EMG activity. In noting that both groups were equally unable to estimate their tension levels, Fowler and Kraft pointed out that the patient's standard deviation of moment-to-moment tension levels was more than three times larger than the control's, and that "It is easier to estimate the magnitude of a variable which varies widely than a variable which varies little" (p. 30). This early attempt at experimental assessment failed to support the hypothesis that tension impairs perception but suggested that a possible impairment of sensory function in the patients could not be ruled out, because these patients may have had an advantage due to the large variability of the tension levels they were estimating. Additionally, constraining subjects to estimate their level of tension on a 1 to 10 scale and applying statistical tests for linear correlations ignores Stevens' (1975) power law, which indicates that the relationship between stimulus intensity and subjective estimates of that intensity is nonlinear, and that imposition of an interval scale is an inappropriate metric for scaling those subjective estimates (Stevens, 1951).

In a further investigation relevant to perception of tense muscles, Sime and DeGood (1977) employed a variation of the two-interval forced-choice procedure in which female subjects responding to ads for relaxation training estimated whether their frontalis muscle tension during a 20-second interval was higher or lower than the immediately preceding interval, with a 10-second intertrial interval. Three groups of subjects were than retested after four sessions of EMG biofeedback, modified progressive muscle relaxation (PMR; Jacobsen, 1938), or listening to music. Although both the EMG feedback and the PMR groups succeeded in significantly reducing their tension levels, the biofeedback group demonstrated greater increases in the proportion of correct estimates given on the awareness assessment task. Because the PMR and the biofeedback groups achieved equivalent reductions of tension, this result suggests that the improvement in awareness was not entirely due to the reduction in tension, but perhaps to some "calibrating" function performed by the feedback stimulus (Brener, 1974, 1977). Some effect of relaxation on perception was also indicated, in that the PMR group showed greater increases in correct responses than did the music control group, which achieved significantly less tension reduction.

The question arises, however, as to just what was being calibrated by biofeedback. Sime and DeGood noted that swallowing and movements of the eyes or jaw produced sharp increases in frontalis muscle activity. The biofeedback subjects would have been most capable of observing this effect and therefore may have acquired additional cues from which to estimate tension. This also presents a problem in the modified two-interval forced-choice procedure, because subjects may have deliberately produced these responses in one interval or another and been able to make correct choices without relying on actual perception of tension levels. This phenomenon has been observed by Ross and Brener (1981) in subjects making similar estimates of cardiac activity. Sime and DeGood observed nonsignificant correlations between frontalis EMG and proportion correct choices pretraining but observed a significant inverse relationship (-.45) between these variables posttraining for all groups combined (individual treatment groups had nonsignificant correlations), suggesting confirmation of Reich's hypothesis that tension decreases sensitivity. However, we will shortly have additional cause to disregard these results.

Stilson, Matus, and Ball (1980) assessed accuracy of motor control (presumably related to accuracy of tension perception) using the magnitude production procedure of S.S. Stevens (1975). In this method, subjects were required to squeeze a hand dynamometer or produce an isometric contraction in the biceps with a force corresponding to each of several numerical subjective magnitudes. Stilson et al. derived two measures of accuracy from the resulting psychophysical function. *Sensitivity* was defined as the rate of change in EMG activity per unit increment of subjective magnitude, i.e., the slope of the function. *Imprecision* was defined as the extent to which EMG activity differed for repeated productions of the same subjective magnitude.

Data for the biceps showed no effect of biofeedback relaxation training on sensitivity or imprecision in psychiatric inpatients or normal controls.[3] An additional study of 36 normal subjects investigated the relationship between frontalis tension levels and awareness. A significant inverse correlation between pretraining tension levels and sensitivity was observed; subjects with the highest tension levels demonstrated the lowest sensitivity, and low-tension subjects demonstrated the highest. Sensitivity was also significantly improved in all groups following biofeedback relaxation training. These results are the strongest confirmation to date of Reich's hypothesis and indicate that accuracy of perception of a muscle group is inversely proportional to the amount of tension present in these muscles. It is not clear whether the additional finding that biofeedback relaxation training improved sensitivity is related to the lower levels of tension achieved through biofeedback, or whether this procedure enhanced sensitivity through some other means.

---

[3]Interestingly, biofeedback resulted in a significant *decrease* in both sensitivity and imprecision in the patient group when the functions for dynamometer force production were analyzed. Although the dynamometer task represents a unique case due to the involvement of tactile receptors, this result is contrary to the hypothesis. It is also perplexing that sensitivity should decrease at the same time that precision is increased, suggesting that accuracy of control is increased at low tension levels but is inversely related to this measure of sensitivity.

Stilson et al. further assessed awareness using a modified two-interval forced-choice procedure similar to that employed by Sime and DeGood (1977) but employed a mathematical procedure (lacking in the earlier study), designed to separate the subject's true sensitivity from their bias for guessing a particular response. A bias toward guessing that progressive intervals had lower tension over the course of relaxation might result in an inflated proportion of correct responses (such a bias was in fact observed, making the earlier results of Sime and DeGood suspect). Although the correlation of pretraining tension levels and the adjusted proportion correct was not significant, feedback training produced a significant improvement in awareness of tension levels. The failure of the forced-choice data to reflect the pretraining differences in awareness observed when the previously defined measure of sensitivity was used as a dependent variable suggests either that the proportion-correct measure is a less sensitive estimator of awareness, or that the two measures are assessing different things.

Again, a methodological difficulty precludes confident acceptance of the magnitude production measure as employed by Stilson et al. to demonstrate reduced sensitivity in the presence of high tension. Stilson et al.'s application, called ratio scaling, requires that the experimenter assign an initial subjective magnitude to a given tension level and thus represents a departure from the more accurate method of absolute scaling (Hellman & Zwislocki, 1961; Zwislocki & Goodman, 1980), where no subjective magnitudes are imposed by the experimenter. It is unclear whether the differences between high- and low-tension groups in Stilson et al.'s study would be preserved if sensitivity were assessed by this more accurate method.

In summary of the results on EMG tension levels and awareness, it is disappointing that, for the reasons noted, the research to date is incapable of convincingly addressing the important question of whether sensitivity is reduced in the presence of high tension. Of course, the caveats noted earlier regarding electromyography as a measure of tension level are equally operative for awareness research: Such studies are not entirely capable of assessing the effects of longstanding chronic tension. Alternative assessments of tension are a much needed component for future research. Nonetheless, it is compelling that Reich's contention that chronic tension impairs local sensory acuity is a by-now commonplace clinical observation reported almost universally by practitioners of the numerous therapeutic practices designed to integrate mind/body functioning. Hefferline's (1958) account of his work presented in Perls, Hefferline, and Goodman (1951) makes particularly interesting reading in this regard. Hefferline engaged undergraduates in "exercises in self-awareness" in which they were encouraged to make extended internal observations of all parts of their skeletal musculature:

> The first report of a subject is likely to be that . . . he can feel . . . every part of his body. When further inquiry is made, it often turns out that what he took to be proprioceptive discrimination of a particular body part was actually a visualization

of the part or a verbal statement of its location . . . . With further work, if he can be persuaded to continue, the subject may report certain parts of his body to be proprioceptively missing. Suppose it is his neck. He may discriminate a mass that is his head and a mass that is his trunk with what feels like simply some empty space in between. At this stage the subject is apt to remember more important things to do and his participation in the silly business ends. (p. 747)

Those subjects persevering with exploration of such lacunae occasionally reported a gradual return of sensation, although it appears that more often the area "suddenly became the locus of sharp pain, paresthesias of one sort or another, 'electric sensations', or the unmistakable ache of muscular cramp" (p. 747). There followed for Hefferline's subjects the trying and perplexing problem of relinquishing the muscular clinch. For those who were successful, Hefferline noted that "when a muscular block is definitely resolved, it is frequently claimed by the subject that there occurs vivid, spontaneous recall of typical situations, perhaps dating back to childhood, where he learned to tense in this particular manner" (p. 748). This description is remarkably consistent with Reich's observations and provides some justification for the role attributed by him to "body work" in the lifting of repressions. It also indicates that, in some cases, passively experimenting with chronically tense muscle groups may release the tension.

Having considered the evidence relevant to the various assumptions suggested by the motor mimicry hypothesis, we are almost ready to begin an examination of methods through which the perceptual and affective reverberation components of empathy may be trained. However, a bit more work is required. The identification of chronic muscular tension as the mechanism by which internal sensations are inhibited entails a prescription for how the sensation is to be restored. Several of the training methods to be considered accordingly proceed with interventions directed specifically at the musculature.

But it is most unlikely that chronic muscle tension is the exclusive mediator of impaired sensory perception. Ekman and Friesen (1974) have noted that certain individuals may block affective processes by simply not producing a given facial expression, whereas in other individuals "the expression is not blocked, but the feedback is, such that the person is remarkably unaware of having shown the particular expression" (p. 219). Although this phenomenon may occur in conjunction with the "frozen affect" (habitually set facial expressions) described by Tomkins (1963), this remains a matter for research, and one is hard put to attribute it entirely to chronic tension. We accordingly embark on a brief physiological excursion of somatosensory mechanisms, bearing in mind the admonition made at the outset of this chapter that empathy-training methods must consider the etiology and locus of deficits occurring in a given stage of the empathic process if they are to meet with success. In this case the question of locus has to do with where in the nervous system a sensory inhibition is effected. Different training methods are designed to effect change at different levels of the system.

Mechanisms of Sensory Inhibition

Peripheral.   The occurrence of sustained high isometric muscle tension impairs the flow of blood through the region (Bonde–Peterson, Mork, & Nielsen, 1975), placing local sensory receptors in a state of oxygen deprivation (ischaemia) that impairs their transmitting properties (Kenshalo, 1977).

Until fairly recently, accounts of kinesthesia and position sense have denied a role for afferent impulses arising from the muscle itself (e.g., Rose & Mountcastle, 1959). Subsequent work by Goodwin, McCloskey, and Matthews (1972) demonstrated a clear contribution of receptors within the muscle to conscious movement and position perception. Vallbo (1974) and Burke, Hagbarth, and Skuse (1978) have demonstrated that isometric muscle contractions strongly activate these receptors, and Burgess, Clark, Simon, and Wei (1982) have suggested that the possibility of differential recruitment of these receptors at different limb positions is correspondingly reduced. Although this would suggest impaired position and movement sense under conditions of high tension, Gandevia and McCloskey (1976; McCloskey & Gandevia, 1978) have demonstrated that perception of small passive movements in the finger is actually *enhanced* when the muscles are contracted rather than relaxed. It remains to be seen whether this effect would be observed under conditions of chronic rather than acute tension. Given the wide variety of sensory receptors that contribute to "muscle sense" (Burgess et al., 1982; Matthews, 1982), it remains difficult to assess the net effect that muscle tension would exert on these interacting mechanisms.

Central.   Numerous neurophysiologic investigations (cf. Schmidt, 1973, and Towe, 1973) have demonstrated that the brain is capable of influencing transmission of sensory impulses as they enter the spinal cord (Fetz, 1968), are relayed through sensory nuclei at the top of the cord (Gordon & Jukes, 1964; Towe & Jabbur, 1961), or pass through higher relay centers at the trigeminal nucleus (Darian–Smith & Yokota, 1966). Although many of these effects are exerted by activity in the pyramidal system, which also provides some "fine tuning" of motor control, other pathways from the brain can mediate this effect, indicating the potential for sensory inhibition quite apart from increases in muscle tension. This suggests that interventions directed at releasing muscular tension may be incapable of substantially altering a sensory inhibition maintained at more central levels of the nervous system. One of these systems, the reticular formation, is of particular interest in that it comprises a group of neurons within the brain stem that, with the posterior hypothalamus, control the overall level of activation of the ANS. Whatmore and Kohli (1974, p. 40) and Gellhorn (1964) have reviewed evidence indicating that both descending activity in motor control systems as well as proprioceptive activity returning from muscle receptors increase the activity of the posterior hypothalamus and reticular activating system, thereby increasing the overall level of arousal.[4] Hagbarth and Kerr (1954) have demonstrated inhibition of spinal sensory pathways following stimulation of the reticular formation, suggesting impairment of sensory function with high arousal. (Although Duffy, 1977, has reveiwed evidence indicating that in some cases, and up to a certain point, moderate increases in arousal can improve sensory acuity.)

Mechanisms Affecting Perceptual Function

Besides the issue of sensory acuity, level of arousal exerts an important influence on perceptual functioning, and it is from a behavioral analysis of these effects that training methods potentially capable of enhancing this first stage of the empathic process may be identified. Bahrick, Fitts, and Rankin (1952) observed that offering subjects a monetary reward for each correct detection of a change in any of an expansive array of lights and meters actually lowered their ability to detect changes occurring at the periphery of the display, which were easily detected by subjects in nonrewarded conditions. Thus, "tunneling" of the perceptual field is experimentally induced by increases in arousal. Support for the interpretation that Bahrick et al. actually manipulated levels of arousal is lent by Callaway and coworkers (Callaway & Dembro, 1958; Callaway & Thompson, 1953). In a similar series of studies utilizing drugs such as adrenalin, amphetamine, and amyl nitrate, Callaway and Dembro reported that:

> every drug that caused narrowed attention could be classed as a "sympathomimetic." On closer inspection, we found they all evoke an "alert" EEG, presumably by stimulating the brainstem reticular formation, and they have this action in common with fear, strong excitement, and orgasm. (p. 85)

Easterbrook (1959) reviewed this literature and concluded that arousal limits the range of cue utilization per se, regardless of the specific nature of the stimulus: "In general, the range of cue utilization is the total number of environmental cues in any situation that an organism observes, maintains an orientation towards, responds to, or associates with a response" (p. 183).

This concept of cue utilization is of particular value in an examination of the perceptual phase of empathy. The array of nonverbal cues that indicate another's affective state may be thought of as similar to the stimulus array of lights and dials employed by Bahrick et al. We should expect that anxious, tense, or otherwise aroused observers are therefore restricted in the range of such cues they are able to utilize as input data upon which to build a reverberatory response. It follows that any method capable of fostering a relaxed state of low

---

[4]This is why persons suffering from an overdose of central nervous system depressants should be made to get up and move around.

arousal may be conceived of as enhancing the perceptual phase of empathy. Such a speculation awaits empirical verification.

The effects of arousal may be extended to include the affective reverberatory as well as the cognitive analysis phases of empathy by appealing to Hull's (1943) "behavioral law" that the probability of occurrence of an overlearned or dominant response is raised by increases in drive. Whereas drive and arousal refer to different concepts, Easterbrook has noted several similarities in their effects on patterns of cue utilization and response. The import of this observation for affective reverberation lies in the extent to which an individual's motor responses are overlearned or strongly based in habit. In the course of motor mimicry, failures to accurately duplicate the nuances of another's expressive behavior will arise when aspects of this behavior are closely related to an overlearned motor response within the observer. An example of this, the association of motor reactions to laughter and hostility, was considered earlier in connection with Hefferline and Perera's findings. The example may be extended by imagining an observer whose previous expressions of anger were harshly punished. The attempt to reproduce the motoric expressions of anger exhibited by another will also lead to activation of motor responses within the observer that have typified her reactions to punishment, for example hunching the shoulders. Thus, anger expressions will produce a coactivation of overlearned fear responses. Hull's law suggests that such coactivations will be more likely to occur in aroused observers.

Additionally, if we consider habitual or stereotyped cognitive judgments as overlearned responses, we should expect that an aroused observer will be more likely to invoke such judgments than the observer who is relaxed and at ease. Further, such judgments will be erroneous to the extent that they occur in response to cues for which they are not entirely appropriate or accurate. As Easterbrook has noted: "The obverse of (Hull's) principle is that the probability of reaction to the cues for other responses is simultaneously reduced" (p. 196). Or, as stated by Hebb (1955): "The greater bombardment may interfere with the delicate adjustments involved in cue function, perhaps by facilitating irrelevant responses" (p. 250). Thus, it is suggested here that arousal impairs the ability to "hold cognition in abeyance" in the interests of accurately identifying relevant cues and shaping a response uniquely appropriate to them. Relaxation accordingly inhibits the tendency to respond with reflexive, ill-considered, and preconceived judgments, as anyone who has tried to reason with a "hot-head" can attest. This analysis is directly applicable to Smith's (1973) observation that sensory impressions give way to more perceptually adulterated expressive impressions in tense interpersonal situations, a topic considered in detail in Chapter 8. Recent examinations of the effect of emotion and arousal on observer's memory and perceptions of affectively toned material may be found in Bower (1981), Laird, Wagener, Halal, & Szegda (1982), and Clark, Milberg, & Erber (1984).

The points to be drawn from this brief foray are that substantial ability exists to inhibit sensory function apart from muscle tension. However, muscle tension can increase central levels of arousal that, if great enough, may inhibit sensory function. Further, arousal delimits the perceptual field and decreases ability to draw upon and creatively integrate a wide range of cues.

TRAINING METHODS

With the exception of meditation and biofeedback, none of the training methods described in this section have, to this author's knowledge, been subjected to experimental investigation relative to their ability to enhance empathic function or sensitivity to nonverbal communication. Indeed, many of these methods were not originally designed with these outcomes in mind. For the time being, assessment of their potential effectiveness must rest on the extent to which they impact the processes involved in the model of perception and affective reverberation described previously. By the same token, experimental tests of the ability of such methods to influence these phases of empathic functioning would provide an important evaluation of the model itself.

Consistent with the preceding attempt to describe different levels at which sensory inhibition could be effected, the training methods that follow have been divided according to whether their effects are directed primarily to peripheral levels, a combination of peripheral and central levels, or central levels alone. This distinction can only be approximate, because it is inevitable that peripheral changes affect central functioning, and because even such internally directed methods as meditation can involve substantial changes in muscular functioning, even through the maintenance of an erect, relaxed sitting posture. Although our concern with these methods is primarily directed to their potential to enhance affective reverberation, we may expect them to exert effects on the perceptual phase in those cases in which either the ability to recognize and reproduce more differentiated, subtle patterns of motor activity is enhanced, or where the method is capable of lowering arousal through relaxation as described previously.

This chapter has consistently emphasized a somewhat one-sided model of affective reverberation based on the role of motor mimicry and somatic sensation. Whereas the training methods described here reflect this emphasis, it should be noted that various psychotherapies and group sensitivity training methods also have potential for enhancing both perception and reverberation. The attention to affective experience evident in these methods may improve awareness of affective displays in others and often involves exposure by the individual to previously unacknowledged emotional experiences. All psychological conflicts and defenses involve some alteration of affective awareness, and it is reasonable to expect that cognitively based procedures designed to alter these defenses and provide supportive conditions for emotional experience should enhance ability to accurately perceive and reverberate to affect.

However, as should be evident by now, such cognitively oriented methods address only half the equation. To the extent that body experience is the "sounding board" for affective perception, therapeutic attention must also be directed to limitations of this perception that are *maintained at the level of the body*. Such limitations include chronically contracted muscles, the persistence of old, stereotyped movement patterns, and possibly, simple sensory neglect. Conversely, body-oriented therapies should, wherever possible, avail themselves of discussion and insightful understanding of the life situations and psychological issues of the individual. As noted, the training methods described here reflect this chapter's emphasis on somatic sensory function, and they should be considered with the preceding provisos in mind. These methods represent a small selection from a large array of promising procedures, many of which may be found in the *consumers guide* to mind and body therapies provided by Feiss (1979).

ENHANCING PERCEPTION AND AFFECTIVE
REVERBERATION AT PERIPHERAL LEVELS

Structural Integration (Rolfing)

Structural Integration, popularly known as Rolfing, after it's originator Ida Rolf (1977), is based on the observation described earlier of structural changes occurring in the connective tissue of the body. These tissues include ligaments attaching bones, tendons connecting bone to muscle, and fascial tissue that surrounds and connects muscle fibers. These changes occur following physical trauma or sustained periods of muscle tension and effectively encase the muscles in an inelastic "envelope" of fascial tissue, distorting the bodies efficient alignment with respect to gravity, and forcing compensatory (and chronic) similar tensions to occur throughout the body.

Proceeding through a typical series of ten 1-hour sessions, the practitioner (Rolfer) systematically loosens thickened fascial tissues and separates points of adhesion between the fascia or tendons. This is accomplished by applying strong pressure to the fascia and muscles along the planes of movement for which they were structurally designed to function. Although superficially resembling massage, the goals and methods of Rolfing are more ambitious: A Rolfer will typically employ fingers, knuckles, and even elbows in an effort to effect structural change in the tissues. The first seven sessions are directed at specific body areas and proceed from releasing the rigidity of superficial or extrinsic fascial and muscle layers to working on deeper or more intrinsic tissues. Consistent with the fundamental insight of Rolfing, that changes in one body area produce compensations in others, the last three sessions are devoted to integrating the changes im major body segments produced earlier. The goal of these sessions is the efficient vertical alignment of the major body segments with gravity, as well as achieving lateral symmetry of the head, shoulders, and pelvis. In some cases, this often painful process has been described as inducing recovery of traumatic early memories and "deep emotional discharge" (Johnson, 1977; Keen, 1970). The influence of this method on the musculoskeletal system is demonstrated by clear alterations of posture in the direction of more efficient and effortless alignment with gravitational forces (Rolf, 1977).

The analysis presented earlier of the effects of muscular tension and restricted mobility on sensory acuity and the potential range of affective experience suggests that Structural Integration may have substantial potential for enhancing affective reverberation. Noting that "highly stressed individuals, such as novice parachutists, schizophrenics, depressives, do not change their levels of physiological responsiveness to correspond to changing stimulation in the same way as less stressed subjects [e.g., Buchsbaum & Silverman 1968; Epstein, 1967; Fenz & Velner, 1970]," Silverman et al. (1973, p. 202) reviewed several lines of evidence suggesting a relation among anxiety, muscular tension, and inability to modulate sensory stimulation. Silverman, Rappaport, Hopkins, Ellman, Hubbard & Kling recorded cortical-evoked potentials in response to light flashes of varying intensity in 15 male subjects before and after 10 sessions of Structural Integration extending over a 5-week period. Results showed increased response amplitudes in all subjects at all light intensities, which the authors related to an increased openness or receptivity to environmental stimulation. There was also a decrease in the variability of responses to repeated stimulations, which Silverman et al. interpreted as indicating greater efficiency in sensory processing. Interestingly, these subjects also exhibited a significant trend toward reduced amplitudes in response to progressively higher light intensities. Silverman et al. had cited research describing this feature as being typical of "hypersensitive normal and psychiatric subjects . . . . (and) nonparanoid schizophrenic and retarded depressive patients" (pp. 205–206).

Although this latter finding might pose something of an embarrassment, Silverman et al. noted that the first two features (greater overall amplitude and decreased variablity) were not typical of these patient groups, and that this overall profile indicated "both a sensitivity to stimulation and a capacity to efficiently modulate strong stimulation" (p. 216). This highly suggestive study deserves replication and, in conjunction with more applied measures of affective sensitivity or empathic functioning, would be an important evaluation of aspects of the model of affective reverberation developed here.

Reichian Therapy and Bioenergetics

Although they are different procedures, with separate programs for training therapists, Reichian Therapy and Bioenergetics have several affinities and common practices. Their common proposition that chronically tense muscles represent specific conflictual inhibitions and suppressions of feelings have been described in detail earlier. Reichian therapists distinguish seven body segments perpendicular to the body's long axis in which armoring occurs; ocular, oral, cervical, thoracic, diaphragmatic, abdominal, and pelvic. Over the course of numerous sessions, therapeutic attention is roughly focused on a sequential progression from ocular to pelvic segments, with the intent of releasing armor and restoring the full range of feeling and expressive movement. Both Reichian therapy and Bioenergetics employ deep breathing, vocalization, and expressive movements (making faces, kicking, hitting, and biting) to induce catharsis (emotional release), which frequently cooccurs with release of chronically tense muscle groups.

It is important to realize that these procedures are intermediary steps in the therapeutic process, and not end points. Nor are they intended as mechanical cookbooks for inducing emotional health. The choice of where and when to employ a particular physical intervention is determined as much by the current affective state and verbalizations of the patient as on the programmatic identification of armored muscles and adherence to procedure. These methods are linear descendents of psychoanalysis and retain strong neo-Freudian affinities. The body work is typically employed in conjunction with insight-oriented or gestalt psychotherapy, and much empahsis is placed on the containment and insightful understanding of feelings rather than their unconnected catharsis. Deep breathing in these methods reliably produces strong tingling or electric sensations that have diagnostic value in locating areas of sensory inhibition, as patients discover areas in which they cannot feel the sensations. Extensive attention is given to the role of respiration in affecting energy level and sensation.

Bioenergetics, developed by Alexander Lowen after several years as a student of Reich's, has extended the focus of these procedures to include the legs and devotes considerable attention to "grounding," developing a sense of connectedness with the ground and an ability to let sensations flow connectedly from the feet to the head. Lowen has also developed individual exercises designed to place unusual stress on specific muscles, inducing them to enter a period of tremor and release of tension (cf. Lowen & Lowen, 1977). Recent descriptions and applications may be found in Lowen (1975), Baker (1967), Keleman (1974), Konia (1975), and Rosenberg (1973).

METHODS COMBINING SOMATIC CHANGE AND CULTIVATED AWARENESS

The Alexander Technique

The Alexander Technique was developed in the late 1800s by F. Matthias Alexander (1969) on the basis of his attempts to correct a recurring loss of voice that threatened his avocation as a recitationist. Alexander observed that, over a lifetime, people developed habitual ways of performing even the simplest movements that were often inefficient and led to fatigue and poor posture. Noting a widespread tendency to tense unrelated muscles in preparation for a movement, Alexander found that such preparatory ''sets'' were entirely unconscious and had the effect of pulling the various body segments, particularly the head, neck, and shoulders out of alignment with each other. In the Alexander technique, starting with the relation of the head and neck to each other and the force of gravity, the entire body is eventually realigned through a series of gentle manipulations of the musculature to reflect equally distributed load requirements of upright posture across muscle groups. Subsequent sessions engage the student in refining and maintaining this alignment while learning to move in ways that sustain improvement. This involves conscious perception and inhibition of previously learned postural habits accompanying movements such as sitting, standing, and walking. Alexander viewed the development of the student's awareness of kinesthetic activity involved in such movements as an essential component of this process.

The emphasis on directing attention to previously unconsious internal sensory states and the development of precise, efficient movement again suggests that this method may enhance affective reverberatory capability. Although no research of this effect has been attempted, consistent clinical reports suggest that this may be the case (Tinbergen, 1974).

Feldenkrais Training

Developed by Moshe Feldenkrais (1970, 1972, 1981) and influenced by the Alexander Technique, Feldenkrais Training involves a series of directed moving -and sensing exercises designed to release chronic tension, teach the efficient, discrete use of muscles, and develop new movement patterns. Very small movements are performed with a minimum of effort and an emphasis on awareness of the sensory changes accompanying each activity. Instructions to ''relax'' the muscles are notably missing from the Feldenkrais procedures; emphasis is placed instead on establishing clear sensory awareness of a body area. Significantly, students of the method regularly report experiencing a marked decrease in tension after a period of establishing this sensory contact, suggesting that the degree of awareness may itself be an internal ''biofeedback'' signal that increases as tension decreases.

Many mental imagery exercises are used in this training method to cultivate awareness of dimly perceived body parts as well as the connections between them. For example, a student may imagine a steel ball slowly rolling from a clearly perceived area, paying close attention to the temperature and weight of the ball, and noting how it displaces the skin as it passes over it. Such exercises represent training in internal awareness and should facilitate perception of sensory changes.

Dance Therapy

A diverse and burgeoning field, dance therapy has spawned a professional organization, a journal, and seven officially recognized certification programs. Whereas embracing numerous applied practices and theoretical orientations, the central tenets of dance therapy involve a belief in the therapeutic value of expressive body movement carried out in a supportive group or individual context (Alperson, 1974; Bernstein, 1975; Canner, 1968; Davis, 1973; Dryansky, 1974; Pesso, 1969). Such activities are designed to facilitate the range and style of expressive movement, provide material for discussion, enliven and integrate emotional expression, and provide a nonverbal basis for sharing with others. The expressive movements employed in dance therapy are typically larger and more vigorous than those employed in the Alexander and Feldenkrais methods, and more attention and discussion is given to their emotional meaning and role in the psychological life of the individual. However, little of the direct intervention seen in Bioenergetics or Reichian therapy is employed. Again, it remains to be demonstrated whether such practice in the affective meaning of movement can significantly impact affective reverberation.

Phenomenological studies of improvisational dance (Levi, 1975) have provided unique descriptions of altered states of consciousness accompanying improvisational duets that speak strongly to the establishment of a sense of shared experience that moves and changes with an immediacy reminiscent of the microsynchrony described by Condon and Ogston (1966).

Biofeedback

Biofeedback, the electronic amplification and display of selected physiological activity, would be expected to enhance affective reverberation by (1) facilitating relaxation or lower levels of arousal as described previously, and (2) enhancing sensory awareness.[5] While few investigations have been made of the influence of this procedure on affective sensitivity per se, several studies have failed to demonstrate any effect on this or other components of the empathic process.

Investigating a counseling student population, Walters (1977/1978) found no effect of 12 hand temperature biofeedback training sessions over 4 weeks on Kagan's (1972) Affective Sensitivity Scale or the Recognition Assessment-Empathy Inventory. Pre and posttest change scores were insignificant, as were differences between groups receiving biofeedback, verbal instructions for hand warming, and a no-treatment control. No significant training effect on hand

---

[5]This last proposition remains controversial (cf. Brener, Ross, Baker, & Clemens, 1979, and Lacroix, 1981). Whereas the results of Stilson et al. (1980) suggest such an effect for muscle tension feedback, the case is especially implausible for organ systems that do not have afferent innervation, such as the brain (alpha wave feedback) and sweat glands (electrodermal activity). Although biofeedback may calibrate awareness of cognitive or efferent activity that typically increases or decreases the feedback stimulus, this is *not* the same as enhancing sensory awareness.

temperature was observed, indicating that the feedback procedure was not effective in changing sympathetic innervation of the peripheral vasculature.

In a decidely creative application, Aylward (1981) gave 4 half-hour sessions of alpha brain wave feedback to 3 professional counselors and 18 respondents to advertisements for a study on biofeedback and counseling. Following this, the clients were divided into 3 treatment groups, and each of the 3 counselors was assigned 2 of the clients from each group, for a total of 6 clients per counselor. In the alpha-only condition the counselors and clients underwent individual alpha biofeedback immediately prior to their first counseling session. In the conjoint-alpha condition the procedure was similar, except that the feedback stimulus was delivered only when the counselor and client simultaneously exhibited alpha frequencies and phase synchrony in their EEG activity. The third group received no biofeedback immediately prior to the first session. Results indicated no effect of treatment conditons on the Empathy scale of the Barret–Leonard Relationship Inventory completed by both participants after the session, or on the Truax Empathy Scale completed by two independent raters scoring tapes of the session.

Ober (1980) compared three groups of eight counseling students receiving (1) 25 minutes of frontalis EMG feedback and three 25-minute sessions of taped Autogenic Training relaxation instructions (Schultz & Luthe, 1959) per week for 4 weeks; (2) 85 minutes of taped counseling information and 15 minutes per week of discussion with the experimenter as an attention placebo; and (3) no treatment. The biofeedback group showed a trend ($p < .063$) toward higher scores relative to the no-treatment group on Carkhuff's Empathic Understanding Scale scored from taped interviews with coached clients. The difference between the treatment and placebo groups was nonsignificant, and the statistical reliability of differences between the placebo and no-treatment groups was not reported. All tests were made following treatment and cannot assess the possibility of pretreatment group differences.

Although not employing biofeedback, Weits (1980) compared a group of counseling students receiving 3 weeks of progressive muscle relaxation training (Jacobsen, 1938) ($N = 13$), with counseling students receiving no training ($N = 16$). Although the PMR group showed significant reductions in EMG tension levels and trait anxiety on the State Trait Anxiety Inventory (Spielberger, Gorsuch & Lushene, 1970) relative to pretraining levels, no training effect was observed on trait anxiety or scores on Kagan's Affective Sensitivity Scale. No significant differences were observed between the groups on any of these measures.

The consistent failure of these studies may be due to several factors. Although the possibility that biofeedback simply does not improve affective reverberation must be considered, it is also conceivable that improvements in reverberatory ability would not be reflected in the subject's verbal statements from which empathy ratings were obtained. This possibility points to the desirability of assessment and training methods directed at all phases of the empathic process, a viewpoint operationalized in considerable detail in Chapter 8.

It is noteworthy that the direct assessment of biofeedback's effect on affective sensitivity provided by Walters also failed to demonstrate significant changes in hand temperature, the feedback variable used in this study. In this case, the biofeedback did not "work." It remains to be seen whether biofeedback applications that did successfully alter their intended physiological activity would also show effects on affective reverberation when more direct measures of this phase are employed. It should also be noted that the effect ascribed to biofeedback earlier of enhancing sensory awareness of internal activity remains a matter of some dispute. It is quite possible that biofeedback generally does not have this effect.

METHODS PRIMARILY INVOLVING CULTIVATED AWARENESS

Meditation

Although several aspects of meditation are relevant to enhancing affective reverberation, Maupin (1972) has probably summarized its most salient feature:

> In general many of the traditions of prayer and meditation within Christianity have consisted of a kind of blabbing at God or some apart-from-nature being about which one has all sorts of preconcevied ideas. The present Western interest in meditation tends to be directed toward Eastern forms of practice, where there is a radical commitment to experiencing what one experiences-even God. Oriental rejection of verbal and conceptual substitutes for experience seems to appeal to our own growing investment in living experience. (p. 182)

This commitment to experiencing one's experience in the absence of verbal or conceptual mediators has clear relevance to affective reverberation as described in this book.

Whereas many different methods and teachings exist (see Maupin, 1972, and Goleman, 1977 for introductions), a practical consideration of meditation as a training method is facilitated by the emphasis on concentration or attentiveness evident in all practices. This is particularly true for the beginning stages of meditation, after which various schools become more divergent. Because most people do not reach the advanced stages of meditation (Goleman, 1977; Lesh, 1970; Maupin, 1965), these variations are not considered here.

Many meditation practices begin by concentrating on a single object, sense perception, or thought, whereas others involve *samatha,* or mindfulness. Mindfulness entails maintaining a direct perception of the flow of sensations or thoughts as they occur in each moment, without becoming caught up in reacting to them, and is sometimes begun after proficiency in concentration is achieved. Chaudhuri (1965) states: "Watch your ideas, feelings and wishes fly across the mental firmament like a flock of birds. Let them fly freely. Just keep a watch. Don't allow the birds to carry you off into the clouds" (p. 31).

A different method, *vipasyana,* or awareness, entails something of a combination of concentration and mindfulness, in that awareness is passively concentrated on the process of mindfulness itself. According to Trungpa (1976), awareness is "the willingness not to cling to the discoveries of mindfulness, and mindfulness is just precision" (p. 50). Eventually one comes to the point of "watching the watcher," and ultimately, to realize that no separate watcher exists, there is only watching. These practices exert three effects of interest for affective reverberation; *sensory awareness, confrontation of self,* and *relaxation.*

Concentrative meditation is often focused on a particular sense, and mindfulness entails establishing a clear, unitary perception of the flow of sensation throughout the body, whereas vipasyana cultivates awareness of the processes of mindfulness itself. Sensory awareness accordingly plays a prominent role in mediation, and this influence may be traced in part to the writings of the Abhidharmakosa, an extensive and detailed account of Buddhist philosophy and practice composed around 200 B.C. by Vasubandhu. This work and its relation to the role of sensory awareness in the Buddhist meditative tradition has been examined in detail by Simmer (1977), from whom much of the present analysis is drawn. Although large portions of the Abhidharma literature consist of technical philosophic discussions, other portions were intended as a pragmatic psychology that provided guideposts and descriptions for experiences encountered in meditation (Guenther, 1974). This work also included analyses of sensory experience in many ways as sophisticated as those arising from Western phenomenological schools. In so doing, it sought to provide a framework in which sensation was not something experienced by a separate self perceiving an external physical reality, but a nondualized immersion in the fabric of experience itself (Guenther, 1974; Simmer, 1977). This description captured the holistic quality experienced in meditation, and, whereas central to Buddhist conceptions of enlightment (cf. Hirakawa, 1973, p. xxxiii), its difficult philosophic implications need not concern us here. Watts (1961) has provided a readable introduction to the nondual perspective.

As previous sections have attempted to outline, this primary and nonreflective encounter with the senses perforce entails a confrontation with the self, at least that fictionalized, separate self maintained through denial or dissociation of unwanted aspects of experience. The suggestion that, buried within the full range of internal sensory experience are unpleasant or terrifying realms of existence, avoidance of which creates a sensory constriction that impairs our ability to function within that full range, was central to Reich's work and has great implications for the explorer who would go traveling in these realms. Meditation represents just such an exploration.[6]

---

[6]It should be noted that at more advanced stages of meditation awareness of body sensations largely ceases to exist (Goleman, 1977, p. 14; Maupin, 1965, p. 141), although potential remains for confrontation of self.

Consider the responses of Hefferline's subjects who, upon encountering missing areas of internal awareness, suddenly remembered that they had more important things to do. Those more conflicted individuals who could be persuaded to continue were apt to describe the process as "fatuous" or "immoral," and Hefferline as a "concentration camp doctor" given to reckless experimentation with dangerous procedures (Hefferline & Bruno 1971, p. 168). While the not infrequent vituperativeness of undergraduates toward assignments precludes a strict conclusion, it is noteworthy that Hefferline received such invective in response to so (superficially) innocuous a procedure.

In the course of dealing with sensory distractions while attempting to focus elsewhere in concentrative meditation, or in attempting to stay with the flow of sensation in mindfulness practice without getting caught up in reacting to the emerging material, the meditator must come to nondefensive terms with unpleasant aspects of self. Similar to Hefferline's subjects, beginning meditators often experience an overwhelming desire to quit and go do something else (Goleman, 1977). The relevance to affective reverberation is clear: If a person confronts us with psychically loaded material we cannot get up and run away from it but instead invoke various cognitions and affect-laden judgments whose primary purpose is conflict management (Fingarette, 1965, pp. 115–145). If, on the other hand, we have through meditation learned to deal calmly and equably with such material, we are more capable of reverberation and realistic understanding, rather than preempting our experience with defensive operations.

Meditation has been described in terms of Kris' (1952) concept of "regression in the service of the ego," which, according to Maupin (1962), "implies suspension of some ego functions such as defensive or logical functions and sometimes emphasis on genetically primitive mechanisms" (p. 370). Lesh (1970, p. 47) has noted that, far from being a psychotic decompensation, this process entails an opening to inner experience while maintaining the ability to consciously and adequately integrate the experience.

Support for the applicability of this concept to meditation has been provided by Maupin (1965), who observed a significant (tau = .49, $p < .001$) correlation between the level of successful response to a 2-week course of zazen meditation and capacity for adaptive regression as scored from Rorschach responses (Holt & Havel, 1960). The meditation investigated by Maupin is a beginners form of zazen, a sitting meditation practiced by the Soto Zen sect of Buddhism (Wienpahl, 1964). The emphasis in this beginner's form is to maintain awareness of the breath, counting each breath from one to 10 and then starting over. As concentration improved, subjects were instructed to imagine the count of each breath descending into the stomach. Instead of trying to force distracting thoughts out, they were merely to be noted and attention gently returned to the breath.

Using this procedure, Lesh (1970) investigated the effects of a half hour of zazen every weekday for 4 weeks on the affective sensitivity of students in a graduate counseling program ($N = 16$). Lesh compared pre and posttraining scores on the Affective Sensitivity Scale (ASS) (Kagan, 1972), a videotape of actual counseling segments from which the subject must detect and describe the feelings experienced by the client. Control groups were counseling students who wanted nothing to do with the meditation ($N = 11$), and a second group who volunteered to meditate but were assigned to listen to music for the same period, after being provided a contrived explanation of the benefits of this procedure ($N = 12$).

The meditators exhibited significant improvements on the ASS ($t = 7.23$, $p <$ .001), whereas the music controls increased only minimally ($t = 0.29$, n.s.), and the no-treatment control exhibited a nonsignificant decrease. The practice of zazen for a relatively short time yielded clear improvements in the ability to accurately detect and describe the affective state of others. Consistent with Maupin's observations, Lesh reported a significant positive correlation (tau = .56, $p < .01$) between the degree of success achieved during meditation and capacity for adaptive regression as measured by Fitzgerald's (1966) Experience Inquiry. Instructions for beginning zazen meditation may be found in Wienpahl (1964) and Kapleau (1967).

Sensory Awareness

Sensory Awareness was brought to the United States and developed by Charlotte Selver (1957, also see Brooks, 1974 and Gunther, 1968), on the basis of her separate contacts with Else Gindler and Heinreich Jacoby (1925) in Germany. Although Sensory Awareness involves small changes in postural activity, its primary focus involves the cultivation of a passive, open, noncritical attitude to body experience. In this regard it shares a strong affinity with zazen meditation (Simmer, 1977; Watts, 1974). Initial exposure to this work may also produce responses that it is trite or shallow. Simmer (1977) states:

> In a three hour session the group might be led to examine their standing relationship to the floor. Explorations might include rotating slightly on the ankles to discover what balance is, what relationship ankles have to standing, or what rotation of the ankle does to standing. The inner attitude encouraged is that of responsiveness, to discover what standing might entail. (p. 38)

The indication here is that with sustained patience and practice the processing of sensory experience becomes subtly yet substantially altered. Roche (1974) asserts:

> Sometimes in class a gong or bell is struck, and we allow this to sound, and resound, within us. So, too, can the words we say, or those said by another—sound and resound through our entire being: the sound of the words themselves, the sound of the words as spoken out by the speaker, and the echoing sound of associations which we hear with another ear. (p. 8)

Selvers' students have included Erich Fromm, Clara Thompson, and Fritz Perls, and some of her methods have been employed by clinical behavior therapists as a relaxation procedure (Goldfried & Davison, 1976, p. 102).

Focusing

Focusing was originated by Eugene Gendlin (1981, 1984), who developed the process on the basis of his research on the abilities that individuals who experienced successful outcomes in psychotherapy seemed to display during their sessions. This method is somewhat arbitrarily divided into six separate stages (through which one may pass within a single session). Initially, the student is involved in "clearing a space"; simply staying as quiet and detached as possible and making a mental list of discomforts or life problems until he or she can step back and say "except for these I feel fine." A particular problem or feeling is then selected, and the student attempts to cultivate a "felt sense" of the problem. Gendlin (1981) suggests:

> Stand back from (the problem) and sense how it makes you feel in your body when you think of it as a whole just for a moment. Ask, What does this whole problem feel like? But don't answer in words. Feel the problem *whole*, the sense of *all that* . . . . Let your sensing go inwardly down past all the details that can distract and sidetrack you, past all the squawking and jabbering, *until you feel the single great aura that encloses all of it*. (pp. 53–54; emphasis in original)

Following clear achievement of the felt sense, the student generates a word, phrase, or image that captures the complete meaning of the felt sense. There follows a resonating stage, which in its description by Gendlin is almost a blueprint for the transition between the affective reverberation and cognitive analysis stages of empathy outlined in this book. This stage proceeds with the student moving back and forth in his or her awareness between the label/image and the felt sense, attempting to determine if the cognitive label completely matches and describes the felt sense. Often, several labels may be generated and discarded before one that truly "resonates" with the felt sense is found. Subsequent stages entail maintaining a passively questioning attitude toward the experiences coming from the previous stages, as if asking them what about them makes them feel that way, and then *waiting for*, rather than supplying, an answer. Gendlin (1981) says: "There is a distinct difference between forcing words or images *into* a feeling and letting them flow *out* of it" (p. 59, original emphasis). Particularly in the later stages of Focusing, there often occurs a distinctive physical experience of movement, well-being, and insight; the "felt shift."

Electroencephalographic (EEG) recordings made during this process (Don, 1977) have demonstrated distinctive patterns of brain electrical activity during the felt shift, with increased amplitude of alpha and theta frequencies. These findings are consistent with EEG changes recorded during meditation (Hirai, 1974).

A MULTILEVEL APPROACH TO PERCEPTUAL AND AFFECTIVE TRAINING

The Work of Rudolf Laban and Irmgard Bartenieff

The Laban/Bartenieff Institute of Movement Studies (LIMS) maintains two certification training programs in movement analysis. These programs involve a 9-month intensive exposure to the theory and application of Laban's and Bartenieff's work. Laban devised extensive systems for the description of body movement. Of these, perhaps the most relevant for an analysis of affective reverberation is his concept of "effort" (Dell, 1977; Laban & Lawrence, 1947), which involves a description not of *what* happens in a movement, but the *how* of the movement, the quality with which it is executed.[7]

The four "efforts" that may occur singly or in combination are Flow, Weight, Time, and Space. Flow may be either "free" or "bound" and describes the "ongoingness" of movement, or how easily it may be stopped. Weight may be either light (1) or strong(st), and a subeffort distinguishes between active and passive weight. Time is either quick(q) or sustained(s). Space describes the focus or intent of the individual with regard to the surrounding area and is either direct(d) or indirect(i), which is reflected in the nature of their movements. If a movement simultaneously shows clear components of two of the efforts combined, it is called a "state," and three efforts combined is a "drive." For example, a movement with well-developed components of weight, space, and time is termed action drive.

Because each effort can express itself in two ways, each drive can contain eight different combinations of the three efforts. Returning to the example of action drive and running through the permutations, you produce or describe the actions float(l,i,s), wring(st,i,s), press(st,d,s), glide(l,d,s), dab(l,d,q), flick(l,i,q), slash(st,i,q), and punch(st,d,q). In any practical sense, these distinctions can only be appreciated by actual movement on the part of the student (or reader), for whom these exercises quickly become engrossing. Similarly, a systematic exploration of the three other drives reveals 24 additional combinations of efforts, not counting applications with strong components of all four efforts, or two, or one.

---

[7]Drawing on and extending Laban's work, Kestenberg (1965a,b, 1967, 1977) has identified precursors of these movement features in neonates and children and traced their developmental relation to trust and empathy. Interrater reliabilities for trained observers coding these patterns are acceptable (Sossin, 1983), and Sossin has demonstrated their relationship to the development of aggression in the first year.

The student is led through a series of exercises that promote the ability to recognize, describe, and emit these movement features. This systematic exploration of effort quickly reveals that certain emotional states are characterized by particular effort combinations, and, moreover, that individuals consistently exhibit preferred constellations of efforts. Notably, beginning students often show consistent individual preferences for detecting particular effort combinations in the movements of others, a possibly related perceptual bias (P. Schick, personal communication, Feb. 11, 1984). Deliberate attempts to produce movements using efforts outside their habitual effort "signature" is an attention and time-consuming procedure through which the student gains recognition of affective variations and nuances in themselves and others of which they may previously have been unaware.

The LIMS certification program also involves didactic work in which students are trained in the application of the elaborate description and notation systems devised by Laban to score these and other movement features. As such, this component represents training of both the perceptual and cognitive analysis phases. Students develop ability to visually differentiate subtle movement and effort features and also become proficient in the application of a sophisticated conceptual system for interpreting their meaning.

Recent investigations of interrater reliabilities for the coding of effort qualities have yielded encouraging results (Diggins, 1982; DuNann, 1983), and experimental investigations of training outcome on nonverbal sensitivity and empathic functioning are an important next step.

An additional component of the LIMS certification program is work in Bartenieff Fundamentals (Bartenieff & Davis, 1965/1972; Bartenieff & Lewis, 1980; Hackney, in press). Proceeding from an anlysis of the structure and function of the somatoskeletal system, Bartenieff developed an approach to movement training that attempted to integrate these anatomically derived principles with the expressive aspects of movement. Initially, slow, deliberate movements may be performed in ways designed to employ the muscles and limbs in rotational motions most compatible with their anatomic structure. When combined with those aspects of Laban's work having to do with the analysis of space, the potential of this work for exploring the full range of body movement becomes as extensive as the approach to effort described previously. The full range of movement suggested by the spherical shape of the femur-pelvic or shoulder-arm joint produces intriguing combinations when integrated with a three-dimensional description of geometric space. For example, a student may engage in rotating the arm in a carving motion as it is extended in an up-back-right vector. The expressive nature or feeling tone accompanying such a movement might be noted, and the process repeated for an arc-like movement in a down-forward-left vector, and so on. Movements incorporating principles such as opening–closing and advancing–retreating are explored, and the student might then perform these using various of the different effort combinations described previously.

The Fundamentals work engages in such explorations with an eye to establishing awareness and integration of the sequencing and phrasing of movements; attention is directed to the subtle preparations one makes in initiating a movement, as well as the patterns of recuperation that follow it. Other movement combinations are based on the developmental sequences appearing in childhood, enhancing the opportunity for significantly relearning old movement habits. This work shares the emphasis of Feldenkrais and Sensory Awareness on cultivated awareness of body changes and employs specific techniques designed to teach the efficient, integrated use of muscle groups previously not used or employed in a gross, undifferentiated fashion. Throughout, emphasis is placed on the expressivity and feeling associated with such movements.

SUMMARY

The historical emphasis on motor mimicry, the adoption of the postural tensions and movements exhibited by another, suggests that affective reverberation may be trained by enhancing both the ability to accurately reproduce the nuances of such movements, as well as the acuity with which the sensory impressions produced by this activity is perceived by the observer.

Most experimental investigations of the motor mimicry process have demonstrated a correlation between the occurrence of shared postures and ratings of the degree of rapport present in the interaction. However, this finding has not been consistently replicated, and some investigators have reported that postural congruence may cooccur with signs of "alienation" and feelings of awkwardness. Although this relatively gross method of assessing motor mimicry has generally supported its relation to rapport (and by extension, empathy), the inconsistent findings indicate the not-suprising conclusion that other factors or components must be present for an interaction to be an empathic one.

The proposition that motor mimicry plays an active role in producing internal affects similar to those the other is experiencing requires acceptance of models of emotion proposed by Darwin and particularly by James. These authors stated that the subjective experience of emotion was caused by perception of physiological changes that themselves largely constituted the emotion. Whereas this model continues to be controversial, several lines of evidence support it, and its detractors have yet to provide convincing evidence to the contrary. Independent work by Fisher has demonstrated that the relative sensory prominence of various body landmarks plays an important role in the perceptual and defensive transactions of the personality with psychologically conflictual stimuli.

This work indicates that affective distortions and suppressions within an individual will be mirrored by similar distortions and suppressions of sensory signals arising in body areas previously associated with such affects. We must expect that such distortions will impair the ability to accurately reverberate with the affective experiences of another person. The work of Wilhelm Reich provided extensive clinical observations of this relation between body sites and affective perception and suggested that the presence of chronic muscle tension identified conflictually related body areas. Moreover, chronic tension was held to be responsible for impairing sensory perception of the tense area. Experimental investigations of Reich's hypotheses have moderately confirmed his observations, although the prediction that chronic tension impairs awareness of the activity of the muscle has so far eluded a methodologically valid test. Apart from the as yet inconclusive evidence that chronic tension impairs sensory perception, it does represent a reduction in the range and differentiation of expressive movement and, as such, constitutes an impedance to the ability to accurately reproduce a wide range of the affective displays likely to be encountered in other persons.

Although experimental investigations of methods that may enhance affective reverberation are exceedingly rare, numerous potentially effective methods can be identified. Such potentially effective training methods include those that release chronically tense muscles and facilitate the differentiated, precise use of muscle groups in ways not previously employed. An additional group of methods employ a variety of procedures designed to enhance sensory perception of kinaesthetic and proprioceptive activity; some methods take chronic tension as their starting point, while others cultivate an internal receptiveness to sensory activity. Studies of biofeedback have so far failed to show any effect of this procedure, while one investigation of Zen meditation indicated significant increases in affective sensitivity in subjects practicing this method.

ACKNOWLEDGMENTS

I am gratefully indepted to Judith Simmer–Brown for several helpful discussions of meditation, and to Pam Schick and Peggy Hackney, who provided invaluable insight into the Laban/Bartenieff movement perspective. Any errors of interpretation remain my own.

4 The Cognitive Analysis Component

We seek in this chapter to examine and put in proper perspective the stage of the emphatic process that immediately follows affective reverberation and that immediately precedes accurate communication, namely cognitive analysis. We briefly introduced this analytic stage in our definition-establishing introductory chapter, describing it as the "detachment (Reik, 1949) and decoding (Danish & Kagan, 1971) phase [in which] the worker seeks to distinguish among, sort out and label his or her own feelings and [especially] those he or she perceives as being experienced by the other person." (Macarov (1978), it is recalled, similarly described this postexperiencing, precommunication stage as "Being adept at reading nonverbal communication and interpreting the feelings underlying it." The observer has, as Keefe (1976) notes, (1) perceived the cues reflecting the actor's feeling state, (2) allowed and encouraged an as-if-they-were-my-own-feelings "trying on" of actor affect, and now, using this perceptual and reverbatory information, (3) seeks to cognitively comprehend, analyze, and label these actor emotions. This chapter seeks to describe how such cognitive analysis may most accurately be accomplished. As is made clear, the broad answer to "how" is primarily but not exclusively by means of judgment of facial expression. A wide array of other nonverbal cues to emotion—gestural, proxemic, postural, paralinguistic—all play a role in this affective decoding effort, but a role clearly subsidiary to that provided by facial expressiveness (Dittman, 1972; Izard, 1971; Rosenthal, Hall, DiMatteo, Rogers, & Archer, 1979; Zuckerman, DeFrank, Hall, Larrance, & Rosenthal, 1979).

AN HISTORICAL PERSPECTIVE

The study of facial expression as a means for deciphering an individual's emotions has a long history in psychology. Over 100 years ago, Duchene (1876) conducted a series of creative if rudimentary studies, utilizing electrical stimulation techniques, in seeking to trace the expressive functions of specific facial muscle groups. Several other early investigators also concerned themselves with various physiological antecedents and concomitants of facial expressiveness, including "nervous excitement" (Spencer, 1910), quantity of stimulation and susceptibility to innervation (Mosso, 1896), the mechanics of facial musculature (Dumas, 1904), and facial tensions (Moore, 1926).

In one of the first expressions of interest in facial "components," in which specific facial characteristics were held to be associated with specific emotional states, Bell (1886) prepared a series of facial muscle diagrams and by means of these proposed that, in all of what he termed the *exhilarating emotions,* the eyebrows, eyelids, nostrils, and angles of the mouth are raised, whereas in the *depressing passions* the reverse is true. Work such as Bell's clearly anticipates, if only in very beginning form, more recent and comprehensive presentations to be examined shortly of facial expressive cues purportedly denotative of a full array of primary affects (eg., Ekman & Friesen, 1975). Another important early contribution to this component's domain was made by Piderit (1886). As was true of the efforts of several of his contemporaries, he sought to describe facial muscle function during emotional activity. Elaborating considerably upon Bell's work, Piderit put forth a "geometry of expression" in which major facial features could be interchanged to produce a wide range of facial expressions. His methods and diagrams found considerable usage as the scientific work of others in this realm grew. Hughes (1900) built upon Piderit's work and was one of the first to make systematic use of photographs in doing so. Frappa (1902) was one of the first to attempt to synthetically construct facial expression variations, all of which derived from his conceptualization at the time of the three "fundamental" emotional expressions, joy, sadness, and astonishment. As the early 1900s unfolded, the technology of facial expression portrayal whose rudimentary beginnings we have just described flowered still further. As Frappa (1902) had done earlier, several investigators sought to portray their versions of the "basic" emotions or the "basic" expressions. Others, by means of some form of interchangeable parts mechanism, tried to make available apparatus for depicting the fullest possible array of human facial expressions—numbering, depending on one's viewpoint, as few as 12 (Moore, 1926) and as many as 3000 (Guilford, 1929). In these diverse portrayal attempts, both of basic emotions and a comprehensive array of expressions, use was made of physical models (Boring & Titchner, 1923; Guilford, 1929), photographs (Feleky, 1914; Frois–Wittmann, 1930; Kline & Kline, 1927; Ruckmick, 1926; Schultze, 1912), and a variety of types of drawings and diagrams (Moore, 1926; Rudolph, 1903; Wundt, 1911).

As the technology of facial expression portrayal progressed, a central, validating question was raised, reraised, and repeatedly examined in a long and extended series of investigations; namely, can facial expressions portrayed in these diverse ways be accurately judged, recognized, or categorized. It is a simple-appearing but in actuality quite complex question whose multifaceted nature has become increasingly obvious as its examination has continued over the past 80 years. It is, at its roots, a question of cognitive analysis and thus the key question of relevance to our understanding of this phase of the empathic process. We examine the conditions associated with accurate recognition of facial expression in the remainder of this chapter and by doing so hope to develop a full appreciation of the task, actor, observer, and related considerations that bear upon recognition accuracy in any affective judgment situation.

The first quasisystematic study of recognition of facial expression (Feleky, 1914) had to await much of the technological development described in the preceding sections. Feleky used as stimulus materials photographs (of herself) in an extended series of posed emotional expressions. One hundred (unspecified) judges were provided with a list of 110 ''names of emotions,'' a list generated by Feleky. Her results showed moderate trends toward interjudge agreement in terms of their categorization into emotional names and grouping of the posed photos. Langfeld (1918) showed 105 of the Rudolph pictures to six judges and requested that they indicate the emotion portrayed. Only a third of the judgments were correct. Allport (1924) and Kanner (1931) in parallel investigations reported judgment accuracy rates of about 50%. Other investigators in this period similarly found only moderate *overall* success for their judges in accuracy of recognition (Buzby, 1924; Jarden & Fernberger, 1926; Landis, 1929). Such average effects, however, mask almost as much information as they convey. Although mean accuracy of recognition in these studies was approximately 50%, considerable variability emerged across judges and across affects. Allport's (1924) judges, for example, varied from 21 to 72% accuracy, and Jenness' (1930) ranged from 20 to 89%. In terms of variability as a function of emotion being judged, Ruckmick (1921) reported much greater recognition success for love, hate, joy, and sorrow (his ''primary'' emotions) than for repulsiveness, surprise, distrust, and defiance (his ''secondary'' emotions). Landis (1929) reported similarly variable success across emotions judged, as did Langfeld (1918) who, based on his findings, arrayed emotions in the following order of ease of recognition, easiest to most difficult: joy, amazement, bodily pain, hate, fear, disgust, doubt, and anger. Such variability provided important clues for later investigators who sought to discern not so much overall accuracy effects but, instead, a fuller picture of judge, stimulus, and actor conditions that functioned to improve or diminish recognition accuracy.

Similar conclusions regarding both accuracy and the conditions seemingly responsible for its variability have also emerged from more recent research on the judgment of facial expression. *Average* accuracy rates appear to be substantial, hovering around 65%, whether the facial expression stimulus being judged was candid photographs (Hanawalt, 1944; Munn, 1940; Vinacke, 1949), spontaneous behavior (Ekman, 1965; Lanzetta & Kleck, 1970), or posed behavior (Drag & Shaw, 1967; Kozel & Gitter, 1968; Osgood, 1966). Yet, as in the earlier studies, variability across emotions is substantial. For example, nine investigations[1] of judgments of posed facial expressions yielded the following mean accuracy scores for what—as we see later—may be considered six primary emotions:

Emotion	Mean Accuracy
Happy	79%
Surprise	65%
Fear	62%
Sad	57%
Anger	55%
Disgust	54%

Such variability as a function of the emotion being judged, as well as other task, observer or actor sources of variability to be considered shortly, are clearly the clues to better understanding and accuracy of facial expression decoding. It is, thus, appropriate in broad conclusion to these judgmental accuracy studies, to concur with the view of Ekman, Friesen, and Ellsworth (1982), that there now clearly exist:

> consistent evidence of accurate judgments of emotion from facial behavior . . . it seems unnecessary to continue to question whether accurate judgments are possible. More useful research would determine under what conditions, for what kinds of people, in what kinds of roles and social settings, and with what types of accuracy criteria facial behavior provides correct information about emotion; and, conversely, research would also determine in what kinds of settings and roles and for what kinds of people facial behavior provides either no information or misinformation. (p. 86)

Ekman et al.'s (1982) call has begun to be answered. In the sections that follow, we describe what is currently known about just such task, actor, and observer characteristics as they bear upon judgmental accuracy.

TASK CHARACTERISTICS

As noted previously and as has been replicated in a substantial number of investigations, judgmental accuracy is in part a function of the particular emotion being displayed. In addition, the recognition task is consistently easier (higher average judgmental accuracy) when less is required of the observer, such as judgments of

---

[1]Drag & Shaw, 1967; Dusenbury & Knower, 1938; Ekman & Friesen, 1975; Feleky, 1914; Kanner, 1931; Kozel & Gitter, 1968; Levitt, 1964; Osgood, 1966; Woodworth, 1938.

pleasant versus unpleasant rather than specific emotions (Ekman & Bressler, 1964; Ekman & Rose, 1965). Conversely, accuracy level is likely to suffer when more than one affect, i.e., blends, are displayed simultaneously by the actor (Plutchik, 1962). The face may express not only more than one emotion at a time but also may simultaneously or sequentially express information of a nonaffect-related type. Ekman and Friesen (1975), in a paper devoted to why recognition errors occur in facial judgment tasks, describe the face as a multisignal, multimessage system. The face, they propose, is a multisignal system in that it displays static, slow, and rapid characteristics. The static are the essentially permanent aspects of the face (e.g., bone structure, fatty deposits, location of features). Slow signals are those facial appearance changes that occur gradually over time (e.g., permanent wrinkles, muscle tone, skin texture). The rapid facial signals, produced by movement of facial muscles, result in temporary and typically quite brief changes in facial features. Facial signals of emotion are rapid signals, although there are some types of rapid signals that are not affect relevant. Ekman and Friesen (1969a, 1975) distinguish among three classes of rapid facial signals. The first, our primary concern, are signals reflective of the actor's emotional state. The second, largely affect irrelevant, are emblematic messages. These are culturally agreed upon facial signals carrying specific meanings—the eye wink that communicates "hello," the raised eyebrow that indicates questioning. Punctuators are a second, affect-irrelevant category of rapid facial expression. Ekman and Friesen (1975) comment: "Everyone knows people who use their hands to accent or italicize a word or phrase as they speak. People can do the same thing with the rapid facial signals, punctuating what is being said in words with facial accents, commas and periods" (p. 13).

The complexity of the emotional recognition task has begun to emerge. Beyond the central matter of what affect any given constellation of facial signals denote, if a blend of affects is being displayed, it's separate components must first be discerned. In addition, the rapid facial signals must be discriminated from their static and slow signal facial context, and, among the rapid signals alone, emblems and punctuators must be perceptually separated from emotion-reflecting rapid signals. And there is more that may add to stimulus complexity and decoding difficulty. As our later discussion of actor characteristics relevant to the recognition process makes clear, actors vary in their expressive styles, the display rules they utilize, their motivation to deceive, and the facial management techniques they utilize.

But several task characteristics, unlike emotional blends and the multisignal and multimessage qualities of facial expressions, often serve to enhance the probability of recognition accuracy. The blends, the static and slow facial signals and the emblem and punctuator messages described previously were pictured by us as likely augmenters of recognition inaccuracy to the degree that they provided a context of excessive complexity, confusion, distraction or conflicting, contradictory information. The stimulus context of a given facial expression, however, may clarify rather than confuse, add consistent and thus useful rather than inconsistent and hence confusing information. The confusion-augmenting context just discussed consisted of an array of facial characteristics. But there are broader relevant contexts. One is other, nonfacial characteristics of the actor himself or herself; the other is the actor's situation, i.e., the people and events in the actor's environment antecedant to and concommitent with the occurrence of a given facial expression. The nature and possible positive contextual impact on recognition accuracy of aspects of the actor other than facial expression is captured well in Ekman and Friesen's (1975) discussion of the communication barrage:

> When listening, you gather information from at least three sources in the *auditory* channel: the actual words used; the sound of the voice; and such things as how rapidly the words are spoken, how many pauses there are, how much the speech is disrupted by words like 'aah' or 'uumh.' When looking, you gather information from at least four sources in the *visual* channel: the face; the tilt of the head; the total body posture; and the skeletal muscle movements of the arms, hands, legs, and feet. Every one of these sources in both the auditory and visual channel can tell you something about emotion. (p. 17)

Thus, the nonfacial visual context and a range of auditory information—both of which emanate from the actor himself or herself—may provide substantial aid in the task of decoding facial expression. We examine such actor clues to the affect recognition process more closely later in this chapter. For purposes of the present discussion, they represent one important sense in which context may aid recognition.

The external situation in which the facial expression occurs—where, with whom, when, preceded by what events, accompanied by what events—is the second, possible positive contextual contribution to the decoding effort. When they are substantially discordant, evidence suggests that sometimes contextual cues will dominate the judgmental process, sometimes facial cues. But in the more typical circumstance, in which external context and facial expression are concordant, a mutually augmenting interpretive effect on recognition seems to occur (Bruner & Tagiuri, 1954; Hunt, 1941; Taguiri, 1968). Studies reported by Munn (1940), Frijda (1958), and Goldberg (1951) further confirm the value of external contextual information for accurate recognition of facial expressions of emotions—although, as we noted earlier was the case for recognition accuracy independent of context, face plus context accuracy also may vary as a function of the emotion displayed.[2] Such emotion-specific variability notwithstanding, we concur in this domain with Frijda's (1958) broad conclusion:

---

[2]See, for example, Mc V. Hunt, Cole, & Reis' (1958) investigation of the influence of situational cues in the recognition of anger, fear, and sorrow.

Recent experimental research suggests that facial expression of emotion can be made with reasonable correctness. At the same time, knowledge of the situation that gives rise to the emotion expressed seems to modify interpretation and to add to its correctness. (p. 150)

Task contributions to recognition accuracy have been examined. Aspects of the facial expression stimulus itself, as well as its actor and external context, may serve to make more difficult the judgmental process or, contrariwise, may clarify, supplement, or otherwise enhance on observer's ability to correctly analyze and label an actor's emotion. In an analogous manner, the actor characteristics we now wish to consider may function to aid the recognition process in a variety of ways, or alternatively may confuse, deceive, or by other means diminish the probability of accurate recognition.

ACTOR CHARACTERISTICS

Just as an observer's ability to judge accurately a given actor's facial expression appears to be a dual function of general observer traits (e.g., "emotional sensitivity" or "recognition skill") *plus* an emotion—specific ability (e.g., judging surprise in Actor Smith's face), so too is the actor's portrayal a joint result of both a general underlying expressive style and emotion and situation-specific abilities. Let us turn first to stylistic contributions.

Ekman and Friesen (1975) propose eight styles, or behavioral predispositions, which they suggest underlie facial expressiveness:

1. Revealer: This is the sheer tendency to be openly and frequently expressive. Revealer's "wear their feeling on their sleeves" (actually, on their faces), rarely modulate their expressions, often break cultural display rules about appropriate facial expressiveness.

2. Withholder: In marked contrast to revealers, a withholding expressive style leads to little facial movement, very infrequent emotional facial displays, and an apparent phlegmatic demeanor.

3. Unwitting expressors: This is the tendency to be unaware that one's face is revealing the given emotion one is experiencing. Ekman and Friesen suggest that, when present, this style will tend to be reflected in one or two emotions in particular for any given individual.

4. Blanked expressor: Also typically centered on one or two emotions, blanked expressors tend to believe they are displaying the given emotion when, in fact, their face appears neutral or highly ambiguous to observing others.

5. Substitute expressor: Ekman and Friesen ask, for example, "Do you look sad to others when you feel angry, or angry when you feel sad?" The substitute

expressor, they hold, typically substitutes the appearance of one emotion for another without awareness that he or she is doing so.

6. Frozen-affect expressor: This expressive style may result from the static and slow facial expressive qualities examined earlier. Both permanent facial features and those that change gradually over time may, in a pseudoemotional manner, represent one or more facial qualities indicative of an emotion that the actor is actually not experiencing.

7. Ever-ready expressor: This expressive style is reflected in the tendency to display a given emotion as an initial response to diverse stimuli, including those for which the particular emotion is an inappropriate response. "An ever-ready expressor might, for example, show a surprise face to good news, bad news, angry provocation, threats, etc."

8. Flooded-affect expressor: For individuals with this expressive style, a given emotional expression or features thereof is constantly present. If another affect is aroused, the flooded affect colors it and both are components of the resultant emotional blend.

Thus, Ekman and Friesen (1975) assert that stylistic predispositions to facial expression regularities exist and are concretely reflected in overt facial expressive behavior. Whereas their list rests on little in the way of an empirical base, it does reflect their creative observational skills and, furthermore, underscores for all of us the need to include trait-like qualities when seeking to understand more fully the processes of emotional expressiveness and recognition accuracy.

What other actor qualities combine with expressive style to influence facial expression and recognition? Ekman and his research group (Ekman, 1982b; Ekman & Friesen, 1975) have devoted considerable attention in this context to actor intent to control, disguise, or deceive. The degree to which any given facial expression is controlled, disguised, or a deception, in their view, appears to be a resultant of three processes: (1) the display rules that govern the control effort, (2) the facial management techniques utilized, and (3) the leakage of "true" affect that nevertheless occurs. Let us examine these processes in turn.

Display Rules

Ekman, Friesen, and Ellsworth (1982) describe display rules as guidelines, usually learned early in life, specifying for an array of real-life circumstances the nature of appropriate and inappropriate facial expressiveness. They comment:

> for each facial behavior [display rules] specify what management technique should be applied by whom in what circumstance. The display rule dictates the occasion for the applicability of a particular management technique in terms of (1) static characteristics of the person within the situation (e.g., age, sex, physical body

size), (2) static characteristics of the setting (e.g., ecological factors, social definition of the situation . . .), (3) transient characteristics of the persons (e.g., role,
attitude), and (4) transient regularities during the course of the social interaction
(e.g., entrances, exists, transition points . . .).

Four categories of display rules are suggested. *Cultural* display rules—guidelines for facial expressiveness and its management shared by essentially all
members of a given community, subculture, or society. *Personal* display rules—
idiosyncratic facial expression regularities or habits, deriving from the actor's
individual developmental history. Functionally, "personal display rules" appears to overlap considerably with the expressive styles considered earlier. *Vocational* display rules—this third basis for basis for facial expression control relates
to the dictates, requirements, or role demands of the actor's occupation. Ekman
and Friesen (1975) cite as relevant occupational examples: actors, diplomats,
attorneys, salesmen, politicians, physicians, and nurses. *Momentary need* display rules—rules for facial expressiveness utilized by the actor not on an habitual
basis (cultural, personal), nor for reasons of vocational requirement (vocational)
but, instead, for the demands, goals, or requirements of a particular, usually
transient, situation: the guilty prisoner proclaiming his innocence, for example.
Given the context of one's expressive style and the display rule guidelines
pointing in particular expressive control directions, what facial management
techniques are at the actor's disposal for enhancing the likelihood of this or her
success in creating and communicating the facial expression he or she considers
desirable and optimal?

Facial Management Techniques

The sometimes conscious, sometimes near-automatic effort by the actor to control, disguise, or manage his or her facial expression will, according to Ekman
and Friesen (1975), typically take one of three forms. The actor may seek to
qualify the appearance of an emotion he or she has just both experienced and
accurately expressed:

> An emotional expression can be a qualifier when shown immediately after the first
> one, either as a social comment called for by a cultural or personal display rule or as
> a genuine expression of further feeling. . . . The smile is the most frequent
> qualifier, added as a comment to any of the negative emotions. The smile qualifier
> gives a clue as to the likely consequences, or limits, of the negative emotion. It tells
> the other person how seriously to take it. It informs the other person you are still in
> control. (p. 140)

Modulation is a second, oft-used facial management technique. Here the actor
neither comments expressively on his or her own emotions (as in qualifying) nor
changes the nature of his or her expression (as in falsifying) but, instead, adjusts

the intensity of the expression to portray either more or less than what is actually being felt. Modulation is expressed concretely by varying the number of facial areas involved in the affective portrayal, varying the duration of the expression, and/or varying the excursion or extent of pull of the facial muscles.

Falsifying is a third facial management technique that Ekman and Friesen (1975) suggest may concretize the individual's governing display rules. Falsifying may take three forms. The actor may seek to simulate, that is, express a feeling when it in fact does not exist. He or she may neutralize, that is, show nothing when the emotion does exist. Or, in masking, the actor may seek to cover a felt emotion with the apparency of another emotion not actually being experienced. Though the display rules may dictate their selection and usage, the facial management effort at control, disguise, of deception may wholly or partially fail. When it does, it may be because the actor's actual emotion is being communicated facially nevertheless, by a process Ekman and Friesen (1975) term *leakage*.

Leakage

Four types of facial leakage clues have been proposed. *Morphological* clues are changes in the configuration, shape, or dimensions of facial features, accomplished by such actor management techniques as modulation (intensification, deintensification) and falsification, but which are discernable to the observer because the features constituting the configuration 'don't fit.'' Ekman and Friesen's (1975) description of the morphological leakage of the six primary emotions may be exemplified by their examination of the simulation of sadness:

> When sadness is simulated, it will probably be shown in the lower face and a downward cast of the eyes. The absence of the sad brow/forehead and upper eyelid would be a good clue that the sadness was simulated. . . . the sad brow/forehead is a particularly reliable indicator that sadness is genuinely felt, because this expression is hard to make voluntarily; it is not part of a facial emblem, and it is rarely used as a punctuator. Some people, however, never show the sad brow/forehead, even when they are genuinely sad. As we emphasized [earlier], you must know whether or not a particular muscular movement is part of the person's usual repertoire to infer leakage or deception clues reliably. If the brow/forehead is not part of the person's repertoire when he is actually sad, then its absence won't tell you that an otherwise sad expression is a simulation. With such people you will have to look at the shape of the upper eyelid. It should be pulled up at the inner corners if the person is actually sad. (pp. 149–150)

In a manner parallel to the morphological discordance of facial features, *temporal* discordances may also provide important leakage clues. How long a given facial expression takes to appear in a particular context, how long it remains on the face, and how long it takes to disappear are each matters relevant to facial expression timing that may serve as clues to leakage or deception.

The *location* of a facial expression, that is its occurrence and spacing in relation to ongoing conversation, body movement, and related unfolding events, may provide further leakage clues. As with morphological and temporal discordance, the social and interpersonal context in which the facial expression is displayed should markedly influence the interpretation of location clues to leakage and deception.

Microexpressions, a final type[3] of clue to the affect actually being experienced during efforts to deceive, are very brief expressive interruptions. The microexpression may come must before, or during, the appearance of the deintensified, neutralized, or masked (i.e., deceptive) emotion.

The cognitive analysis of facial affective displays is, we have held, a resultant not only of the display per se, but also of a host of other task, actor, and observer characteristics. The complexity and interrelatedness of these characteristics has clearly emerged in our preceding consideration, that of the judging task and of the actor displaying the expression. We turn now to cognitive analysis considerations associated with the individual performing the analysis, the observer. As becomes clear in the next section, observer characteristics, too, may serve as significant determinants and crcorrelates of recognition accuracy.

OBSERVER CHARACTERISTICS

Of the three broad categories of casual influences and concommitants of recognition accuracy—task, actor, and observer characteristics—least is yet known about the observer. Still, enough relevant research has been conducted that a number of at least substantial leads, if not yet firm conclusions, have emerged. The cognitive analytic task we are addressing is the decoding of nonverbal (especially facial) expressive communications for their emotional meanings. Such analytic ability, early research suggests, increases with age in children (Dymond, Hughes, & Raabe, 1952; Gates, 1923); is moderately but consistently better in females than males (Buzby, 1924; Kellogg & Eagleson, 1931); relates positively if modestly to socioeconomic status (Sweet, 1929), family size (F. Allport, 1924), intelligence (G. Allport, 1937; Taft, 1950), and esthetic interest (Vernon, 1933); and correlates positively with emotional adjustment (Fields, 1953; Lindgren & Robinson, 1953) and quality of social relations (Gage, 1953; Van Zeldt, 1952). Much of this early research on accuracy of affective and related judgments has been critically evaluated by Taft (1955).

More recent research on individual differences in nonverbal decoding ability builds further in clarifying directions upon that just depicted. Hall (1979) reports that 84% of 61 relevant investigations show females to be better decoders than

---

[3]In the present section, our focus is upon facial clues to leakage and deception. As later sections make clear, inconsistencies among speech, body movements, and facial expression may provide yet additional, important leakage and deception information.

males of nonverbal affective messages. The female advantage remains with age and is somewhat greater for visual than for auditory nonverbal cues. Women are also more likely than male observers to overlook or ignore leaked nonverbal cues of actor deception (Rosenthal & Paulo, 1979). Several investigators have examined in considerable depth a question visited but briefly by us earlier, namely the degree to which recognition accuracy is a general observer trait or more a function of task-specific abilities. The early view of F. Allport (1924), G. Allport (1937), Vernon (1933), and Wedeck (1947) that it is in fact both seems to be further supported by more recent research. The general trait component, for example, is clearly demonstrated in Beldoch's (1964) finding of positive relationships among the abilities to accurately recognize emotions expressed graphically, musically, and vocally; in studies showing similarly positive relationships in the ability to judge posed versus spontaneously posed emotions (Cunningham, 1977; Zuckerman, Hall, De Frank, & Rosenthal, 1976); and in a series of investigations reporting positive correlations among the abilities to identify nonverbal cues communicated by the face, the body, or the tone of voice (Cunningham, 1977; Zaidel & Mehrabian, 1969; Zuckerman, Lipets, Koivumaki, & Rosenthal, 1975). Yet De Paulo and Rosenthal (1979) and Rosenthal, Hall, Di Matteo, Rogers, & Archer (1979) have also quite substantially demonstrated the companion importance of task-specific abilities to the success of the judgment task. For example, in their factor analytic analysis of their Profile of Nonverbal Sensitivity (PONS), Rosenthal et al. (1979) report:

> Along with a 'general' factor of nonverbal decoding skill, we also found four more specific factors: (1) skill at decoding pure and briefly exposed face and body cues: (2) skill at decoding pure audio cues; (3) skill at decoding mixed face and body cues; and (4) skill at judging mixed audio cues and discrepant cues. (p. 232)

Much of the more recent research on emotional decoding has sought to add further to our understanding of personalogical correlates in the observer of such (general plus specific) decoding ability. Skilled decoders, in contrast to their less accurate counterparts, appear to be less Machiavellian, more comfortable in seeking help from others, and more likely to see themselves as attractive and having good same-sex interpersonal relationships (Rosenthal, et al., 1979). These same investigators also found no relationships among decoding skill and esthetic involvement, religious involvement, and self-rated quality of opposite-sex relationships. In a manner parallel to the general plus situation-specific *abilities* findings cited earlier, there are—in addition to the observer trait-like correlates of decoding ability—also very likely state-like concomitants of such ability. Schiffenbauer (1974) found that the emotional state of the observer at the time of his or her participation in the decoding task exerts a substantial influence upon the content of his or her judgments. More specifically, aroused observers were more likely to attribute to the actor the specific emotion he or she was feeling than were nonaroused or differently aroused observers. Furthermore, the level of observer arousal also directly influenced the intensity of the emotion judged in the actor. These findings held for both positive and negative observer affects. Beyond Schiffenbauer's (1974) study, only a few studies of the influence in social perception tasks of observer state exist (e.g., Feshbach & Feshbach, 1963; Feshbach & Singer, 1957; Hornberger, 1960). Clearly, this too is a potentially very fruitful path for future research on the observer in the cognitive analysis of emotional messages.

FACIAL COMPONENTS OF SPECIFIC EMOTIONS

To this point in the present chapter we have presented and examined the array of task, actor, and observer characteristics that may function to influence the accuracy of judgments of facial expressions of emotion. With these several guidelines as context, we now turn to the facial expressions per se and the manner in which specific facial components are indicative of specific actor emotions. The several investigations that we utilized to form the research base of our task, actor, and observer discussions were primarily *judgement* studies. These were essentially efforts to identify the conditions under which observers, looking at a facial expression, accurately identify the actor's emotional state. We now shift our interest to a second type of facial expression research, *component* studies, in which the effort is made to identify specific facial expression features denotative of a particular emotion.

Component studies are a somewhat more recent development than judgment investigations in the history of facial expression research, but a substantial number have been conducted (e.g., Ekman & Friesen, 1975; Fulcher, 1942; Landis & Hunt, 1939; Leventhal & Sharp, 1965; Rubenstein, 1969; Thompson, 1941; Trujillo & Wartkin, 1968). These several investigations combine to provide considerable information about emotion-specific qualities and configurations of the forehead, browns, eyelids, eyes, nose, mouth, and other facial features. A major increment to this component understanding of facial expression was provided by Ekman, Friesen, and Tomkin's (1971) development of the Facial Affect Scoring Technique (FAST). Unlike the procedure for judgment studies, coders utilizing the FAST procedures do not judge the emotion in the face they are coding. Instead, utilizing motion pictures of the face, coders are required to score each observable movement in each of three areas of the face: (1) brows/forehead, (2) eyes/lids, and (3) lower face including cheeks, nose, mouth, and chin. Ekman et al. (1971), based upon the component studies cited previously and their own considerable research in this domain (e.g., Ekman, 1972, 1973; Friesen, 1972), have derived the FAST Atlas, a document presenting pictorial examples of the various specific characteristics of these three facial areas that denote happiness, sadness, surprise, fear, anger, and disgust. Coders score each movement within each of the three facial areas, determine its exact duration, and classify the movement observed by comparing it with FAST Atlas criterion photographs. A score or categorization is thus assigned to the movement based on the criterion picture it most closely resembles, the score is combined with the other scores similarly derived for the particular expression being coded, the scores are cast into FAST formula format, and the affect is thus identified. Averill, Opton, and Lazarus (1969), Ekman, Friesen, and Ellsworth (1982), and Hjortsjo (1970) have provided further validity information in support of the affect-identifying adequacy of FAST.

In the FAST Atlas as well as in their very useful book *Unmasking the Face,* Ekman and Friesen provide both the criterion photographs for the six primary emotions, as well as descriptions of facial component features in each of the three facial component areas. We have, with their generous permission, reproduced these "blueprints of facial expression." In the context of the several ways that task, actor, and observer characteristics may increase or diminish recognition accuracy, the facial components identified here are the heart of the cognitive analysis task. It is these features that the observer must accurately discern, through both the fog and the light ot task, actor, and observer characteristics, if accurate decisions are to be reached about the other person's feelings.

Happiness.

FIG. 4.1.
(From Ekman & Friesen, 1975, p. 112)

1. Corners of lips are drawn back and up.
2. The mouth may be parted, with teeth exposed.
3. A wrinkle (the naso-labial fold) runs down from the nose to the outer edge of the top corners.
4. The cheeks are raised.
5. The lower eyelid shows wrinkles below it, and may be raised but not tense.
6. Crow's-feet wrinkles go outward from the outer corners of the eyes.

Sadness.

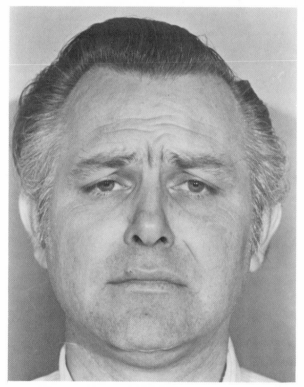

FIG. 4.2.
(From Ekman & Friesen, 1975, p. 127)

1. The inner corners of the eyebrows are drawn up.
2. The skin below the eyebrow is triangulated, with the inner corner up.
3. The upper eyelid inner corner is raised.
4. The corners of the lips are down or the lip is trembling.

Surprise.

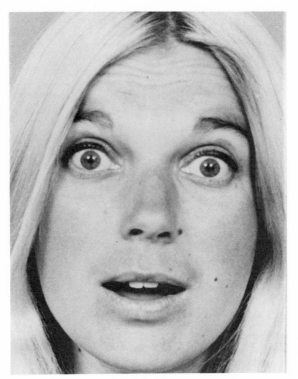

FIG. 4.3.
(From Ekman & Friesen, 1975, p. 45)

1. The brows are raised, so that they are curved and high.
2. The skin below the brow is stretched.
3. Horizontal wrinkles go across the forehead.
4. The eyelids are opened; the upper lid is raised and the lower lid drawn down; the white of the eye shows above the iris, and often below as well.
5. The jaw drops open so that the lips and teeth are parted, but there is no tension or stretching of the mouth.

Fear.

1. The brows are raised and drawn together.
2. The wrinkles in the forehead are in the center, not across the entire forehead.

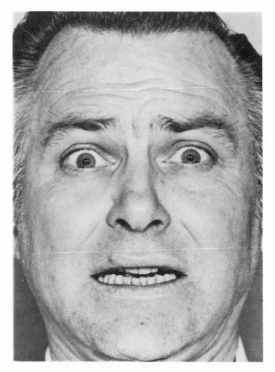

FIG. 4.4.
(From Ekman & Friesen, 1975, p. 62)

3. The upper eyelid is raised, exposing sclera, and the lower eyelid is tense and drawn up.
4. The mouth is open and the lips are either tensed slightly and drawn back or stretched and drawn back.

Anger.

1. The upper lid is tense and may or may not be lowered by the action of the brow.
2. The eyes have a hard stare and may have a bulging appearance.
3. The lips are in either of two basic positions: pressed firmly together, with the corners straight or down; or upen, tensed in a squarish shape as if shouting.
4. The nostrils may be dilated, but this is not essential to the anger facial expression.

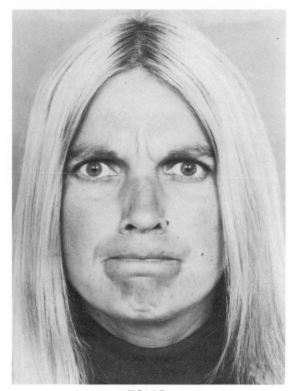

FIG. 4.5.
(From Ekman & Friesen, 1975, p. 97)

Disgust.

1. The upper lip is raised.
2. The lower lip is also raised and pushed up to the upper lip, or is lowered and slightly protruding.
3. The nose is wrinkled.
4. The cheeks are raised.
5. Lines show below the lower eyelid, and the eyelid is pushed up but not tense.
6. The brow is lowered, lowering the upper lid.

This presentation of facial components denotative of primary facial expressions completes our consideration of the cognitive analysis of facial information. As noted earlier, our primary focus has been on the face in response to substantial evidence that the face is actor's and observer's primary, nonverbal means of, respectively, encoding and decoding emotion-relevant information.

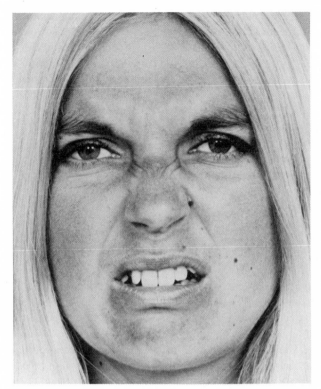

FIG. 4.6.
(From Ekman & Friesen, 1975, p. 76)

But actor sends and observer receives via other channels also, channels that may be less declarative and less well-studied than the face, but which nevertheless may combine with facially communicated emotional information to yield a clearer, more comprehensive, and more accurate picture of actor affect. It is these nonfacial, nonverbal affective channels we now consider.

OTHER NONVERBAL EMOTIONAL COMMUNICATION

The array of nonverbal human behaviors that are at least potentially relevant to the encoding and decoding of emotional contents is broad indeed. Duncan (1969) suggests that nonverbal communication modalities include: (1) body motion or kinesic behavior, such as gestures, posture, eye movement; (2) paralanguage, such as voice qualities, speech nonfluencies, vocal qualifiers; (3) proxemics, concerned with the use of personal space; (4) olfaction; (5) skin sensitivity; and (6) the use of artifacts, such as dress and cosmetics. Duncan's (1969) examination of the experimental history of these several communication channels is a valuable statement of the historical context and development of work in these domains. Mehrabian (1969a) proposed a largely similar series of nonverbal communication possibilities. Argyle's (1972) also sought to provide a comprehensive listing of nonverbal communication channels. In addition to facial expression, he includes:

1. Bodily contact
2. Proximity
3. Orientation
4. Appearance (voluntary aspects of)
5. Posture
6. Headnods
7. Gestures
8. Gaze
9. Nonverbal aspects of speech

Although it may appear reasonable to propose that each of the nonverbal communication channels in the preceding listings is a likely route for the transmission of affective messages, in no instance has this conclusion been demonstrated with anything approaching the comprehensiveness of research done on facial expressiveness of emotion. In fact, with the partial exception of nonverbal aspects of speech, it is fair to observe that the investigation of nonverbal (and nonfacial) communication of emotion is still in its early stages. But let us look at what has been reported.

Fairbanks and Pronovost (1939), building upon the early, parameter-defining research of Cowan (1936), Gray (1926), Lynch (1934), and Ortleb (1937), conducted an investigation in which a group of six actors, reading the same test passage (constant content), each sought to portray by means of nonverbal, vocal characteristics a series of five emotions, namely contempt, anger, fear, grief, and indifference. The 30 phonographic recordings of their portrayals were played to 64 judges who were required to select, from a list of 12 emotions, that one depicted by each record. The percentage of correct judgments, across judges and actors, was quite high—indifference (88%), contempt (84%), anger (78%), fear (66%). Fairbanks and Pronovost (1939) propose that the essential vocal quality upon which judges made their (largely accurate) selections of the emotion portrayed was pitch, its level, range, and shifts. Twenty years later, Davitz and Davitz (1959a) successfully conducted a near replication of this earlier investigation. Eight speakers each expressed 10 different feelings by reciting parts of the alphabet. Accuracy of identification by a panel of 30 judges was well beyond chance expectancy, and in the order: anger, nervousness, sadness, happiness, sympathy, satisfaction, fear (tied with), love, jealousy, and pride. Davitz and Davitz (1959b) suggest that the vocal qualities utilized by their judges in differentiating among and identifying the emotions portrayed were tone, volume, and rate. In this same investigation, they were able to show that the subjective similarity of two expressions influences the ease with which they can be discriminated, the more similar the more difficult the discrimination.

In contrast to the constant content, nonverbal research sampled previously, Soskin and Kauffman (1961) employed a filtered speech paradigm in which high-frequency sounds that carry the semantic portion of communication are filtered out of the communication. The investigations employed, as stimulus materials, (filtered) recordings of real-life emotional communications. Their judges, as in the constant content studies, were required to categorize each passage into one of an array of alternative emotions. Their results clearly indicate that judges can do so well beyond chance expectancy. Soskin and Kauffman (1961) conclude:

> Although the precise nature of the vocal cues which make such judgments possible is unclear, the experiments do establish that the sounds within a relatively narrow carrier band (100–550 CPS), at least for the kinds of voice samples used in this study, are sufficient for the transmission of generally identifiable cues to the emotional state of the speaker. (p. 80)

Thus, an overall effect is discernable: Evidence does exist to demonstrate significant levels of emotional recognition accuracy based upon nonverbal, vocal information. In addition, more denotative—if only initial—evidence regarding which vocal qualities are indicative of which emotions has begun to emerge. Costanzo, Markel, and Costanzo (1969) report that: "peak–pitch voices were judged as portraying grief; peak-loudness as anger or contempt, and peak–tempo as indifference" (p. 267). Davitz and Davitz (1961) provide evidence that subjectively rated "active" emotions, such as anger or joy, are expressed with a relatively loud voice, high pitch, blaring timbre, and fast rate. "Passive" emotions, such as boredom or despair, in contrast, are expressed with a relatively quiet voice, low pitch, resonant timbre, and slow rate. Feldstein and Jaffe (1962) and Mahl (1956) have investigated the relationship of speech disruptions to certain affective states and found certain disturbances in word-to-word progression to characterize anxiety, but not anger. In a similar vein, other investigators have examined speech and breathing rates (Goldman–Eisler, 1955), silences (Dibner, 1956), intrusive nonverbal sounds (Krause & Pilisuk, 1961), and non-lexical aspects of speech (Pittenger & Smith, 1957). Though a moderate number of such investigations have been conducted, oriented toward the identification of specific emotion-associated vocal qualities, it is a domain still largely unclarified, with much valuable work to be done.

Beyond the considerable information we have presented regarding facial expressiveness of emotion and our brief excursion into vocal cues to a speaker's affect, there is relatively little existing experimental information bearing upon other nonverbal channels of emotional communication. The work of Hall (1964), Mehrabian (1968, 1969a,b), and Sommer (1967) dealing with posture, position, body orientation, and related proxemic dimensions is pregnant in its implications for the transmission and cognitive analysis of emotional information. Most proxemics research to date, however, has examined the relationship of such nonverbal behaviors to individual and dyadic status and attitudinal characteristics, and not the affective state of the individual's involved.

Similarly in its early research stages are investigations of emotional communication transmitted by gesture or hand movements (Bauml & Bauml, 1975; Friesen, Ekman, & Wallbott, 1979; Mahl, 1968; Wylie & Stafford, 1977), by leg motions (Ekman & Friesen, 1969b), by touching (Henley, 1977; Montagu, 1971), gaze (Argyle & Cook, 1976), and pupil size (Hess, 1975). Finally, and perhaps most veridical with real-life communication of messages of emotion, there are a small series of investigation that examine and compare, singly and in combination, several different channels of affective expression employed simultaneously (Burns & Beier, 1973; Dittman, Parloff, & Boomer, 1965; Ekman, Friesen, O'Sullivan, & Scherer, 1980; Graves & Robinson, 1976; Rosenthal, 1966). Beyond basic findings of the additivity of consistent messages (Rosenthal et al., 1979), the primacy of visual over auditory cues (Mehrabian & Ferris, 1967; Rosenthal et al., 1979) and the confusion-engendering effect of inconsistent cues (De Paulo, Rosenthal, Eisenstat, Rogers, & Finkelstein, 1978), not a great deal may yet be concluded from studies thus far on the processing of such multimodal cues of emotion. This line of research, we feel, is especially worthy of further investigative inquiry.

SUMMARY

This chapter has focused upon the cognitive analysis phase of the empathic process. The affective reverberatory information experienced by the actor in the preceding phase will optimally be combined with the observer's interpretation of the actor's facial expression and other verbally and nonverbally transmitted cognitive analytic information to yield a conclusion, a decision, a label, a summary impression regarding the actor's emotional state.

5 Psychotherapeutic Consequences

We have organized much of this book around the notion offered by Keefe (1976), Macarov (1978), and others that empathy is optimally defined as a four-stage process. The perceptual, affective reverberation and cognitive analysis stages of this process have been examined in earlier chapters. In this and the three chapters that follow, our focus is upon the final empathic stage—accurate communication—and its purportedly beneficial consequences. As becomes clear, this chapter's emphasis on communication is especially relevant to psychotherapy, so much so in fact that certain definitions of empathy in psychotherapy stress in particular the communication component. Truax and Carkhuff (1967) state:

> Accurate empathy involves more than just the ability of the therapist to sense the client or patient's private world as if it were his own. It also involves more than just his ability to know what the patient means. Accurate empathy involves both the therapist's sensitivity to current feelings and his verbal facility to communicate this understanding in a language attuned to the client's current feelings. (p. 46)

And, even more explicitly, according to Lambert, DeJulio, and Stein, 1978:

> Accurate empathy . . . is the degree to which the therapist is successful in communicating his awareness and understanding of the client's current feelings in language attuned to that client. (p. 468)

In seeking to trace and understand the import of empathy in the psychotherapeutic context, it is to the seminal role of Carl Rogers to which we must turn first. Building upon the then (and now) prevailing view regarding the central role

131

for psychotherapeutic outcome of the therapist–patient relationship, Rogers (1957) proposed what Parloff, Waskow, and Wolfe (1978) correctly describe as the "startling hypothesis" that a combination of only a very small number (six originally, subsequently reduced to four) of therapy-relevant conditions were necessary and sufficient to produce constructive personality change. These conditions were three specific attitudinal characteristics of the therapist: (1) empathy, (2) unconditional positive regard, and (3) genuineness that were (4) accurately perceived by the patient. Roger's (1957) definition of empathy stressed the therapist's experiencing of an accurate understanding of the client's private world as if it were his or her own, but without ever losing the "as if" quality. For Rogers, unlike many who later sought to build upon his proposal of necessary and sufficient conditions, empathy was primarily a therapist *attitude,* a way of being, of experiencing that could, in turn, be communicated to the client in any one of a number of ways. Unlike the later researchers who largely equated empathy with one (but only one) of its possible concretizations, Rogers believed that an array of channels existed for its accurate expression. As Parloff et al. (1978) observe:

> he dismissed any notion that the techniques of the various therapies were important other than as vehicles for achieving one or another of these conditions. Consistent with this formulation, he abandoned the view that the nondirective therapy technique of 'reflecting feelings' had any unique or specific therapeutic impact; instead, he proposed that like such techniques as free association, analysis of transference, and suggestion, it was simply a mechanism for communicating the therapist's sensitive empathy and unconditional positive regard. (p. 244)

EARLY INVESTIGATIONS

It is to Rogers special credit that as a joint outcome of the attractiveness of his proposal, his explicit calls for its empirical scrutiny and his own research involvement and leadership, a large number of relevant investigations were subsequently conducted. It is not unimportant to note in this regard that, as often occurs in the sociology of science, these initial studies were conducted mostly by young researchers who were disciples working with, or who had worked with, Rogers directly. Halkides (1958), in perhaps the first such investigation, employed a variety of change measures and found, as Rogers had predicted, significant therapist empathy—client change relationships. Several investigations by Charles Truax and his coworkers appeared in the early and mid-1960s, almost all of which substantially supported the relationship between therapy outcome and what by then was termed the *facilitative conditions.* These findings held for hospitalized inpatients receiving group psychotherapy (Truax, Carkhuff, & Kodman, 1965), two juvenile delinquent patient sample (Truax & Wargo, 1966;

Truax, Wargo, & Silber, 1966), an adult outpatient sample (Truax & Carkhuff, 1967), and emotionally disturbed college students (Dickenson & Truax, 1966). Further such support also emerged from investigations by Altmann (1973), Bozarth and Rubin (1976), Cairns (1972), Minsel, Bommert, Bastine, Langer, Nickel, and Tausch (1971), Truax (1970), and Truax and Wittmer (1971). Additional early evidence for the Rogers prediction also appeared in the form of results suggesting that low levels of therapist empathy, regard, and genuineness were nonfacilitative and, in fact, led to negative patient change, i.e., deterioration (Truax & Carkhuff, 1967; Truax & Mitchell, 1971). Based upon such literature, Truax and Mitchell in 1971 drew the following conclusion:

> These studies taken together suggest that therapists or counselors who are accurately empathic, nonpossessively warm in attitude, and genuine are indeed effective. Also, these findings seem to hold with a wide variety of therapists and counselors, regardless of their training or theoretic orientation, and with a wide variety of clients or patients. . . . Further, the evidence suggests that these findings hold in a variety of therapeutic contexts and in both individual and group psychotherapy or counseling. (p. 310)

As Parloff et al. (1978) observe, these "initial results of research efforts based on Rogers' hypothesis were, with few exceptions, exhilarating. They suggested that the field of psychotherapy research had achieved a major breakthrough" (p. 245). As we see, however, subsequent research, subsequent reexamination of the earlier research, and newer perspectives on psychotherapy research itself had led to less effusive and rather more modest claims, and to still useful but more realistic conclusions.

A REEXAMINATION

As a new generation of psychotherapy researchers became active and began to scrutinize the array of earlier empathy-outcome studies, a substantial number of serious conceptual and methodological criticisms were put forth, with regard to both empathy itself as well as therapeutic outcome. The tape ratings scales utilized as the operational definition of empathy, appeared to reflect substantial movement away from Rogers' empathy-as-attitude conceptualization toward a more technological stance in which empathy-as-technique—a very specific technique—prevailed. Lambert, et al. (1978) comment:

> the focus for training has shifted from a somewhat philosophical, existential emphasis on therapist attitudes and beliefs to a technology for teaching effective and concrete therapist responses. This trend appears to be an outgrowth of research efforts that have attempted to specify and measure the three original facilitative conditions proposed by Rogers. Once it was considered possible to discriminate

between high and low levels . . . it was a natural step to begin training counselors to give specific responses that would be rated high on the research scales. (p. 474)

Beyond these definitional concerns, both the validity (Rappaport & Chinksy, 1972; Shapiro, 1969) and reliability (Shapiro, 1969) of the more popularly used scales for measuring therapist empathy from tape-recorded therapy sessions were seriously challenged, as was the exclusive reliance on audiotapes and thus client verbal behavior, ignoring the complete array of demonstrably relevant therapist nonverbal behaviors (Fritz, 1966; Haase & Tepper, 1972; Shapiro, Foster, & Powell, 1968). Further, a number of artifactual influences upon rated empathy, i.e., factors influencing therapist empathy ratings quite aside from therapist empathy per se, were shown to be operative. These included the length (Gurman, 1973) and location in the therapy session (Mitchell, Bozarth, & Krauft, 1977) of the segment selected for rating, the therapeutic experience or naivity of the judges (Lambert et al., 1978), the sex of the judge vis a vis the sex of the client (Olesker & Balter, 1972; Sweeney & Cottle, 1976), and the startling finding (Chinsky & Rappaport, 1970; Shapiro, 1969; Truax, 1966) that therapist empathy judged from tape recordings on which the patients' statements had been deleted (i.e., the raters heard *only* therapist responses) were essentially judged no differently ($r = .68$) from the same tapes played so that judges heard patient statement–therapist statement–patient statement sequences, i.e., judges could hear to what patient contents the therapist was responding. This result led some investigators (Bozarth & Krauft, 1972; Chinsky & Rappaport, 1970; Lazar, 1976; Muehlberg, Pierce, & Drasgow, 1969; Wenegrat, 1974) to wonder whether ''empathy'' was being judged at all or, instead, therapist involvement, commitment, focus upon affect, or even merely his or her verbal activity level. Further, it appears to matter considerably who is doing the ratings. Therapists ratings of their own empathy appear to be consistent overestimates that, in addition, tend to correlate not at all or negatively with therapist empathy ratings obtained from independent judges or the client (Barrett–Lennard, 1962; Kurtz & Grummon, 1972). It also appears to be the case that a somewhat stronger and more reliable empathy-outcome relationship is demonstrable for client-perceived ratings of therapist empathy that for those obtained from independent judges (Lambert et al., 1978).

The measurement of outcome in these earlier studies also received considerable tempering critique. Measures varied considerably from study to study and suffered from the substantial array of psychometric problems to which all therapy outcome measures are vulnerable (Shapiro, 1969), and, as just noted, empathy did appear to relate to outcome when the empathy ratings were obtained from patients (as Rogers, 1957, had originally predicted), but less frequently so when empathy was rater judged (Chinsky & Rappaport, 1970; Mehrabian & Ferris, 1967; Rappaport & Chinsky, 1972). With considerable frequency it was the case that both empathy and outcome data were obtained from the same source. As Parloff et al. (1978) note:

Since the patient's ratings of therapist and outcome are likely to be reflections of the patient's overall satisfaction with the therapy, and therefore highly interrelated, the usefulness of these studies as independent tests of the facilitative conditions hypothesis must further be questioned. (p. 251)

In addition to such conceptual and methodological concerns, Blackwood (1975), Chinsky and Rappaport (1970), Parloff et al. (1978), and Rachman (1973) have each questioned whether some of the early investigators had permitted their enthusiasm to cloud their objectivity, whether sufficient weight had been given to apparent inconsistencies, whether nonpredicted findings had been too greatly deemphasized. We concur with these critiques; there indeed exist errors in judgment in the analysis and presentation of a not insignificant portion of the early empathy-outcome research. Although we in no sense wish to rationalize or explain away such investigator behavior, we nevertheless wish to put forth the view that the harshness of judgments made vis a vis these early studies should be at least somewhat tempered by awareness that all research must in part be understood and evaluated in the temporal and philosophical context in which it is conducted. The 1960s were a time in which all psychotherapy research, including empathy-outcome studies, occurred in the particular zeitgeist of research philosophies, strategies, and tactics that then prevailed. The psychotherapy research atmosphere of the 1960s was one in which many investigators labored under the uniformity myths (Kiesler, 1966) then in effect, myths that operationally treated all therapists as more or less equivalent, all patients as more or less equivalent, and all utilizations of any given therapeutic approach as more or less equivalent. Researchers generally were embarked on a preprescriptive search for main effects. Thus, in the early empathy studies and in most other therapy research of this era, there was essentially no attempt to pose and test *differential* predictions, e.g., about for whom high empathy was facilitative versus for whom such therapist attitudes might in fact be irrelevant or harmful. In subsequent years, psychotherapy research in general has moved discernably toward becoming more prescriptive, seeking to identify therapist, patient, and treatment characteristics that combine to enhance therapeutic outcome. As we see later, such differential thinking is increasingly reflected in more recent empathy-outcome research also. Truax, Carkhuff, Mitchell, and their early empathy-outcome research collaborators, we are suggesting, were *in part* in their efforts responsive to their times. We should judge their works rigorously, but also with the softening of the historical perspective we have put forth.

RECENT INVESTIGATIONS

As was true for much of the early empathy-outcome research, a portion of the later studies has also failed to prescriptively break out targeted subsamples of patients or therapists from larger samples to test differential predictions. By pursuing such a homogenizing course, global relationships more often than not failed to emerge (Beutler, Johnson, Neville, & Workman, 1972; Beutler, Johnson, Neville, Workman, & Elkins, 1973; Garfield & Bergin, 1971; Kurtz & Grummon, 1972; Mintz, Luborsky, & Auerbach, 1971; Mullen & Abeles, 1971; Sloane, Staples, Cristol, Yorkston, & Whipple, 1975). As early as 1973, this moderation of global effects became evident. Mitchell, et al. (1973) at that time noted that of 109 possible relationships between empathy and outcome tested in (mostly) early 1970s studies, only 24 were significantly positive. Similarly moderate data and tempered conclusions emerged in the decade that followed. Review articles appearing throughout this recent period (Blackwood, 1975; Gladstein, 1977a; Mitchell, Bozarth, & Krauft, 1977; Lambert et al., 1978; Parloff et al., 1978) have consistently led to the more accurate conclusion that, according to Mitchell et al. (1977):

> The recent evidence, although equivocal, does seem to suggest that empathy, warmth and genuineness are related in some way to client change but that their potency and generalizability are not as great as once thought. (p. 481)

Lambert et al. (1978) state:

> The generally well designed and executed studies . . . present only modest evidence in favor of the hypothesis that such factors as accurate empathy, warmth and genuineness relate to measures of outcome. (p. 472)

Yet to know that high levels of therapist empathy relates to substantial degrees of positive patient change only in a moderate number of instances, rather than more uniformly as had been claimed earlier, still has rather little applied consequence for the actual practice of psychotherapy unless one can specify for which therapists, patients, and therapies the positive association holds. As noted earlier, the 1960s was a period of global outcome research in psychotherapy. The investigative question characteristically asked was "Is treatment A superior to treatment B?" (Or, of relevance to our theme, "Is a high level of therapist empathy superior—across diverse therapists, diverse patients, and diverse therapies?"—to a low level of therapist empathy?) In the late 1970s and early 1980s, psychotherapy research was in large measure shifting to a prescriptive stance, one in which the goal was to learn enough about the potential contribution to outcome of particular therapist, patient, and therapy variables, individually and in diverse combinations, so that increasingly the outcome question that could be addressed was "Which type of patient, meeting with which type of therapist, for which type of treatment, will yield which outcomes?" (Bergin, 1967; Goldstein & Stein, 1976; Kiesler, 1966).

In this prescriptive, differentiated, or tailored psychotherapies context, the late 1970s and early 1980s, then, may appropriately be viewed as a prerequisite period in which considerable research was directed toward the identification of specific, potentially active therapeutic ingredients, that is, qualities of the therapist, the patient, and the therapy that individually and in combination bore a causal or concommitant relationship to a positive therapeutic outcome. As we have noted elsewhere, accoridng to Goldstein and Stein (1976):

> In its third and most progressive stage thus far, the stage of 'outcome-related process studies,' psychotherapy research began more fully to identify the patient, therapist, and treatment variables relevant to increasing the success of therapeutic outcomes. It is these active therapeutic ingredients—these characteristics of the participants, the treatment offered, and the outcomes obtained—which form the building blocks [for perspective psychotherapies]. (p. XI)

With more direct reference to empathy, it became increasingly the case that research questions posed, and sometimes answered, addressed such prerequisite matters as: For which type(s) of patients is high therapist empathy likely to occur? For which type(s) is it facilitative? For which type(s) is it neutral or deteriorative? Is the level of therapist empathy a therapist "trait" as it were, more or less constant across his or her caseload, or is it more typically variable and client specific, i.e., client determined? To the extent that therapist empathy is not only client specific, but also a reliable therapist characteristic, are there other therapist qualities predictive of or associated with it? Is the import for outcome of therapist empathy in part a function of the type of therapy being offered, e.g., does it matter a great deal for the consequences of client-centered therapy, but rather little for more psychodynamically oriented treatments? The foregoing preprescriptive, active ingredient-identifying questions are what we have termed *unidifferential* questions (Goldstein & Stein, 1976). Each seeks to identify a single therapist, patient, *or* treatment characteristic likely to contribute significantly to outcome (or other dependent variable), especially when combined with yet other to-be-identified potential active ingredients. Ingredients identifying questions may also be raised about combinations of two ("bidifferential," e.g., patient type 1 matched with therapist type X) or three ("tridifferential," e.g., patient type 1 matched with therapist type X matched with treatment type A) combinations. As one shifts from examining the impact on dependent variables of single ingredients to the impact of two or three or more such ingredients, one is shifting from the preprescriptive, ingredients-identifying phase to, progressively, the testing of increasingly more complex and complete full prescriptions, i.e., one is increasingly actually addressing the patients X therapists X treatments contemporary ideal outcome question in psychotherapy research noted previously. Again with regards to therapist empathy, such bidifferential and tridifferential questions will (and are beginning to) take form in a few ways, especially however around the therapist–patient relationship. Are there therapists qualities that when matched with particular patient qualities result in enhanced therapist empathy for the client? Are there empathy-enhancing consequences of therapist–client similarity, complementarity or differences on certain psychological dimensions? Parallel questions can be and have been raised about the relevance for therapist empathy of therapist–client degree of similarity–dissimilarity on an array of demographic qualities—sex, race, socioeconomic status. Let us see what the evidence to data reveals. What follows, therefore, is a statement reflecting unidifferential and bidifferential (there have been no three-way factorial studies) research seeking to identify therapist, patient, relationship, and therapy antecedants and concommitants of therapist empathy.

The level of psychotherapist or counselor empathy appears to be associated, first of all, with certain trait-like therapist qualities, ingredients of potential utility for the prescriptive selection and matching purposes at the heart of this section. The therapist's level of empathy has been shown to be positively associated with his or her cognitive flexibility (Brewer, 1974; Passons & Olsen, 1969), cognitive differentiation (Huth, 1979), conceptual level (Kimberlin & Friesen, 1977), perceptual sensitivity (Brewer, 1974), field dependence (Huth, 1979), tolerance of ambiguity (Jones, 1974), dominance (Bergin & Solomon, 1963), and to relate negatively to therapist dogmatism (Tosi, 1970), depression (Bergin & Jasper, 1969; Bergin & Solomon, 1963), psychasthenia (Bergin & Jasper, 1969; Bergin & Solomon, 1968), and need for consistency and order (Bergin & Solomon, 1963). No significant relationships have emerged between therapist empathy and his or her open-mindedness (Passons & Olsen, 1969), state anxiety (Huth, 1979), or intelligence or academic achievement (Bergin & Jasper, 1969; Bergin & Solomon, 1963). On an array of demographic criteria, therapist empathy has been shown to be associated with a therapist history of having personally experienced the same core problem as the client (Nehr & Dickens, 1975), with being a professional rather than paraprofessional (Brannon, 1976) an experienced rather than inexperienced therapist (Mullen & Abeles, 1971), and with the number of hours of personal therapy experienced (Peebles, 1980). No doubt artifactually, rated therapist empathy has also been significantly associated with the rated physical attractiveness, but not rated vocal attractiveness, of the therapist (Munig, 1979).

We have described a nomethetic net depicting who the empathic therapist is— cognitive, perceptual, and personality correlates of rated empathy. How else is he or she to be known? A series of behaviorally oriented investigations have studied the linguistic, paralinguistic, positional, gestural, proxemic, and other nonverbal covariates of therapist empathy. This research not only bears further on prescriptive markers but provides an array of beginning clues to understand just how broadly empathy—in Rogers' (1957) terms, an attitude—finds overt, concrete expression within the psychotherapeutic encounter. Hargrove (1974) found that high-empathy in contrast to low-empathy therapists had longer response times and were more likely to remain silent when the client paused, i.e., in both ways they allowed the client more time to express himself or herself, they interrupted many fewer times, and talked fewer times but for longer periods when they did speak. This last finding may point to an especially noteworthy aspect of the empathic therapist's verbal behavior, because several studies have reported significant correlations between therapist empathy and the total length or duration of his or her statements in the therapeutic hour (e.g., Carothers & Inslee, 1974; Hargrove, 1974; Matarazzo & Wiens, 1977).

In the nonverbal realm, Smith–Hanen (1977) showed that both therapist arm and leg position significantly effected his or her rated empathy, though degree of body movement did not. Arms crossed and legs crossed so that the ankle of one leg rests on the knee of the other were the two positions rated least empathic. Tepper and Haase (1978) found positive evidence for facial expression, vocal intonation, eye contact, and trunk lean correlates of therapist empathy, as have Brown (1980) (for facial expression and vocal intonation), Seay and Altebruse (1979) (for smiling), and Haase and Tepper (1972) (for eye contact, trunk lean, and close distance). The relative potency of these findings, as well as the price heretofore paid by the almost singular reliance upon *audio-only* recordings of therapist behavior in past psychotherapy studies of empathy, is made clear by Haase and Tepper's (1972) comment that:

> The most significant finding centers around the fact that with respect to the main effects, the nonverbal components in the model accounted for slightly more than twice as much variance in the judged level of empathy as did the verbal message. This finding suggests that empathy is communicated in more than one channel and moreover that to rely solely on the verbal content of the message reduces the accuracy of the judgment by 66%. (p. 421)

These then are therapist qualities that have been identified as antecedants, correlates, and consequents of therapist empathy. But is it only the therapist who determines the level of his or her own empathy toward a given patient? Truax thought so (Truax, 1963; Truax & Carkhuff, 1967). In his research:

> different therapists produced different levels of accurate empathy when interacting with the same set of patients ($p < .01$). In sharp contrast, different patients did not receive different levels of accurate empathy when interacting with the same set of therapists ($p < .40$). The data, then, suggest that it is the therapist who determines the level of accurate empathy. (p. 258)

Whereas some independent research exists that has been viewed as supporting this position (Bleyle, 1973; Cochrane, 1972; Mitchell, Truax, Bozarth, & Krauft, 1973; Pengel, 1979; Prager, 1970; Taylor, 1972), much of this research is interpretable in a manner similar to Mitchell, Bozarth, and Krauft's (1977) reflection upon the Mitchell et al. (1973) investigation:

In the Mitchell et al. (1973) study, then, in which the clients were chosen for therapy by their therapists, the levels of empathy, warmth, and genuineness received by the pairs of clients of the therapists were moderately consistent. It should be noted, of course, that the percentage of variance accounted for was only 24%, 21%, and 17% respectively. Clearly there were other factors which affected the levels of interpersonal skills received by the clients (p. 492)

To take a singular position in this domain, to claim that it is *only* the therapist (or *only* the patient) who determines the level of therapist empathy, is patently to reinvent the uniformity myth. Of course, the therapist is a major determinant of his or her own level of empathic skill in any given psychotherapeutic encounter. But it has also been more than amply demonstrated that patients, too, may differentially "pull" diverse empathic responses from therapists (Alexik & Carkhuff, 1967; Carkhuff & Alexik, 1967; Friel, Kratochvil, & Carkhuff, 1968; Houts, MacIntosh, & Moos, 1969; Moos & MacIntosh, 1970; VanderVeen, 1965). In fact, beyond these few demonstrations that either experimentally primed or actual clients are able to successfully influence the facilitative offerings of therapists with whom they are interacting, *which* patient characteristics may differentially influence therapist empathy has to a considerable extent already been empirically established. Therapists differ in the empathy they offer as a function in part of client affective ambivalence (Kimberlin & Friesen, 1977), friendliness (Rappaport, 1975), hostility (Blakeley, 1973; Roberts, 1977; Taylor, 1975), experiencing level (Abec, 1975), anxiety (Adams, 1980), depression (Steinitz, 1976), compliance (Ham, 1980), degree of disturbance (Dubnicki, 1977), degree of subjective discomfort (Steinitz, 1976), and such demographic characteristics as client sex (Cartright & Lerner, 1963; Petro & Hansen, 1977; Yergensen, 1978), socioeconomic status (Jones, 1975; Yergensen, 1978), and physical disability (McKay, 1979).

Thus it appears that a broad array of both therapist characteristics and qualities of the patient influence or covary with therapist empathy. Just as it has been shown that therapist empathy gains its significance for therapeutic outcome only to the degree that it is actually a perceptual reality for the client, client variables too, including those just enumerated, can only have their influence upon therapist empathy dyadically, as they are perceived, processed, and responded to by the therapist. In this sense, all the therapist and client antecedants, concommitants, and consequents presented to this point are also appropriately viewed as relationship variables. Their influence upon empathy is mediated by reciprocal therapist–patient perceptions of one another. There are a few studies of the network of variables that influence, covary with, or grow from therapist empathy that examine therapist–patient relationship variables even more directly.

Therapist–patient relationship studies of empathy are those in which a characteristic of *both* members of the dyad—sometimes the same characteristic, sometimes not—is examined for its conjoint influence upon or covariation with the level of therapist empathy. There have not been many such studies, and those that have been conducted are primarily matching studies of one of two types. In the first, the degree of therapist–patient similarity or sameness on a given dimension is examined for its effects upon therapist empathy. As has been true for most therapist–patient similarity investigations in other realms of psychotherapy research (Goldstein, 1971; Mendelsohn, 1966; Pepinsky & Karst, 1964; Welkowitz, Cohen, & Ortmeyer, 1967), those in the empathy domain have generally failed to find support for their major predictions (Bleyle, 1973; Lesser, 1961; Lubin, 1979; Pitt, 1979; Tully, 1974). As we and others have noted elsewhere, such research appears to suffer from a problem of conceptualization. The antecedants of dyadic compatability, or other relationship consequent—such as heightened empathy—seem to us to be generally multiply determined. Whether a husband and wife are reciprocally attracted, whether a parent disciplines a child satisfactorily, whether a therapist deeply understands a client's affective meanings results, in each instance, from the similarity, complementarity, and difference of the two members of the dyad on *several* dimensions and not, as overly simply operationalized in the studies just cited, their similarity on a single dimension.

The second type of matching study is that in which a therapist characteristic and a *different* patient characteristic are predicted to lead to optimal affective, cognitive, or unspecified compatability, with such heightened compatability functioning as an intervening variable that in turn results in specific beneficial consequences—such as enhanced levels of therapist empathy. Beutler, Johnson, Neville, and Workman (1972) conducted one such investigation. Utilizing the Whitehorn and Betz (1954) procedure for categorizing psychotherapists, they found substantial support for their differential prediction that A-type therapists would be significantly more empathic than B-type therapists with schizophrenic patients, and that the reverse would be the case for neurotic patients. In our schema (Goldstein & Stein, 1976), this result is an important, prescription-building, bidifferential finding and represents precisely the type of investigation we feel is especially needed in this domain. This conclusion is underscored by the results of the final matching studies we report. Heck and Davis (1973) were interested in the relationship of therapist conceptual level, a cognitive style characteristic, and therapist empathy. Their's was a unidifferential study in which two categories of conceptual level, high and low, were compared for their association with empathy. Although their result, as predicted, showed high-conceptual level therapists to be significantly more empathic, the suspicion emerged that this result might well not hold across all types of patients. In fact, taking the same view that we have in the present chapter, namely that therapist empathy level is *both* therapist and patient determined, Heck and Davis (1973) comment: ''Presumably, between different counselors there are different base levels of empathic capability, but this is quite different from assuming that empathy remains constant for any single counselor across different clients'' (p.

101). Responding bidifferentially to these results, Kimberlin and Friesen (1977) studied the interaction between therapist conceptual level (high vs. low) and the ambivalence reflected in client affective statements (present vs. absent). As they had predicted, high-conceptual level therapists were significantly more empathic than their low-conceptual level counterparts in response to ambivalent, but not nonambivalent, client standards.

In our earlier description of a prescriptive orientation toward psychotherapy research, we portrayed it ultimately as an effort to optimally match patients with therapists with treatments. Our specific focus thus far, however, has been only on patients and therapists (and their relationship), and not upon the treatment ingredient in the prescriptive mix. What of treatment? Truax (1966) claimed early that empathy mattered for outcome in a broad array of different treatments. Has his claim been substantiated? Perhaps it is yet too early to tell. Findings reported by Bergin and Suinn (1975), Garfield and Bergin (1971), and Mitchell et al. (1973) combine to suggest that in therapies conducted, for example, by analytic, client-centered and eclectic therapists, it is mainly for the client centered that therapist empathy and patient change were related. Yet analog format comparisons of psychodynamic, behavioristic, and humanistic interventions tend to yield a different conclusion, that intervenor empathy may be consequential across such diversely oriented therapies (Fischer, Paveza, Kikerty, Hubbard, & Graysen, 1975; Traemeo–Ploetz, 1980). This tentative view gains at least the beginnings of nonanalog support in findings of the importance of therapist empathy for patient change in actual therapies as diverse as time-limited group psychotherapy (Truax, Wargo, & Silber, 1966) and rational restructuring (Smith, 1979). Finally, it may be noted that the ''therapy'' may be a significant prescriptive ingredient not only in the usual ''what type of'' sense, but also with regard to special aspects of its utilization. Gurman (1973), for example, proposes in his ''empathic specificity hypothesis'' that therapist empathy matters most (or only) for outcome as that empathy is directed toward the client's core emotional problems. Mitchell et al. (1977) speculate that there may exist stage-of-therapy effects, such that the empathy-outcome relationship will vary as a function of how early or late in the psychotherapeutic sequence it is—with these authors placing special importance upon early therapy empathy.

SUMMARY

Early psychotherapy research too sweepingly concluded that high levels of therapist empathy enhanced therapeutic outcome whoever the patient and therapist were, and whatever the therapy was. Subsequent investigation and reflection led to a more moderate view, one that saw therapist empathy being facilitative in some instances, not in others—but which, and when, with whom, by whom? Empathy-in-psychotherapy research has entered a prescriptive phase. A beginning has been made at pointing toward therapist, patient, relationship, and to a lesser extent, treatment variables as prescriptive markers, that is, participant qualities whose reflection in the matching of therapists and patients, and in the implementation of their psychotherapy, are likely to lead to heightened levels of psychotherapist empathy and the beneficial outcome consequences that often derive therefrom.

6 Educational Consequences

Humanistic education has emerged as a major philosophical and applied direction in American educational thinking in recent decades. Its roots include the existential writings of May (1969) and Maslow (1962, 1971), self-theory (Kelley, 1962), the person-centered perspectives of Combs (1962) and Rogers (1983), and the diverse expressions of interest in what has come to be called, collectively, affective education (Chase, 1975; Ringness, 1975; Weinstein & Fantini, 1970). It is generally an experiential perspective, one in which the teaching–learning process is not something done *to* the learner but, instead, in which growth emerges largely from the facilitative consequences of a special teacher–pupil relationship (Brookover, 1945; Davidson & Lang, 1960; Dixon & Morse, 1961; Gage & Suci, 1951; Lewis, Lovell, & Jessee, 1965). Rogers (1983) more recently articulated this perspective with particular clarity:

> the initiation of such learning rests not upon the teaching skills of the leader, not upon scholarly knowledge of the field, not upon curricular planning, not upon use of audiovisual aids, not upon the programmed learning used, not upon lectures and presentations, not upon an abundance of books, though each of these might at one time or another be utilized as an important resource. No, the facilitation of significant learning rests upon certain attitudinal qualities that exist in the personal relationship between the facilitator and the learner. We came upon such findings first in the field of psychotherapy, but now there is evidence that shows these findings apply in the classroom as well. (p. 121)

As he had earlier proposed held true for psychotherapy, Rogers (1983) similarly suggested that facilitator (teacher) empathy was a central ingredient in these growth-enhancing relationships. He comments:

144

A further element that establishes a climate for self-initiated, experiential learning is empathic understanding. When the teacher has the ability to understand the student's reactions from the inside, has a sensitive awareness of the way the process or education and learning seems *to the student*, then again the likelihood of significant learning is increased. . . . When there is a sensitive empathy. . .the reaction in the learner follows something of this pattern, 'At last someone understands how it feels and seems to be *me* without wanting to analyze or judge me. Now I can blossom and grow and learn. This attitude of standing in the other's shoes, of viewing the world through the student's eyes, is almost unheard of in the classroom. One could listen to thousands of ordinary classroom interactions without coming across one instance of clearly communicated, sensitively accurate, empathic understanding. But it has a tremendously releasing effect when it occurs. (p. 125)

In putting forth this view, Rogers both echoes and elaborates upon earlier champions of the significance of teacher empathy in the learning process (Chambers, 1957; Clayton, 1943; Melton, 1965; Thelen—see Withall & Lewis, 1963). These earlier writers, however, did not have available to them, as we do now, a substantial series of empathy-in-education empirical studies. These several investigations form the primary substantive concern of the present chapter, allowing us to speak evidentially about the degree and circumstances of facilitativeness upon learning of teacher-initiated and student-perceived empathy.

RESEARCH EVIDENCE

In the chronology of empathy outcome research examined in this book, that occurring in the context of psychotherapy began and flourished first. As these psychotherapy studies unfolded—particularly the earlier, especially enthusiastic research reports—some writers began to propose that empathy might have similarly facilitative effects in still other contexts in which an individual's growth, broadly defined, appeared (to some at least) to depend in substantial part on a special interpersonal relationship. As noted earlier, several humanistically oriented writers, including especially Carl Rogers, provided the philosophical rationale and impetus for this view. As had also largely been true in the psychotherapy domain, one of the initial ''bridging'' studies was conducted by Truax (Truax & Tatum, 1966).

Truax and Tatum (1966) hypothesized that preschool children receiving high levels of teacher empathy, warmth, and genuineness would exhibit greater positive change in socialization adjustment than would youngsters receiving low amounts of these teacher conditions. Twenty 4-year-olds participated as study subjects. It is recalled from Chapter 5 that in the psychotherapy realm the level of relationship between empathy and outcome varied greatly depending on from whose perspective—therapist, rater, or patient—empathy was judged. So, too, apparently in an educational context. No significant relationship emerged between empathy as rated by independent classroom observers and student change toward positive social adjustment. Such student behavior did relate significantly, however, to teacher self-rated empathy. With a tone of the same "creeping significance" (mixed findings in the results section summarized as unequivocally positive by the conclusion) characteristic of some of the early empathy-in-psychotherapy studies, the authors (Truax & Tatum, 1966) (over) conclude:

> The importance of unconditional warmth and empathic understanding in facilitating constructive personality change in the human encounter is clear, regardless of the age of the human beings involved, regardless of the reason for the encounter, and regardless of the setting in which the encounter takes place. (p. 462)

Because our enthusiasm for the broad impact of empathy on human behavior is made explicit at many points in this book, we hope we have by this point made equally clear our objection to the overly expansive, "one-true-light," "empathy-is-good-for-all, everywhere" type of thinking reflected in the foregoing quotation. Its potency is broad and diverse but not pervasive and encompassing. A number of the other empathy-outcome studies conducted in educational contexts add further support to what we perceive as a more balanced and prescriptive view of the role of empathy in human relations.

Empathy and Outcome: Achievement Criteria

Wagner (1969) found a significant empathy-achievement relationship at the college student level, but for student-perceived teacher empathy, not teacher-perceived, a finding replicated by Robinson, Wilson, & Robinson (1978) at the sixth-grade level. This relationship not only varied, as noted, by locus of empathy rating, but also by type of course. For reasons Wagner (1969) speculates may have to do with achievement anxiety and its reduction, the empathy-achievement (final examination score) relationship was strongly positive in algebra classes, essentially absent in introductory business courses. While both the Wagner (1969) and Robinson et al. (1978) studies add to the robustness of the empathy-achievement relationship, it must be noted that both also suffer from the same type of measurement circularity not infrequent in psychotherapy empathy investigations, circularity present when, as here, one respondent (here the student) is the source for both the independent variable (empathy) and dependent variable (achievement) data.

One further moderator of the empathy-outcome relationship that emerged in the context of psychotherapy concerned when in the course of treatment such therapist behavior was manifest. Gurman (1977), it is recalled, proposed that early in therapy, during the initial rapport-building phases and before the full emergence of the client's core problems, helper empathy may be especially important. In an empathy-outcome study also looking at stage of intervention, but in an educational context, Stoffer (1970) found directly contrasting results. Working in this instance with elementary schoolchildren, no relationship emerged early in the school term between teacher empathy and student achievement, but a substantial positive relationship between these variables did appear later in the term. In addition to this finding, two of Stoffer's (1970) concluding speculations are of special interest in that they also help us further extend certain of our psychotherapy-relevant prescriptive inferences to the realm of the teacher–student relationship. In Chapter 5, we found ourselves in agreement with those holding that in each therapist–patient dyad, *both* participants share responsibility for the level of therapist-offered, patient-perceived empathy that emerges. Further, we held that some (unknown) portion of the level of therapist empathy is attributable to the diagnostic type of client involved. Stoffer (1970) observes in these regards:

> This study has assumed that the helpers [teachers] are primarily responsible for the level of conditions present in the relationship. There is considerable evidence which suggests that the level of conditions are a result of dynamic interaction between helper and child. . . . This study has not investigated the possibility that certain types of behavior disorders profit more or less from the therapeutic conditions. For example, shy, withdrawn children seem to respond better than acting-out children to this kind of relationship. (p. 227)

Our discussion thus far has begun to make clear that in contemplating the nature and strength of the empathy-achievement relationship in educational contexts a number of methodological provisos, stipulations, qualifications, moderator variables, or prescriptive considerations must be factored into our thinking. In these regards, we have thus far mentioned a tendency toward "creeping significance", overreliance on a "one-true-light' perspective, circularity of measurement, and variation in results as a function of source of data, timing in measurement, type of academic course, and diagnostic considerations. And there is more. Whereas Morgan (1979) is correct in pointing out substantial potential differences for the role of empathy between psychotherapy and education, it is nevertheless the case that most of the methodological issues raised vis a vis therapy—empathy research also apply here. In addition to those just enumerated, a substantial number are as yet even unraised by educational researchers of the empathic process. The role of segment or observation sampling and length, the underrepresentation of teacher nonverbal behaviors, the contribution of rater sex and experience, treating very different achievement indices as essentially equivalent, diversity in the conceptual and operational definition of empathy itself, and, as part of this, confusion of empathy-as-attitude with empathy-as-behavior, are among these several sources of possible methodological bias, and each in turn deserves careful consideration and operational attention.

Yet, in spite of all we have just proposed, and in spite of two reported failures to find the predicted relationship (Aspy & Roebuck, 1972; Christenberry, 1974), the evidence already presented and to be presented nevertheless underscores the robustness of the empathy-achievement relationship. Scheuer (1971) examined the teacher empathy—student academic gain relationship in a study involving 278 secondary school students, most of whom were minority-group members and their 20 teachers. A strong, positive relationship obtained. Mantaro (1971) reported similarly significant results in a large sample ($N = 435$) study involving fifth- and sixth-grade elementary school children. Two investigations at the college student level yielded further confirming results (Chang, 1973; Perkins, 1971). Perhaps the most substantial investigative contribution to conclusions about the educational consequences of empathy has come from the active re-search program of Aspy and his coworkers. Although certainly not free from the methodological concerns just examined, their collective findings add substantially to our belief that teacher empathy relates strongly and positively to student achievement. Aspy (1972), in his first such investigation, administered selected subtests of the Stanford Achievement Test to 120 third-grade students at the beginning and conclusion of the academic year. Reading groups conducted by their teachers throughout the year were tape recorded and reliably rated for teacher empathy by independent judges. Change scores on four of the five achievement tests revealed significantly greater gain for those youngsters receiving high, as compared to low levels of teacher empathy. Aspy and Hadlock (1966) found that elementary school students taught by teachers high in accurate empathy gained 2.5 years in reading achievement during the 5-month study period, whereas those taught by low-empathy teachers gained only 0.7 years. Not unimportantly, the investigators also report that the truancy rate in the latter classes was twice that for those taught by high-empathy teachers. Thus encouraged, Aspy and Roebuck (1977) conducted a substantially larger investigation, involving 600 teachers and 10,000 students from kindergarten through twelfth grade. As before, significant positive relationships obtained for teacher empathy and student (math and reading) achievement scores. In several empathy-outcome studies, as we examine shortly, significant associations have been found between teacher empathy and educationally significant outcome criteria other than achievement per se. In this regard, Aspy and Roebuck (1977) report that students of high-empathy teachers, compared to their low-empathy counterparts, (1) miss fewer days of school during the academic year, (2) have increased (more positive) self-concept scores, (3) commit fewer acts of vandalism, and (4) present fewer disciplinary problems. Of perhaps special interest, the investigators also report that a number of the apparent achievement and nonachievement benefits associated with high levels of teacher empathy are cumulative, i.e., the more consecutive years that given students had high-empathy teachers, the greater the associated gains. Finally with regard to student achievement criteria, cross-cultural replications and extensions of the Aspy program by Tausch

(Tausch, Kettner, Steinbach, & Tonnies, 1973; Tausch & Tausch, 1980; Tausch, Witter, & Albus, 1976) successfully demonstrate the significant teacher empathy—student achievement association in a substantially different educational context.

Empathy and Outcome: Nonachievment Criteria

What else may be said about empathy and both its correlates and consequences in educational settings? Diskin (1956) reported that teacher trainees high in empathy had classes evidencing high levels of harmonious peer relationships, a finding replicated by Walter (1977) 20 years later. Not just interpersonal relations, but also more intrapsychic qualities seem to benefit from a relationship with a highly empathic teacher, e.g., a variety of self-concept changes (Berens, 1976). Emmerling (1961) found significant positive intercorrelations between teacher empathy, acceptance of students, congruence, and pupil centeredness.

Female students were more prone to view their teacher as empathic than were males, according to Brown (1980), and the younger the student—in this study of first, third, and fifth graders—the greater the likelihood the teacher would be seen as highly empathic. Hawks and Egbert (1954), Dixon and Morse (1961), and Lifton (1958) all reported significant relationships between teacher empathy and his or her rated competence. A small number of interesting and at times provocative correlates of teacher empathy have been reported at the college level. Rector (1953) found a moderate inverse relationship between instructor empathic ability and years of teaching experience. A parallel negative association emerged between empathic ability and professional rank. Instructor empathy also correlated negatively and significantly with class size, the smaller the class the higher his or her average empathy level. Perhaps the most consequential result emerging from Rector's (1953) work is a substantial, significant positive correlation between instructor–student empathy toward one another, suggesting precisely the type of reciprocal influence upon mutual empathy in teacher–student pairs that we proposed earlier was the case for psychotherapist–patient dyads. Perkins (1971), in addition to finding female professors to be more empathic than their male colleagues, also reported results somewhat more welcome to this book's senior author than Rector's (1953) inverse relationships between empathy and both experience and professorial rank. In Perkins' (1971) findings, empathy was significantly positively correlated with both the professor's age and length of time at his or her institution of employment.

We have thus far in this chapter articulated a humanistic educational philosophy and one of its overt expressions, accurate empathic communication, and cited studies largely supporting—their methodological faults notwithstanding—both the student-achievement and nonachievement correlates and consequences of such teacher empathy. But a large piece of the puzzle is still missing. If one subscribes to the Rogerian position that facilitator (therapist, teacher, parent) empathy is most appropriately considered an *attitude,* it becomes central for both understanding and implementation purposes to inquire how this attitude finds behavioral expression. What does the high-empathy teacher actually do? What overt processes mediate between teacher empathy and the broad potpourri of achievement and nonachievement empathy correlates and consequences we have just reported?

MEDIATING PROCESSES

Aspy and Roebuck (1975), in a significant empathy process study, found that high-empathy teachers, in comparison to teachers rated low in classroom expression of empathy, use significantly more praise and encouragement, use less criticism, more frequently accept student expressions of feeling, elicit more student-initiated talk, have fewer instances of silence or confusion, and smile more at their students. High-empathy teachers, according to this research report, also use fewer controlling behaviors, fewer time deadlines, place more emphasis upon creativity and productivity than evaluation, rely more on cooperative goal planning between teacher and student, and more fully individualize both the contents of their instructional communications and the nature of classroom projects and displays. Clearly, teacher empathy is embedded in an impressive cluster of diverse "good teacher" behaviors, a conclusion that is altered at most moderately by Wisdom's (1978) only partial success in replicating the array of Aspy and Roebuck (1975) findings.

How can identified correlates and mediators of teacher empathy such as these be organized into a coherent, investigatable and, ultimately, teachable framework. Two educational theorists have tried. As part of an effort to better understand differences in the nature and role of empathy in teacher–student relationships involving disturbed versus more typical children, Morgan (1979) proposed a theoretical model describing the channels by means of which teacher empathy may be expressed. According to this model, teacher empathy is reflected in sensitivity to the child's stress, a sensitivity demonstrable via four alternative channels, each of which has several possible behavioral expressions. This model is depicted in Fig. 6.1.

Morgan (1979) comments:

> According to this model, a teacher expresses empathy in four ways: (1) through the management of instruction; (2) by the organization of the environment, (3) with verbal responses and actions that show understanding and caring for the child's feelings and emotional well-being, and (4) employing their own human qualities as part of the program for the child. (p. 451)

Examples of the concrete teacher behaviors that may be employed as overt expressions of these four channels include, according to Morgan (1979):

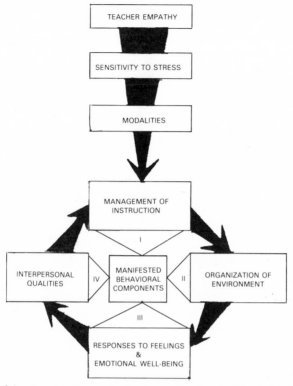

FIG. 6.1.   Empathic Process for Teachers of Emotionally Disturbed Children

I. MANAGEMENT OF INSTRUCTION
   A. Devises legitimate reasons to change an activity when the child is frustrated.
   B. Begins with a guaranteed success.
   C. Personalizes lesson to teach concepts.
II. ORGANIZATION OF THE ENVIRONMENT
   A. Gives the child a time and a place to be alone and quiet.
   B. Does not send the child to someone else for punishment.
   C. Room itself (space and furnishings) is organized and uncluttered.
III. RESPONSES TO FEELINGS AND EMOTIONAL WELL-BEING
   A. Senses when the child is on the verge of trouble and offers help before it's requested or a blow-up occurs.
   B. Identifies for children feelings they are unable to verbalize.
   C. Stays physically close and lavishes assurances.
IV. INTERPERSONAL QUALITIES
   A. Has a sense of humor.
   B. Is warm and can openly show affection to the child.
   C. Appears calm, relaxed, speaks softly and smiles frequently.

Morgan's (1979) proposal is an important heuristic statement. It is one thing to know, as much of the empathy-outcome research tells us, that teacher empathy under a variety of conditions is associated with an array of positive student achievement and nonachievement outcomes. But to be better able to specify the conditions under which such findings obtain, to be better able to understand the several possible processes that mediate between empathy and outcome, and to be better able to train teachers in these processes, a mediation model is necessary. Morgan's (1979) is a very substantial step in this direction, and it well deserves serious research scrutiny.

Another such attempt at suggesting a mediational model for the empathy-outcome relationship has been provided by Kieran (1979). She, too, essentially asked the question, "What do highly empathic teachers actually do?" Her response, as we see, is of the same multiprocess, behavioral specificity as Morgan's (1979), but goes well beyond Morgan, and in a variety of ways thus seems to us to have special clarifying potential.

Bringing this chapter, in a sense, full circle, Kieran (1979) begins by placing her effort squarely in the purview of a humanistic orientation to the teaching–learning process. She comments:

> The role of the teacher in this process is that of facilitator, one who forms a relationship with the learner that, according to Combs (1962) 'assists, helps, sides, ministers to a growing, living, dynamic organism already in the process of becoming.' (p. 70) From this vantage point teaching is seen as one of the helping professions. As 'helpers' do in other such professions, for example, guidance counseling, the ministry, psychotherapy, the teacher uses herself . . . as an instrument to form a relationship with another human being which helps him to grow. (p. 17)

In Kieran's (1979) investigation, research subjects were five teachers selected by both their school's administration and independent measurement as highly empathic. Each teacher in this preschool context had a class of 15 to 18 three- to 5-year-old children from diverse cultural and socioeconomic backgrounds. Extensive videotaped behavioral observation was made in each of the five participating classes, yielding a total of 12½ hours of taped teacher–child interaction across classes, across activities, and across teachers and children. Teacher–student exchanges were systematically content analyzed by a panel of judges asked to sort the raw data (145 teacher–student interactions) dichotomously into those that did and did not fit the study's definition of empathy. Forty interactions were reliably judged to reflect teacher empathy, and it is these interactions that in the second and finer grain content analysis that then followed formed the basis for the empathic response classification system then developed. Kieran (1979) proposed that the empathic process might be both best understood and comprehensively described if the classification system reflected both *how* the teacher communicated, i.e., Process Categories, and *what* she elected to communicate about, i.e., Content Categories. In the content analysis system of mediational processes that thus resulted, six process categories and six content categories emerged. These categories, describing both the "how" and the "what" of what empathic teachers actually do, are presented next.

Process Categories

1. Verify.   The teacher states what she believes are the child's feelings or intentions and offers it as a guess to the child for verification. The purpose of her question is to confirm or disconfirm her interpretation of the child's verbal or nonverbal messages and to make the child more aware of his feelings or how to express his feelings in an appropriate way for the situation. Examples: "Are you feeling _____ this morning?" or "Do you want to _____?"

2. Reflect.   The teacher makes a statement that describes or mirrors the child's feelings that have been expressed or have been implied by his actions. Sometimes her statement is a repetition or paraphrase of what the child has said with emphasis on a key word. Example: "That really makes you angry."

3. Accept.   The teacher makes a statement that communicates to the child that it is natural for him to feel the way he does. She does not, however, communicate that she shares these feelings or perceptions. Her statement might take the form of: "It's OK to feel _____" or "You can do _____ if you want to."

4. Validate.   The teacher makes a statement that communicates to the child that it is natural or appropriate for him to feel the way he does and she shares or could share the same feelings or perceptions. Examples: "I would feel the same way" or "I don't blame you for feeling that way" (meaning 'I would feel the same way.'). Occasionally a form of validation occurs indirectly when the teacher makes her statement by speaking to a second child. Examples: "No wonder she felt that way."

5. Extend.   Once the child's feelings or intentions have been expressed and/or explored, the teacher responds to the child's experience in a way that extends or further pushes the child's *thinking* about his feelings or his actions based on his feelings. The teacher's statements may either be declarative or interrogative. A form of extending can occur even though the child's feelings are not directly expressed or explored. In these instances the understanding of the feelings or intentions is implied indirectly by the teacher's communication to the child that consists only of statements or questions that facilitate the child's thinking.

6. Prescribe.   Once feelings or intentions have been expressed and/or explored, the teacher gives the information or makes suggestions for *actions* that might help the child cope with his feelings or intentions. These prescriptions might include suggestions about what the child alone could do, or what the child and someone else could do, or what someone else alone could do to respond to, alleviate, or act upon the child's feelings or intentions. A form of prescription can occur even though the child's feelings are not directly expressed or explored. In these instances the understanding of the feelings or intentions is implied indirectly by the teacher's statement that consists only of helpful information or suggestions of what could be done. Examples of Prescriptive teacher statements might be: "You can say _____, or "You and _____ could _____."

Content Categories

1. Child's Psychological or Emotional State of Being.   Teacher's statement refers to: (1) the psychological state of the child. Topics might include competence, affiliation (caring for someone), ego strength (being in control or having a strong sense of self); (2) the emotional state of the child. Topics might include loneliness, sadness, anger, frustration, boredom; (3) the child's positive or negative feelings or how the child might feel about an activity; e.g., enjoyment, ease or difficulty of participating in some aspect of an activity, the relief that an activity did or did not take place.

2. Child's Physical State of Being.   Content of teacher's statement refers to the physical state of being of the child. Topics might include pain, sickness.

3. Child's Involvement in an Activity.   Subcategories:

A. Initiation of Activity:
Teacher's statement refers to child's participation in an activity that may begin momentarily or sometime in the near future.
B. Engagement in Ongoing Activity:
Teacher's statement refers to child's participation in an activity already underway. Might include the conditions of involvement.
C. Continuation of Involvement in Ongoing Activity:
Teacher's statement refers to child's continued involvement in an activity. Might include the conditions of continuation.
D. Variation of Involvement or Change to Another Activity:
Teacher's statement refers to the conditions under which the child could or might change the nature of his involvement, terminate his involvement or change to a different activity.

4. Child's Possessions or Products of Activities.   Teacher's statement refers to something the child possesses, has made or is going to make.

5. Child's Coping with Emotions or Feelings. Teacher's statement contains: (1) a suggested insight or perspective on a situation or reinforces child's perspective; (2) suggested possibilities for acting upon a feeling; (3) suggested consideration of a specific action (verbal or behavioral); (4) suggestion(s) for carrying out a specific action to cope with an emotion or feeling.

Kieran (1979) presents satisfactory evidence that this content analysis system can be applied reliably by trained judges. She speculates creatively on both the demonstrable and the probable interrelationships between and among process and content categories, thus giving us at least a beginning sense of the flow or stream of empathic teacher–student interactions. These interrelationships are summarized succinctly by Kieran (1979) in Fig. 6.2. She comments:

> The larger boxes represent the Process categories. Two Process categories which have similar general functions share a common border: *Verify* and *Reflect* share the function of describing the child's emotions or feelings. *Accept* and *Validate* share the general function of communicating the naturalness, acceptability or validity of the child's feelings/emotions. *Extend* and *Prescribe* share the function of communicating information or suggestions to the child to help him cope with his emotions/feelings. Each Process box contains the Content categories which appeared in combination with the occurrence of the particular Process. Content boxes which overlap the shared border between two Process categories indicate that a given Content category appeared in combination with both Processes. (p. 81)

Kieran (1979) has thus provided an especially heuristic set of apparent process and content mediators of the empathic teacher–student interaction. Hopefully, her ground breaking effort will stimulate others to continue, elaborate, and carry forward this domain.

SUMMARY

We have held in this chapter that in spite of a series of yet to be resolved (and, in some instances, yet to even be raised) methodological problems, teacher empathy frequently appears to be substantially associated with student achievement gains as well as a variety of positive, nonachievement outcome criteria. How such a empathic attitude is behaviorally communicated by the teacher and, in response to which student behaviors, has been the target of both speculation and beginning investigation in important statements by Morgan (1979) and Kieran (1979). We closed our presentation of somewhat similar facts and events in the realm of empathy in psychotherapy on a prescriptive theme and would like to do so here also. A prescriptive orientation toward the educational process is not new, and those who have preceded us in this regard have had much to offer of use in the context of empathy in education research. The eventual questions to be answered must seek to specify which types of teachers paired with which types of students and engaging in which manifestations (process and content) of empathic

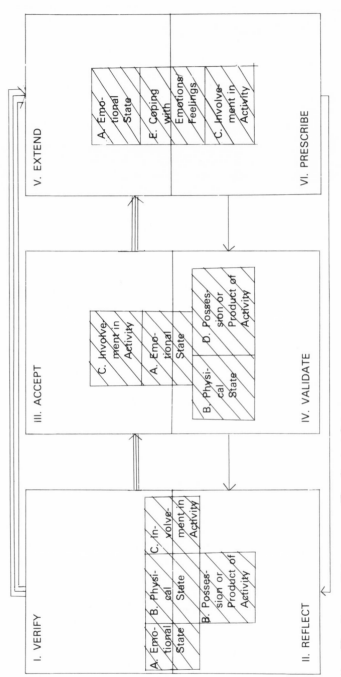

I. VERIFY

II. REFLECT

A. Emo-
tional
State

B. Physi-
cal
State

C. In-
volve-
ment in
Activity

B. Posses-
sion or
Product of
Activity

III. ACCEPT

IV. VALIDATE

C. Involve-
ment in
Activity

A. Emo-
tional
State

B. Physi-
cal
State

D. Posses-
sion or
Product of
Activity

V. EXTEND

VI. PRESCRIBE

A. Emo-
tional
State

E. Coping
with
Emotions/
Feelings

C. Involve-
ment in
Activity

Key: ☐ = Process Category   ▨ = Content Category

FIG. 6.2.   Model of Empathic Behavior in Teachers of Young Children

behavior will most effectively yield which types of educational outcomes. In planning, executing, and reflecting upon such prescriptive empathy research, we hold, one would do well to draw heavily upon the prescriptive thinking at the heart of Cronbach and Snow's (1977) work on aptitude treatment interactions, Hunt's (1971) conceptual systems matching model, Salomon's (1972) differential model of teaching, Stern's (1970) research on "people in context," and Harootunian's (1978) examination of all these perspectives for their teacher training implications. Clearly, the initial conceptual groundwork regarding prescriptiveness in education has been done. Its application to the domain of teacher empathy and its consequences is our logical next step.

7

Parenting Consequences

This chapter examines the theoretical and research literature on empathic parenting. Empathy in the domain of parenting shares common characteristics with the two other domains of adult empathy that we have discussed: empathy in psychotherapy and empathy in education. However, as we see, there are also important differences. These have mainly to do with the uniquely and intensely emotional, long-lasting, ever-developing investment that both parents and children have in their relationship. In the discussion to follow we first focus on the major theoretical approaches to understanding parent empathy. We then explore a number of important conceptual and methodological issues that need to be addressed by researchers in this area. And finally, we examine what is still a relatively small body of research on the development, consequences, and training of parental empathy.

THEORETICAL FRAMEWORKS FOR PARENTAL EMPATHY

The major theoretical underpinnings for understanding the importance of parental empathy have, historically, come from two main schools of personality development: the psychoanalytic-object relations school, which has focused on the role of maternal empathy and sensitivity in the very early parent–child relationship and the client-centered school, which has focused on parent empathy during childhood and adolescence. These approaches have influenced, and are reflected in, much of the ongoing parent-empathy research. We therefore review some of the major ideas of key writers within these two traditions.

Psychoanalytic and Object Relations Approaches

Orthodox psychoanalytic theory underplayed the importance of the real parent–child bond and focused, instead, on the viscissitudes of the developing child's fantasy life as he moved from the earliest dependence on the pleasure principle, to the later reliance on the reality principle. Yet, Freud did, at points, acknowledge the importance of the parent's ability to provide a stable, nurturing environment to the child, which at least implies an interest in, and attention to, the child's feelings and needs. Furthermore, it has been noted that there are elements of the successful practice of psychoanalytic therapy that are similar to our conceptions of empathic parenting. Both provide a safe, nurturant environment in which either the client or child can work through his problems. As Modell (1976) writes:

> There are actual elements in the analyst's technique that are reminiscent of an idealized maternal holding environment. The analyst is constant and reliable, he (sic) responds to the patient's affects, he accepts the patient; and his judgment is less critical and more benign: he is there primarily for the patient's needs and not for his own; he does not retaliate; and he does at times have a better grasp of the patient's inner psychic reality than does the patient himself and therefore may clarify what is bewildering and confusing (p. 261)

Kesterberg and Buelte (1977) have noted that aspects of nonverbal communication in psychotherapy and mothering are very similar, including the communication of empathy through mirroring, in which the infant and mother or client and therapist reflect back to each other a smile, a sigh, their rate of breathing, and even adjust their bodily postures to one another. Winnicott (1970) compares the parent's need to cope with "massive response processes" to the infant's needs with the therapist's attempts to cope with countertransference reactions to his patients. Once identified and analyzed, the therapist or parent is in a better position to respond empathically.

Psychoanalytic and object relations theorists tie the emergence of parental empathy to the earliest contacts that a parent (and in these writings it has been almost exclusively the mother that is the focus) has with the new infant. Primary in their thinking is that the mother and infant constitute an empathic unit such that it makes little sense to view the parent's empathic capacity separate from her intimate interactions with her very young child. Interestingly, although this approach was developed without a strong empirical base, we see later when we address the research on parent empathy that it is quite consistent in many respects with current literature on the transmission of emotions by parents to their children, as well as the literature on recognition of emotions by infants and young children.

Sullivan (1953) was one of the earliest personality theorists to address the importance of the mother–infant empathic system in the mother's ability to provide "tenderness" or nurturant caregiving. He believed that the infant's needs for tenderness were reciprocated by the mother's motivation to provide sensitivity and tenderness to her child:

> Even though the needs which I include when I speak of the generic need for tenderness are direct derivatives of disequilibrium arising in the physiochemical universe inside and outside the infant—that is, making up the infant and the necessary environment—nonetheless these generic needs all require cooperation from another; thus, the need for tenderness is ingrained from the very beginning of things as an interpersonal need. And the complementary need of the mothering one is a need to manifest appropriate activity, which may be called a general need to give tenderness or to behave tenderly, and thus, whatever tension and energy transformations may be mixed up in it, is again interpersonal in kind, if not in all details. (pp. 40–41)

Sullivan believes that a major threat to the infant's adaptation is caused by the mother's transmission of her own anxiety to her child. This anxiety is experienced differently by the infant than other types of tension states that are more specific and, therefore, more manageable. It is only when the maternal figure can provide an appropriate tender response, which Sullivan equates with empathy, that the infant can experience a reduction in tension and an increase in basic "interpersonal security."

From an object relations theoretical framework, Winnicott (1960, 1965, 1970) writes that in early infancy the "infant and the maternal care together form a unit . . . at the earliest stages the infant and the maternal care belong to each other and cannot be disentangled" (1960, pp. 39–40). Within this close-knit bond of mother–infant "mutuality" the mother provides the infant with a facilitative environment that consists especially of "holding." The term holding is a figurative one that connotes the entire spectrum of maternal activities that provide a facilitative environment to the infant, in addition to the actual physical contact of mother and infant when the child is being held. Winnicott (1965) states:

> Holding includes especially the physical holding of the infant, which is a form of loving. It is perhaps the only way in which a mother can show the infant her love. There are those who can hold an infant and those who cannot; the latter quickly produce in the infant a sense of insecurity, and distressed crying. All this leads right up to, includes, and co-exists with the establishment of the infant's first object relationships and his first experiences of instinctual gratification. (p. 49)

Winnicott (1965, 1970) believes that the mother's ability to provide such a holding environment is facilitated by a heightened "primary maternal preoccupation" that occurs toward the end of the pregnancy and for a few weeks after the birth, during which time the mother is especially given over to the care of the baby, which is first experienced like a part of herself, and with whom she is very much identified. During this period, Winnicott believes that the mother uses her own experiences as a very young child as the basis for her empathy with her baby, and she is herself in a dependent, vulnerable, and somewhat regressed state (Winnicott, 1965). However, whereas there does occur a natural preoccupation with mothering during the infant's first weeks and months, overall, adapting to the infant's maturational processes in a way that preserves mutuality and creates the optimal facilitating environment is a very complex process that makes tremendous demands on the mother.

Recently, the emphasis on the fused, dependent, and regressive nature of the mother's early empathy for her child has been criticized by several female writers who, nevertheless, view their work from the object relations perspective. Kaplan (1983) criticizes Winnicott's views of the "good enough mother" as a mother who can "fuse" with her infant in such a way as to be responsive to the child's need and feeling states. The problem with this, she argues, is that traditional views of development describe psychological maturation as involving self–other differentiation, firm ego boundaries, and the capacity for differentiation. Fusion and merger are seen as failures to attain such developments. She particularly criticizes Winnicott's discussion about the merger of mother and infant into a single unit, which can't be disentangled. At this point the mother is said to rely on identification with the infant to know what the infant feels like. Kaplan argues that, at best, the process described by Winnicott may be "regression in the service of empathy," in which temporary fusion is followed by separation. However, Kaplan believes that the emphasis is too much on regression and immaturity and that this does not give credit to the high level of maturation and competence that is required in true parent empathy. She writes: "[that this]. . .belies the mother's sense of a mature self co-existing with this intense affective connectedness and minimiz[es] the complexity of decision making and processing that also occurs" (p. 15). Instead, Kaplan proposes a model of empathy for both parenthood and psychotherapy, in which, rather than linking the affective regression and fusion with empathy's affective component and separation and differentiation with empathy's cognitive component, both affective connectedness and cognitive differentiation exist simultaneously in the mature empathic response. In this way, the parent or therapist "is both intimately connected with the other person and yet, without losing that connectedness, is in touch with her own individuality" (p. 14).

In a book that attempts to integrate psychoanalytic and object relations theory with the new and burgeoning research on infant development, Lichtenberg (1983) notes a major difference in both goals and orientation. The psychoanalytic and object relations tradition focuses on conflict, aggressive struggles, and primitive mechanisms. The new infant research, on the other hand, focuses on the developing mutuality and fit between mother and child. Thus, the former approach is oriented to what the infant has to overcome in order to engage in satisfactory object relations, whereas the new infant research focuses on the naturally occurring tendencies of parents and infants to actively seek out and secure the kinds of interactions and relationships that will lead to successful psychological and social development.

Client-Centered Theoretical Views of Parental Empathy

Although the psychoanalytic and object relations approaches emphasize the importance of empathy-like behaviors during the earliest phase of parenting, there is little attention given to the role that parent empathy might play during the childhood years and during adolescence. Furthermore, in the writings of these theorists it is difficult to differentiate those specific qualities that constitute empathy from other aspects of successful parenting, all of which ensure the maintenance of a facilitative environment in which the child can adaptively progress through the normal stages of psychosocial development. Finally, there is relatively little attention to individual differences in parent empathy, or its causes.

In contrast, Carl Roger's theory of personality development and client-centered therapy provides a theoretical account of the importance of parental empathy that does distinguish between parents' empathy and other parent attitudes and behaviors, and Rogers links parental empathy directly to the child's and adolescent's development of a basic sense of self. It therefore provides an integrated model of the importance of parent empathy during the course of a child's entire development.

Rogers (1951) defines the "self" as "an organized, fluid but consistent conceptual pattern of perceptions of characteristics and relationships of the 'I' or the 'me' together with values attached to these concepts" (p. 498). The child begins to develop the self-concept in infancy, as he begins to interact with the environment, at first nonverbally, and often unconsciously. Also, closely associated with the development of the self is an innate, but low-strength, motive toward fulfillment of the self called the *organismic valuing process,* which leads the child to positively value those experiences that he perceives as enhancing the self and to negatively evaluate experiences that are perceived as threatening to the self, or which do not enhance or maintain the self. Thus, the child's growing awareness of the self (e.g., "I experience") is accompanied by the further awareness of which activities enhance the self ("I like") and which activities block expression and fulfillment of the self ("I dislike").

As long as the child's environment provides a situation in which he receives unconditional positive regard from parents and significant others, he will perceive himself as lovable, worthy of love, and as having loving parents. These perceptions will become a core element of the developing structure of the self, which will be free to pursue "self-actualization" in line with the organismic valuing process. However, not all the child's behaviors will meet with parental approval. Rogers uses the example of a child who finds it satisfying and enhancing to hit or try to do away with his baby brother. However, punitive words and actions of his parents lead him to feel that, because he has these thoughts, he must be bad, his behavior must be bad, and that he cannot be loved or lovable when he thinks or behaves in this way. These "conditions of worth" are a serious threat to the child's developing sense of self. He is left with the dilemma that if he were to admit to awareness how hitting or wishing to do away with his baby brother would be satisfying, this would be inconsistent with an image of himself as being loved or lovable.

This type of dilemma usually results in the child's denial or repression of the original satisfactions. Also, another likely outcome is the occurrence of a distortion of the child's perceptions about his original behaviors and thoughts so that, rather than experiencing these as being undesirable to the parents, he perceives the behaviors and thoughts as undesirable to himself. In Rogers' example, the child's anger toward his baby brother becomes experienced as bad, even though the more accurate symbolization would acknowledge that experiencing anger is often satisfying and enhancing to the self, and that it is not he but his parents who find these feelings intolerable. Rogers (1951) writes:

> It is here, it seems, that the individual begins on a pathway which he later describes as 'I don't really know myself.' The primary sensory and visceral reactions are ignored, or are not permitted into consciousness, except in distorted form. The values which might be built upon them cannot be admitted to awareness. A concept of self based in part upon a distorted symbolization has taken their place. (p. 501)

Based on this theoretical formulation, Rogers (1951) proceeds to outline the qualities of child caregiving that would promote the healthy development of the self.

> The parent who is able (1) genuinely to accept these feelings of satisfaction experienced by the child, and (2) fully to accept the child who experiences them, and (3) at the same time to accept his or her own feeling that such behavior is unacceptable in the family, creates a situation for the child very different from the usual one. The child in this relationship experiences no threat to his concept of himself as a loved person. He can experience fully and accept within himself and as a part of himself his aggressive feelings toward his baby brother. He can experience fully the perception that his hitting behavior is not liked by the person who loves him. What he then does depends upon his conscious balancing of the elements in the situation—the strength of his feeling of aggression, the satisfactions he would gain from hitting the baby, the satisfactions he would gain from pleasing his parent. The behavior which would result would probably be at times social and at other times aggressive. It would not necessarily conform entirely to the parent's wishes, nor would it always be socially 'good.' It would be the adaptive behavior of a separate, unique, self-governing individual. Its greatest advantage, as far as psychological health is concerned, is that it would be realistic, based upon an accurate symbolization of all

the evidence given by the child's sensory and visceral equipment in this situation. (p. 501)

Rogers' prescription for empathic parenting is essentially the same as his prescription for empathic psychotherapy. In client-centered therapy the therapist attempts to provide unconditional positive regard to an individual who, during his formative years, was not able to obtain this sufficiently from his parents. In the context of the therapist's empathy, the client then can feel safe to reintegrate the formerly unconscious, unacceptable elements of his self-concept with those aspects of the self-concept that have always been conscious.

Later writers who followed within the client-centered tradition have addressed the particular kinds of parent behaviors and communications that tend to allow the child to experience acceptance and unconditional positive regard. For example, from the standpoint of Rogerian theory, how the parent responds to the child in discipline encounters where the child's behavior must be corrected is especially important. Invariably, these types of situations evoke strong emotions in both the parent and the child. Yet, although the parent may be upset with the child, he or she must be able to show disapproval and attempt to change the child's immediate and long-term behavior, in a way that does not result in the splitting off and denial of a part of the child's self-concept. Administering discipline in an empathic manner presents a difficult challenge. Stollak (1978) suggests that in problem situations there often occurs a reflexive chain of negative parent–child communications. The parents "instinctively" react to a nondesirable behavior in their child with a "reflexive" attack response and defense of their own point of view. Thus, Stollak (1974) found that in problem situations where mothers replied with both "effective" and "noneffective" communications the ineffective message was more likely to be expressed first. Stollak (1978) then put forth a sequence of five types of verbalizations that, when communicated in sequence, constitute an empathic response to a child in a problem situation:

1. clear and unambiguous, verbal and non-verbal, communications which indicate that the adult is aware of and understands the child's feelings, wishes, and desires, and how the child's social actions derive from these inner experiences.

2. clear and unambiguous, verbal and non-verbal, communications which indicate that the adult acknowledges the child's feelings, needs, wishes and desires as natural and valid human experiences.

3. clear and unambiguous, verbal and non-verbal, communications which indicate what the adult thinks and feels about the way the child is expressing his or her inner experiences. The child's feelings and needs are indeed natural and valid human experiences but the way the child is expressing them might be unacceptable;

4. if the child's actions are not acceptable, clear and unambiguous, verbal and non-verbal communications indicating alternative ways for the child to express his or her feelings in the present. These alternatives should be provided immediately, not after some period of delay;

5. if the child's actions are not acceptable, clear and unambiguous, verbal and non-verbal communications indicating how the child can express his or her feelings, needs or desires in the future. Again, several alternatives should be offered (p. 68–69).

Stollak called this sequence of effective parental responses "discipline communications." He believes that they will not arouse a level of anxiety or fear that is so high that the child will want to escape the discipline encounter and all further parent–child interactions. Rather, the preceding communications will result in the child feeling loved and validated, so that he then will want to confront the problem and work toward compromises out of his own competence motivation.

It is interesting to note how these discipline communications are similar to, yet go beyond, the "inductive discipline" techniques explored by Hoffman (1970) and others that, as we discussed in Chapter 2, have been found by developmental psychologists to be related to enhanced empathy in the child. In inductive discipline the focus is on making the child aware of how his or her actions have made somebody else feel. Stollak's sequence of five empathic responses acknowledges and validates the child's feelings and then indicates how the *parent* feels about the child's actions, including a statement of whether the current behavioral expression of these feelings is acceptable, and if not, what alternative behavioral expression would be acceptable. Presumably, these responses incorporate inductive discipline, because the fact that the child's actions have caused distress in the other would be pointed out by the parent as one important reason why the child's behavior has been found unacceptable. However, inductive discipline techniques do not go the extra step of emphasizing the validity of the child's feelings, even if they caused the other hurt. It is this acknowledgment that, from the standpoint of Rogers' theory, prevents the splitting off and denial of a part of the child's self that leads to the emergence of many child behavior problems in the first place.

Not all client-centered writers agree with all five of Stollak's parental communications in discipline situations. Gordon (1976) advocates different kinds of parental responses in child-centered and parent-centered problem situations. Child-centered skills like "active listening" should be used when the problem situation is owned by the child, that is, when the child has a problem because he is frustrated in attempting to satisfy a need, but his behavior in no way interferes with the parent's satisfying his or her own needs. Examples of child-owned problems are a child being rejected by friends, being sad because he is not able to earn a place on a sports team, and feeling upset because he does poorly on a test. Gordon (1976) gives the following example of a parental response that involves active listening to a child-centered problem:

Johnny: Tommy won't play with me today. He won't ever do what I want to do.
Mother: You're kinda angry with Tommy. (ACTIVE LISTENING.)

Johnny: I sure am. I never want to play with him again. I don't want him for a friend.

Mother: You're so angry you feel like never seeing him again (ACTIVE LISTENING.)

Johnny: That's right. But if I don't have him for a friend, I won't have anyone to play with then.

Mother: You would hate to be left with no one (ACTIVE LISTENING).

Johnny: Yeah, I guess I just have to get along with him some-way. But it's so hard for me to stop getting mad at him.

Mother: You want to get along better but it's hard for you to keep from getting mad with Tommy (ACTIVE LISTENING).

Johnny: I never used to—but that's when he was always willing to do what I wanted to do. He won't let me boss him anymore.

Mother: Tommy's not so easy to influence now (ACTIVE LISTENING).

Johnny: He sure isn't. He's not such a baby now. He's more fun though.

Mother: You really like him better this way (ACTIVE LISTENING).

Johnny: Yeah. But it's hard to stop bossing him—I'm so used to it. Maybe we wouldn't fight so much if I let him have his way once in a while. Think that would work?

Mother: You're thinking that if you might give in occasionally, it might help (ACTIVE LISTENING).

Johnny: Yeah, maybe it would. I'll try it'' (p. 68).

Gordon believes that active listening in the preceding situation was effective because it kept ownership of the problem with the child (rather than having the problem taken over by the parent), because it resulted in a dissipation of the child's anger, because it led to an initiation of problem solving by the child, because it led to the child's taking a deeper look at himself, and, finally, because the child is able to arrive at a solution that indicates that he has become a little more mature, responsible, and independent.

On the other hand, Gordon does not advocate active listening as the proper approach for parent-owned problems, i.e., problems where the child's attempts to satisfy a need interfere with the parent's attempts to satisfy a need. Gordon believes that confrontational skills should be used in instances of parent-owned problems. This involves the use of an ''I-message'' that includes a description of the unacceptable behavior, a statement of the feeling the parent has, and a description of the tangible effect the child's behavior has on the parent, or the consequences of the behavior. Stollak (1978; Cottrill & Stollak, 1984) disagrees with such an immediate focusing on the parent's reactions to the problem situation, which he believes would likely evoke the child's defensive reactions and ultimately cause the child to engage in the type of denial of feelings and inner experiencing that could lead to alienation from the self.

The theorists and researchers who view parental empathy from the client-centered approach believe that it is no easy task to communicate empathically with children over the long term, especially in situations that evoke that parents' own needs, such as the parent-owned problem situations Gordon describes. From the perspective of Rogers' client-centered theory, some important prerequisites of being an empathic parent are identical to those for being an empathic therapist: The parent must accept himself and must himself have an integrated self-concept, based on sufficient positive self-regard. To this, Stollak (1978) adds the following additional requirements: (1) The empathic parent must not be frightened off by the child's feelings and needs; (2) to be consistently empathic the parent must be able and willing to look to the child's behavior for evidence about whether previous attempts at empathy were successful and be willing to adjust these attempts when the child is not responsive to them, even if the parent himself/herself feels that the previous attempts have been empathic.

Child Effects on Parental Empathy

The developing awareness that children are not passive recipients of parents' caregiving but also initiate parent–child interaction sequences (e.g., Bell, 1968) has led to the consideration of how the child's response to the parent's attempt to communicate empathically can influence the parent's future attempts. For example, Michaels, Messe', and Stollak (1983) examined children's behavior in relation to a parent's ability to accurately judge how he or she was being preceived by the child. They hypothesized that accurate perceptions of the child's experience could set in motion a "benign" cycle of parent–child interaction. In the benign cycle accurate parent inferences lead to more positive child behavior that, in turn, encourages more involvement and hence greater accuracy on the part of the parent, leading to even more adaptive child behavior, and so on. On the other hand, these authors hypothesized that inaccurate parent perceptions could lead to a negative parent–child interaction cycle in which, due to the inability to judge how his or her behavior appears to the child, the parent will be unable to regulate caregiving behavior effectively. The child will then develop fewer adaptive behaviors and more numerous maladaptive behaviors. These in turn will discourage the parent from moving closer to, and becoming more involved with, the child that will lead to still more inaccurate perceptions, more maladaptive behavior from the child, and so on.

A new model of parental empathy by Bell and Bell (1982) also stresses the reciprocal nature of parent–child interaction. In this case, the development of parent empathy is seen to both influence, and depend on, the development of child empathy. Like Michaels, Messe', and Stollak's work, this model stresses the significance of accuracy of parental perception. In addition, the model also stresses what Bell and Bell (1982) call "mutual validation" between parent and child, which includes the ability to acknowledge the other (e.g., "I heard what you said; what you are saying makes sense to me."), and the ability to respond to the other (e.g., "What you are doing and saying has a specific effect on me; here is how I react.") (pp. 1–2). The sequence of events is as follows: Parents who are able to acknowledge and accept themselves will not have to perceive their children from the standpoint of their own needs and will not have to project their own needs onto the child. They will also be able to attend to all aspects of the child's personality and behavior, rather than only to those aspects that satisfy their own needs. Because their children will respond in a loving manner and will be capable to increased caring themselves, this will lead to mutual validation between parent and child. Finally, because the focus of the model is on the family system, both the parents and the child are seen as achieving greater self-acceptance, self-efficacy, and individuation, and, in fact, these qualities can be viewed as family variables, rather than individual variables, with some families further along the process of individuation than other families.

Enhancing Empathy through Attention to One's Own Emotional History

Each of the theoretical approaches we have discussed up to now would agree that one characteristic that is associated with difficulties in achieving and maintaining a high level of empathy is parents' inability to attend to, and stay in touch with, their own emotional histories. Paul (1970) wrote that difficulty in doing this may sometimes reflect a parent's identification with his or her own parents' lack of empathy while he or she was growing up:

> Surely both parents have lived through situations comparable to those through which their son is charting his hesitant course; surely the events, at the time they were fresh, generated important emotional responses. Yet the memories of these feelings have been relegated to the silent past as though they were no longer pertinent. They are either forgotten or at least not recalled in words. The parents' silences, their failure to revivify past moments of doubt, guilt, or grief and to share fully these recollected feelings may be repetitions of similar silences on the part of their own parents. They are behaving toward their son as their parents behaved toward them. A habit of restraint, a stifling of empathic potential, can run through a family from generation to generation as each new set of parents accords its young the treatment that it received earlier. And so each child is left to traverse life's problems alone, as though his responses were so unique and uncharacteristic that they must be kept private. (p. 343)

Paul remarks that sometimes parents feel that they will contaminate their child's happy environment if they express their own feelings, especially feelings of disappointment or worry. Moreover, he believes that attempting to isolate children from such feelings does not succeed, because a child will usually sense that something has gone wrong. However, when the feelings are not out in the open, the child will not be able to explain what has gone wrong, and this can lead to a widening of the emotional distance between parent and child.

Paul believes that one of the most effective, though indirect, ways by which the parental empathy can be enhanced is through sharing one's emotional history with one's spouse. During courtship it is important that the man and woman share their emotional histories with each other because this will help each person respect the other's individuality and will later help the couple acknowledge the separateness of their own child and the validity of his feelings. Another important time for the couple to share feelings is during the pregnancy itself. Paul believes that, if the couple can share their fears, anxieties, and discomforts of adjusting to the pregnancy, this can lead to increased empathic potential for the forthcoming child. Furthermore, through an empathic sharing of feelings in the marriage, emotional resources can be replenished and this can prevent the later development of hidden resentments toward the child for taking up so much of the couple's emotional energy. Paul also believes that such emotional sharing will make it possible for each parent to accept the child's preference of the other parent in some situations, as well as the child's having needs for people outside the family.

CONCEPTUAL AND METHODOLOGICAL ISSUES

Although the theoretical perspectives discussed previously each hold that parental empathy plays an important role in parent–child relations and in the child's psychological development, these perspectives do not describe parent empathy with sufficient conceptual clarity to allow the kind of intensive research effort warranted by its importance in parent–child relations. Some critical conceptual and methodological issues surrounding the investigation of parent empathy are now discussed.

A major problem is what Feshbach (1982a) has described as the overuse of the term empathy "to take on the property of an all-embracing 'good' " (p. 319). As parental empathy becomes equated with such broad concepts as love, nurturance, morality, and effective parenting, its unique definition as a multicomponent process consisting of affective perception, affective reverberation, comprehension of the other's emotion, and communication of understanding and shared feeling gets lost. Thus, many studies of parenting styles and practices include empathy-like behaviors among the measures employed, but, as we see later, it is often extremely difficult to disentangle the impact of empathy on the child from the impact of several other closely related, but distinct parenting variables.

Another little-dealt-with conceptual issue is whether a parent's empathy for his or her child constitutes a unique kind of empathy, different, for example, than a teacher's or therapist's empathy for a child who is not an offspring. There are a number of reasons for expecting that parental empathy includes some aspects that are unique. First, it is based on a long-term, continuous relationship with a child.

The accumulation of experiences that a parent has with his or her child is far greater than for any other kind of interpersonal relationship in which empathy is hypothesized to play an important role, except possibly the relationship between husband and wife. This leaves the parent with access to a very large store of historical and situational cues to use in making judgments about how the child is feeling in any current affect-producing situation.

Another important distinction between parental empathy and other forms of empathy concerns the nature of the motivation to use one's full empathic abilities. In the case of parental empathy one can hypothesize that the naturally occurring bonding and attachment process between parent and child is usually sufficient to produce the motivation necessary for a parent to want to perceptually, affectively, cognitively, and communicatively empathize with his or her child. It can even be argued that the concept of altruism, which has often been linked theoretically to empathy, starts to become meaningless in the context of parent empathy, because helping one's child often feels like helping one's self. In the research literature the term altruism is usually reserved for helping behavior outside of the parent–child relationship.

Whereas the preceding qualities should work toward enhancing empathy and making a high level of empathy easier to achieve, there are also a number of unique aspects of parent empathy that may make the task of the parent more difficult. Furthermore, the same unique quality that enhances parent empathy in some situations may interfere with the expression of empathy in other situations. First, more so than with most other long-term relationships, the parent's own needs are inevitably involved in many situations where the child is having an affective experience that calls for empathy. We have already discussed "parent-owned" problems in which the child's behavior impacts directly on the parent's needs. More problems arise when the parent is called on to be empathic in situations where the child is causing a negative response in the parent that could interfere with his or her attempt to also be empathic. Furthermore, just as it is difficult for the parent to maintain an empathic stance when the child's behavior is impinging on the parent's needs, it is also very difficult to remain empathic in situations where the parent is aware that his or her own behavior may be the cause of the child's experienced distress. Feelings of guilt may interfere with empathy when, for example, the parent must be away from the child for an extended, but unavoidable, out-of-town trip. These same feelings may even occur in situations where the parent is purposely causing the child some immediate distress, as in the case of punishment for some misdeed. Here, the parent must try to express understanding of the child's distress and anger without having this empathy overwhelmed by other feelings about the situation.

Thirdly, whereas close involvement and knowledge of how one's child responds over a long period of time may serve to enhance a parent's empathic ability, the fact that children are constantly changing and developing in both the affective and cognitive realms must surely challenge the parent's ability to recognize the more subtle, qualitative changes in his or her child's experience. For example, the experience of hunger by a helpless infant with no internalized concept of a parental figure who will come into the room to feed him must be much more traumatic than the experience of hunger in an older child who now realizes that he has the power to relieve the hunger himself through a trip to the refrigerator. The empathic parent must have the flexibility to make adjustments for the changing nature of children's experiences and abilities.

As the child grows older, the degree to which a parent can rely on his or her own experience with the child in order to understand the child's emotional reaction probably lessens. Once the child enters preschool or nursery school, many emotionally arousing situations occur that the parent does not observe and for which the parent has no direct situational cues. At this point, the parent probably must become less reliant on situational cues to help understand what the child is experiencing and more reliant on person cues, such as the child's verbalizations, facial expressions, tone of voice, posture, etc. However, whereas fewer cues are now available to the parent, it is also true that when the child experiences feelings outside the family context the parent is less likely to be personally involved, and the problem is more likely to be child centered than parent centered.

RESEARCH FINDINGS

The body of research on parent empathy is very small. One reason for this may be the difficulty in bridging the somewhat broad and vaguely set forth theoretical concepts with the need to operationalize these concepts. Although we believe that the general multidimensional view of empathy presented in this book can apply to parental empathy, it has been mainly one component—empathic communication—that has been addressed in the existing research literature.

Factors Related to High- and Low-Parental Empathy

As we have seen, several writers have hypothesized that the transition to parenthood is a time of naturally increasing empathic capacity. Some support for this has come from a study by Michaels, Hoffman, and Goldberg (1982), who interviewed primaparous mothers and fathers 3 months after the birth of their first child about whether changes had occurred in their most important personal and social values. A large percentage of parents reported an increased valuing of "caring for others," which they believed was reflected in better quality contacts with their close circle of family, friends, and acquaintances. However, based on those interviews and on two objective values measures given to the new parents pre and postpartum, it appeared that the increase in empathy did not lead to greater concern for other people generally. Values reflecting societal concerns, such as the value "Equality–brotherhood, equal opportunity for all," tended to decline in importance among the new parents. A person's valuing of social justice and equality may be less influenced by level of empathy than values of concern and caring for those one knows personally. The authors speculated that increased empathic concern might be a source of motivation for increased participation in the life of their community by the new parents.

Balser (1980) investigated the relationship between level of parental empathy and a variety of personality, parental, and relationship variables. Parental empathy was conceptualized as a multicomponent process consisting of affective, cognitive, and behavioral components. The affective and cognitive components were assessed by an audiotaped interview with each parent. The behavioral component was assessed with a Video Empathy Scale that was scored from videotaped parent–child play sessions. Subjects were white middle-class parents who were seen in their homes within a month of their child's second birthday.

Parents' scores on the audiotape measure of empathy were significantly positively correlated with scores on the Revised Locke–Wallace Marital Adjustment Inventory, with socioeconomic status of the parents, with successful adaptation to the pregnancy, and with early postpartum adjustment (scored from an earlier assessment of these parents). Mothers scored higher on overall empathy than did fathers. For mothers, empathy tended to be related to competence in measures of ego strength, whereas for fathers, empathy tended to be related to measures of social competence. No relationships were found between parental empathy and the children's functioning, but the author believes this may have reflected a limited range in empathic and nonempathic parenting among the participants. There was no relationship between parental empathy on the videotape measure and the various measures of parent characteristics, and, in fact, the correlation between the audiotape and videotape empathy measures, whereas significant, was low. As we have seen, the problem of low relationships between various measures of empathy has been a recurring one across the many domains of empathy discussed in this book.

There is some evidence that parents may bring particular person perception biases to their interactions with their children that may interfere with their ability to accurately perceive important behavioral cues, and, hence, to be empathic. Although not studying parental empathy directly, Stollak, Messé, Michaels, Buldain, Catlin, and Paritee (1982) found that particular perception biases in the parents of 8- and 9-year-old children were associated with specific patterns of parent–child interaction and with child adjustment problems. These perceptual biases were in the area of judging the occurrence of positive and negative behaviors in a child. To assess these biases, videotapes of a child interacting with an adult in a playroom setting were presented to the parent subjects. The pair were actors and their behavior together followed a prepared script in which approximately equal numbers of adaptive and maladaptive child behaviors occurred. It was found that the greater the parent's (especially the father's) tendency to perceive maladaptive or negative child behavior in the videotapes, the more likely the parent was to display distancing behaviors toward his or her child. Furthermore, parental acts that connoted superior status were more likely to be negatively correlated with negative perceptual style than were egalitarian or subordinated parental behaviors. However, the children's displays of disagreement and/or antagonism toward their parents tended to be inversely related to parental negative perceptual bias. It has been suggested (Guerney, 1964) that such a relationship is to be expected, because it is only when the child feels accepted that he or she will feel safe enough to express anger openly. In a follow-up study of problem and nonproblem third-grade children and their parents, fathers of teacher- and peer-rated problem children were found to be more negatively biased in their perceptions of child behavior than were fathers of either "adequate" or "highly adjusted" children.

Whereas the results of this research suggest that perceptual bias influenced the parents' behavior with their children and, ultimately, their children's adjustment, this study could not rule out the possibility that the relationships found were due mainly to the negative impact on a parent's perceptual judgments of numerous negative experiences with a poorly adjusted child. In an attempt to clarify the causal direction of these findings, Messé, Stollak, Watts, Perlmutter & Peshkess (1982) performed a prospective study in which parental perceptual styles were assessed prenatally and then related to subsequent caregiving behaviors in a group of primaparous mothers and fathers. Based on two home observations when the children were 4- and 9-months-old, four categories of parenting behavior were scored: sensitivity, acceptance, noninterference, and accessibility. Perceptual bias was found to be negatively related to responsive parenting. Again, this relationship was stronger for fathers than for mothers. The concept of parental perceptual bias, as it has been used in these studies, has been conceptualized as a general inability to form balanced, complex perceptions of a target person as possessing negative and positive attributes. It remains to be seen whether either such a general bias or more specific perceptual biases operate in the area of parental perceptions of their children's emotions.

Earlier, the theoretical argument was made that the parent's task of empathizing with his or her child may frequently be complicated by the fact that problem situations for the child also impinge on the parent's needs. Stollak and his colleagues have investigated empathic communications by parents to their children in problem situations where the problem was either the child's alone, the parent's alone, or where problem ownership was both parent's and child's. In studies discussed in Chapter 2 (Kallman & Stollak, 1974; Stollak, Scholam, Kallman, & Saturnasky, 1973), it was found that mothers most often responded to their children in conflict or problem situations with questions, logical persuasion, and orders or commands. These are categories that Gordon (1970) called "ineffective" parental communications in such situations. In a recent study, Cottrill and Stollak (1984) examined both "instinctual" and optimal maternal responses to fourth- and sixth-grade children in problem situations, using the semiprojective items of Stollak's Sensitivity to Children Questionnaire. This questionnaire consists of 9 vignettes, 3 focusing on the child's need, 3 focusing on the parent's needs, and 3 focusing on the needs of both parent and child. The mothers were first asked to respond verbally as they would to the actual situation. Then, at a later date, they were asked to respond to the same items, but with thought-out written responses about how they would actually respond and how they think they ideally should respond to the child. Their responses were then coded along 20 categories of effective and ineffective communication.

The results showed that problem ownership appeared to be the most influential variable in determining parental responses. The mothers' communications only appeared to focus on the child's inner experiences when the problem situation aroused the child's needs, but not the mother's. When the mother's own needs were involved in the problem situation, these mothers were more likely to engage in destructive and defensive verbal responses to the child. Furthermore, when their own needs were involved, mothers tended to respond differently to sons and daughters. Sons were responded to with more psychologically harmful responses such as "name-calling, ridiculing, and shaming" and "withdrawing, ignoring, or distancing," whereas the use of negative evaluations and simple ignoring was more characteristic of the mothers' responses to daughters. Finally, the "ideal" responses given to the "should" instructions did, overall, yield more communications that focused on the child's feelings, but there was no difference between the immediate and thought-out responses as a function of problem ownership. Again, as in previous reserach by Stollak and his colleagues, there was very little use of higher level empathy responses such as "relating of the child's feelings to adult's feelings," or "relating child's feelings to adult's behavior."

To summarize, there is little existing research addressing the question of what qualities in the parent or the situation are likely to be associated with either high or low levels of parental empathy, although the theoretical writings on parent empathy suggest numerous areas for exploration. To the extent that parental empathy is similar to adult empathy outside the parental role, it is likely that person and situation factors that have been found to be related to adult empathy in other realms will also be shown to influence parental empathy, but this is yet to be demonstrated. There are also fairly strong theoretical reasons to expect that at least some important determinants of parental empathy are unique to this domain. For example, one group of variables that may provide fertile ground for future research are those relevant to family structure and to the reciprocal nature of parent–child interaction. Finally, we do not yet know how general an ability parental empathy is, and future research will certainly need to address the question of whether the determinants of parent empathy operate only in specific situations or are operative across the various situations in which parents interact with their child, as well as across different periods in the child's and family's development.

In Chapter 2 we discussed the impact of parental empathy on children's own development of empathic abilities. To the extent that parental empathy is an important socialization variable, its presence or relative absence should be related to a wide spectrum of other adaptive and maladaptive behaviors in children. In the next sections we review the research that has explored the relationship between parents' empathy and children's psychological and behavioral development.

Studies of Parents' Affection and Involvement with their Child

A large body of research now exists that quite conclusively demonstrates the beneficial impact of parental affection and nurturance on children's psychological and social development. To cite but a few examples, Ainsworth and Blehar (1975) say that during infancy, secure attachment has been found to be related to such parental behaviors as "initiation of affectionate contact, acceptance of the infant's behavior, and sensitivity to infants' signals and communications" (p. 7). Social responsiveness at 6 months has been related to parental smiling, talk, vocalization, and play (Yarrow, Rubenstein, Pederson, & Jankowski, 1972). Also, in 6-month-olds, performance on the Bayley Scales of Infant Development has been found to be related to such parental variables as level and variety of social stimulation and prompt and contingent responsiveness to distress (Ainsworth, Bell, & Stayton, 1974). In toddlers, child competence, including such characteristics as mature play and language competence, was found to be related to caregiving variables of verbal stimulation, responsiveness to social signals, playing with the child, and positive emotional expression (Clarke–Stewart, 1973). At 54 months, IQ performance was related to emotional and verbal responsivity of mother and maternal involvement with the child (Bradley & Caldwell, 1976). However, as we have pointed out earlier, whereas affectionate and nurturant parent behavior surely includes elements of empathy, it is very difficult to distinguish which behaviors specifically indicate one of the components of empathy from those behaviors that are indicative of general parental involvement and affection. Recognizing this problem, we nevertheless discuss two areas of recent research in more detail because of their direct relevance to the theoretical writings on the role of parental empathy discussed previously. The first area is the literature on the relationship between behavioral indices of maternal sensitivity and infant–mother attachment. The second area is the literature on the relationship between behavioral indices of parental empathy and children's prosocial and altruistic behavior.

Empathy in the Context of Mother–Infant Attachment.   The psychoanalytic and object relations theorists linked empathy's development directly to the formation of an early and strong mother–child bond. Similarly, high levels of parent empathy may facilitate the development of such a bond. Recently, empirical support for this position has become available in the form of research demonstrating a relationship between quality of an infant's attachment to its mother (Bowlby, 1969) and various indices of maternal sensitivity. Attachment researchers have generally used a laboratory procedure developed by Ainsworth and her colleagues (Ainsworth & Blehar, Waters, & Wall, 1978; Ainsworth & Wittig, 1969) called the *strange situation*. It comprises a standardized series of eight episodes in which an infant, accompanied by his or her mother, is first introduced to an unfamiliar room, then confronted by an adult female stranger, then separated from the mother and briefly left alone in the unfamiliar room, and finally reunited with the stranger and the mother. Analysis of the child's interactive behavior in the strange situation leads to the child being classified into one of three attachment categories: anxious avoidant (group A), secure (group B), or anxious resistant (group C). It has been found that anxious-avoidant infants tend to avoid their mothers in the reunion episodes and often cry very little when they are separated from their mothers. Anxious-resistant infants show a pattern of ambivalence toward their mothers, showing both anger and resistance and a wish to remain in close proximity and have contact with the mother. Securely attached infants all show interest in gaining proximity and contact with their mothers when the two are reunited. Evidence is mounting that securely attached infants develop more adaptively than nonsecurely attached infants. Securely attached infants have been found to show greater sociability with peers (Easterbrooks & Lamb, 1979), social competence in the preschool peer group (Waters, Wipman, & Sroufe, 1979), and more competent behavior in problem-solving situations and with social and cognitive problems (Arend, Gove, & Sroufe, 1979; Matas, Arend, & Sroufe, 1978).

Although empathy as we have conceptualized it in the multicomponent model presented in this book has not been investigated with respect to infant attachment, the parent's general "sensitivity" to the infant's cues has been implicated in the development of a secure attachment of infant to mother (Ainsworth, Bell, & Stayton, 1971, 1974; Blehar, Lieberman, & Ainsworth, 1977; Smith & Pederson, 1983). Two illustrative studies are described.

Ainsworth, Bell, and Stayton (1971, 1974) examined the relationship between quality of attachment and maternal sensitivity to the cues of infants in the last quarter of their first year. They measured four aspects of maternal sensitivity. The first aspect was the mother's awareness of her infant's signals. Here, her accessibility to the infant and her threshold of awareness of the infant's cues were assessed. Mothers with low thresholds of awareness were alert to very subtle cues, whereas mothers with high thresholds were aware only of the infant's most blatant cues. The second aspect of maternal sensitivity to be assessed was the mother's ability to correctly interpret the infant's cues. This aspect focused on maternal empathy and the extent to which the mother's interpretations were undistorted by projection, denial, and other defense mechanisms. Mothers with the most distorted perceptions seemed to bias their interpretations of the infant's needs with their own feelings and desires, whereas mothers with low distortion could recognize their own feelings and desires and how these affected their infant's behavior.

The third aspect of sensitivity was the mother's appropriateness in giving the infant what she felt the infant wanted, as well as the mother's capacity to regulate the stimulation of the infant during interactions with him or her. Sensitive mothers perceived, interpreted, and responded to cues of boredom when understimulated and to cues of overexcitement when stimulation was too intense. The sensitive mothers successfully completed these responses to the infant's cues, whereas nonsensitive mothers often tried a range of different responses that seemed to indicate the lack of a planned response to the infant's cues. Finally, the fourth aspect of sensitivity measured was the promptness of the maternal response, with sensitive mothers responding quickly enough so that the infant could view the response as contingent on his or her communication. Ainsworth et al. found that mothers of securely attached infants were rated as more sensitive than mothers of anxiously attached infants.

In a later study, Smith and Pederson (1983) examined mothers' behavioral sensitivity to their 12-month-old infants in a laboratory situation in which they had to complete a questionnaire while their infant was allowed to explore the room in which she worked, which did not have any child toys. The demand to complete the questionnaire was expected to compete with attentional demands from the infant. The authors classified maternal responses to the infant into three broad sensitivity dimensions: appropriate, insufficient, and intrusive responses to the infant. The authors (Smith & Pederson, 1983) gave the following examples of these categories:

> For example, a mother who looked at, and vocalized to an infant who was whimpering, would be scored as providing an appropriate response. A mother who did not look at, vocalize, or reach toward an infant who was looking at her, vocalizing, and in close proximity would be scored as providing an insufficient response. A mother who looked at, vocalized, and reached toward an infant who was not looking at her, not vocalizing, and not in close proximity to her, was scored as providing an intrusive response. (p. 9)

The authors found that mothers of securely attached infants were more likely to provide appropriate responses to the infant, generally, and more likely to do so when an active response was required than were mothers of anxious-avoidant infants. However, mothers of anxious-avoidant infants were more likely to use appropriate responses than were mothers of anxious-resistant infants. The use of insufficient responses was higher for mothers of anxious-resistant infants than for mothers of infants in the other two attachment groups, whereas the use of intrusive responses was higher in the mothers of the anxious-avoidant infants. Finally, mothers of securely attached infants usually checked their infants more than did mothers of anxious-avoidant and anxious-resistant mothers, who did not differ in this. Using discriminant analysis, 94% of the infants were classified correctly to their attachment group on the basis of the maternal sensitivity scores.

Parental Empathy and Children's Prosocial Behavior.   Again, using behavioral measures that overlap with our conceptualization of empathy, Zahn–Waxler, Radke–Yarrow, and King (1979) assessed, as empathic caregiving, the following maternal characteristics: (1) anticipating dangers and difficulties (2) responding promptly to the child's hurts, and (3) nurturant caregiving associated with specific hurts and needs. The ratings of these behaviors were made in the home, based on naturalistic observations of mothers and their 1½- to 2½-year-old children. The results showed that empathic caregiving behaviors were associated with significantly higher recorded altruism and reparation in the children. Furthermore, the prosocial responses of the children of empathic mothers were also more frequently associated with concerned emotional expression on these children's part than was true of the children whose mothers were rated low on empathic caregiving. The authors (Zahn–Waxler et al., 1979) then suggest that mothers of reparative and altruistic children use high-intensity, clear communications when their children transgress, side by side with these empathic behaviors.

> The effective induction is not calmly dispensed reasoning, carefully designed to enlighten the child; it is emotionally imposed, sometimes harshly and often forcefully. These techniques exist side by side with empathic caregiving. Mother's nurturance may be an important condition for the effectiveness of the induction and power. (p. 327)

A study by Eisenberg–Berg and Geisheker (1979) with older children found evidence that exhortations to engage in generous behavior are more effective when they include an empathic component. These authors examined the relative influence of three kinds of adult preaching, as well as the influence of the adult's power status, on third- and fourth-grade children's willingness to donate a portion of their earnings to poor children. More relevant to the topic of this chapter were the findings for type of preaching. The children were exposed to either an empathic exhortation, a normative exhortation that emphasized the rightness and goodness of sharing, or a neutral statement. The three types of exhortations were as follows: (Eisenberg–Berg & Geisheker, 1979):

> (Empathic condition) Well now, I think that people should share with the poor children. They would be so happy and excited if they could buy food and toys. After all, poor children have almost nothing. If everyone would help these children maybe they wouldn't look so sad.
>   (Normative condition) Well now, I think that people should share with the poor children. It's really good to donate to poor boys and girls. Yes, we should give some money to others poorer than ourselves. Sharing is the right thing to do.

(Neutral condition) I've never seen a toy like that before. It reminds me of a dart game, but different because you use balls. It's not that easy to play it well. You have to aim very carefully and hit the ball just right. (p. 170)

These statements were presented at the end of a videotape of a game being demonstrated by an adult, which the children were told they would later play and evaluate.

The results showed that the empathic preaching elicited the most sharing by the children. This finding is consistent with the research discussed in Chapter 2 that indicated that the development of altruism is enhanced by parental verbalizations that point out what the consequences are of a child's behavior toward another person (e.g., Hoffman, 1970; Hoffman & Saltzstein, 1967). Interestingly, the normative exhortations, which did not include an empathic component, proved ineffective in eliciting more generosity than the neutral verbalizations could elicit. Although the adults doing the exhorting were not parents, the findings suggest that effective preaching that includes references to the victim's emotions and unhappy situation is more effective than preaching that invokes normative expectations without such empathic references.

Parents' Understanding of How their Children View Them

Earlier it was suggested that, because many of the child's most salient emotional experiences occur during direct interaction with their parents, a crucial arena for parental empathy may be the child's feelings and perceptions related to the parent–child relationship and to parent caregiving. Examining empathy from a cognitive perspective, the parent's ability to infer or comprehend how the child feels about his mother and father can be assessed. A study by Michaels, Messé, and Stollak (1983) hypothesized that a parent's ability to accurately judge how the child views his or her parenting behavior is an important parent–child relationship variable, with consequences for the child's psychosocial development. First, eighty 7-year-old children and one of each one's parents completed versions of the Bronfenbrenner Parent Behavior Questionnaire, giving their judgments about the extent to which the parent engaged in "loving," "punishing," and "demanding" behaviors with the child. Children completed the questionnaire about their parents while the mothers and fathers answered first with their self-perceptions of caregiving behavior with that child, and secondly with inferences about how they thought their children would perceive them. To assess inferences the instructions read: (Michaels et al., 1983):

Now please imagine that you are your child, the one who participated in the study, and you are asked to comment upon the following statements about you—his/her mother or you—his/her father. That is, we'd like to know how you think your child sees you. These statements are the same as before, only this time put yourself in your child's place. (p. 12–13)

The first set of findings indicated that parents and children, on the average, viewed parenting behavior differently. Parents perceived themselves to be, and inferred that their children would perceive them, as less loving than their children actually viewed them. Mirroring this, the parents also perceived themselves, and inferred that they would be perceived, as more punishing than they were actually viewed by their children. The results for demanding parenting behavior also showed parent–child perception differences. In this case, children perceived their parents as more demanding than the parents viewed themselves, whereas parents inferred that they would be perceived as less demanding than the children actually perceived them.

With this demonstration that children and parents tend to view parent behavior "through different eyes," the next step was to determine whether, within a particular family, a parent's ability to infer how he or she was perceived by the child would be related to the child's social adjustment. Adaptive and nonadaptive child behavior was rated during a half-hour playroom interaction with an adult, who was a stranger. The child and adult performed play, teaching, and cooperative work tasks. The results showed that "parental accuracy" on each of the three parenting behavior dimensions—loving, punishing, and demanding—was significantly positively related to children's adaptive behavior during the playroom interaction and significantly negatively related to some nonadpative behaviors.

Empathy as an Inhibitor of Dysfunctional Parenting

Parental empathy may also play a role in impeding potential dysfunctional or even neglectful and abusive parenting. Letourneau (1981) predicted first, that parents who had lower abilities to perceive their children's needs, intentions, or feelings would be more likely to respond punitively in conflict situations with children. This prediction was based on Feshbach and Feshbach's (1969) position that the ability to comprehend a conflict from the other person's perspective would result in a lessening of the conflict itself. Secondly, she predicted that the parent's tendency to experience affective empathy (e.g., feeling distress in the presence of the child's cries, groans, or tears) would limit or halt abusive behavior on the part of the parent. She speculated that such an affective empathic response could account for why some children are bruised but are not battered. Furthermore, she hypothesized a mediating role for empathy in the previously observed relationship between child abuse and stress (Garbarino, 1976; Gelles, 1973; Gil, 1973). It was expected that a combination of high empathy and low stress would be associated with little or no child abuse, whereas low empathy and high stress would account for the highest frequency of abusive incidents.

Three measures of empathy were administered: the Hogan Empathy Test, which operationalizes empathy from a cognitive role-taking perspective; the Mehrabian and Epstein Empathy Scale, which conceptualizes empathy as a vicarious emotional response, and a role-play inventory developed by Rothbart and Maccoby (1966). This last instrument assesses the subjects' responses to a series of situations in which a child seeks comfort, seeks help, or becomes angry. Parents' responses were coded along scales of help withholding, comfort withholding, sensitivity to the child's needs, and aggression.

As predicted, abusive mothers were found to be less empathic than nonabusive mothers. Abusive mothers were also more help withholding (e.g., likely to reply to a child's request for help with "Wait a minute," or "I'm busy") and less comforting (e.g., rather than replying to a statement by the child that he is hurt with a comforting response, the abusive mother was more likely to give a neutral response such as "It was an accident"). Furthermore, empathy appeared to be the critical variable influencing the rate of abuse; it was more influential than level of stress. When empathy was high, mothers appeared to be able to adapt to high-stress levels without resorting to abusive behavior, but when empathy was low, abuse was more likely to occur in both the high- and low-stress levels. Letourneau suggests, on the basis of these findings, that programs that focus primarily on helping families deal with stress would not prevent the recurrence of abuse and suggests, as a possible alternative, a structured group experience that provides a series of role-taking opportunities.

Parents of Adolescents

Miller (1976) investigated the relationship between eighth-grade children's self-esteem and their parents' use of what Rogers (1951) and Carkhuff (1969a&b) have termed the core facilitative conditions of empathy, genuineness, and positive regard. Rogers considers these conditions to be both essential and sufficient components in effective interpersonal functioning. In the study, self-esteem was measured by Coopersmith's (1967) Self Esteem Inventory, whereas the Relationship Inventory-B (Bierman, 1967) was used to assess affective and empathic responses in family interaction. The results indicated that these facilitative conditions of maternal empathy, genuineness, and positive regard for the child were all significantly related to the adolescent's self-esteem, suggesting that the presence of parental empathy is related to the general self-image and social image of the child.

Bell and Bell (1982) attempted to operationalize some important aspects of parental empathy in a way that would allow a more detailed analysis of empathy's role in parent–child interaction and in the child's personal development. They utilized a revealed differences task in which parents and their adolescent daughters were asked to attempt to achieve consensus on a number of items from a questionnaire focusing on family environment, on which they disagreed. The verbal interaction was analyzed at the level of the single sentence and subsentence unit. For example, "validation" was scored as the percentage of replies to the adolescent that acknowledge her speech minus the percentage of parental replies that ignored or in some way undermined her speech. A second way of scoring validation was the percentage of statements by the parents that focused on the process of the adolescent's thinking, figuring, or understanding, rather than on particular information or attitudes. However, the results of the investigation showed only mixed support for the expected relationship between these and similar empathy indices, and adolescent girls' scores on introversion–extroversion, self-esteem, ego development, school achievement, and socialization, with only a small number of significant correlations. Empathy-related behaviors by fathers seemed to be more strongly related to the adolescent girls' achievement of these important developmental tasks than were empathy behaviors shown by mothers. Whereas their findings were somewhat disappointing, the authors note that their approach permits more refined analyses in the future through combining scales (e.g., combining "statement of facts" with "statements about another's feelings" to form "statements of facts about another's feelings"). Their methodology also permits analysis of the nature and role of parent empathy in families with different kinds of coalitions, or during interactions within the same family, where coalitions among family members change (e.g., items on the revealed differences task where the daughter and mother are opposed to the father, where both parents are opposed to the daughter, etc.).

TRAINING PROGRAMS FOR PARENTAL EMPATHY

Training programs designed to enhance empathic communication form a major portion of the parent-empathy literature. These studies are relevant to our discussion in two ways. First, they may answer the question of whether empathy skills can be successfully taught to parents, and, secondly, the studies potentially provide a method for experimentally investigating the impact of empathic parenting on the child's adjustment.

Many parent-training programs that have included education for empathy have not distinguished the empathy training from other aspects of parenting instruction. In such cases, it is impossible to distinguish what role empathy enhancement may have played in behavioral changes that are found in either the parent trainees or their children. On the other hand, there have been some programs that have attempted to increase empathy directly, and the findings from these do bear on the research questions raised previously.

Most empathy training programs for parents have been built from the following theoretical propositions stated by Carkhuff (Carkhuff & Bierman, 1970):

(a) the core of functioning or dysfunctioning (health or psychopathology) is interpersonal;
(b) the core of helping processes (learning or relearning) is interpersonal;
(c) group processes are the preferred mode of working with difficulties of interpersonal functioning.

(d) systematic group training in interpersonal functioning is the preferred mode of working with difficulties in interpersonal functioning (p. 157).

In a study with parents of emotionally disturbed children who were seeking intervention, Carkhuff and Bierman (1970) explored the effectiveness of an interpersonal skill training program, a large component of which focused on empathy training. Mothers and fathers in the training group were first taught to discriminate different levels of accurate empathy and then to communicate at high levels of accurate empathy (Carkhuff, 1969). Only parents attended the training sessions, which used role playing and communication training between spouses of the same family and between members of different families, with each member of the pair in turn playing the role of the child.

The results of the study revealed that parents in the training group showed greater increases in empathic discrimination and communication with their spouse than was true for either participants in a traditional counseling group or participants in a time-control group. However, the parents in the training group did not become more empathic toward their children than parents of the other groups, though the training parents did perceive themselves as improving in interpersonal skills. The authors suggest that the limited generalizability of the training to parent–child interaction may have been caused by the failure to include the children in the training sessions. They suggest that a more effective approach would have parents being trained directly in accurate discrimination and communication with their own children.

It should be noted that in developing the program of discrimination training in the preceding study, the authors conceptualized affective discimination somewhat differently than it has been used in other places in this book. The parents were trained to discriminate levels of empathy according to whether or not the helper's responses were an interchangeable reflection of the feelings and personal meaning expressed by the helpee (level 3 of accurate empathy). They then learned to discriminate whether noninterchangeable responses were "additive" (levels 4 and 5 of accurate empathy) or subtractive (levels 1 and 2 of accurate empathy), according to the type of effect the helper's response had on the helpee's subsequent response. The question, here, was whether the helpee could utilize the helper's response to enable him to explore and understand himself at a deeper level. This conceptualization of affective discrimination offers an interesting direction for future investigation of this component of empathy. Similarly, the communication component that was taught involved more than "affect labeling." Carkhuff writes, "The initial goal of communication training, the formulation of interchangeable responses, served as the basis for later shaping additive responses" (p. 158).

Filial Therapy.   One of the more adequately studied parent-empathy training programs is filial therapy, developed by Bernard Guerney (1964) and his research group. It seeks to train parents of emotionally disturbed children to themselves use techniques of Rogerian client-centered play therapy directly with their children in the hopes of alleviating the child's psychological and behavioral problems. Guerney believes this to be an effective approach despite the probability that the parents have played some role in the development of the child's problems in the first place. Stover and Guerney (1967) list a number of reasons why training parents to be client-centered therapists to their children ought to be effective. First, parents have more emotional significance to a child than do professionals. Secondly, anxieties that the child has learned in the context of the parent–child relationship, or as a result of the parent's attitudes and behaviors, could be more easily unlearned or extinguished in filial therapy. Thirdly, the filial therapy situation should facilitate the correction of misperceptions by the child as to exactly what is expected of his/her behavior at particular times or places.

The filial therapy situation also frees up the professional's time to the extent that the parent conducts the play therapy sessions. It avoids possible feelings of rivalry in parents who witness their child becoming more independent of them and more attached to the therapist. The parents are also less likely to suffer from feelings of guilt and helplessness over the fact that they had to give the child up to an expert for help. Finally, in filial therapy, the parents are directly encouraged to develop new, more empathic response patterns that are more appropriate to the parenting role.

Training in filial therapy takes place in groups of six to eight and practice in developing empathy skills with the child is done both in the clinic playroom and in the home. The training techniques of Filial Therapy were modeled after Rogerian client-centered play therapy, with the focus on developing an empathic relationship with the child. Stover and Guerney (1967) describe the training process as follows:

> The first step was to discuss the possible benefits to be derived for the child, and for parent–child relationships, that might be expected to accrue from the application of the method of filial therapy. The mothers in the E group then observed demonstrations through a one-way screen, and were encouraged to model their behavior after that of the group leader, a psychologist who demonstrated the process of following the child's lead in the initiation and direction of activities. The mothers were encouraged to attempt not only specific techniques, but to seek to express a genuine empathy with the child. Following three to five such demonstrations with non-clinic children, the mothers each demonstrated with their own child, and received comments on their techniques by the other group members and the trainer. Mothers' feelings about accepting their reflective role were explored in the group meeting, with a view to developing insight into their relationship with their children. Their reactions to the demonstrated play sessions, and a growing awareness of their child's needs, formed the basis of subsequent weekly mothers' group meetings. The therapist was reflective, also, and sought to provide an empathic understanding of their feelings, much as they were being expected to provide in play sessions with their children. The training groups met at the Clinic for ten one-and-a-half-hour sessions of discussion and observation. (p. 112)

The question may well be raised whether parents of poorly adjusted children can possibly learn the skills of a client-centered therapist. First of all, the parents of a disturbed child are living in a highly volatile situation where the child's problems may evoke such nonempathic feelings as hostility. Maladaptive interaction patterns may have already been established that would make developing new, empathy-oriented interactions more difficult. Furthermore, to the extent that there is a relationship between child and parental psychopathology, one would expect a higher frequency of low adjustment and psychological problems in the parents who are referring their children, which also would interfere with the capacity to develop empathy skills. However, despite these obstacles, assessments of the effectiveness of the Filial Therapy program show it to be quite effective in helping both the parents and their referred child.

Guerney and Stover (1967) conducted a study that examined whether parents of clinic-referred children could, in fact, use filial therapy training to develop greater empathic skills with their children, and whether filial therapy training would lead to changes in the child's behavior patterns. Change in empathy and child behavior in a group that received filial therapy was compared to changes in a control group who were also clinic referred, but who did not undergo treatment until after the study's data were collected. The results showed that parents in the filial therapy group increased their reflective communications in a category that included reflective leads, restatement of content, clarification of feeling, and reflective structuring. Children in the filial therapy group also changed their behavior by the fourth session in ways predicted by the authors on the basis of previous research with child client-centered therapy, i.e., the children in both the training groups expressed more nonverbal aggression and, in one training group, more verbal negative feeling. According to Guerney and Stover, this increase in negative behaviors on the part of the children has previously been found to occur prior to an increase in positive attitudes and is thought to be related to the permissive climate engendered by the acceptance and respect the parents were showing for the child's feelings (Moustakas, 1955).

Sywulak (1977) evaluated the effectiveness of filial therapy training using a design in which subjects served as their own controls. Subjects were tested four times. Paper and pencil tests were used to assess both parental acceptance and the child adjustment at each testing time. The results supported the effectiveness of the Filial Therapy program in both areas. Parental acceptance improved markedly by the second month of treatment, as did some aspects of child adjustment, with withdrawn children improving in adjustment more quickly than aggressive children. These changes then continued through the fourth month of treatment.

Another study, by Sensue (1981), provided follow-up data on families who had 3 years earlier completed the Filial Therapy program. These families had previously been evaluated on level of parental acceptance and on child adjustment as perceived by the parents. These same measures were completed again at followup, and in addition a follow-up questionnaire, a measure of skills usage, and a parent and child interview was administered. Data were also collected from a group of control families who were similar to the follow-up group on demographic variables but had not sought, or received, either psychological services for their child or parent education training. The results showed that the treatment families improved on parental acceptance and child adjustment from pretreatment to both a point 6 months into treatment and to the 3-year follow-up assessment. At followup the parents reported that they used the skills they had learned with other children, and that their involvement in Filial Therapy had promoted positive changes in their family. There was also no difference in child adjustment between the children of the treated families at followup and the children of the control group families who had never sought professional help.

Parent–Adolescent Relationship Development.   Guerney and his coworkers have developed a general Relationship Enhancement Group intervention approach designed to improve important interpersonal relationships of various kinds. Empathy training is distinguished as an important component, but not the sole component, of this general approach. Guerney, Coufal, and Vogelsong (1981) describe the general Relationship Enhancement method as follows:

> Within a context of very high levels of empathy, warmth, and genuineness, the Relationship Enhancement method attempts to change clients' attitudes, perceptions, and interpersonal behaviors through demonstration, modeling, reinforcement, vicarious reinforcement, various kinds of prompting, supervision, feedback, and home assignments. Relationship Enhancement teaches clients to resolve problems and conflicts and to enrich their relationship by using certain skills, primarily: (a) the Expression mode; (b) the Empathic Responder mode; (c) Mode Switching; and (d) the Facilitator mode. (p. 929)

Thus, empathic techniques by the group leader, along with specific skill training, are used to promote empathic responding by the group participants. This, in turn, is thought to lead to a better interpersonal relationship, generally.

One type of Relationship Enhancement program designed specifically for parents is the Parent–Adolescent Relationship Development (PARD) program (Ginsberg, 1977; Grando & Ginsberg, 1976), which systematically teaches communication and problem–conflict skills. Results of a study investigating the effectiveness of the PARD program done by Guerney, Coufal, & Vogelsang (1981) indicated that empathic responding can be trained in parents and their adolescent children, and that the PARD program, with its empathy component, leads to more successful parent–adolescent child relationships. However, once again this finding does not separate the impact of changing empathy levels from the impact of the other skills that the PARD program and Relationship Enhancement teach.

Other Empathy Training Programs for Parents.   Earlier, we discussed the theoretical belief that parental empathy is enhanced when the parent has access to his or her own childhood experiences. Ware (1977) points out that recalling one's own experiences of being a child involves more than a cognitive process. In part, it involves getting in touch with "the child that is still within ourselves." Ware's own parental-empathy training program (Ware, 1977) included a component that focused on reexperiencing childhood experiences. The parents were asked to interact with each other in an activity playroom that contained materials such as paint, crayons, paste, dolls, and other play equipment. They were told to try to recall themselves or other children at the preschool years while they interacted with each other. The workshop leaders also interacted with the parents as participants during the play period. Ware reports what with these instructions interaction patterns soon emerge that are typical of preschool children's play. The play period is then followed by a group discussion about the feelings that were evoked. Frequently heard are comments such as "It was like you had to force something," illustrating the barrier between adulthood and childhood, and the strangeness of the prelogical and primary process experience of very young children. The discussion also typically focused on the process of repression and amnesia for experiences during the preschool years. Further discussion is then directed to other aspects of the adult's experiences as they engaged in role taking of preschool children, including short attention span, the differences in adult and child time perspectives, the desire for stable and firm limits from adults, and the development of reaction formations to initial pleasure in making a mess with the finger paints and clay.

Some training programs have been developed around specific problems or domains of parent empathy. Gladding (1978) studied the relationship among "trait empathy," gender, and training on the ability to identify four kinds of infant cries; birth cries, hunger cries, cries of pain, and cries of pleasure. The subjects were college students, rather than parents, and only students with little prior experience as caregivers to infants were selected. Trait empathy was measured with the Hogan Empathy Scale and students who scored at least one standard deviation above or below the mean were assigned to the high- and low-empathy conditions, respectively. Half the subjects from each group were then randomly assigned to a control group. Subjects in the training condition listened in small groups to a 15-minute training tape focusing on how to recognize the four types of infant cries. Immediately after, they were asked to identify 24 infant-cry signals from a previously developed audiotape that presented instances of the four cries in random order. Subjects in the control group identified the cries in a similar manner, but without the prior training session. The results showed that training was positively related to correct identification of all but the pleasure cry. Furthermore, females and males performed equally well after training, despite the fact that an earlier study by Wasz–Hockert, Partanen, Vuorenkoski, Valanne, and Michelson (1964) had shown that experienced females were more accurate than experienced males in identifying these same cries. This suggests that, with training, males may be as effective as females in identifying infants' cries. However, the study also produced two puzzling findings: the negative relationship between empathy measured on Hogan's scale and identification of the birth cry signal and the finding of no relationship between empathy scores and identification of the other type of cries.

Murphy (1979) developed a videotape for parents with disabled children that was designed to enhance their empathy for the concerns and feelings of the *siblings* of these children. Ten couples who were parents of a disabled child and at least one other, nondisabled child were shown the videotape, whereas 10 additional couples formed a comparison group that did not view the videotape. The videotape was designed to enhance empathy in the following five areas: (1) perception of children's concerns and feelings, (2) ability to identify children's feelings, (3) acceptance of children's feelings, (4) awareness of negative feelings about having a disabled sibling, and (5) factual information. Based on a series of paper and pencil measures administered 1 week prior to and 1 week following the showing of the videotape, parents who had viewed the program compared to the control group, had increased their awareness about possible negative feelings their nondisabled children might be having toward the disabled child. There were no significant increases in the other four aspects of parental empathy that were measured.

Differential Effectiveness and Generalizability of Parent-Empathy Training Approaches. Existent investigations of parental-empathy training programs hold out promise that the components of empathy can be taught to parents who can then utilize them in their interactions with their children. However, there have been almost no attempts to systematically compare the effectiveness of different parent-empathy approaches, either with regard to short-term or long-term effects. There has also been very little attempt to determine whether the increased empathy skills shown by the parents in the training situation transfer to family life outside the training situation.

One of the few studies comparing the effectiveness of two parent-empathy training approaches was performed by Klock (1977). The first approach was a microtraining program. This was a prestructured, directive program that included didactic presentation of materials, video models of specific behaviors, role-playing exercises, and home practice. The second approach was a nondirective discussion group that included reading materials related to empathic communication, as well as group discussion. Assessment of change in empathic skills was based on ratings of empathic communication behavior in pre and posttraining videotaped play sessions of each parent and one of this parent's children. Changes in knowledge about the principles of empathic communication and a follow-up measure assessing the parents' perceptions of the impact of the program were also administered. The results indicated that both groups showed significant gains in empathy, but not differential gains. However, a small sample size and the fact that the participants self-selected into groups are important problems with this study. As we make clear in the chapter on empathy training, the process of evaluating techniques and processes for increasing parents' empathic skills is a long-term undertaking that eventually requires, not the comparison of one whole program with another whole program, but sophisticated methodological designs in which the individual elements and components of a training package can be validated separately and in combination with other elements.

The problem of transfer of training was addressed in a study by Guzzetta (1976), using Goldstein's structured learning program, which includes components of modeling, role playing, and social reinforcement. In this study, the training was directed toward teaching parents of adolescents to respond empathically to their children. The parents were volunteer mothers who were assigned to one of four groups. In one group the mothers participated without their children, in a second group both mothers and children participated separately, and in the third group the mothers and children participated together. The fourth group was a control group whose members did not receive structured learning training. Empathy was assessed with a Parent Training Questionnaire that presented 15 situations likely to result in a breakdown in communication between parents and teenagers. In each situation the adolescent makes a statement to which the parent must write a response.

The training procedure consisted of showing the subjects a videotaped model responding with a highly empathic statement to the 15 situations in one form of the Parent Training Questionnaire. After viewing the model's response two times, the parents were asked to give their own responses to the situations to either the trainer of their group, or in the group where the children were participating, to their own children. All responses by the parents that were judged as either empathic (i.e., they were scored at Carkhuff's, 1969a&b level 3, 4, or 5) were given social reinforcement by the trainers. When a parent gave a nonempathic response (i.e., one scored at Carkhuff's level 1 or 2), she was provided with more high-empathy modeling. This sequence of modeling with the videotape and role playing by the group members was repeated once more. Following this, the group members engaged in further role playing, with their own children, or with another parent, or with the trainer, who played the adolescent's part. The adolescents who were participating without their parents received information about structured learning training, saw films of parent–adolescent problems, and participated in listening and communication exercises.

After the third week of training, all groups completed a second form of the Parent Training Questionnaire with both old and new situations. The results showed that the training groups scored significantly higher in empathy after the 3 weeks (6 hours total) of empathy training. The parents then participated in a behavioral test of empathy in which they were asked to make a response to 10 situations role played by their children. Both the questionnaire and these responses were then scored according to the Carkhuff scale.

The behavioral measure was considered the test of transfer of training. All the training groups showed higher empathic communication on this measure than the control group. Although presence of the children did not increase transfer of training, Guzzetta speculated that other transfer enhancers inherent in all the structured learning groups, such as general mediating principles to govern performance, stimulus variety, and performance feedback, may have led to a ceiling effect, with all groups responding at an equally high level on the measure designed to test transfer of training. It should be noted, however, that the transfer of training measure used was an analogue situation, rather than a naturalistic situation, and future research will need to investigate more fully the ability of parent empathy training to transfer to real-life family interaction. The issue of transfer of training remains a crucial one for this, as well as for other domains of empathy training, as we see in the next chapter.

8 Training

Our presentation thus far has sought to define and describe empathy as a process constituted of four sequentially related components. We have explored its theoretical structure, developmental antecedants, and substantial consequences in psychotherapy, education, and parenting. Though much still remains to be clarified regarding its nature, enough now appears to be understood about what empathy is, and enough has been demonstrated regarding its potency in significant interpersonal relationships, that the issue of means for its enhancement is appropriately raised. Who shall be trained, all or those demonstrating at least certain levels of empathic capacity? Who shall conduct the training, and are there consequences for trainee empathy enhancement of the level of trainer empathy? What do the major empathy-training methods consist of, and how much do they actually differ operationally? How can we interface our components perspective on empathy with available training techniques to yield optimal training method recommendations for each phase of the empathy process? What experimental designs will effectively further this effort, leading to ever more potent, prescriptive, and enduring empathy component training? These are among the several questions relevant to empathy training that we seek to raise and explore in the present chapter.

SELECTION

In recent decades, empathy training of one sort or another has become an especially frequent undertaking. Trainees have included young children (Feshbach, 1982c; Hatch & Guerney, 1976; Moore, 1980), adolescents (Avery, Rider, &

191

Haynes-Clements, 1981; Janoka, 1977; Lehman, 1972), undergraduates (Albert, 1974; Bath, 1976; Berenson, 1971), parents (Carkhuff, 1969a&b; Guzzetta, 1974; Vogelsong, 1975), senior citizens (Becker & Zarit, 1978; Isquick, 1978; Moyer, 1981), teachers (Aspy, 1975; Goud, 1975; Harman, 1978), nurses (Law, 1978; Layton, 1978), a variety of allied health professionals (Beale, 1978; Greensberg, 1981), and, most especially, counselors and counselor trainees (Birk, 1972; Carkhuff, 1969a&b; Pierce, Carkhuff, & Berenson, 1967). Almost without exception, these several dozen programmatic attempts to enhance levels of empathy have done so via an exclusive focus on training, with little or no companion concern with selection. It is as if an underlying assumption of each training program is that empathy—or rather, the capacity or potential to become highly empathic—is distributed equally throughout the population of potential trainees. Given this implicit assumption, attention to selection of those most likely to benefit from training does not occur. Instead, being viewed as of equal capacity, trainees are chosen randomly, or are self-selected, or become involved because of membership in a "natural" group (all members of a class, all employees, all residents). Yet empirically it is clear that trainees do *not* benefit equally from empathy training, some advancing a great deal, others very little or not at all. Because training resources—time, effort, funds, facilities—are finite, such a typical training outcome is inefficient at best and often quite wasteful. The fault here lies, we believe, in the implicit operating assumption of equal empathic potential. Rather than being equally distributed, we would propose that the capacity to be empathic, like most psychological qualities, is normally distributed. Efficiency and effectiveness, particularly given the availability of limited training resources, are best promoted by selecting for training those individuals (and perhaps *only* those individuals) most likely to benefit therefrom, i.e., those with demonstrable empathic capacity. Walstedt (1968) takes a similar position in urging that empathy training be essentially reserved for those people:

> who already have empathic capacity or innate endowment. It is not clear whether a high 'empathy quotient' is biologically determined, is a function of the mother–child interaction, and/or is socially acquired. It is Greenson's contention that we can be taught to use our empathic capacity . . . but that people with low empathic capacity cannot be taught. (p. 608)

How many high-potential individuals be identified? Two efforts to do so with Hogan's (1975) scale, a purported measure of empathic capacity, were unsuccessful (Charles, 1975; Courtois, 1973). We know of no measures thus far successful in this regard, and thus must fall back in this identification-selection effort upon reliance on marker variables. These are biographical and psychological qualities of the individual demonstrated to (or, in some instances, speculated to) serve as either antecedants or correlates of empathic capacity. They may each have little (or much) to do with empathy and empathic capacity *causally* but do seem to be part of the nomothetic network in which empathy lies and thus are an aid to identification of high-potential persons.

Allport (1961) postulated that empathy correlated with intelligence, esthetic attitude, breadth of experience, similarity with the other, intraceptiveness, and self-insight. Weinstein (1969) stressed cue sensitivity in this regard, which he described as a constitutionally determined level of attentiveness to environmental stimuli. Weinstein (1969), as well as Kerckhoff (1969), and Christiansen (1979) especially emphasized that "exposure to a breadth and variety of experiences [and their attendant social relationships] will promote the development of role-taking tendencies" (p. 29). Closely related to this broad predisposer to empathic capacity, others have included field dependence (Moore, 1978), sociability and extraversion (Hogan, 1969), and later born ordinal position (Stotland, 1971) and greater number of siblings (Moore, 1978) (more sibling availability as models and companions). Foote and Cottrell (1955), Hogan (1975), and Weinstein (1969) have each pointed strongly to empathic parental models as yet one other likely substantial marker useful in the identification of persons with high-empathic capacity. Not only may highly empathic parental models (as described in Chapter 2) enhance an individual's empathic capacity, there is also some reason to suspect a contrasting influence, one in which motivation and skill in empathic behaviors is fostered self-defensively by having egocentric, manipulative, or even aggressive parents. Hall (1979), examining the type of decoding ability at the heart of the cognitive analysis component in our definition of empathy, proposes a similar mechanism in her "responding to oppression" hypothesis:

> one possible explanation for women's superior decoding ability is that they develop fine skills in nonverbal judgment as a way of saving their skins. The hypothesis states that oppressed or subjugated people need to be alert and responsive in order to know how more powerful others are feeling from moment to moment. (p. 54)

This response to oppression explanation of sensitivity to other's affect has also been put forth by English (1972), Thomas, Franks, and Calonico (1972), and Weitz (1974).

In addition to these several biographical and psychological markers, one further cluster of qualities appears to be reflective of empathic capacity. Chief among these qualities, described by Carkhuff (1969a&b) as "traditionally femi-nine response patterns," are "high scores on social service interests and nur-turant inclinations as well as on indexes of restraint, friendliness, deference, intraception, affiliation . . . and low scores on more aggressive, assertive, and achievement-oriented traits" (Carkhuff, 1969, (p. 80). How may additional markers predictive of empathic responsiveness be identified? We are not op-timistic about the value of psychological testing in this regard. As Carkhuff (1969) observes, and we largely agree: "These is no evidence to indicate that performance on traditional tests does anything but predict performance on traditional tests" (p. 80). We have long been in general agreement with this viewpoint and strongly favor an alternative assessment strategy. Drawing historically on the pioneering efforts at situational testing developed by the Office of Strategic Services during World War II, we and others sought in the 1960s to further the conceptual underpinnings and operational technology at the heart of such alternative, behavioral assessment (Goldstein, Heller, & Sechrest, 1966). Here, a physical-interpersonal environment is created replicating the real-world task to be faced by the testee. In such a simulation or trial setting, the testee is given the opportunity to display the very behaviors that constitute the selection criterion. In more recent work of this type, full-scale "Assessment Centers" have been created to process large numbers of testees across a diversity of behavioral selection tasks (Moses & Byhem, 1978). To Robert Carkhuff (1969a&b) goes the credit for incorporating this perspective into the realm of empathy training. He, as we, view empathy and behavioral assessment selection for high capacity therein from a components perspective:

> Those who are concerned with selection, therefore, must develop relevant indexes that discern those prospective helpers who can most meaningfully employ their training experiences and most effectively discharge their treatment functions. This goal can best be accomplished by breaking down both training and treatment into their critical process variables and assessing the level of functioning of the prospective helpers on these dimensions. The most relevant indexes that emerge for both training and treatment, then, are those which assess the helper trainee's level of communication and discrimination (p. 85)

By means of use of "standard helpees" (simulated clients) representative of the population(s) for which the trainee is being prepared, the trainee is "cast into the helping role" and behavioral assessment of trainee performance may then proceed. Clearly, behavioral assessment on empathy components criteria is a strategy for selection vis a vis empathy training that we strongly endorse.

TRAINER CHARACTERISTICS

In the preceding section we briefly examined a series of issues relevant to the selection of empathy trainees. We similarly wish to highlight our concern about the empathy trainer. We do so largely to underscore our belief that those concerned with the increased effectiveness of empathy training have given short shrift to both the selection process and trainer-relevant two concerns we believe to be as central to the outcome of such training as the training method itself.

Who shall the trainer be? Surely two decades of widespread employment plus substantial empirical evidence of effective performance (Durlak, 1979) have made clear the relative unimportance of level of credentials. All manner, background, and type of professional, paraprofessional, and nonprofessional change agents have shown their competence in a variety of treatment, teaching, and training endeavors, including empathy training (Carkhuff, 1969a&b). What personal qualities might the effective empathy trainer optimally process? One approach to answering this question is the long list of positive attributes combining to yield a near superhuman psychotherapist (Krasner, 1962), teacher (Getzels & Jackson, 1964), parent (Ginott, 1969), or other change agent. Because such composite persons are more an idealized abstraction than a realizable reality, the positive attribute listing answer is only minimally useful at best. We believe, however, that the prescriptive viewpoint we have adopted throughout this book suggests a better answer, or at least a better formulation of the question. Rather than ask about optimal trainer qualities in isolation from trainee and training method considerations, a more heuristic question vis a vis empathy enhancement is: What personal qualities might the effective empathy trainer, training type A trainees by means of method Y, optimally possess? The very few attempts thus far to be responsive to this prescriptive strategy in the context of empathy training have been at best only beginning approximations of effective trainer x trainee x training method matches. The best existing example is the effort of Carkhuff (1969), who comments with regard to training via his didactic-experiential method:

> Perhaps the most critical variable in effective counselor training is the level at which the counselor–trainer is functioning on those dimensions related to constructive helpee change. In relation to helpee change, research has led us to discern what we term both facilitative and action-oriented interpersonal dimensions (empathy, respect, concreteness, genuineness, self-disclosure, confrontation, immediacy) as the critical ingredients of effective interpersonal processes. . . . Hopefully, the trainer is not only functioning at high levels on these dimensions but is also attempting to impart learnings concerning these dimensions in a systematic manner, for only then will he integrate the critical sources of learning—the didactic, the experiential and the modeling. (pp. 152–153)

For Carkhuff (1969a&b) then, the answer regarding optimal trainer qualities is clear. The empathy trainer must, perhaps above all, be a highly empathic individual. This assertion finds considerable empirical support, especially from Carkhuff's own research group, e.g., Carkhuff (1969), Carkhuff & Berenson (1967, 1969). That these findings emerge in the context of a particular training method, the didactic experiential, is at least an important step forward in a prescriptive direction. Which personal trainer qualities should optimally be present for the effective training of which trainees by means of other empathy-training methods remains a high-priority question for future research.

TRAINING METHODS

In contrast to the relatively scant attention devoted to the trainer and his or her selection and qualifications in the empathy-training literature, training methods have been the focus of voluminous theorizing, speculation, and empirical scrutiny. Though as earlier chapters revealed, psychotherapy, education, and parenting have been the major contemporary realms of empathy training, the bulk of both theory construction and research examination vis a vis empathy training has occurred in the psychotherapy arena, and it is primarily to this literature to which we now turn.

Six major training approaches, or training "packages," have been developed in the past several years designed to enhance the level of psychotherapist or counselor empathy, and/or that of persons not in helper roles (couples, parents, teachers, adolescents, etc.). Because these are, in essence, "empathy training today," we describe and illustrate them in some detail. But we are also deeply concerned with "empathy training tomorrow," and thus we seek to critically evaluate these packages and chart directions for the future of such training that we believe will be far more productive of reliable and enduring empathy enhancement than results from even the better of the present methods.

Didactic-Experiential Training

In the mid-1960s, Truax, Carkhuff, and their research team introduced the didactic-experiential approach to the training of that small cluster of purportedly facilitative helper behaviors that constituted the heart of the Rogerian approach to the helping process (Truax & Carkhuff, 1967; Truax, Carkhuff, & Douds, 1964). Chief among these training goals was high levels of helper empathy. Truax et al. (1964) held that traditionally didactic and traditionally experiential approaches each had much to offer, but that neither alone was sufficient for the task at hand. They comment:

> The didactic orientation emphasizes passing down an accumulated store of knowledge in the traditional learning setting. Clearly, the flow is downward. That is, for the student the experience is one of accepting and incorporating a set of 'established' premises, from which he may deduce certain modes of doing things in therapy. In contrast, while the experiential approach nurtures, elicits and even predicts behavioral change on the part of the supervisee, it focuses upon instituting certain attitudinal conditions. The belief is that growth, born of the trainee's own experience, will follow. In generalizing from experience, the flow is upward. Thus, the didactic orientation is largely deductive and the experiential orientation is largely inductive. The approach set forth . . . incorporates both the didactic and the experiential: the therapist supervisor brings to bear his knowledge of therapy accumulated from his own experience and the experiences and work of others in the context of a therapeutic relationship which provides for the trainee the conditions which . . . are essential for psychotherapeutic personality change. (p. 242)

Implementation and evaluation of this training philosophy became an active pursuit of this research team, and in 1967 Truax and Carkhuff presented a detailed operational statement of the training orientation reflected previously. The didactic-experiential training approach, circa 1967, contained several constituent procedures. Sequentially, it began with didactic input seeking to provide trainees with a base of relevant knowledge and then proceed to a series of experiences (some didactic, some experiential, some an admixture of both), further reflecting the overriding training philosophy. Concretely, its procedures were:

1. Reading list: Extensive readings from a diverse range of psychotherapy theorists and practioners.
2. Tape library: To supplement the readings, trainees listened to 25 hours of individual and group psychotherapy sessions of various orientations.
3. Discrimination practice: Trainees were given copies of the Accurate Empathy Scale (see page 199) and asked to rate specific excerpts from the therapies of experienced therapists included in the tape library listening.
4. Reflection of feeling: Series of tape-recorded patient statements were presented to trainees who, first privately and then out loud as called upon during group supervision, were required to provide interchangeable responses indicative of Level 3 empathy on the Accurate Empathy Scale.
5. Live role play: Trainees paired off and, alternately in the role of helper and helpee, sought to respond when in the helper role with high levels of empathy. This experience provided opportunity for role-played empathic responding for larger units of time than had the responding to taped excerpts.
6. Feedback: Live roleplay responses were tape recorded, brought to group supervisory sessions, and rated by group members on the Accurate Empathy Scale—thus providing feedback to the responding trainee, and both further modeling and further empathy discrimination training to all other members of the training group.
7. Therapeutic interviews: Trainees met with actual clients for first single interviews and then extended series of interviews of a psychotherapeutic nature.
8. Feedback: As with the role played experiences, the therapy interviews were tape recorded and utilized for feedback purposes in group supervision.
9. Quasigroup psychotherapy: In parallel with all the foregoing, and as one major reflection of the experiential thrust of this method, all trainees met regularly in a group therapy-like experience designed among other goals to enhance trainee's awareness of their own affective functioning.

A second formulation of the didactic-experiential approach appeared in 1969 (Carkhuff, 1969a&b), and we here present it in somewhat greater detail. We do so in response to the manner in which its format moves discernably and importantly in the direction of a components view of empathy—a perspective also at the heart of the present book. In later sections of this chapter we propose that an especially effective approach to empathy training appears to be a components approach, i.e., one in which each of the phases that constitute empathy is sequentially taught to trainees by means of one or more training methods *tailored to* the contents and processes that constitute the given phase. The 1969 formulation by Carkhuff of the didactic-experiential approach, with its dual empahsis on separate training for the discrimination of empathy and the communication of empathy, is a significant step in this components strategy direction.

Carkhuff (1969b) comments:

> There is substantial evidence to support the proposition that a high level of discrimination, insufficient in and of itself for a high level of communication, is nevertheless critical to a high level of communication. Since a high level of communication is the basic goal of training [Carkhuff & Berenson, 1967], it is meaningful to focus upon discrimination as a first stage of effective communication in the helping process. (p. 167)

The first phase of the training effort, therefore, is didactic-experiential empathy discrimination training. For purposes of building an initial knowledge base, trainees begin with discussions regarding the nature of empathy, its functions and consequences. In tandem with this didactic beginning, the program provides an in-depth exposure to a wide variety of taped counseling and psychotherapy sessions. In-session and homework assignments involve not only tape listening but also require trainees to rate taped helper responses on the Accurate Empathy Scale (Table 8.1). The procedure involved goes beyond rating per se. Trainees record their ratings, their reasons for them, and discuss these estimations in group feedback sessions with supervisors and peers.

Carkhuff (1969b) summarizes the discrimination training phase:

> We have found it most effective to begin with the dimension of empathy. Empathy is the key ingredient of helping. Its explicit communication, particularly during early phases of helping, is critical. Without an empathic understanding of the helpee's world and his difficulties as he sees them there is no basis for helping. In focussing upon training in the discrimination of the level of communication of empathic understanding in interpersonal processes, then, we first emphasize the critical nature of this necessary ingredient. We study its functions and effects as well as its qualification and modifications. Finally, we study those scales relevant to the assessment of the level of empathic understanding and apply them to taped material. (p. 173)

Moving on to the second component of empathy represented in this formulation, this essentially didactic series of empathy discrimination-enhancing experiences is then followed by intensive training in the effective communication of empathic understanding—a jointly didactic and experiential undertaking. The experiential facet finds overt expression primarily via the empathic, warm, genuine relationship that trainers functioning at high levels of these facilitative condi-

TABLE 8.1
Empathic Understanding in Interpersonal Processes a Scale
for Measurement

Level 1

The verbal and behavioral expressions of the helper either do not attend to or detract significantly from the verbal and behavioral expressions of the helpee(s) in that they communicate significantly less of the helpee's feelings and experiences than the helpee has communicated himself.

EXAMPLE: The helper communicates no awareness of even the most obvious, expressed surface feelings of the helpee. The helper may be bored or disinterested or simply operating from a preconceived frame of reference which totally excludes that of the helpee(s).

In Summary, the helper does everything but express that he is listening, understanding, or being sensitive to even the most obvious feelings of the helpee in such a way as to detract significantly from the communications of the helpee.

Level 2

While the helper responds to the expressed feelings of the helpee(s), he does so in such a way that he subtracts noticeable affect from the communications of the helpee.

EXAMPLE: The helper may communicate some awareness of obvious, surface feelings of the helpee, but his communications drain off a level of the affect and distort the level of meaning. The helper may communicate his own ideas of what may be going on, but these are not congruent with the expressions of the helpee.

In summary, the helper tends to respond to other than what the helpee is expressing or indicating.

Level 3

The expressions of the helper in response to the expressions of the helpee(s) are essentially interchangeable with those of the helpee in that they express essentially the same affect and meaning.

EXAMPLE: The helper responds with accurate understanding of the surface feelings of the helpee but may not respond to or may misinterpret the deeper feelings.

In summary, the helper is responding so as to neither subtract from nor add to the expressions of the helpee. He does not respond accurately to how that person really feels beneath the surface feelings; but he indicates a willingness and openness to do so. Level 3 constitutes the minimal level of facilitative interpersonal functioning.

Level 4

The responses of the helper add noticeably to the expressions of the helpee(s) in such a way as to express feelings a level deeper than the helpee was able to express himself.

EXAMPLE: The helper communicates his understanding of the expressions of the helpee at a level deeper than they were expressed and thus enables the helpee to experience and/or express feelings he was unable to express previously.

In summary, the helper's responses add deeper feeling and meaning to the expressions of the helpee.

Level 5

The helper's responses add significantly to the feeling and meaning of the expressions of the helpee(s) in such a way as to accurately express feelings levels below what the helpee himself was able to express or, in the event of on going, deep self-exploration on the helpee's part, to be fully with him in his deepest moments.

EXAMPLE: The helper responds with accuracy to all of the helpee's deeper as well as surface feelings. He is "tuned in" on the helpee's wave length. The helper and the helpee might proceed together to explore previously unexplored areas of human existence.

In summary, the helper is responding with a full awareness of who the other person is and with a comprehensive and accurate empathic understanding of that individual's deepest feelings.

tions are purportedly able to offer trainees. According to Carkhuff (1969), this training context, it is held, provides "the trainee with the experience of having his own communications understood in depth with a fineness of discrimination that extends his communications and allows him to understand himself at ever deeper levels" (p. 200). The opportunity to interact with one or more such facilitative trainers also provides, it is important to note, a significant empathy-modeling experience for trainees.

The primarily didactic component of empathy-communication training involves (1) responding to taped materials, (2) role playing, and (3) participation as helper in interviews with actual clients, plus receiving feedback on these communication efforts. In carrying forward these tape, role play, and real client interactions, the trainee is urged to utilize the following communication guidelines:

1. The helper will find that he is most effective in communicating an empathic understanding when he concentrates with intensity upon the helpee's expressions, both verbal and nonverbal.

2. The helper will find that initially he is most effective in communicating empathic understanding when he concentrates upon responses that are interchangeable with those of the helpee.

3. The helper will find that he is most effective in communicating empathic understanding when he formulates his responses in language that is most attuned to the helpee.

4. The helper will find that he is most effective in communicating empathic understanding when he responds in a feeling tone similar to that communicated by the helpee.

5. The helper will find that he is most effective in communicating empathic understanding when he is most responsive.

6. The helper will find that he is most effective in communicating empathic understanding when, having established an interchangeable base of communication, he moves tentatively toward expanding and clarifying the helpee's experiences at higher levels.

7. The helper will find that he is most effective in communicating empathic understanding when he concentrates upon what is not being expressed by the helper.

8. The helper will find that he is most effective in communicating empathic understanding when he employs the helpee's behavior as the best guideline to assess the effectiveness of his responses.

The didactic-experiential approach to empathy (and other facilitative conditions) training has been widely utilized since its initiation and also has been the focus of numerous studies seeking to evaluate its efficacy. With relatively few exceptions (e.g., Spadone, 1974), these several investigations have yielded results that support the value of the didactic-experiential training program as an effective means for enhancing empathy (Avery et al., 1981; Bath, 1976; Beale et al., 1978; Becker & Zerit, 1978; Berenson, 1971; Bierman, Carkhuff, & Santilli, 1972; Carlson, 1974; Deshaies, 1974; Gustafson, 1975; Housley & Magnus, 1974; Isquick, 1978; LaMonica, Carew, Winder, Haase & Blanchard, 1976; Pierce, Carkhuff & Berenson, 1967). Although it thus appears probable, even highly probable, that the didactic-experiential approach to empathy training—as operationalized previously—is an effective program for empathy training, it is not without its drawbacks. Chief among these, as is also true to varying degrees for the other training packages to be described later, are unanswered questions regarding the contribution of each of the package's separate methods to the training outcome. Almost all the evaluation research cited earlier compares the didactic-experiential package as a whole to either other packges or to control groups. Of the several separate training processes that constitute the didactic-experiential package, do all contribute to the apparently effective outcome, or just a few and, if a few, which ones? The program is long, involved, and expensive of time and other resources. If all its constituent processes contribute appreciably to outcome, fine; if not (as seems quite likely), further potency-identifying research seems necessary. We recommend in this context a research approach that Kazdin (1980) describes as a dismantling treatment strategy:

> The dismantling treatment strategy refers to analyzing the components of a given treatment. . . . Once a treatment package has been shown to 'work,' research may begin to analyze the precise influence of specific components. The purpose of dismantling treatment research is to understand the basis for behavior change. To dismantle a given technique, individual treatment components are eliminated or isolated from treatment. Comparisons usually are made across groups that receive the treatment package or the package minus the specific components. (p. 84)

The apparent need for a dismantling research strategy via a vis the didactic-experiential training package not withstanding, it is clear that the approach—both conceptually and operationally—stands as a major contribution to the domain of empathy training. To at least some significant extent, most of the remaining empathy-training packages that we now consider have been importantly influenced, directly or implicitly, by the didactic-experiential approach and its ramifications.

Interpersonal Living Laboratory

The interpersonal living laboratory, developed by Gerald Egan in 1976, represents an effort to bring together, for purposes of the training of empathy and a host of other human relations skills, the essence of two contemporary movements in the United States. The first, known variously as the encounter group, sensitivity group, T-group, or human relations group movement, was an effort to employ the opportunities inherent in the samll group structure when designed for purposes of interpersonal exploration, experimentation, and learning. The second and newer movement, still largely taking shape at the time Egan (1976) published his *Interpersonal Living: A Skills Approach,* is the psychological skills training movement, a now widely popular utilization of social learning and related instructional techniques for the purposeful teaching of discrete interpersonal and other behaviors. By bringing these two streams together in the manner he has, and in ways quite different from Carkhuff (1969a&b), we may fairly characterize Egan's (1976) effort as an experiential-didactic training package approach to empathy training. The essence of this approach is the simultaneous didactic instruction of trainees in a spectrum of interpersonal skills, while at the same time providing a group experience in which the newly learned skills may be experimented with—tried, provided with feedback, modified—in a semiprotective human context. Hence, an interpersonal living laboratory.

Group members (trainees) contractually commit themselves to certain types of behaviors and goals as a condition of participation in an interpersonal living laboratory group. According to Egan (1976), goals include:

> 1. Exploration. You will use your time in the group, first of all, to examine your own interpersonal style [in the operational sense of the psychological skills which constitute the individual, didactic training].
>
> 2. Experimentation. You will also use your time to alter your interpersonal style in ways you deem appropriate. One mode of altering will be to check out and strengthen basic interpersonal skills. Your work in the group should help you to consolidate and develop your interpersonal strengths while beginning to work at eliminating or coming to grips with your weaknesses. (p. 24)

These interpersonal learning goals are to be achieved, according to Egan (1976), by the (contractually stipulated) effort each trainee is expected to put forth toward establishing and developing relationships with other laboratory group members:

> Your first and overriding means of achieveing these goals is to participate actively in the process of establishing and developing relationships with your fellow group members. This process demands that:
>
> a. In everything you do, throughout the training and in all of the exercises, you are attempting to establish and develop a relationship with every other member of your group.
>
> b. As you move through the process of attempting to establish and develop these relationships, you observe at first hand your own interpersonal style.
>
> c. At the same time, you receive feedback from your fellow group members on your style, including your strengths and your weaknesses.

d. You have the opportunity to experiment with 'new' behavior—that is, to attempt to alter dimensions of your interpersonal style in order to become, in your own eyes, more interpersonally effective (pp. 24–25)

In order to facilitate a group culture promotive of member movement towards these goals, group leaders seek to help create a variety of group characteristics. The successful interpersonal living laboratory group is a psychologically safe and semiprotected environment in which experiential learning and a climate of experimentation are fostered. Its focus is "here and now" on within-group interpersonal relating. Its leaders are part facilitator, part member. It is a place where risktaking becomes possible, and interpresonal growth may result. Many of these characteristics, however, also describe the traditional sensitivity, encounter, or T-group. As noted earlier, what is different about the interpersonal living laboratory is its conjoint attention to didactic instruction in the array of interpersonal skills to be tried out and developed in the living laboratory of the small group.

Thus, concurrent with the establishment and development of the interpersonal living laboratory group, trainees participate in individual interpersonal living skills training and commit themselves to such skill training via stipulation of such commitment in the group participation contract. For each of the several skills constituting this effort, trainees (1) learn the theory underlying skill usage, (2) study a host of relevant examples, (3) practice the skill through a series of written exercises, (4) practice further in dyadic, face to face contexts, and (5) utilize the skill in the experimental–exploratory senses described earlier within the setting of the interpersonal living laboratory group. The skills thus taught, i.e., the interpersonal living laboratory "skills curriculum" or, as Egan (1976) puts it, "core interpersonal skills" consists of:

a. *Self-presentation skills.*   Included here are the skills of appropriate self-disclosure, concreteness, and expression of feeling.

b. *Response skills.*   Included here are the skills of attending and listening, the communication of empathic understanding, and the behavioral communication of genuineness and respect. Training in these two groups of skills will take place through the subgroupings made from your basic training group.

c. *Challenge skills.*   You will be trained in a set of advanced skills, including skills of higher-level empathic understanding, confrontation, and immediacy (direct "you-me" talk). Much of this training will take place in the larger group.

d. *Group-specific skills.*   You will be trained in how to use both self-presentation and response skills in the larger group. Initiating is more difficult in a group than in one-to-one dialogue. (p. 25)

As this abbreviated skills listing suggests, two levels of accurate empathic responding are taught in this training program. The first, "Primary Level Accurate Empathy," is equivalent in its process to Level 3, the level of interchangeable responding, in the Carkhuff (1969) system (See Table 8.1). The second, "Advanced Accurate Empathy,"—analogous to Carkhuff's (1969a&b) Levels 4 and 5, is defined by Egan (1976) as communicating "to the other person an understanding of not only what he actually says but also what he *implies*, what he hints at, what he fears to state more clearly" (p. 29). We now illustrate, in concrete terms, the materials and exercises utilized by interpersonal living laboratory trainees in learning these two levels of empathic communication.

Primary Level Accurate Empathy. Egan (1976) defines this first level of empathy as:

> a communication to the other person that you understand what he says *explicitly* about himself. In AE I, you don't try to dig down into what the other person is only half-saying, or implying, or stating implicitly. You don't try to interpret what he is saying, but you do try to get inside his skin and get in touch with *his* experiencing. (p. 10a)

The exercise whose segments illustratively follow are designed to sequentially and systematically build toward trainee competence in empathy thus defined (Egan, 1976):

Exercise 27: The Communication of Understanding of Feelings (One Feeling)
These are the kinds of statements you might hear in your group. Picture yourself listening to the speaker. This exercise should give you some experience of responding directly to the feelings of another.
Directions
Read the statement, pause for a moment, and then write down the description of the speaker's feelings that comes to mind immediately. Then reread the statements and check yourself for accuracy. The second time, see if you can come up with a better response to each statement. Feel free to use not only individual words but phrases as well.
Note that in the next few exercises you will use the somewhat artificial formula "You feel (word or words indicate feelings) because (words indicating the content, experiences, and/or behaviors underlying feelings)." This formula will get you used to identifying both feelings and content. Later on you will be asked to do it in your own way, using your own language.
  1. This is a hell of a mess! Everybody here's ready to talk but nobody is ready to listen. Are we all so self-centered that we can't take time to listen to one another?
     a. Your immediate response: You feel _____."
     b. Your response on reflection: "You feel _____."
  2. You and I have been fighting each other for weeks—not listening to each other, pushing our own agendas, being competitive. I think today we did what we feared the most. We talked to each other. And you know, it's been very good talking to you, or with you, rather than at you.
     a. Your immediate response: "You feel _____."
     b. Your response on reflection: "You feel _____."

Exercise 28: The Communication of the Understanding of Content
This exercise is the next step. You are asked not just to identify but also to communicate understanding of the experiences and/or behaviors that underlie the speaker's feelings.

In order to enable you to focus on just the content, the stems below will provide the "feeling" words or phrases. You supply merely the "because" part of the response. The stimulus phrases are the same as those for Exercise 27. You are still responding to those ten statements.

1. You feel angry because _____ .
2. You feel at peace because _____ .
3. You feel very pleasantly surprised because _____ .
4. You feel safe enough to risk yourself because _____ .

Exercise 29: The Communication of the Understanding of Feelings (More Than One Distinct Feeling)
When people speak to one another, they don't limit themselves to the expression of just one emotion. Often, conflicting or contrasting emotions are expressed, even in a relatively short statement. For example:
I love him a lot, but sometimes he really drives me up a wall!
The purpose of this exercise is to help you communicate primary-level accurate empathy—first with respect to feelings—to someone who expressed two different emotional states.

Read the following statements. Imagine that the person is speaking directly to you. In this exercise, limit yourself to responding to the two distinct emotions you see being expressed (in the next exercise you will be asked to deal with content). For the present, use the formula "You feel both . . . and. . . ."

1. George, I keep telling myself not to move too quickly with you. You are so quiet, and when you do talk you usually start with a statement about how nervous you are. It's obvious to me that right now you're pretty fidgety and probably wish that I hadn't said anything to you. It's like a checkmate; if I move I lose, and if I don't move nothing will happen between us, and I'd lose.
   "You feel both _____ and _____ .
2. Elaine, in the two weeks we've been together here my response to you has been very positive. It's a little hard to say this to you. My tendency is to get to know the men first in a social situation, since I feel more comfortable and accepted initially by men than by other women. I like you, though, and want to trust that feeling instead of waiting to see if you'll somehow "prove youself."
   "You feel both _____ and _____ .

Exercise 30: The Communication of the Understanding of Content (More Than One Distinct Feeling)
This exercise concludes the previous exercise and asks you to "put it together"—that is, to hook up distinct feelings with content. Distinct experiences and/or behaviors give rise to the distinct feelings.

Once you have shared your responses to Exercise 29, you have already identified the distinct emotions expressed by the speakers in the statement. Now that you have correctly identified the emotions, tie each emotion in with content, as in the example below. Continue to use the formula "You feel . . . because . . . and/but you also feel . . . because. . . ." The first one is an example.

1. You feel cautious with George because you want to respect his pace, but you also feel on edge because you're afraid that nothing is going to happen in your relationship.

Now continue to respond to the rest of the statements.

Check your responses with those of your fellow group members and with the suggested responses given in the Appendix. How accurate have you been? How "lean" are your responses? Are they too long?

Exercise 31: The Full Communication of AE 1, Both Feeling and Content

This exercise is designed to achieve two goals: First, you are asked to "put it all together" and respond completely with accurate empathy—that is, to respond to both feelings and content. Second, you are asked to begin to use your own language—your own verbal style—instead of the formula "You feel . . . because. . . ." By now this formula should have begun to outlive its usefulness. Genuineness demands that you respond to others naturally, using your own style.

Directions

Read the following statements. Try to imagine that the person is speaking directly to you. You have two tasks:

a. Respond with accurate empathy (primary-level), using the formula "You feel . . . because. . . ."

b. Next, write a response that includes understanding of both feelings and content but is cast in your own language and style. Make this second response as natural as possible. The first is an example.

Group Member A: I had a hard time coming back here today. I felt that I shared myself pretty extensively last week, even to the point of letting myself get angry. This morning I was wondering what kind of excuse I could make up for not being here.

a. You're feeling awkward about being in the broup tonight because—given last week—you aren't sure how I, or the others, will receive you.

b. It's not easy being here tonight. You've been asking yourself how you're going to be received. In fact, you're so uneasy that you almost didn't come.

1. John, why do you have to compare me to Jane and Sue? I do that so much myself—always trying to measure up to someone else's standards. It's something I'm really trying to break myself of. And then you come along and compare me, too.

    a. _____

    b. _____

2. Gary, you seem to have everything so together. You're good at all of these skills, and you even seem strong when you're talking about your vulnerabilities. Or, at least, when you're talking about some weak point I allow myself to hear only how you are on top of it, how you have it under control. And then I just take another long look at my own inadequacies.

    a. _____

    b. _____

Exercise 32: The Full Communication of AE 1: Contrasting Emotions

This exercise is an expansion of the previous exercise. Therefore, it also has two goals. You are asked to "put it together" again and respond with full primary-level accurate empathy. This time, however, the speaker will express two distinct or contrasting emotions. We don't lead simple emotional lives. We very often feel two sets of emotions in our transactions with others (for example, approach and avoidance). Accuracy demands that we be able to identify and respond to both, for responding to only one distorts the picture. Second, you are again asked to cast your response into your own language and verbal style.

Read the following statements. Try to imagine that the person is speaking directly to you. Then:

a.   Respond with AE I, using the formula "You feel . . . because. . . ," keeping in mind that the speaker will express more than one emotional state.

b.   Second, write a response that expresses your understanding in your own language and verbal style.

The first is an example.

> Group Member A: I've never experienced anything quite like this before. I can speak my mind in this group. I can be utterly myself, and even see myself in a kind of mirror through the feedback I get. I get encouraged to be more assertive because that's what I want and need; but people here aren't afraid to tell me that when I become more assertive I also become more controlling. I wonder why then, I still act a bit defensive here. Almost in spite of myself, everything I do here still says "Be careful of me."
>
> a.   You feel a great deal of satisfaction here because you can entrust yourself more fully than ever to us, and yet you feel uneasy because the trust isn't complete, and you find yourself still instinctively on guard.
>
> b.   You trust people here; you trust the direct way they deal with you, and you like that very much. But something is still making you cautious, and this need to be cautious seems to be making you uneasy.

1.   I always thought that doing exercises in groups would be very phony, but certainly can't say that about the exercise we just did. I'm still not sure that the physical touch part is really ''me,'' but maybe it would do me good to be freer in the ways I express myself. If exercises can help me be more myself or what I want to be, well, maybe they're all right—at least some of them.

   a.   _____.
   b.   _____.

2.   I don't know what to do with you! You look so sincere, and I believe you're sincere. I think you actually have my interests at heart. You talk to me here. You make me look at myself—my fears of getting close to others, my use of boredom as a defense. But the way you do it! You keep after me. You make the same point over and over again. Sometimes I want to run out of here screaming!

   a.   _____
   b._____

Exercise 33: The Practice of Primary-Level Accurate Empathy in Everyday Life

If responding with accurate empathy is to become part of your natural communication style, you will have to practice it outside the formal training sessions. If accurate empathy is relegated exclusively to officially designed helping sessions, it may never prove genuine. Actually, practicing accurate empathy is a relatively simple process.

1. Begin to observe conversations between people from the viewpoint of the communication of accurate empathic understanding. Does a person generally take the time to communicate this kind of understanding to another person? Try to discover whether, in everyday life, the communication of accurate empathic understanding (primary-level) is frequent or rare. As you listen to conversations, keep a behavioral count of these interactions (without changing your own interpersonal style or interfering with the conversation of others).

2. Try to observe how often you use the communication of accurate empathic understanding as part of your communication style. In the beginning, don't try to increase the number of times you use accurate empathy in day-to-day conversations. Merely observe your usual behavior.

3. Increase the number of times you use accurate empathy in day-to-day conversations. Again, without being phony or overly preoccupied with the project, try to keep some kind of behavioral count. Use accurate empathy more frequently, but do so genuinely. You will soon discover that there are a great number of opportunities for using accurate empathy genuinely.

4. Observe the impact your use of primary-level accurate empathy has upon others. Don't use others for your own experimentation, but, once you increase your use of genuine accurate empathy, try to observe what it does for the communication process.

Exercise 34: The Identification of Common Mistakes in Phase I

The following exercise deals with some of the common mistakes people make when responding to another person. These faults or mistakes consist, in effect, of poor execution of primary-level accurate empathy. Before you do the exercise itself, let's review briefly what some of these common mistakes are:

- responses that imply condescension or manipulation
- unsolicited advice-giving
- premature use of advanced-level accurate empathy
- responses that indicate rejection or disrespect
- premature confrontation
- patronizing or placating responses
- inaccurate primary-level empathy
- longwindedness
- cliches
- incomplete or inadequate response (such as "uh-huh")
- responses that ignore what the person said
- use of closed, inappropriate, or irrelevant questions
- use of inappropriate warmth or sympathy
- judgmental remarks
- pairing or side-taking
- premature or unfounded use of immediacy
- defensive responses

This list is certainly not exhaustive. Can you think of other mistakes? Some of these errors are demonstrated in the exercise that follows. You are asked to identify them.

However important it is to understand a person from his own frame of reference, there is still a tendency not to do so—to do many other things instead. One function of this exercise is to make you aware of the many different ways in which it is possible to fail to communicate basic empathic understanding to others.

Directions

Following are a number of statements made by various group members, followed by a number of possible responses.

a.   First, if the response is good—that is, if it is primary-level accurate empathy—give it a plus (+) sign. However, if it is an inadequate or poor response, give it a minus (−) sign.

b.   Second, if for any reason you give the response a minus (−), indicate briefly why it is poor or inadequate (disrespect, premature confrontation, defensiveness, judgmentalness, condescension, and so on). A response may be poor for more than one reason. Make your reasons as specific as possible.

Study the example following and then move immediately to the exercise.

Example

Group Member A: I have high expectations of this group. I think we've developed a pretty good level of trust among ourselves, and I'd like to start taking greater risks. The longer I'm here the more desire I have to learn as much as possible about myself. I want you to help me do this, and I want to do the same for you.

a.   (−) Hey, I wish you wouldn't speak for me. I'm not at all sure that my
expectations are the same as yours. I think you're being pretty
idealistic.
Reason: <u>defensive, judgmental, accusatory</u>   .

b.   (+) Your enthusiasm is growing. There are a lot of resources here, and
you'd like to take advantage of them.
Reason: <u>(none because it is a plus)</u>   .

c.   (−) Do you think we're ready to do this sort of thing?
Reason: <u>inappropriate, closed question; vague</u>   .

d.   (−) Now, John, you've always been a good member, very eager; I appreciate your eagerness very much, but festina lente, as the Romans
said—"make haste slowly."
Reason: <u>condescending, parental, advice-giving</u>   .

e.   (+) Your enthusiasm's infectious, John—at least for me. I think that I,
coward that I am, am ready for a bit more risk, myself.
Reason: <u>(none because it is a plus)</u>   .

1.   I didn't feel right barging in on Paul and Marie's conversation, so I waited until I thought they were finished. I keep thinking that people will get angry if I interrupt. It may be the wrong way to be, but I don't interrupt people outside the group, and it's hard for me to think that it's okay here.

a.   ( ) It seems that you're afraid of being rejected if you interrupt. And
rejection really hurts you, because you don't see yourself as a worthwhile person.
Reason: _____ .

b.   ( ) I think that's pretty unfair of you, since you don't give Paul and
Marie much credit.
Reason: _____ .

    c. ( ) Peter, you know the contract here. What you call "barging in" is merely "owning" one of the interactions. I know you're timid, but I think you should push in anyway.

Reason: _____.

    d. ( ) Direct "owning" of another conversation just doesn't seem right to you—so it's really hard for you to move in.

2. I think my skill level has improved significantly within the last two or three weeks. I'm able to express my feelings much more openly and honestly, and feeling more confident has helped me to become less defensive.

    a. ( ) You feel half-finished because you haven't been able to lick your defensiveness completely.

Reason: _____.

    b. ( ) Yeah. I can see that.

Reason: _____.

    c. ( ) How have you managed to become less defensive?

Reason: _____.

    d. ( ) I know your skills are improving, but I can't say that I see you as less defensive.

Reason: _____. (pp. 112–113)

Advanced Accurate Empathy.   Once the trainee has shown mastery of Primary Level Accurate Empathy and its sister initial skills, training advances to deeper levels of accurate empathic communication. Such communications may take several forms (Egan, 1976):

Expressing What is Only Implied
    The most basic form of advanced accurate empathy is to give expression to what the other person only implies as he communicates ideas to the group.
    Group Member D: I've gotten in touch with resources for relating here that I never realized I had. At least in any full way. I see that I'm caring, that I can talk concretely, that I'm unafraid to reveal myself to others who give me half a chance. I'm not trying to blow my own horn. I'm just saying that these discoveries are important to me.
    Group Member E: These resources are very real, and their discovery has been— well, exciting for you.
    Group Member F: I hear a note of determination. Now that you've gotten in touch with these resources, you're going to make them a part of your interpersonal life. And that's even more exciting than doing well in the group.

The Summary
    You can also communicate advanced accurate empathy by bringing together and summarizing what the other has presented in bits and pieces during the group experience. This summarizing helps the other person focus on his interpersonal behavior in a new way. He sees himself from a different frame of reference.
    Group Member B: Let me see if I can put some of this together. Different things seem to keep you from making contact with different people here. George and Jim are too strong, too assertive, and their strength makes you keep your

distance. On the other hand, you're afraid that Sarah might become dependent on you—for this is her tendency anyway. You and Mary haven't been able to find any "common ground." You want to establish a closer relationship with me, but you hesitate because you're not sure that I want any kind of relationship. I don't think that I'm misrepresenting what you yourself have said in your interactions here, but I'd like you to check me out on it.

Group Member A: Oh boy! I really hadn't realized that in one way or another I was saying "No!" to everyone here.

Identifying Themes

AE II includes the identification of behavioral and emotional themes as group members go about the business of exploring their interpersonal styles and establishing relationships. For instance, without saying so explicitly, a group member may intimate through what he reveals about himself and through the way he behaves in the group that he tends to be a dependent person.

Group Member B: I've been thinking of some of the things you've said here, Ned and trying to hook up these up with the ways I see you acting here. You're hesitant to challenge anyone, especially the "strong" members in the group. You say things like "I've been quiet because other people haven't given me the kind of feedback I need." You've asked me outside the group for feedback on how you are coming across. The message I tend to get out of much of this from you is "I'm not my own person. I depend on others quite a bit. I don't value myself; I wait to see how others value me first." Perhaps this is too strong. I'd like to find out how you're reacting to what I'm saying.

Ned: What you're saying is very painful for me to hear. It's even more painful because of the truth in it.

Helping Another Draw Conclusions from Premises

Still another way of conceptualizing advanced accurate empathy is to help another person draw his own conclusions from the premises that he himself lays down.

Group Member E: I know I'm quiet here, but I don't believe that's any reason for people to pick on me, to make me feel like a second-class citizen. I've got resources. I can say a lot of the things that others say, but they move in first.

Group Member F: The logic of what you're saying seems to be: one, I don't want to appear to be a second-class citizen; two, I have what it takes to be an active member; three, I'm going to begin to take my rightful place in this group. I'm not sure whether I'm saying too much.

"Drawing a conclusion" will often deal with how the other person wants to behave within the group (or in interpersonal relations generally.) If the "conclusion" you help your fellow group member draw is not in his premises, your empathy will be seen as an attempt to make him behave in ways that are acceptable to you. Again, accuracy is extremely important, as are tact and timing.

To develop competence in these diverse expressions of Advanced Accurate Empathy, the following exercises are utilized.

Exercise 40: Advanced Accurate Empathy: An Exercise in Self-Exploration

One way of making sure that you are careful in using confrontational skills is to use them on yourself first. The purpose of this exercise is to make you think about some dimensions of your interpersonal style and behavior at two different levels (roughly corresponding to AE I and AE II). Self-understanding and being in touch with your own feelings and emotions should (at least logically) precede being in touch with deeper dimensions of the interactional style of others.

Directions

1. Read the examples given below.
2. Choose some situation or issue or relationship having to do with your interpersonal style that you would like to take a deeper look into. Choose something that you will be willing to share with your fellow group members.
3. Briefly describe the issue (as is done in the examples).
4. As in the examples below,

    a.   Write a statement that reflects a primary-level accurate empathic understanding of the issue you have chosen. This statement should reflect understanding of both your feelings and the behaviors/experiences underlying these feelings.

    b.   Write a statement that reflects your advanced accurate empathic understanding of this issue. This understanding should go deeper into the issue.

Example 1

Issue. I'm concerned about the quality of my "being with" others in interpersonal and social situations.

    a.   I enjoy being with people. I meet people easily, and I'm generally well received and well liked. I make others feel at home. I'm outgoing and, to a degree, uninhibited when I'm with others—I'm humorous, I try to understand the world of others, I show an interest in what they are doing. I also try to be careful with others; that is, I try not to be "too much" (AE I).

    b.   When I'm with people, even though I'm outgoing, I'm not "all there." I don't tend to share myself deeply with others. Therefore there is something almost superficial (perhaps this is too strong a word) about my "being with" others. In my deepest moments, I am alone with myself. Perhaps I haven't learned to share my deeper self with anyone. I may even be afraid to do so (AE II).

Exercise 41: Advanced Accurate Empathy: Understanding Others More Deeply

Before trying to use advanced accurate empathy "on the spot" in your group, you can, through this exercise, prepare yourself at a leisurely pace for such empathy. This exercise should help you look before you leap into advanced accurate empathy.

Directions

This exercise is the same as the previous one, except that your attention is now directed toward your fellow group members instead of yourself.

1. Read the examples given below.
2. Consider each of your fellow group members one at a time. Choose some dimensions of each one's interpersonal style that you would like to explore at both the AE-I and the AE-II level. Remember, you are trying to understand the person more deeply, not "psych him out."
3. Briefly describe the issue for each (see the examples).
4. As in the examples below,

    a.   For each, write a statement that reflects a primary-level accurate empathic understanding of the issue you have chosen (feelings and content). Write the statement as if you were speaking directly to the person.

b. For each, write a second statement that reflects your advanced accurate empathic understanding of this issue. Write the statement as if you were speaking directly to the person.

Example 1

Issue. John is both satisfied and dissatisfied with the strengths in interpersonal relating he manifests in the group.

a. John, you come across in the group as very self-assured. Most of the group members seem to enjoy interacting with you, and they do so frequently. You are understanding. You reveal how you feel about each of the group members without "dumping" your emotions on them. At one level, you seem to enjoy your position in the group. You get a great deal of respect and even admiration, and you find something satisfying in this (AE I).

b. John, even though you share yourself a great deal, by telling others how you are reacting to them as the group moves along, you don't speak much about your own interpersonal style. It may be that you are hesitant to do so, or that others box you in by putting you on a pedestal. Whatever the case, I sometimes see you wince slightly when you get positive feedback. I'm beginning to suspect that you feel you aren't allowed to share your vulnerabilities here, and that you're beginning to resent it (AE II). (pp. 161–170)

We have provided extensive examples of the diverse materials and creative exercises that constitute the empathy-training components of the interpersonal learning laboratory approach. Although this creative, systematically sequenced, and apparently comprehensive training package appears to be most useful, it has (unlike the other packages to be examined) given rise to very little empirical research evaluating its training impact. It most deservedly warrants such scrutiny.

In the early 1970s, there began to emerge in the United States the development of a new style of psychological intervention. It had its historical beginning in both education and psychology. Education's contribution was diverse but expressed itself in the spirit of various efforts to teach nonacademic, personological qualities, e.g., Character Education (Bain & Clark, 1966; Hill, 1965; Trevitt, 1964), Moral Education (Kohlberg, 1969, 1970, 1972, 1976), Affective Education (Miller, 1976). This belief in the value of didactic, instructional techniques for the purposive teaching of personal attributes also found concrete expression in both the hundreds of highly diverse personal development courses taught in America's over 2000 community colleges, as well as in the several hundred self-instructional self-help books so popular in the United States today. These several historical and contemporary educational strands—each reflecting both processes and contents targeted toward personal change or personal growth—interwove with complementary themes long present in psychology. We refer in particular to the enduring and pervasive concern in American psychology with the learning process—its theoretical bases, its empirical context, its applied implications. Psychology's deep interest in learning and its more recently emerging broad attention to social learning combined in the early 1970s with the educational perspectives and technologies mentioned earlier to yield the beginnings of the psychoeducational skills training movement. It has been a movement captured by several names—psychological education, psychological skills training, interpersonal skills training, social skills training, and more. At least two dozen programmatic expressions of this orientation have been formulated and implemented. In the present context, we present and examine the three psychoeducational skills training programs that have devoted greatest attention to the training of empathy. Though the development of the three approaches occurred in a manner largely independent from one another, their shared philosophy and overlapping procedures justifiably enable us to view them as an empathy-training method constellation.

Relationship Enhancement

The psychoeducational skills training program we consider first is the product of the sustained and creative efforts of Bernard Guerney and his research group. Guerney (1977) helps orient us to his approach with his statement of purpose that:

> Relationship enhancement (RE) therapy and programs are educational services designed to enhance relationship between intimates, especially between family members. RE programs can be conducted with individuals, with dyads, or with larger groups. The purpose of the programs is to increase the psychological and emotional satisfaction that can be derived from such intimate relationships and, in addition, to thereby increase the psychological and emotional well-being of the individual participants. (p. 1)

and further:

> The purpose of RE programs is to give the participants skills that will allow them to be empathic when they want to be and to try to encourage them to try to use these skills at a variety of times and in a variety of situations. (p. 19)

The curriculum or training objective of the RE approach consists of four sets of skills: (1) the expressive,(s) the empathic responder, (3) mode switching, i.e., skill in the ability to switch between expressive and responsive, and (4) facilitator skills, which concern the ability to teach the first three skills to others. Guerney (1977) concretizes empathic skill as follows:

> The Empathic Responder Mode
> This mode might be explained to clients as follows.
> Eliminating fear and creating an atmosphere of respectful acceptance is the function of the empathic responder. Even when you totally disagree, it is still possible to show respect, appreciation, and understanding of another person. In

effect, the empathic responder says to the expresser: I will respect and value you as a person, regardless of what your feelings and wishes may be, and whether I disagree with them or not. I appreciate the opportunity to assist you in your efforts to understand your wishes and feelings because I want you to communicate them to me more and more openly, honestly, and nonspecifically. Such communication affords me the opportunity to understand you better and work more realistically toward enhancing our relationship. The more you can convey such an attitude to your partner, the more your partner will be able to do likewise in response to your communication of your own needs and feelings.

In the empathic responder mode, the attitude that you adopt is the most important thing. You must strive to put yourself in a receptive frame in mind. Your attitude must be: Nobody can help seeing things the way they see them, and nobody can help feeling the way they feel. You must say to yourself:

'If my partner's perceptions are wrong, or if I think that these faulty perceptions have given rise to feelings that need not be there, or that should be different than they are, I will soon have my turn to say so. I can very shortly be the expresser and express my perceptions and the feelings I wish that my partner would be able to experience if only my partner perceived the situation as I do. But while my partner is expressing his own outlook, I can best help my partner, myself, and our relationship by completely understanding how my partner does perceive the situation and how he does feel. It is on this basis that we can best proceed to enhance our relationship in an enduring way. I can do this best by temporarily setting aside my own perceptions, and my own reactions, and my own feelings. If I do have strong feelings, I will not have to put them aside for more than a moment. In a moment I can take the role of expresser myself.'

I must strive to put myself in my partner's shoes and to try with all the energy and heart I can muster to see the world through my partner's eyes at this moment in time. I must try to understand exactly how my partner is perceiving the situation and exactly what my partner's feelings are about the situation.

Because I can never be sure that I have fully grasped another's views or feelings, I must check out my understanding with my partner. Moreover, my feedback to my partner must do much more than establish the accuracy of my understanding. In the tone and in the manner of my feedback, I must also try to convey my sincere interest in my partner's viewpoint. I must try by the tone and manner of my statement to convey that I accept unconditionally my partner's right to express honestly his or her own unique feelings and view of the world.

The word empathy epitomizes what you are trying to do. By empathy we mean putting yourself inside the skin of another person and being able to share the world that he sees and feels. The highest level of empathic understanding is reached when you have put together what has been said and the manner in which it has been said in a way that goes beyond the words used. You can then articulate your partner's views and feelings in a way that expresses them even more accurately and fully than he has been able to do himself. You must then communicate this deep level of understanding to your partner in a warm and accepting manner. We don't mean that you will have detected something that will come as a surprise to your partner, but rather that you've focused his feelings in a clearer way than he has been able to do as he struggled to understand and express them himself.

When you are responding only with empathy, as we wish you to do, there are many things that you will not be doing:

1.   You cannot be asking your partner questions. For example, you cannot be asking: "What makes you think that? How do you feel about that? How long have you felt this way? Do you always feel this way? and What do I do to make you feel that way?" Questions have the effect of diverting your partner's attention from his or her own stream of communication by seeking information that your partner has not freely chosen to give. To ask such questions would violate the expresser's right to maintain complete direction over the flow of the communication, to explore what he wants to explore, and to say what he thinks needs to be said in the way, and in the order he prefers. Often your attempt to clarify your partner's views and feelings should be stated in a questioning tone of voice. It is appropriate to be tentative in your empathic reflections of your partner's views; but not appropriate, as the empathic responder, to seek new information. If you feel the need for such information in order to later express your own needs and views, then when you become the expressor you should tell your partner the information you wish to have.

2.   You cannot present your own opinion, perception, and viewpoint about what your partner is saying. We will make it easy for you to switch from being a responder to being an expresser whenever you have a strong urge to present your own viewpoint or feelings, but while you are the responder you do not express your own feelings.

3.   You must not interpret things for the speaker. That is, you must not add your own reasoning as to causality, make connections between different events, or between events and feelings, in a way that presents things in a different perspective from that in which your partner seems to be viewing the situation.

4.   You must not make suggestions about how your partner might alter the situation in a favorable way or solve a problem.

5.   Above all, you must avoid making judgments about what your partner has said. Your own evaluation of the validity of your partner's viewpoint, or the correctness, effectiveness, or morality of your partner's statements must not enter into your empathic statements.

When your partner takes the risk of an honest expression of needs and feelings and meets with your acceptance, there is an increase in his expectation that he can afford to be open and honest with you about his needs and feelings. Each time you provide accepting understanding, you will have increased the probability that your partner will communicate more openly, directly, and honestly with you in future communications. Conversely, each time you fail to be empathic, and instead say something that denies the importance or relevance of any of the speaker's communications, you raise your partner's expectation of future rejections and diminish the probability that your partner will communicate with you in an open and constructive manner. Even a rejecting tone or manner will have this undesirable effect. It is the accumulated weight of thousands of such exchanges—some, of course, having much more impact than others—that will determine whether communication proceeds to become better, remains stagnant, or deteriorates.

It is almost impossible to train a person to speak openly, honestly, and constructively of his innermost interpersonal wishes, needs, and feelings, unless he has acquired faith that such expressions will meet with acceptance rather than with coolness or rejection. Until he has a measure of such faith, he will hardly be aware himself of what these needs and wishes are, in the midst of a dialog, let alone be capable of communicating them. Therefore, in the early phases of your training we will put more emphasis on helping each of you to acquire good empathic responding skills and later on we will put more emphasis on helping you acquire good expressive skills. However, both skills will be taught from the start of the program. (pp. 26–29)

The psychoeducational procedures by which the foregoing contents are taught to RE trainees are collectively describable as social learning techniques. Following opening introductions and early rapport and trust-building efforts, the nature of the RE program, its procedures, contents, and goals are explained to the participating couples, parent–child dyads, families, or other trainees. Such structuring importantly includes presentation, elaboration, discussion, and personalization of the description of empathy presented previously. Incorrect skill use in the context of one or another type of communication conflict is demonstrated by the RE trainer, as is the correct use of empathic responding in the context of the same conflicts. These modeling portrayals are discussed in depth by the participants, who are encouraged to respond with similar skill levels both within the group in interactions therein and outside the group, in practice and homework activities. Ancillary to these training procedures are such trainer-initiated techniques as the use of graded expectations vis a vis skill improvement, social reinforcement for effective skill use, attention to nonverbal expressive accompaniments to verbal behavior, presentation of relevant factual data, and major attention to discriminating appropriate and productive from inappropriate and progress-retarding trainer responses. The Relationship Enhancement approach has taken several programmatic forms: Conjugal Relationship Enhancement, Filial Therapy, Parent–Adolescent Relationship Development, and Pupil Relationship Enhancement.

These diverse operationalizations of the Relationship Enhancement approach to training empathy and related skills have received substantial, rigorous research scrutiny (Collins, 1971; Coufal, 1975; Ginsberg, 1977; Guerney, 1964, 1977; Harrell & Guerney, 1976; Hatch & Guerney, 1975; Preston & Guerney, 1982; Stover & Guerney, 1967; Vogelsong, 1974, 1975). The collective impact of these several evaluative investigations is supportive of the effectiveness of the Relationship Enhancement approach in general, and its specific training procedures in particular. As we noted in our introduction to the psychoeducational training approaches, we revisit most of the same training interventions again as we now turn to sister empathy skills training approaches.

Microtraining: Enriching Intimacy Program

Since their initial publications in the late 1960s, Alan Ivey and his research team have energetically pursued the development of a skills orientation to behavior change that has found concrete expression in counseling, teaching, and training contexts in series of programs termed microcounseling, microteaching, and microtraining. The "micro" quality of these programmatic interventions is the use of social learning techniques to teach highly discrete, segmented behavioral skills. One microtraining subprogram, Enriching Intimacy, focuses substantially on empathy training and thus is the target of our attention here.

In the Enriching Intimacy program (as in all microtraining), the skills to be taught are first operationalized in especially concrete, at times even minute, behavioral form. Ivey & Authier (1971) comment:

> The Enriching Intimacy (E.I.) program [proceeds by] teaching via a microtraining format specific behaviors . . . demonstrated to be aspects of empathy, genuineness and warmth. The program is divided into four stages: (1) teaching the behavioral components of respect, (2) teaching the behavioral components of empathy, (3) teaching the behavioral components of genuineness, and (4) an integrative group phase . . . within each skill learning phase, model tapes, five-minute practice sessions with role playing which are simultaneously videotaped, and immediate feedback during the review sessions are all part of the [micro] training program. Additionally, operational definitions of each behavioral component are discussed, and for the most part the skills are focused on singly. (p. 266)

With this procedural overview as context, how then is empathy operationalized?

> The behavioral components [of empathy] . . . consist of many of the behavioral components of respect [attending behavior, minimal encouragement to talk, open question, paraphrasing], but for the most part, the use of the skills, especially the nonverbal skills, is intensified. Thus, eye contact may be more intense; facial expression may be showing more than interest, perhaps even concern; and seating distance may be closer, perhaps even with touching occurring. The main difference [from respect] with regard to verbal skills is their focus on feelings. The format for the empathy training portion is similar to that of the respect portion of training with two major exceptions. The first exception is that there is a large emphasis given to identification of feelings, and a feeling word list is used for this purpose. Once the trainees have expanded their feeling word vocabulary, they listen to audiotapes of clients' statements of personal concern in an attempt to identify as accurately as possible the feelings the client is expressing. The second exception, related to the above, involves the trainee's viewing silent videotapes as a way of helping them become more aware of the nonverbal components of feelings. Other than these two exceptions, though, the training involves the trainees' focusing on one skill at a time, following the traditional microtraining format. (pp. 267–268)

As was the case for Relationship Enhancement, Microtraining and its Enriching Intimacy operationalization has been examined in some depth in comparative training outcome research and has acquitted itself well (Authier & Gustafson, 1973, 1975; Gustafson, 1975; Gustafson & Authier, 1976; Ivey & Authier,

1971). Both further study and use of the microtraining package and its constituent training components for empathy-training purposes is clearly to be encouraged.

Structured Learning

A third skills-oriented approach to empathy training finding substantial use in recent years in Structured Learning, developed by the senior author of this book and his research group (Goldstein, 1973, 1981; Goldstein & Goedhart, 1973; Goldstein & Sorcher, 1974; Goldstein, Sprafkin, & Gershaw, 1976; Goldstein, Sprafkin, Gershaw, & Klein, 1980, 1983). The Structured Learning method consists of most of the same psychoeductional-social learning procedures that essentially constitute Relationship Enhancement and Microtraining. These procedures, in the sequence utilized, include:

Modeling. Small groups of trainees are shown a series of specific and detailed displays—on audiotape, videotape, film or live—of a person (the model) performing the empathic or other skill behaviors constituting the group's training goal.

Role Playing. Trainees are then provided with extended opportunity and encouragement to rehearse the specific behaviors comprising the target skill, e.g., empathy, which they have seen or heard the model perform. The role playing is enacted in a manner as relevant as possible to each trainee's intended real-life use of the target skill.

Performance Feedback. Following each role play, the trainee actor is provided with recoaching and prompting as needed for improved performance and positive feedback, approval, or reward as his or her role played enactment of the skill becomes more and more similar to that of the model's.

Transfer Training. The three processes just sketched as well as certain additional procedures (see pages 230–233) are implemented in such a manner as to maximize the likelihood that what the trainee learns in the training context will be available as equally skilled behavior in his or her own real-world settings, e.g., home, school, work, etc.

This series of procedures, Structured Learning, has been demonstrated to be an effective means for training empathy to parents (Guzzetta, 1974), counselors (Cominsky, 1981), aggressive adolescents (Berlin, 1977; Trief, 1977), undergraduates (Shaw, 1978), teachers (Gilstad, 1978), nurses (Goldstein, Cohen, Blake, & Walsh, 1971; Goldstein & Goedhart, 1973), ministers (Perry, 1970), mental hospital attendants (Sutton, 1970), mental hospital patients (Goldstein, Sprafkin, & Gershaw, 1976), and home aides (Robinson, 1973).

Some examples of part of the empathy modeling displays used in certain of the preceding investigations include:

To psychiatric nurses (Goldstein & Goedhart, 1973):

1. Nurse: Here is your medicine, Mr. _____.
Patient: I don't want it. People here are always telling me to do this, do that, do the other thing. I'll take the medicine when *I* want to.
Nurse: So it's not so much the medicine itself, but you feel you're bossed around all the time. You're tired of people giving you orders.
2. Patient: My father and mother used to get into terrible fights. He'd come home and they'd really go at it. I'd have to pull the pillow over my head so I wouldn't hear the noise.
Nurse: It sounds like something that would really be upsetting, especially to a child.
3. Patient: I've been here for years, and what's it done for me? Things are the same, nothing's changed much. I don't think it ever will.
Nurse: You really feel discouraged. Not much has happened, and it doesn't seem like much will.

To home aides (Robinson, 1973):

1. Client: When my husband was alive I never really believed he cared about me . . . My doctor never seemed too sure what kinds of medicine I should have. . . . And the nurses seemed more interested in themselves than me. . . . So why should I believe *you* when you say you're interested in me?
Home aide: You've been disappointed by a lot of people who *said* they cared about you but really didn't seem to care. And you're wondering whether you should trust one more person who says she wants to help.
Client: Don't take it personally. It's just that people say they care, but I never feel they really do.
Home aide: I can understand how you don't know whether to believe a brand new person who's going to be helping you. You want to be sure that I'm *really* interested in you, that I really care.
2. Client: My kids could care less if I exist. They're only in Rochester, but somehow that's too far away to visit me. . .
Home aide: You'd really like them to visit, but somehow they don't seem interested enough in you to drive only 90 miles to see you.
Client: Yeah, you got the idea. If they were interested in me they'd make the short trip to come see me. But They don't even call. And I'll be damned if I'll invite them one more time.
Home aide: You're not about to beg them to visit you if they aren't interested. But you seem pretty hurt that your own children don't seem to care about you.
3. Client: (lovingly stroking cat on her hap while looking at him) This house is so empty and quiet. . . . Thank goodness for my cat.
Home aide: He gives you some company—someone to talk to, play with, be with. . . . And that comforts you in a lonely house.

Client: Yeah, I don't feel *so* lonely with him here, but it's still lonely.
Home aide: You enjoy spending time with him instead of being alone. But that's still lonelier than having *people* friends around.

To hospitalized mental patients (Goldstein, Sprafkin, & Gershaw, 1976):

Responding to the Feelings of Others (Empathy)

I'm Dr. Harris, Director of the Regional Psychiatric Center. You are now going to hear a tape which will show you how a number of people, many of whom have been hospitalized, successfully handle a skill which is very important in getting along well with other people. This skill is responding to the feelings of others or empathy. When we empathize with a person we try to figure out what the other person is feeling. If we think it may be helpful we then tell the other person our impressions. In the examples of responding to the feelings of others which you will hear, the main speaker does four things. He observes the other person's words and actions; decides what the other person might be feeling and how strong the feelings are; decides whether it would be helpful to let the other person know he understands his feelings, and tells the other person in a warm and sincere manner how he thinks he is feeling. When the speaker does these four things, he gains a new understanding of why people act the way they do. He makes others feel that they are understood and in this way makes them feel more comfortable. It is then more likely when other people feel understood that they will want to have further closer contact with him. If he does not attempt to understand how others are feeling, however, the other people may feel less comfortable with him and will be less likely to desire future contact. So, when you want to respond to the feelings of others better, you will benefit by following these steps. Remember:

1. Observe the other person's words and actions.
2. Decide what the other person might be feeling and how strong the feelings are.
3. Decide whether it would be helpful to let the other person know you understand his feelings.
4. Tell the other person in a warm and sincere manner how you think he is feeling.

You will now hear examples of these good steps in responding to another person's feelings. The people on these tapes are actors but what you will hear them say has actually occurred in real situations. We would like you to learn these steps in order to get the benefits of responding to the feelings of others well. So please pay close attention. Thank you.

1. Person 1: There's Jane, the new patient that came in this morning. I've been watching her for about an hour and she just sat there with her hands folded in her lap and her head bent forward and her hair is covering her eyes. She hasn't said a word to anybody. She looks as if she might be feeling really down. I wonder if I should go up and speak to her. She might want to just be alone for now. It's her first

day. But then, again, I'd kind of like to let her know that someone's here and that someone does care. Yeah, I'll go up and tell her. Jane, I was watching you this morning and you just sat there and haven't said a word to anybody. You look as though you're really down.

Person 2: Yeah, you're right.

2. Person 1: I just had such a great visit from my family. Next week when I go home on my home pass they promised that they'd take me out to the movies and, um, I'm looking forward to it. It's the nicest time I've had with them, since I've been up in the hospital.

Person 2: Gee, Jane's voice sounds different. It's . . . it's kind of lighter, clearer, uh, the way she's standing there, she just seems a lot different. She really seems to be happy. I think I'll tell Jane how . . . how much her happiness and her pleasantness really come through. Jane, you know that there's . . . the way that you just feel so happy, it just comes right through in the way you speak.

Person 1: I'm glad you noticed.

3. Person 1: Mr. Johnson, can you take a look at these orders, please?

Person 2: Um, not now.

Person 1: Boy, he . . . he just didn't even have time to talk to me. Wouldn't give me the time of day. But . . . he's really been busy lately. And I bet he's really been feeling a lot of pressure. Bet he's really feeling kind of hassled. And it's understandable why he wouldn't have time to talk to me. But . . . but maybe it would be helpful if I told him that I understand that he's feeling pressured. Mr. Johnson, this inventory time must really put some pressure on you. Maybe tomorrow you might have about ten minutes to go over these back orders.

Person 2: Yeah, I hope so. I really am feeling the pressure today. And, and I'm glad you noticed and understand.

Each of the five training packages presented to this point has received considerable research scrutiny, and each has received considerable positive support. Most of this research scrutiny has been in the form of comparisons of a total package against one or more of its constituent procedures and/or control groups, rarely one training package against another. When the latter has been true, i.e., comparison between training packages, the result has usually been that both are equally potent, and superior to controls. We believe this experimental outcome has resulted because the training packages, regardless of their differing names, are in actuality quite similar operationally and, in several instances, actually identical as far as their skills training components are concerned. Almost all contain some form of instructions or structuring, modeling, role playing or behavioral rehearsal, and performance feedback. Thus, it becomes appropriate to generalize about these training packages as a collective. The combined outcome research examining their efficacy is indeed impressive, and we later in this chapter have the opportunity to recommend the set of approaches collectively represented by these training packages as the optimal means for training the communication component of the empathic process.

Programmed Self-Instruction

Although not yet as common as trainer-led group or individual empathy training, a number of programmed self-instructional approaches toward this goal have emerged in recent years (Bullmer, 1972; Keenan, 1976; Kozma, 1974; Laughlin, 1978; Saltmarsh, 1973). Bullmer's (1972) *The Art of Empathy* has proven to be the more widely used of these alternatives and thus will serve as our illustrative example. Just as the psychoeducational skills training approaches described earlier each essentially concern themselves with teaching but a single phase of what Keefe (1976) and we view as the four-phase empathic process, e.g., communication, the programmed self-instructional approaches are for the most part means for training the initial, perceptual phase of empathy, plus some elements of the discrimination phase. Such is the case for Bullmer's (1972) approach.

Both Bullmer's (1972) aspiration and the style of his methodology are captured by his introductory commentary:

Empathy means many things to many people, but most properly it is defined as a process whereby one person perceives accurately another person's feelings and the meaning of these feelings and then communicates with sensitivity this understanding to the other person. This definition makes clear the important role played by accurate interpersonal perception in the empathic process. No matter how well phrased or sensitive a response may seem, a true state of empathy between individuals cannot exist unless the responses are based on accurate percepts. In other words, people who are considered to be highly empathic are both empathic perceivers and empathic responders.

The purpose of this book is to facilitate the development of empathic perception. The development of empathic response is left for other equally important training programs. (Pg. VI)

The book is designed so that you will learn a single principle concept or idea at a time. Each of the units deals with one such principle or idea. It is very important that these units be learned in the order in which they are presented. Units I and II are designed to provide background knowledge concerning the nature of interpersonal perception and the common causes of errors that occur when an individual makes inferences concerning others. This knowledge will assist you in analyzing your own perceptual skills and in determining how errors might occur and influence your perceptions of others. In addition, this knowledge will increase the sgnificance of what you learn as a result of Units III, IV, V and VI and will thus increase the probability that your interpersonal perceptual skill will be improved.

If the procedure outlined here is followed, upon completion of this book you will be better able to understand the meaning and hidden dispositions of those with whom you are working and living and consequently be more effective in your interpersonal endeavors. (p. VII)

The self-instructional sequence proceeds through a series of programmed exercises in which the attempt is made to move the trainee through awareness of interpersonal perceptual processes, sources of error therein, antecedants and correlates of affective states (e.g., needs, desires, motives), "hidden meanings" reflected by diverse emotions, and the utilization of the foregoing in seeking to accurately perceive the emotions of another individual. Substantively, the sequenced lessons consist of explanations of relevant concepts, programmed exercises, and graduated proficiency tests. Bullmer's materials do not readily lend themselves to illustrative excerpting, as they should be considered as a gestalt of sequentially arranged informational bits. Thus, we refer the reader to Bullmer (1975) for direct inspection of his work. Although this orientation to empathy training has not yet received extensive evaluation of its efficacy, the relevant research that has been conducted has indeed proven promising (Bullmer, 1972, 1975; Keenan, 1976; Saltmarsh, 1973). This initial evidence combines with the marked inexpensiveness of this approach to clearly warrant its further examination.

Other Empathy-Training Approaches

We have described and illustrated what we view as the major approaches to empathy training. Many, many other procedures and packages of procedures have been utilized for such purposes. Although their sheer number may surprise the reader, their broad diversity should not—given the equally broad diversity of conceptual definitions of empathy described in Chapter 1. Before enumerating these several approaches, it is consistent with the theme of this chapter to emphasize that the vast majority of them seek to enhance but a single component of the empathic process—usually communication, occasionally discrimination, rarely perception, and never affective reverberation.

Certain of these additional empathy training programs are training packages, e.g., Danish and Hauer's (1973) Helping Skills Program and Kagan's (1972) Interpersonal Process Recall. Others rely on a single, usually social learning, procedure. Modeling is chief among these, and its record of a positive contribution to the learning of empathy is substantial and reliable (Albert, 1974; Berenson, 1971; Bierman, 1967; Dalton & Sundblad, 1976; Fraser & Vitro, 1975; Gulanick & Schmeck, 1977; Hodge, 1976; Isquick, 1978; Josephson, 1979; Layton, 1978; Lehman, 1972; Perry, 1970; Ronnestad, 1977; Rosen, 1978; Uhlemann, Lea, & Stone, 1976). Role playing or behavioral rehearsal fares less well when used as a sole instructional procedure (Pruden, 1976; Wentink, 1975). Sensitivity groups, T-groups, or encounter groups, implemented without the companion interpersonal skills training employed by Egan (1976), appear to yield positive results, but the supportive evidence is largely anecdotal (Deshaies, 1974; McAuliffe, 1974). As noted above, empathy training has occurred via many other methods. These include "short term empathy communication training" (Law, 1978), "action training" (Howard, 1975), "modified, theme-centered interactional training" (Larabee, 1980), "clinical pastoral training"

(Strunk, 1960), "flexibility training" (Berenson, 1971), "dyadic programmed instruction" (Berenson, 1971), "CUE: communication, understanding, empathy" (Hundleby, & Zingle, 1975), "psychodramatic doubling" (Kipper & Ben-Ely, 1979), "interview skills training program" (Fine, 1980), "videotape focused feedback" (Morrison, 1974), "role play reversal" (Miller, 1980), "sequential refocusing" (Moore, 1978), "desensitization reappraisal plus communications skill training" (McLean, 1979), "controlled regression" (McLean, 1979), and by story telling, game activities, and other age-graded, prescriptive techniques for empathy training with children (Feshbach, 1981).

What may be concluded from our presentation of empathy training today? We have examined a small number of rather widely used training packages, a few single technique methods, and a parade of largely innovative but not widely studied or implemented procedures. The operational diversity of the latter, we held, followed logically from the equally diverse manner in which empàthy has been defined. Both these lesser used methods, as well as the more frequently used training packages, have most typically been means for empathy-*communication* training. We have held throughout this book that empathy (and its training) requires attention to more than just certain classes of overt, verbal behavior by the trainee, i.e., empathic communication. From our belief that empathy is a four-stage process follows the companion position that empathy training most effectively entails a components-specific training program, one in which each component of empathy is taught by means of that method or methods optimal for or prescriptive for the given component. In the section that follows, we seek to concretize this empathy components training perspective.

EMPATHY COMPONENTS TRAINING

It is our proposal that the training of empathy is optimally operationalized via a six-stage training program whose ingredients we now present and examine.

Readiness Training

An optimal empathy-training program, in our view, commences with training activities designed to maximize the likelihood that the trainee is fully prepared to understand, acquire, and utilize the four component skills that constitute empathy per se. Such preparatory training, we believe, would ideally take two complementary forms. The first concerns efforts to help the trainee acquire a series of what might be termed *empathy-preparatory* skills, i.e., abilities potentiating empathy-skills acquisition. Frank (1977) has developed and evaluated just such a readiness program. In it, trainees were successfully taught (1) imagination skills, which significantly increased accurate identification of implied meanings, (2) behavioral observation skills, which significantly increased accurate predictions of other person's overt behavior, and (3) flexibility skills (in shifting from 1 to 2), which significantly increased the use of differentiated levels of social reasoning.

The likelihood that training in the perceptual, affective reverberation, cognitive analysis, and communication stages will proceed effectively may be enhanced not only by the augmentation or enhancement of propadeutic skills, such as offered by Frank (1977). Such training may also be potentiated by the reduction or elimination of what might be termed *empathy skill-acquisition inhibitors*. Bullmer's (1972) programmed self-instructional approach to training the perceptual component of empathy contained at least one such inhibition-reduction component, i.e., the effort to help trainees understand and ameliorate the influence of perceptual biases and certain types of implicit interpersonal theorizing. Pereira (1978) contributed a second such effort in his use of Interpersonal Process Recall (Kagan, 1972) not to teach aspects of empathy per se, but to reduce "affect-associated anxiety," making trainee approach to such affects more possible. Clearly, the potentiation of empathic skill development by means of training in readiness skills and the reduction of empathy-inhibitors are valuable paths for future empirical efforts.

Perceptual Training

We have had rather little to say thus far in this book about the initial, perceptual stage of the empathic process. As we noted in Chapter 1, Keefe (1976) proposed that empathy commences with the perception of the other person, as the empathizer nonevaluatively observes and records an array of verbal and nonverbal behaviors, physical characteristics, environmental attributes, and other aspects of the ongoing interpersonal context. We agree with this perspective and thus wish to propose that in optimal empathy training it is desirable that the readiness stage be followed by purposeful, effective perceptual training. The existing training technology for doing so is not large, but promising possibilities do exist. One is the programmed, self-instructional approach developed by Bullmer (1972). As our earlier presentation of this approach sought to make clear, the thrust of Bullmer's (1972) materials is the training of more accurate, less distorted, less inferential, and more objective perception.

A second promising approach to enhancing perceptual accuracy in interpersonal contexts is described by Henry Smith in his important works, *Sensitivity Training* (Smith, 1973) and *Sensitivity to People* (Smith, 1966). As we have done with empathy, Smith takes a components perspective to the target behaviors of concern to him, in his instance, sensitivity. He (Smith, 1973), as we, does so for reasons of potentially enhanced training effectiveness:

> Should we take a general or components view of sensitivity? The answer depends, in part, on whether the purpose is to select sensitive people or to train them. If selection is the aim, then the general answer is to be favored. What we wish in

selection is to place individuals on a single scale that ranges from the least to the most sensitive. If training is the aim, however, then a component view is very helpful. Viewing sensitivity as a general ability gives us no clues as to where to begin training, what to train for, or how to train. (p. 23)

To be sure, sensitivity, as empathy, in the real world of their expression, are expressed as gestalts, not individuated components. A components view, though in this sense artificial, is in our view—and Smith's—heuristically superior in the functional sense of utility for training. As with programmed instruction, the pieces may be learned first and then sequentially combined to the whole.

It is the first component of Smith's concept of sensitivity that interests us here, i.e., "observational sensitivity" that, as is soon seen, is identical to the perceptual accuracy component of empathy in Keefe's (1976) and our definition of the concept. Smith (1973) states:

We define and shall use observational sensitivity in a specific way as the ability to look at and listen to another person and remember what he looked like and said. Observation is sometimes pictured as a quite passive affair: the eye is a motion-picture camera; the ear, a tape recorder. What we see a person do and hear him say is transcribed on the slate of our awareness. The records are then sorted, edited, and evaluated. No picture could be further from the truth, for we do not observe people; we perceive them. And we perceive what we want to perceive, what we expect to perceive, and what we have learned to perceive. Perceivers differ widely in their ability to discriminate what they see and hear from what they feel and infer about a person. It is an important task of training to develop the ability to make such discriminations. (p. 24).

Smith (1973), accordingly, distinguishes between sensory impressions, the enhancement of which is the goal of perceptual accuracy training, and expressive impressions, which interfere with perceptual accuracy. The goal of Smith's (1973) observational sensitivity training—our perceptual accuracy training—is to increase trainee competence in recording sensory impressions (what the other person looked like, said, and did) and discriminating them from the inferential, derivative, interpretive expressive impressions (how the other felt, believed, their motivations, traits). As Smith (1973) describes it:

To become a good observer, the trainee must learn to shift his attention from the subjective to the objective, from himself to the other person. (P. 78) The goal of observational training should be to develop the trainee's ability to discriminate sensory from expressive qualities. The critical problem in observational training is not that we make poor observations that lead to faulty inferences; it is that we do not make observations or inferences at all. We do not merely see or hear a person, we perceive a quality in the person. . . . We do not see a redhead and hear a loud voice; we perceive an 'interesting,' 'intelligent,' and 'level-headed' person or one who is 'narrow-minded,' 'irritating,' and 'insincere.' (p. 242)

How is this training goal to be sought? Smith (1973) proposes that an effective means for observational sensitivity training might be responsive to the apparent difficulties that individuals have in maintaining objectivity in anxiety-arousing interpersonal contexts: "*The* problem of observational training is to teach trainees to maintain the observer role in tense interpersonal situations. It is then that the perception of sensory qualities fade and expressive qualities intensify" (p. 79).

Perhaps, then, observational sensitivity training participants ought to be exposed to progressively more intense levels of interpersonal stress and even confrontation, in companion with trainer efforts to have trainees keep their focus on the other and his/her objective qualities, not the other's inferred characteristics nor the internal reactions of the trainee. Such a training effort, Smith (1973) suggests, might for example make use of the affect stimulation films developed by Kagan and Schauble (1969). In the filmed portrayal, the speaker addresses the viewer with progressively heightened negative affect-rejection, hostility, etc. The trainee's task in the face of such escalating affect is to continue to report what the person in the film looked like, said, and did. Smith (1973) suggests that interpersonal stress levels could be heightened yet further by use of simulated and then actual real-life, face-to-face implementations of the hierarchical training strategy. While Smith's (1973) proposal for effective observational sensitivity training has not yet received extensive empirical scrutiny, an initial examination of its value by Danish and Brodsky (1970) was clearly encouraging.

Affective Reverberation Training

An extended series of procedures of potential utility for purposes of affective reverberation training were examined in depth in Chapter 3. These included mediation (Goleman, 1977; Lesh, 1970; Maupin, 1965, 1972), structural integration or Rolfing (Johnson, 1977; Keen, 1970; Rolf, 1977), Reichian therapy (Baker, 1967; Lowen, 1975; Reich, 1933/1949), bioenergetics (Lowen & Lowen, 1977), the Alexander technique (Alexander, 1969), Feldenkrais' Awareness through movement (Feldenkrais, 1970, 1972), dance therapy (Bernstein, 1975; Davis, 1973; Pesso, 1969), sensory awareness training (Brooks, 1974; Guenther, 1968; Selver, 1957), focusing (Gendlin, 1981, 1984), and the Laban–Bartenieff multilevel method (Bartenieff & Lewis, 1980; Laban & Lawrence, 1947). All these several somatapsychic methods oriented toward the enhancement of affective reverberation (and, in some instances, toward enhancing perceptual accuracy also) have been, at best, at the fringes of scientific psychology. Yet that is precisely where some of psychology's most profound and most effective interventions began their existence—in the wisdom and experience of creative clinicians. Whether some or any of these techniques, and which ones, will prove on experimental scrutiny to be of substantial and reliable value for teaching the affective reverberation component of empathy is an empirical question whose pursuit seems to us to be especially worthwhile.

Cognitive Analysis Training

It is recalled from our earlier presentation of a components definition of empathy that following perception, i.e., the nonevaluative recording of the other's behavior (Stage 1), and affective reverberation, i.e., the trying-on, or as-if experiencing of the other's affects (Stage 2), the observer steps back from the other's behavior and his/her own reverberatory experiencing to cognitively discern the nature of the other's affects and to label them. Training for high levels of competence in this cognitive analysis stage is currently optimally provided, we believe, by the Carkhuff (1969a&b) discrimination training procedures that we examined and illustrated in detail earlier in this chapter (see pages 196–201). Such discrimination training, it appears to us, rests on a reasonably firm foundation of supportive evaluation evidence, has been adaptively applied to diverse trainee populations, and has been shown to be a necessary prerequisite for adequate skill at the final, communicative stage of empathy.

Beyond Carkhuff's (1969a&b) discrimination training method and materials, there exist additional potential techniques of possible value for cognitive analysis enhancement. Both some very old research (Allport, 1924; Davitz, 1964; Guilford, 1929; Jenness, 1932) and some quite recent studies from our own research group (Berlin, 1974; Healy, 1975; Lopez, 1977) combine to suggest that a combination of exposure to an array of facial expressions plus guided practice and feedback provided regarding the accuracy of judgments made (i.e., cognitive analysis) regarding the affective labeling of the expressions provided is an effective technique for enhancing judgmental accuracy. Readers interested in pursuing further this ancillary means for the possible enhancement of the cognitive analysis phase of empathy will find ample experimental materials for doing so in the creative work put forth by the Ekman (1965, 1972) and Rosenthal (1966; Rosenthal & DePaulo, 1979) research groups, described in detail in Chapter 4.

Communication

Earlier in this chapter, we described in considerable detail a number of existing and widely used empathy-training packages, as well as an extended series of less frequently used techniques. When viewed collectively these major and minor approaches to empathy training—almost all of which focus on the communication aspect of the process—consist largely of a small number of skills-development-oriented social learning techniques plus, in several instances, an experiential opportunity. The social learning methods thus utilized typically include instructions, modeling (an especially popular empathy-training technique), role playing or behavioral rehearsal, and some form of systematic feedback. The experiential component, when offered, typically has been a combination of supervised experience conducting actual counseling sessions plus a group experience of a sensitivity training or quasitherapeutic type. There currently exists little empirical basis for evidentially discriminating among the major training packages available, and we are not convinced that the most productive research path to follow regarding the communication component of empathy would be comparisons between existing training packages. As we suggested earlier in this chapter, the contribution-if any- of each procedure constituting a given training package ideally must first be established by means of studies utilizing dismantling experimental designs. Until such time as such research becomes available and helps us discern which procedures are in fact contributing positively to skill in empathic communication, or until such time as the less valuable but still informative comparative studies of training packages are done, we are not in a position to discriminate in our training recommendation among the Carkhuff (1969a&b), Egan (1976), Guerney (1977), Ivey and Authier (1971), and Goldstein (1973) training approaches.

Transfer and Maintenance Training

It has been substantially demonstrated in the context of psychotherapy that gains made by patients during the course of treatment fail in the majority of instances to manifest themselves either out of the treatment setting (a failure of *transfer* or generalization over settings) or over time (a failure of maintenance or generalization over time) (Goldstein & Kanfer, 1979; Kazdin, 1975; Keeley, Shemberg, & Carbonell, 1976). These writers have held that such infrequency of transfer and maintenance of therapeutic gain is the most telling weakness of contemporary psychotherapy. The severe paucity of follow-up studies on the transfer and maintenance of empathic skill after training, and the essentially negative outcome of the few that do exist (e.g., Billingsley & Giordano, 1980; Collingwood, 1971; Gantt et al., 1980; Guzzetta, 1974) lead us to believe that a similarly dismal postintervention picture exists for such training as for psychotherapy. That is the bad news. The good news, however, is that an emerging array of techniques do exist whose explicit goal is the enhancement of transfer and maintenance. Furthermore, a fair amount of outcome evidence is already available demonstrating the efficacy of these techniques in a psychotherapeutic context and, in at least a few instances, in the context of empathy training (Bath, 1976; Collingswood, 1971; Guttman & Haase, 1972; Guzzetta, 1974; Jones & Neil, 1974; Rocks, Baber, & Guerney, 1982). The particular enhancement techniques we especially recommend (Goldstein et al., 1966) based on their long history of efficacy in other psychological intervention domains and their beginnings of such demonstrable effectiveness in skills training contexts, are described here:

Provision of General Principles.   In laboratory settings transfer of training has been shown to be facilitated by providing the learner, experimental subject, or trainee with the general mediating principles which govern satisfactory performance on both the original and transfer tasks. He is given the rules, strategies, or organizing principles that can lead to successful performance. In the earliest research dealing with transfer-enhancement by means of general principles, Judd (1902) sought to teach boys to shoot darts at a target submerged in water. Boys thus instructed about the principle of refraction did better at the task than boys not so instructed. This finding was later replicated on a related task by Hendrickson and Schroeder (1941). In both studies, positive transfer was attributed to the acquisition of the general principles governing successful task performance. A number of other experiments have further confirmed this conclusion. Woodrow (1927) was able to produce improved performance in memorization on transfer tasks requiring memorizing poetry, prose, and factual material by instructing subjects in specific principles and techniques of memorization. Ulmer (1939) found that a special geometry curriculum designed to arouse critical thinking both connected and unconnected with geometry resulted in better performance on later transfer tasks. Duncan (1959), Goldbeck, Bernstein, Hellix, and Marx (1957) and Miller, Heise, and Lichten (1951) are others reporting similar results. Recent interest in the "New Math" is a more current example of anticipated transfer of training mediated by general principles.

This general finding, that mediating principles for successful performance can enhance transfer to new tasks and contexts has, furthermore, been reported in a number of other domains of psychological research. These include studies of labeling, rules, mediated generalization, advance organizers, learning sets, and deutero-learning. It is a robust finding indeed.

Maximizing Identical Elements.   In perhaps the earliest experimental concern with transfer-enhancement, Thorndike and Woodworth (1901) concluded that when there was a facilitative effect of one habit on another, it was to the extent that and because they shared identical elements. Ellis (1965) and Osgood (1953) have more recently emphasized the importance for transfer of similarity between characteristics of the training and application tasks. As Osgood (1953) notes, 'the greater the similarity between practice and test stimuli, the greater the amount of positive transfer [p. 213].' This conclusion rests on a particular solid base of experimental support, involving studies of both motor (Crafts, 1935; Duncan, 1953; Gagné, Baker, & Foster, 1950) and verbal (Osgood, 1949, 1953; Underwood, 1951; Young & Underwood, 1954) behaviors. Empathy training conducted by Guzzetta (1974) and Rocks et al (1982), in which both the trainee and real-world figures with whom trainees desired to be empathic (spouse, children) were trained together, are examples of effective use of the maximizing identical elements transfer-enhancing technique.

Maximizing Response Availability.   Transfer of training has been shown to be enhanced by procedures which maximize response availability. The likelihood that a response will be available is very clearly a function of its prior usage. We repeat and repeat foreign language phrases we are trying to learn, insist that our child spend an hour per day in piano practice, and devote considerable time in practice seeking to make a golf swing smooth and "automatic." These are simply expressions of the response availability notion, that is, the more we have practiced (especially *correct*) responses, the easier it will be to call them forth in later contexts or at later times. We need not rely solely on every day experience here. It has been well established empirically that, other things being equal, the response that has been emmitted most frequently in the past is quite likely to be emitted on subsequent occasions. This finding derives from studies of the frequency of evocation hypothesis (Underwood & Schulz, 1960), the spew hypothesis (Underwood & Schulz, 1960), preliminary response pretraining (Atwater, 1953; Cantor, 1955; Gagne & Foster, 1949) and overlearning (Mandler, 1954; Mandler & Heinemann, 1956). In all of these related research domains, real-life or laboratory-induced prior familiarization with given responses increased the likelihood of their occurrence on later trials. Mandler (1954) summarizes much of this research as it bears upon transfer by noting that "learning to make an old response to a new stimulus showed increasing positive transfer as degree of original training was increased" [p. 412]. Mandler's own studies in this domain, that is, studies of overlearning, are especially relevant to our present theme, for it is not sheer practice of attempts at effective behaviors which we feel is of most benefit to the transfer needs of the empathy trainee. As will be seen, it is practice of *successful* attempts.

Overlearning is a procedure whereby learning is extended over more trials than are necessary merely to produce *initial* changes in the individual's behavior. In all too many instances of near-successful therapy or training one or two successes at a given task are taken as evidence to move on to the next task, or the next level of the original task. To maximize maintenance and transfer via response availability, and in particular from the perspective of research on overlearning, the foregoing is a therapeutic or training technique error. Mandler's (1954) subjects were trained on the study task until they were able to perform it *without error* (either 0, 10, 30, 50, or 100 consecutive times. As noted earlier, transfer varied with the degree of original learning. To maximize transfer in empathy training via this principle, the guiding rule should not be, practice *makes* perfect (implying simply practice until one gets it right, and then move on), but practice *of* perfect (implying numerous overlearning trials of correct responses *after* the initial success).

Maximizing Stimulus Variability. In our last section, we addressed ourselves to enhancement of maintenance and transfer by means of practice and repetition, that is, the sheer *number* of effective responses to a given stimuli which the patient makes. Turning now to the stimulus member of the event, maintenance and transfer are also enhanced by the *variability* or range of stimuli to which the patient responds. For example, Duncan (1958) has shown that on a paired associates task, transfer is markedly enhanced by varied training. Training on even only two stimuli is better than training on a single stimulus. Other investigators have obtained similar results in concept attainment tasks, showing more rapid attainment when a variety of examples is presented (Callantine & Warren, 1955; Shore & Sechrest, 1961). As we have noted elsewhere in response to studies such as these: The implication is clear that in order to maximize positive transfer, training should provide for some sampling of the population of stimuli to which the response must ultimately be given. (p. 220)

Real-World Reinforcement.

Maintenance of newly developed empathy skill, as is true of the maintenance of any recently learned behavior, is very much at the mercy of real-life reinforcement contingencies. Rewarded behaviors will maintain; those responded to with indifference or punishment will extinguish (Agras, 1967; Gruber, 1971; Patterson, 1971; Tharp & Wetzel, 1969). The likelihood that such in vivo reinforcement is in fact forthcoming may be enhanced by deliberate use of training and other activities targeted to the trainee's real-life reinforcement dispensers, i.e., those persons (spouse, boss, sibling, etc.) in a position to respond rewardingly vis a vis trainee empathic communications. Such programmed reinforcement has actually already been used effectively in the context of empathy training (Bullmer, 1975). The probability of such real-world positive responsiveness may be further increased by the use of hierarchically graduated homework assignments (Goldstein et al., 1980; Shelton, 1979). Empathic skill utilization performed effectively during skills training sessions form the substance of out-of-training-group homework assignments in which the persons who are the targets of skill expression are carefully selected and sequenced to maximize the likelihood that at least the first few trials of skill expression by the trainee will yield reinforcing responses from the targeted others.

Because such hierarchical homework, no matter how carefully arranged, will on some occasions yield not reinforcement, but indifference or punishment, trainee reward for highly adequate skill use may in some instances have to be self-administered. Such use of self-reinforcement usually takes form in teaching the trainee to follow skilled performance by ''saying nice things to yourself'' and, if the skill was used with special competence, also ''doing something nice for yourself.'' Ample evidence exists attesting to the behavior-maintaining potency of such self-reinforcement.

We have described here five well-grounded techniques of probable utility for the transfer and maintenance of newly trained empathic skills. There exist several other, if less frequently tested, promising means for the transfer and maintenance of skilled behavior. A comprehensive listing of all these techniques, examined in depth in two recent books on this topic (Goldstein & Kanfer, 1979; Karoly & Steffen, 1980) and systematically evaluated for efficacy in a skills context by Goldstein (1981), is presented in Table 8.2.

Empathy Training—A Prescriptive Summary

We have utilized a wide variety of research evidence and theoretical materials to propose a six-component view of empathy training. To summarize this perspective, we believe optimal empathy training should attend to the following components (Table 8.3), first individually, and then as a coherent gestalt.

TABLE 8.2
Transfer and Maintenance Enhancers

---

 1. Provision of general principles (Lack, 1975; Lopez, 1977)
 2. Maximizing identical elements (Guzzetta, 1974; Wood, 1977)
 3. Maximizing response availability (Lopez, 1977)
 4. Maximizing stimulus variability (Hummel, 1977)
 5. Real-world reinforcement (programmed, graduated homework, self-administered) (Greenleaf, 1977; Gutride, Goldstein, & Hunter, 1973)
 6. Stimulus control techniques (Marholin & Touchette, 1979)
 7. Teaching self-management techniques (Karoly & Kanfer, 1982)
 8. Helper role structuring (Trainee anticipates trainer responsibilities) (Litwack, 1976; Solomon, 1978)
 9. Building social support networks (Heller, 1979)
10. Building reinforcing ecological climates (Price, 1979)

For each of the several components of the empathy-training process, we have identified at least a few, often several, potentially viable specific training techniques. We earnestly hope that this presentation will help stimulate the research now necessary to sort through this array and yield a training technology consisting of optimal sets of techniques. As we urged in earlier chapters, we here again prefer a goal of not *the* set or the one-true-(training)-light, but of *sets* of optimal techniques to be utilized prescriptively with different types of trainees and trainers. It is already the case that numerous investigators have raised prescriptive questions in their empathy-training studies. Research has been directed toward the relevance for training outcome of such trainee characteristics as initial or "developmental" level of empathy brought to the training (Bath, 1976; Birk, 1972; Geary, 1979; Uhlemann et al., 1976), age (Becker & Zarit, 1978), sex (Freely, 1977), cognitive level (Taylor, 1975), and such personality attributes as dogmatism (Relfalvy–Fodor, 1976), field dependence (Moore, 1980), and the array reflected by the Edwards Personal Preference Schedule (Burnham, 1976). In analogous empathy-training studies, beginning prescriptive matches have been sought not by studying trainee characteristics but by examining the prescriptive implications of the emotions being empathized with (Hayes, 1979), or

TABLE 8.3
Empathy Training Components

---

1. Readiness training
2. Perceptual accuracy training
3. Affective reverberation training
4. Cognitive analysis training
5. Empathic communication training
6. Transfer and maintenance training

---

of qualities of the training techniques themselves (Burnham, 1976; Fauvre, 1979; Feshbach, 1981; Janaka, 1977). As we have said often before in this book, such prescriptive leads appear to us to be especially valuable paths for the future conduct of empathy-training research to pursue.

References

Abec, J. M. (1975). *Therapist level of accurate empathy: A dyadic variable.* Unpublished doctoral dissertation, Illinois Institute of Technology.

Adams, D. R. (1980). *The effects of various levels of counselor-offered empathy on client anxiety in the initial counseling session.* Unpublished doctoral dissertation, Utah State University.

Agras, W. S. (1967). Transfer during systematic desensitization therapy. *Behavior Research and Therapy, 5,* 193–199.

Ainsworth, M. D. S., Bell, S. M. & Stayton, D. J. (1974) Infant-mother attachment and social development. In M. P. M. Richards (Ed.) *The integration of the child into a social world.* Cambridge: Cambridge University Press.

Ainsworth, M. D. S. & Blehar, M. C. (1975). Developmental changes in the behavior of infants and their mothers relevant to close body contact. Presented at Society for Research in Child Development, Denver.

Ainsworth, M. D. S., Blehar, M. C., Waters, E., & Wall, S. (1978). *Patterns of attachment.* Hillsdale, NJ: Lawrence Erlbaum Associates.

Ainsworth, M. D. S., & Wittig, B. A. (1969.) Attachment and exploratory behavior of one-year-olds in a strange situation. In B. M. Foss (Ed.), *Determinants of infant behavior.* London: Methuen.

Albert, S. J. (1974). *The effects of video taped modeling and written materials in teaching affective attending responses to undergraduate students.* Unpublished doctoral dissertation, University of Virginia.

Alexander, F. M. (1969). *The resurrection of the body.* New York: Dell.

Alexik, M., & Carkhuff, R. R. (1967). The effects of the manipulation of client depth of self-exploration upon high and low functioning counselors. *Journal of Clinical Psychology, 23,* 212–215.

Allport, F. H. (1924). *Social psychology.* Boston: Houghton–Mifflin.

Allport, G. W. (1937). *Personality: A psychological interpretation.* New York: Holt.

Allport, G. W. (1961). *Pattern and growth in personality.* New York: Holt, Rinehart, & Winston.

Alperson, E. D. (1974). Carrying experience forward through authentic body movement. *Psychotherapy: Theory Research and Practice, 11,* 211–214.

Altman, B. B. (1973). *Empathy, warmth, and genuineness as reinforcement for patient self-exploration*. Unpublished doctoral dissertation, Columbia University.

Anthony, R. A. (1980). A pilot study of the effect of training in Interpersonal Process Recall on the Affective Sensitivity and Empathy of Hearing Parents of Deaf Children. *Dissertation Abstracts International*, 43266.

Arend, R., Gove, F., & Sroufe, L. A. (1979). Continuity of individual adaptation from infancy to kindergerten: A prediction study of ego-resiliency and curiosity in preschoolers. *Child Development*, 50, 950–959.

Argyle, M. (1972). Non-verbal communication in human social interaction. In R. A. Hinde (Ed.), *Nonverbal communication* (pp. 243–267). Cambridge: Cambridge University Press.

Argyle, M., & Cook, M. (1976). *Gaze and mutual gaze*. Cambridge: Cambridge University Press.

Aronfreed, J. (1970). The socialization of altruistic and sympathetic behavior: Some theoretical and experimental analyses. In J. R. Macauley & L. Berkowitz (Eds.), *Altruism and helping behavior*. New York: Academic Press.

Aronfreed, J., & Paskal V. (1968). *Altruism, empathy, and the conditioning of positive effect*. Unpublished manuscript, University of Pennsylvania.

Aronfreed, J. (1968). *Conduct and conscience: The socialization of internalized control over behavior*. New York: Academic Press.

Aspy, D. (1972). *Toward a technology for humanizing education*. Champaign, IL: Research Press.

Aspy, D. N. (1975). Helping teachers discover empathy. *Humanist Educator*, 14, 56–63.

Aspy, D. N., & Hadlock, W. (1966). *The effect of empathy, warmth, and genuineness on elementary students' reading achievement*. Unpublished manuscript, University of Florida.

Aspy, D. N., & Roebuck, F. N. (1972). An investigation of the relationship between student levels of cognitive functioning and the teacher's classroom behavior. *Journal of Educational Research*, 65, 365–368.

Aspy, D. N., & Roebuck, F. N. (1975, September). A discussion of the relationship between selected student behavior and the teacher's use of interchangeable responses. *Humanist Education*, 3–10.

Aspy, D. N., & Roebuck, F. (1977). *Kids don't learn from people they don't like*. Amherst, MA: Human Resource Development Press.

Astin, H. S. (1967). Assessment of empathic ability by means of a situational test. *Journal of Counseling Psychology*, 14, 57–60.

Atwater, S. K. (1953). Proactive inhibition and associate facilitation as affected by degree of prior learning. *Journal of Emperimental Psychology*, 46, 400–404.

Authier, J., & Gustafson, K. (1973). *Enriching intimacy: A behavior approach*. Unpublished training manual. Omaha: University of Nebraska Medical Center.

Authier, J., & Gustafson, K. (1975). Application of supervised and nonsupervised microcounseling paradigms in the training of paraprofessionals. *Journal of Counseling Psychology*, 22, 74–78.

Averill, J. R., Opton, E. M., Jr., & Lazarus, R. S. (1969). Cross-cultural studies of psycho-physiological responses during stress and emotion. *International Journal of Psychology*, 4, 88–102.

Avery, A. W., Rider, K., & Haynes–Clemments. (1981). Communication skills training for adolescents: A five-month follow-up. *Adolescence*, 16, 289–298.

Ax, A. F. (1953). The physiological differentiation between fear and anger in humans. *Psychosomatic Medicine*, 15, 433–442.

Aylward, J. L. (1981). Effects of alpha biofeedback training on empathy in counseling. *Dissertation Abstracts International*, 42, 85-A.

Bachrach, H. (1968). Adaptive regression, empathy and psychotherapy: Theory and research study. *Psychotherapy*, 5, 203–209.

Bachrach, H. (1976). Empathy: We know what we mean, but what do we measure? *Archives of General Psychiatry*, 33, 35–38.

Bahrick, H. P., Fitts, P. M., & Rankin, R. E. (1952). EFfect of incentives upon reactions to peripheral stimuli. *Journal of Experimental Psychology, 44*, 400–406.

Bain, O., & Clark, S. (1966). *Character education: A handbook of teaching suggestions based on freedom's code for elementary teachers.* San Antonio, Texas: The Children's Fund.

Baker, E. F. (1967). *Man in the trap: The causes of blocked sexual energy.* New York: Avon Books.

Baldwin, J. M. (1895). *Mental development in the child and the race.* New York: Macmillan.

Balser, R. (1980). Parental empathy. *Dissertation Abstracts,* 4650-B.

Barnett, M. A., King, L. M., Howard, J. A., & Dino, G. A. (1980). Empathy in young children: Relation to parents' empathy, affection, and emphasis on the feelings of others. *Developmental Psychology, 16,* 243–244.

Barrera, M. E., & Maurer, D. (1981). The perception of facial expressions by the three-month old. *Child Development, 52,* 203–206.

Barrett–Lennard, G. T. (1962). Dimensions of therapist response as causal factors in therapeutic change. *Psychological Monographs, 76,* 1–36.

Bartenieff, I., & Davis, M. (1972). Effort-Shape analysis of movement: The unity of expression in function. In M. Davis (Ed.), *Research approaches to movement and personality.* New York: Arno Press.

Bartenieff, I., & Lewis, D. (1980). *Body movement: Coping with the environment.* New York: Gordon & Breach.

Bath, K. E. (1976). Comparison of brief empathy training. *Perceptual and Motor Skills, 43,* 925–926.

Bauml, B. J., & Bauml, F. H. (1975). *A dictionary of gestures.* Metuchen, NJ: Scarecrow Press.

Beale, A. V., Payton, O. D., & Zachary, I. G. (1978). The effects of a communications course for health professionals on empathy discrimination. *Journal of Applied Rehabilitation Counseling, 9,* 46–49.

Becker, F., & Zarit, S. H. (1978). Training older adults as peer counselors. *Educational Gerontology, 3,* 241–250.

Bell, C. (1886). *Anatomy and philosophy of expression as connected with the fine arts.* London: G. Bell.

Bell, L., & Bell, D. (1982). *Parental validation as a mediator in adolescent development.* Paper presented at the American Psychological Association, Washington DC.

Bell, R. Q. (1968). A reinterpretation of the direction of effects in studies of socialization. *Psychological Review, 75,* 63–72.

Beldoch, M. (1964). Sensitivity to expression of emotional meaning in three modes of communication. In J. R. Davitz (Ed.) *The communication of emotional meaning.* New York: McGraw-Hill.

Belsky, J., Spanier, G. B. & Rovine, M. (1983). Stability and change in marriage across the transition to parenthood. *Journal of Marriage and the Family, 45,* 567–577.

Berens, G. L. (1976). *Effects of a program imparting teacher empathy, respect, and acceptance on children's self-concepts and perceptions of teacher attitudes.* Unpublished doctoral dissertation, Fordham University.

Berenson, D. (1971). The effects of systematic human relations training upon classroom performance of elementary school teachers. *Journal of Research and Development in Education, 4,* 70–85.

Beres, D. (1968). The role of empathy in psychotherapy and psychoanalysis. *Journal Hillside Hospital, 17,* 362–369.

Beres, D., & Arlow, J. (1974). Fantasy and identification in empathy. *Psychoanalytic Quarterly, 43,* 26–49.

Bergin, A. E. (1967). An empirical analysis of therapeutic issues. In D. Arbuckle (Ed.), *Counseling and psychotherapy: An overview.* New York: McGraw-Hill.

Bergin, A. E., & Jasper, L. G. (1969). Correlates of empathy in psychotherapy: A replication. *Journal of Abnormal Psychology, 74,* 477–481.

Bergin, A. E., & Solomon, S. (1968). Personality and performance correlates of empathic understanding in psychotherapy. In T. Tomlinson & J. Hart (Eds.), *New directions in client-centered therapy.* Boston: Houghton–Mifflin.

Bergin, A. E., & Suinn, R. M. (1975). Individual psychotherapy and behavior therapy. *Annual Review of Psychology, 26,* 509–556.

Berlin, R. J. (1974). *Training of hospital staff in accurate affective perception of fear–anxiety from vocal cues in the context of varying facial cues.* Unpublished masters thesis, Syracuse University.

Berlin, R. J. (1977). *Teaching acting-out adolescents prosocial conflict resolution through structured learning training of empathy.* Unpublished doctoral dissertation, Syracuse University.

Bernstein, P. (1975). *Theory and methods in dance-movement therapy.* Dubuque, IA: Kendall/Hunt.

Beutler, L. E., Johnson, D. T., Neville, C. W., & Workman, S. N. (1972). "Accurate empathy" and the A–B dichotomy. *Journal of Consulting and Clinical Psychology, 38,* 372–375.

Beutler, L. E., Johnson, D. T., Neville, C. W., Workman, S. N., & Elkins, D. (1973). The A–B therapy-type distinction, accurate empathy, nonpossessive warmth, and therapist genuineness in psychotherapy. *Journal of Abnormal Psychology, 82,* 273–277.

Bierman, R. (1967). *The relationship inventory -B. An experimental questionnaire for parents to assess facilitative family interaction.* Discussion Paper 2, The Psychiatric Clinic, Buffalo, New York.

Bierman, R., Carkhuff, R. R., & Santilli, M. (1972). Efficacy of empathic communication training groups for inner city preschool teachers and family workers. *Journal of Applied Behavioral Science, 8,* 188–202.

Birk, J. M. (1972). Effects of counseling supervision method and preference on empathic understanding. *Journal of Counseling Psychology, 19,* 542–546.

Blackwood, G. L. Jr. (1975). *Accurate empathy: Critique of a construct.* Unpublished manuscript, Vanderbilt University.

Blackman, N., Smitl, K., Brokman, R., & Stern, J. (1958). The development of empathy in male schizophrenics. *Psychiatric Quarterly, 32,* 546–553.

Blakely, P. B. (1973). *The relationship between therapist mood and conceptual level and his ability to label and rate client affect and respond empathically.* Unpublished doctoral dissertation, University of Nebraska-Lincoln.

Blehar, M. C., Sielerman, A. F., & Ainsworth, M. D. S. (1977). Early face-to-face interaction and its relation to later infant–mother attachment. *Child Development, 48,* 182–194.

Bleyle, D. M. (1973). *The relationship of counselor–client measured value similarity to client self-concept change and client perception of empathy, warmth, and genuineness after brief counseling.* Unpublished doctoral dissertation, University of Northern Colorado.

Bonde–Peterson, F., Mork, A. L., & Nielsen, E. (1975). Local muscle blood flow and sustained contractions of human arm and back muscles. *European Journal of Applied Physiology, 34,* 43–50.

Boring, E. G., & Titchner, E. B. (1923). A model for the demonstration of facial expression. *American Journal of Psychology, 34,* 471–485.

Borke, H. (1971). Interpersonal perception of young children: Egocentricism or empathy. *Developmental Psychology, 5,* 263–269.

Borke, H. (1972). Chandler and Greenspan's "ersatz egocentrism." *Developmental Psychology, 7,* 107–109.

Botwinick, J., & Thompson, L. W. (1966). Premotor and motor components of reaction time. *Journal of Experimental Psychology, 71,* 9–15.

Bower, G. H. (1981). Mood and memory. *American Psychologist, 36,* 126–148.

Bowlby, J. (1969). *Attachment and lags.* New York: Basic Books.

Bozarth, J. D., & Krauft, C. C. (1972). Accurate empathy ratings: Some methodological considerations. *Journal of Clinical Psychology, 28,* 408–410.

Bozarth, J. D., & Rubin, S. E. (1976). Empirical observations of rehabilitation counselor performance and outcome: Some implications. *Rehabilitation Counseling Bulletin.*

Braatoy, T. (1954). *Fundamentals of psychoanalytic technique.* New York: Wiley.

Bradley, R. H. & Caldwell, B. M. (1976). The relation of infants home environments to mental test performance. *Child Development, 47,* 1172–1174.

Brannon, L. (1976). *Black clients' perceptions of empathy in black professional and paraprofessional therapists.* Unpublished doctoral dissertation, Southern Illinois University.

Brener, J. (1974). A general model of voluntary control applied to the phenomena of learned cardiovascular change. In P. A. Obrist, A. H. Black, J. Brener, & L. V. Dicara (Eds.), *Cardiovascular psychophysiology.* Chicago: Aldine.

Brener, J. (1977). Sensory and perceptual determinants of voluntary visceral control. In G. E. Schwartz & J. Beatty (Eds.), *Biofeedback: Theory and research.* New York: Academic Press.

Brener, J., Ross, A., Baker, J., & Clemens, W. J. (1979). On the relationship between cardiac discrimination and control. In N. Birbaum & H. D. Kimmel (Eds.), *Biofeedback and self-regulation.* Hillsdale, NJ: Lawrence Erlbaum Associates.

Brewer, B. R. (1974). *Relationships among personality, empathic ability and counselor effectiveness.* Unpublished doctoral dissertation, University of North Dakota.

Brookover, W. B. (1945). The relation of social factors to teaching ability. *Journal of Experimental Education, 53,* 191–205.

Brooks, C. V. W. (1974). *Sensory awareness: The rediscovery of experiencing.* New York: Viking Press.

Brown, J. T. S. (1980). *Communication of empathy in individual psychotherapy: An analogue study of client perceived empathy.* Unpublished doctoral dissertation, University of Texas at Austin.

Brown, L. A. (1980). *Teacher empathy and fairness: Elementary school children's perceptions.* Unpublished doctoral dissertation, Iowa State University.

Bruner, J. S., & Tagiuri, R. (1954). The perception of people. In G. Lindzey (Ed.), *Handbook of social psychology* (Vol. 2, pp. 634–654). Reading, MA: Addison–Wesley.

Bryant, B. K. (1982). An index of empathy for children and adolescents. *Child Development, 53,* 413–425.

Buber, M. (1948). *Between man and man.* New York: Macmillan.

Buchheimer, A. (1963). The development of ideas about empathy. *Journal of Counseling Psychology, 10,* 61–70.

Buchsbaum, M., & Silverman, J. (1968). Stimulus intensity control and the cortical evoked response. *Psychosomatic Medicine, 30,* 12–22.

Buck, R. (1975). Nonverbal communication of affect in children. *Journal of Personality and Social Psychology, 31,* 644–653.

Buck, R. (1979). Individual differences in nonverbal sending accuracy and electrodermal responding: The externalizing–internalizing dimension. In R. Rosenthal (Ed.), *Skill in nonverbal communication: Individual differences.* Cambridge, MA: Oelgeschlager, Gunn, & Hain.

Buck, R. (1980). Nonverbal behavior and the theory of emotion: The facial feedback hypothesis. *Journal of Personality and Social Psychology, 38,* 811–824.

Buck, R. W., Miller, R. E., & Caul, W. F. (1974). Sex, personality, and physiological variables in the communication of emotion via facial expression. *Journal of Personality and Social Psychology, 30,* 587–596.

Budzynski, T., Stoyva, J., & Adler, C. (1970). Feedback induced muscle relaxation: Application to tension headache. *Behavior Therapy and Experimental Psychiatry, 1,* 205–211.

Bull, N. (1962). *The body and its mind.* New York: Las Americas.

Bull, N. (1968). *The attitude theory of emotion.* New York: Johnson Reprint corporation. (Original work published 1951)

Bull, R. (1980). Predicting self-reported empathy from dimensions and sources of socialization in adolescence. *Dissertation Abstracts* (5–B) 1905.

Bullmer, K. (1972). Improving accuracy of interpersonal perception through a direct teaching method. *Journal of Counseling Psychology, 19,* 37–41.

Bullmer, K. (1975). *The art of empathy: A manual for improving accuracy of interpersonal perception.* New York: Human Sciences Press.

Burgess, P. R., Clark, F. J., Simon, J., & Wei, J. Y. (1982). Signaling of kinesthetic information by peripheral sensory receptors. *Annual Review of Neuroscience, 5,* 171–187.

Burke, D., Hagbarth, K. E., & Skuse, N. F. (1978). Recruitment order of human spindle endings in isometric voluntary contractions. *Journal of Physiology, 285,* 101–112.

Burnham, T. L. (1976). *Personality and time as factors in the training of preservice teachers in empathy skills.* Unpublished doctoral dissertation, University of Minnesota.

Burns, K. L., & Beier, E. G. (1973). Significance of vocal and visual channels in the decoding of emotional meaning. *Journal of Communication,* 1973, *23,* 118–130.

Burns, N., & Cavey, L. (1957). Age differences in empathic ability among children. *Canadian Journal of Psychology, 11,* 227–230.

Buzby, D. E. (1924). The interpretation of facial expression. *American Journal of Psychology, 35,* 602–604.

Cairns, K. V. (1972). *Desensitization and relationship quality.* Unpublished master's thesis. University of Calgary.

Callantine, M. F., & Warren, J. M. (1955). Learning sets in human concept formation. *Psychological Reports, 1,* 363–367.

Callaway, E., & Dembro, E. (1958). Narrowed attention: A psychological phenomenon that accompanies a certain physiological change. *Archives of Neurology and Psychiatry, 79,* 74–90.

Callaway, E., & Thompson, S. V. (1953). Sympathetic activity and perception. *Psychosomatic Medicine, 15,* 443–455.

Campbell, R. J., Kagan, N., & Krathwohl, D. R. (1971). The development and validation of a scale to measure affective sensitivity (empathy). *Journal of Counseling Psychology, 18,* 407–412.

Canner, N. (1968). *. . . . And a time to dance.* Boston: Beacon Press.

Cannon, W. B. (1927). The James–Lange theory: A critical examination and an alternative theory. *American Journal of Psychology, 39,* 106–124.

Cannon, W. B. (1929). *Bodily changes in pain, hunger, fear and rage* (2nd ed.). New York: Appleton.

Cantor, J. H. (1955). Amount of pretraining as a factor in stimulus predifferentiation and performance set. *Journal of Experimental Psychology, 50,* 180–184.

Carkhuff, R. R. (1969a).*Helping and human relations: A primer for lay and professional helpers* (Vol. 1): *Selection and training.* New York: Holt, Rinehart, & Winston.

Carkhuff, R. R. (1969b). *Helping and human relations: A primer for lay and professional helpers* (Vol. 2): *Practice and research.* New York: Holt, Rinehart, & Winston.

Carkhuff, R. R., & Alexik, M. (1967). Effects of client depth of self-exploration upon high and low functioning counselors. *Journal of Counseling Psychology 14,* 350–355.

Carkhuff, R. R., & Berenson, B. G. (1967). *Beyond counseling and therapy.* New York: Holt, Rinehart, & Winston.

Carkhuff, R. R., & Bierman, R. (1969). The effects of human relations training upon child psychiatric patients in treatment. *Journal of Counseling Psychology, 16,* 117–121.

Carkhuff, R. R., & Bierman, R. (1970). Training as a preferred mode of treatment of parents of emotionally disturbed children. *Journal of Counseling Psychology, 17,* 157–161.

Carlson, K. W. (1974). Increasing verbal empathy as a function of feedback and instruction. *Counselor Education and Supervision, 12,* 208–213.

Carothers, J. E., & Inslee, L. J. (1974). Level of empathic understanding offered by volunteer telephone services. *Journal of Counseling Psychology, 2d,* 274–276.

Cartright, R. D., & Lerner, B. (1963). Empathy, need to change, and improvement with psychotherapy. *Journal of Consulting Psychology, 27,* 138–144.

Chambers, F. M. (1957). Empathy and scholastic success. *Personnel and Guidance Journal 36,* 282–284.

Chandler, M. J., & Greenspan, S. (1972). Ersatz egocentrism: A reply to H. Borke. *Developmental Psychology, 7,* 104–106.

Chang, A. F. (1973). *The relationship of teacher empathy and student personality to academic achievement and course evaluation.* Unpublished doctoral dissertation, University of Southern California.

Charles, C. H. (1975). *Correlation of adjudged empathy as early identifiers of counseling potential.* Unpublished doctoral dissertation, University of Alabama.

Charny, E. J. (1966). Pyschosomatic manifestations of rapport in psychotherapy. *Psychosomatic Medicine, 28,* 305–315.

Chaudhuri, H. (1965). *Philosophy of meditation.* New York: Philosophical Library.

Chase, L. (1975). *The other side of the report card.* Santa Monica, CA: Goodyear.

Chinsky, J. M., & Rappaport, J. (1970). Brief critique of the meaning and reliability of "accurate empathy" ratings. *Psychological Bulletin, 73,* 379–382.

Christiansen, B. (1963). *Thus speaks the body: Attempts toward a personology from the point of view of respiration and postures.* Oslo, Norway: Institute for Social Research.

Christiansen, C. (1979). *The relationship between life history variables and measured empathic capacity in allied health students.* Unpublished doctoral dissertation, University of Houston.

Christenberry, M. S. (1974). *An exploratory study to investigate the relationship between teacher effectiveness and level of empathic undestanding of paraprofessional teachers of young children.* Unpublished doctoral dissertation, Georgia State University.

Chronbach, J. (1958). Processes affecting scores on "understanding of others" and "assumed similarity." *Psychological Bulletin, 52,* 177–193.

Clark, M. S., Milberg, S., & Erber, L (1984). Effects of arousal on judgments of others' emotions. *Journal of Personality and Social Psychology, 46,* 551–560.

Clarke-Stewart, K. A. (1973). Interactions between mothers and their young children: Characteristics and consequences. *Monographs of the Society for Research in Child Development, 38,* No. 153.

Clayton, A. S. (1943). *Emergent mind and education.* New York: Columbia University.

Cochrane, C. T. (1972). Effects of diagnostic information on empathic understanding by the therapist in a psychotherapy analogue. *Journal of Consulting and Clinical Psychology, 38,* 359–365.

Collingswood, T. R. (1971). Retention and retraining of interpersonal communication skills. *Journal of Clinical Psychology, 27,* 294–296.

Collins, J. D. (1971). *The effects of the conjugal relationship modification method on marital communication and adjustment.* Unpublished doctoral dissertation, Pennsylvania State University.

Combs, A. W. (1962). What can man become. In A. W. Combs (Ed.), *Perceiving, behaving, becoming.* Washington, DC: Association for Supervision and Curriculum Development.

Cominsky, I. (1981). *Transfer of training in counselor education programs: A study of the use of stimulus variability and the provision of general principles to enhance the transfer of the skill of reflection of feeling.* Unpublished doctoral dissertation, Syracuse University.

Condon, W. S. (1968). Linguistic-kinesic research and dance therapy. *American Dance Therapy Association Proceedings, Third Annual Conference* (pp. 21–44). (Available from ADTA, 10400 Connecticut Ave., Suite 300, Kensington, MD 20795.)

Condon, W. S. (1970). Method of micro-analysis of sound films of behavior. *Behavior Research Methods and Instrumentation, 2,* 51–54.

Condon, W. S. (1982). Cultural microrhythms. In M. Davis (Ed.), *Interaction rhythms: Periodicity in communicative behavior.* New York: Human Sciences Press.

Condon, W. S., & Brosin, H. W. (1969). Micro linguistic-kinesic events in schizophrenic behavior. In D. V. S. Sankar (Ed.), *Schizophrenia: Current concepts and research.* Hicksville, NY: PJD publications.

Condon, W. S., & Ogston, W. D. (1966). Sound film analysis of normal and pathological behavior patterns. *Journal of Nervous and Mental Disease, 143,* 338–347.

Condon, W. S., & Ogston, W. D. (1967). A method of studying animal behavior. *Journal of Auditory Research 7,* 359–365.

Condon, W. S., & Sander, L. W. (1974). Neonate movement is synchronized with adult speech: Interactional participation and language acquisition. *Science, 183,* 99–101.

Coopersmith, S. (1967). *The antecedents of self-esteem.* San Francisco: Freeman.

Costanzo, F. S., Markel, N. N., & Costanzo, P. R. (1969). Voice quality profile and perceived emotion. *Journal of Counseling Psychology, 16,* 267–270.

Cottrell, L. S. Jr. (1950). Some neglected problems in social psychology. *American Sociological Review, 15,* 705.

Cottrill, C. J., & Stollak, L. E. (1984). *An examination of maternal responses to children in hypothetical problem situations.* Unpublished manuscript, Michigan State University.

Coufal, J. D. (1975). *Preventive therapeutic programs for mothers and adolescent daughters: Skill training versus discussion methods.* Unpublished doctoral dissertation, Pennsylvania State University.

Courtois, S. V. (1973). *Nonverbal cues: Effects of two instructional modes on subjects' choices of empathic responses.* Unpublished doctoral dissertation, University of Missouri-Kansas City.

Coutu, W. (1951). Role-playing vs. role-taking: An appeal for clarification. *American Sociological Review, 16,* 180–184.

Cowan, J. M. (1936). Pitch and intensity characteristics of stage speech. *Archives of Speech, 1,* Suppl. 1–92.

Cowden, R. (1955). Empathy or projection? *Journal of Clinical Psychology, 11,* 188–190.

Crafts, L. W. (1935). Transfer as related to number of common elements. *Journal of General Psychology, 13,* 147–158.

Cronbach, L. J. (1955). Processes affecting scores on "understanding others" and "assumed similarity." *Psychological Bulletin, 52,* 177–193.

Cronbach, L. J., & Snow, R. E. (1977). *Aptitudes and instructional methods.* New York: Irvington Publishers.

Cunningham, M. R. (1977). Personality and the structure of nonverbal communication of emotion. *Journal of Personality, 45,* 564–584.

Curren, J. P., Gilbert, F. S., & Little, I. M. (1976). A comparison between behavioral replication training and sensitivity training approaches to heterosexual dating anxiety. *Journal of Counseling Psychology, 23,* 190–196.

Dabbs, J. M. (1969). Similarity of gestures and interpersonal influences. *Proceedings of the 77th Annual Convention of the American Psychological Association, 4,* 337–338.

Dalton, R., & Sundblad, L. (1976). Using principles of social learning in training for communication of empathy. *Journal of Counseling Psychology, 23,* 454–457.

Danish, S. & Brodsky, S. L. (1970). Training police in emotional control and awareness. *American Psychologist, 24,* 368–369.

Danish, S., & Hauer, A. (1973). *Helping skills: A basic training program.* New York: Behavioral Publications.

Danish, S. J., & Kagan, N. (1971). Measurement of affective sensitivity: Toward a valid measure of interpersonal perception. *Journal of Counseling Psychology, 18,* 51–54.

Darian–Smith, I., & Yokota, T. (1966). Cortically evoked depolarization of trigeminal cutaneous afferent fibers in the cat. *Journal of neurophysiology, 29,* 170–184.

Darwin, C. (1872). *The expression of the emotions in man and animals.* London: John Murray.

Davidson, H. H., & Lang, G. (1960). Children's perceptions of their teachers' feelings toward them related to self-perception, school achievement and behavior. *Journal of Experimental Education, 29,* 107–118.

Davis, F. (1973). Inside intention. What we know about nonverbal communication. New York: McGraw–Hill.

Davis, H. (1973). Classes of auditory evoked responses. *Audiology, 12,* 464–469.

Davis, M. (1972). *Understanding body movement: An annotated bibliography.* New York: Arno Press.

Davis, M. (1973). Clinical implications of body movement research. *International Mental Health Research Newsletter, 15,* 1–7.

Davis, M. (Ed.) (1982). *Interaction rhythms: Periodicity in communicative behavior.* New York: Human Sciences Press.

Davitz, D. (1964). *The communication of emotional meaning.* New York: McGraw–Hill.

Davitz, J. R., & Davitz, L. J. (1959a). The communication of feelings by content-free speech. *Journal of Communication, 9,* 6–13.

Davitz, J. R., & Davitz, L. J. (1959b). Correlates of accuracy in the communication of feelings. *Journal of Communication, 9,* 110–117.

Davitz, J. R., & Davitz, L. J. (1961). Nonverbal vocal communication of feeling. *Journal of Communication, 11,* 81–86.

Dell, C. (1977). *A primer for movement description.* New York: Dance Notation Bureau Press.

DePaulo, B. M., & Rosenthal, R. (1979). Ambivalence, discrepancy, and deception in nonverbal communication. In R. Rosenthal (Ed.), *Skill in nonverbal communication* (pp. 204–248). Cambridge: Oelgeschlager, Hunn, & Hain.

DePaulo, B. M., Rosenthal, R., Eisenstat, R. A., Rogers, P. L. & Finkelstein, S. (1978). Decoding discrepant nonverbal cues. *Journal of Personality and Social Psychology, 36,* 312–323.

DePaulo, B. M., Rosenthal, R., Finkelstein, S., & Eisenstat, R. A. (1979). The developmental priority of the evaluative dimension in perception of nonverbal cues. *Environmental Psychology and Nonverbal Behavior, 3,* 164–171.

Deshaies, G. (1974). *The effects of group sensitivity training and group didactic-experiential training on the accurate empathy of counselor trainees.* Unpublished doctoral dissertation, Boston University.

Deutsch, F. (1952). Analytic posturology. *Psychoanalytic Quarterly, 21,* 196–214.

Deutsch, F. (1974). *The relationship of empathic ability and communicative egocentrism in female preschoolers.* Unpublished manuscript, Pennsylvania State University.

Deutsch, F. (1975). The effects of sex of subject and story character on preschoolers' perceptions of affective responses and intrapersonal behavior in story sequences. *Developmental Psychology, 11,* 112–113.

Deutsch, F., & Madle, R. A. (1975). Empathy: Historic and current conceptualizations, measurement, and a cognitive theoretical perspective. *Human Development, 18,* 267–287.

Dibner, A. S. (1956). Cue-counting: A measure of anxiety in interviews. *Journal of Consulting Psychology, 20,* 475–478.

Dickenson, W. A., & Truax, C. B. (1966). Group counseling with college underachievers: Comparison with a control group and relationship to empathy, warmth, and genuineness. *Personnel and Guidance Journal, 45,* 243–247.

Diggins, D. (1982). Dealing with problems of observer agreement. *Laban/Bartenieff News, 4,* 3–5. (Available from Laban/Bartenieff Institute of Movement Studies, 133 West 21st Street, New York, NY 10011)

Diskin, P. (1956). A study of predictive empathy and the ability of student teachers to maintain harmonious interpersonal relations in selected elementary classrooms. *Dissertation Abstracts, 16,* 1399.

Dittman, A. T. (1972). *Interpersonal messages of emotion.* New York: Springer.

Dittman, A. T., Parloff, M. B., & Boomer, D. S. (1965). Facial and bodily expression: A study of receptivity of emotional cues. *Psychiatry, 28,* 239–244.

Dixon, W. R., & Morse, W. C. (1961). The prediction of teaching performance: Empathic potential. *Journal of Teacher Education, 12,* 322–328.

Don, N. S. (1977). The transformation of conscious experience and its EEG correlates. *Journal of Altered States of Consciousness, 3,* 147–168.

Drag, R. M., & Shaw, M. E. (1967). Factors influencing the communication of emotional intent by facial expressions. *Psychometric Science, 8,* 137–138.

Dryanski, V. (1974). A case study of a chronic paranoid schizophrenic in dance therapy. *Monographs of the American Dance Therapy Association 1973–1974, 4,* 100–119. (Available from ADTA, 10400 Connecticut Ave., Suite 300, Kensington, MD 20795)

Dubnicki, C. (1977). Relationships among therapist empathy and authoritarianism and a therapist's prognosis. *Journal of Consulting and Clinical Psychology, 45,* 958–959.

Duchene, G. B. (1876). *Le mecanisme de la physionomie humaine.* Paris: J. B. Balliere.

Duffy, E. (1977). Activation. In N. S. Greenfield & R. A. Sternbach (Eds.), *Handbook of psychophysiology.* New York: Holt, Rinehart, & Winston.

Dumas, G. Le sourire (1904). *Review of Philosophy, 58,* 1–23.

DuNann, D. (1983). *A reliable model for observing body movement.* Unpublished manuscript, Whitman College, Walla Walla, WA.

Duncan, C. P. (1953). Transfer in motor learning as a function of degree of first-task learning and inner-task similarity. *Journal of Experimental Psychology, 45,* 1–11.

Duncan, C. P. (1958). Transfer after training with single versus multiple tasks. *Journal of Experimental Psychology, 55,* 63–73.

Duncan, C. P. (1959). Recent research on human problem solving. *Psychological Bulletin, 56,* 397–429.

Duncan, S. (1969). Nonverbal communication. *Psychological Bulletin, 72,* 118–137.

Durlak, J. A. (1979). Comparative effectiveness of paraprofessional and professionals helpers. *Psychological Bulletin, 86,* 80–92.

Dusenbury, D., & Knower, F. H. (1938). Experimental studies on the symbolism of action and voice. *Quarterly Journal of Speech, 24,* 424–435.

Dymond, R. F. (1949). A scale for the measurement of empathic ability. *Journal of Consulting Psychology*

Dymond, R. F. (1950). Personality and empathy. *Journal of Consulting Psychology, 14,* 343–350.

Dymond, R. F., Huges, A. S., & Raabe, V. L. (1952). Measureable changes in empathy with age. *Journal of Consulting Psychology, 16,* 202–206.

Easterbrook, J. A. (1959). The effect of emotion on cue utilization and the organization of behavior. *Psychological Review, 66,* 183–201.

Easterbrooks, M. A., & Lamb, M. E. (1979). The relationship between quality of infant–mother attachment and infant competence in initial encounters with peers. *Child Development, 50,* 380–387.

Egan, G. (1976). *Interpersonal living.* Monterey, CA: Brooks/Cole.

Ehmann, V. E. (1971). Empathy: Its origin, characteristics, and process. *Perspectives in Psychiatric Care, 9,* 72–80.

Eisenberg–Berg, N., & Geisheker, E. (1979). Content of preachings and power of the model/preacher: The effect on children's generosity. *Developmental Psychology, 15,* 168–175.

Eisenberg–Berg, N., & Lennon, R. (1980). Altruism and the assessment of empathy in the preschool years. *Child Development, 51,* 552–557.

Eisenberg–Berg, N., & Mussen, D. (1978). Empathy and moral development in adolescence. *Developmental Psychology, 14,* 185–186.

Eisenberg–Berg, N., & Neal, C. (1979). Children's moral reasoning about their own spontaneous prosocial behavior. *Developmental Psychology, 15,* 228–229.

Ekman, P. (1965). Communication through non-verbal behavior: A source of information about an interpersonal relationship. In S. S. Tomkins & C. E. Izard (Eds.), *Affect, cognition and personality* (Chap. XIII, pp 390–442).

Ekman, P. (1972). Universals and cultural differences in facial expressions of emotions. In J. Cole (Ed.), *Nebraska Symposium on Motivation* (Vol. 19), 1971. Lincoln: University of Nebraska Press.

Ekman, P. (1973). Cross-cultural studies of facial expressions. In P. Ekman (Ed.), *Darwin and facial expression: A century of research in review* (pp 169–222). New York: Academic Press.

Ekman, P. (Ed.) (1982a). *Emotion in the human face.* Cambridge: Cambridge University Press.

Ekman, P. (1982b). Methods for measuring facial expression. In K. R. Scherer & P. Ekman (Eds.), *Handbook of methods in nonverbal behavior research.* Cambridge: Cambridge University Press.

Ekman, P., & Bressler, J. (1964). In P. Ekman, *Progress report to National Institute of Mental Health,* Bethesda, MD.

Ekman, P., & Friesen, W. V. (1969a). Nonverbal leakage and clues to deception. *Psychiatry, 32*(1), 88–105.

Ekman, P., & Friesen, W. V. (1969b). The repertoire of nonverbal behavior-categories, origins, usage and coding. *Semiotica, 1,* 49–98.

Ekman, P., & Friesen, W. V. (1974). Nonverbal behavior and psychopathology. In R. J. Friedman (Ed.), *The psychology of depression.* New York: Wiley.

Ekman, P., & Friesen, W. V. (1975). *Unmasking the face: A guide to recognizing emotions from facial clues.* Englewood Cliffs, NJ: Prentice–Hall.

Ekman, P., Friesen, W. V. & Ellsworth, P. (1982). Conceptual ambiguities. In P. Ekman (Ed.) Emotion in the human face. Second edition. Cambridge: Cambridge University Press.

Ekman, P., Friesen, W. V., O'Sullivan, M., & Scherer, K. (1980). Relative importance of face, body and speech in judgments of personality and affect. *Journal of Personality and Social Psychology, 38,* 270–277.

Ekman, P., Friesen, W. V., & Tomkins, S. S. (1971). Facial Affect Scoring Technique (FAST): A first validity study. *Semiotics, 3*(1), 37–58.

Ekman, P., Levenson, R. W., & Friesen, W. V. (1983). Autonomic Nervous System activity distinguishes among emotions. *Science, 221,* 1208–1210.

Ekman, P., & Rose, D. (1965). In P. Ekman, *Progress report to National Institute of Mental Health,* Bethesda, MD.

Elkind, D. (1967). Egocentrism in adolescence. *Child Development, 38,* 1025–1034.

Ellis, H. (1965). *The transfer of learning.* New York: Macmillan.

Ellsworth, P. C., & Tourangeau, R. (1981). On our failure to confirm what nobody ever said. *Journal of Personality and Social Psychology, 40,* 363–369.

Emmerling, F. C. (1961). A study of the relationships between personality characteristics of classroom teachers and pupil perceptions of these teachers. *Dissertation Abstracts, 22,* 1054–1055.

English, P. W. (1972). *Behavioral concomitants of dependent and subservient roles.* Unpublished manuscript, Harvard University.

Epstein, S. (1967). Toward a unified theory of anxiety. In B. Maher (Ed.), *Progress in experimental personality research* (Vol. 4). New York: Academic Press.

Erikson, E. (1950). *Childhood and society.* New York: W. W. Norton.

Fairbanks, G., & Pronovost, W. (1939). An experimental study of the pitch characteristics of the voice during the expression of emotion. *Speech Monographs, 6,* 87–104.

Fauvre, M. (1979). *The development of empathy through children's literature.* Unpublished doctoral dissertation, University of California at Los Angeles.

Fay, B. (1970). *The relationships of cognitive moral judgement, generosity, and empathic behavior in six- and eight-year-old children.* Unpublished doctoral dissertation, University of California, Los Angeles.

Feiss, G. J. (1979). *Mind therapies/body therapies: A consumer guide.* Millbrae, CA: Celestial Arts.

Feitel, B. (1968). *Feeling understood as a function of a variety of therapist activities.* Unpublished doctoral dissertation, Teachers College, Columbia University.

Feffer, M. H. & Gourevitch, V. (1960). Cognitive aspects of role taking in children. *Journal of Personality, 28,* 383–396.

Feldenkrais, M. (1970). *Body and mature behavior.* New York: International Universities Press.

Feldenkrais, M. (1972). *Awareness through movement.* New York: Harper & Row.

Feldenkrais, M. (1981). *The elusive obvious.* Cupertino, CA: Meta Publications.

Feldstein, S., & Jaffe, J. (1962). The relationship of speech disruption to the experience of anger. *Journal of Consulting Psychology, 26,* 505–509.

Feleky, A. M. (1914). The expression of the emotions. *Psychological Review, 21,* 33–41.

Fenz, W. D., & Velner, J. (1970). Physiological concomitants of behavioral indexes in schizophrenia. *Journal of Abnormal Psychology, 76,* 27–35.

Ferenczi, S. (1930). Principle of relaxation and neocatharsis. *International Journal of Psychoanalysis, 11,* 428–443.

Ferguson, M. (1980). *The aquarian conspiracy: Personal and social transformation in the 1980's.* Los Angeles: J. P. Tarcher.

Fernberg, S. W. (1930). Can an emotion be accurately judged by its facial expression alone? *Journal of Criminal Law and Criminology, 20,* 554–564.

Feshbach, N. D. (1975). Empathy in children: Some theoretical and empirical considerations. *Counseling Psychologist, 5,* 25–30.

Feshbach, N. D. (1978). Studies of empathic behavior in children. In B. Maher (Ed.), *Progress in experimental personality research* (pp. 1–47). New York: Academic Press.

Feshbach, N. D. (1980). *The psychology of empathy and the empathy of psychology.* Presidential Address presented at the Meeting of the Western Psychological Association, Honolulu.

Feshbach, N. D. (1981, June). *Empathy, empathy training and the regulation of aggression in elementary school children.* Paper presented to the NATO Advanced Study Institute on Aggression in Children and Youth, Maratea Italy.

Feshbach, N. D. (1982a). Empathy, empathy training and the regulation of aggression in elementary school children. In R. M. Kaplan, V. J. Konecni, & R. Novoco (Eds.), *Aggression in children and youth.* Sijthoff/Noordhoff International Publisher. Alphen den Rijn: The Netherlands.

Feshbach, N. D. (1982b). Sex differences in empathy and social behavior in children. In N. Eisenberg–Berg (Ed.), *The development of prosocial behavior.* New York: Academic Press.

Feshbach, N. D. (1982c). Empathy training and the regulation of aggression in elementary school children. In R. M. Kaplan, V. J. Konecni, & R. Novoco (Eds.), *Aggression in children and youth.* Sijthoff/Noordhoff International Publisher. Alphen den Rijn: The Netherlands.

Feshbach, S., & Feshbach, N. (1963). Influence of the stimulus of object upon the complementary and supplementary projection of fear. *Journal of Abnormal and Social Psychology, 66,* 498–502.

Feshbach, N. D., & Feshbach, S. (1969). The relationship between empathy and aggression in two age groups. *Developmental Psychology, 1,* 102–107.

Feshbach, N. D., & Feshbach S. (in press). Empathy training and the regulation of aggression. *Academic Psychology Bulletin.*

Feshbach, N. D., & Roe, K. (1968). Empathy in six- and seven-year-olds. *Child Development, 34,* 133–145.

Feshbach, S., & Singer, R. D. (1957). The effects of fear arousal and suppression of fear upon social perception. *Journal of Abnormal and Social Psychology, 55,* 283–288.

Fetz, E. E. (1968). Pyramidal tract effects on interneurons in the cat lumbar dorsal horn. *Journal of Neurophysiology, 31,* 69–80.

Field, T., Woodson, R., Greenberg, R., & Cohen, D. (1982). Discrimination and imitation of facial expressions by neonates. *Science, 218.*

Fields, S. J. (1953). Discrimination of facial expression and its relation to personal adjustment. *Journal of Social Psychology, 38,* 63–71.

Fine, J. M. (1980). The effects of an interviewing skills training program on law students' communication of empathy and respect. Unpublished doctoral dissertation, Boston University.

Fingarette, H. (1965). *The self in transformation: Psychoanalysis, philosophy, and the life of the spirit.* New York: Harper & Row.

Fisch, H. U., Frey, S., & Hirsbrunner, H. P. (1983). Analyzing nonverbal behavior in depression. *Journal of Abnormal Psychology, 92,* 307–318.

Fischer, J., Paveza, G. J., Kikerty, N. S., Hubbard, L. J., & Graysen, S. B. (1975). The relationship between theoretical orientation and therapist's empathy, warmth, and genuineness. *Journal of Counseling Psychology, 22,* 399–403.

Fisher, S. (1966). Body attention patterns and personality defenses. *Psychological Monographs: General and Applied, 80*(9), 1–31.

Fisher, S. (1968). Selective memory effects produced by stimulation of body landmarks. *Journal of Personality, 36,* 92–107.

Fisher, S. (1970). *Body experience in fantasy and behavior.* New York: Appleton.

Fisher, S. (1972). Influencing selective perception and fantasy by stimulating body landmarks. *Journal of Abnormal Psychology, 79,* 97–105.

Fisher, S. (1980). Theme induction of localized somatic tension. *Journal of Nervous and Mental Disease, 168,* 721–731.

Fitzgerald, E. T. (1966). Measurement of openess to experience: A study of regression in the service of the ego. *Journal of Personality and Social Psychology, 4,* 655–663.

Flavell, J. H., Botkin, P. T., Fry, C. L., Wright, J., & Jarvis, P. (1968). *The development of role-taking and communication skills in children.* New York: Wiley.

Foote, N., & Cottrell, L. (1955). *Identity and interpersonal competence.* Chicago: University of Chicago Press.

Fowler, R. S., Jr., & Kraft, G. H. (1974). Tension perception in patients having pain associated with chronic muscle tension. *Archives of Physical and Medical Rehabilitation, 55,* 28–30.

Frank, S. J. (1977). *The facilitation of empathy through training in imagination.* Unpublished doctoral dissertation, Yale University.

Franzén, O., & Offenloch, K. (1969). Evoked response correlates of psychophysical magnitude estimates for tactile stimulation in man. *Experimental Brain Research, 8,* 1–18.

Frappa, J. (1902). *Les expressions de la physionomie humaine.* Paris: Libraire generale des arts decoratifs.

Fraser, J. A. H., & Vitro, F. T. (1975). The effects of empathy training on the empathic response levels and self-concepts of students in a teacher-training program. *Canadian Counselor, 10,* 25–28.

Freely, H. D. (1977). *Differential effects of Carkhuff model communications skills training on selected sex-role types.* Unpublished doctoral dissertation, University of Kentucky.

Freud, A. (1966). *The ego and the mechanisms of defense.* New York: International Universities Press.

Fridlund, A. J., & Izard, C. E. (1983). Electromyographic studies of facial expressions of emotions and patterns of emotions. In J. T. Cacioppo & R. E. Petty (Eds.), *Social psychophysiology.* New York: Plenum.

Friel, T., Kratochvil, D., & Carkhuff, R. R. (1968). The effects of the manipulation of client depth of self-exploration upon helpers of different training and experience. *Journal of Clinical Psychology, 24*, 247–249.

Friesen, W. V. (1972). *Cultural difference in facial expression in a social situation: An experimental test of the concept of display rules.* Unpublished doctoral dissertation, University of California, San Francisco.

Friesen, W. V., Ekman, P., & Wallbott, H. (1979). Measuring hand movements. *Journal of Nonverbal Behavior, 4*, 97–112.

Frijda, N. H. (1958). Facial expression and situational cues. *Journal of Abnormal Social Psychology, 57*, 149–154.

Fritz, B. R. (1966). Postural movements in a counseling dyad. *Journal of Counseling Psychology, 13*, 335–343.

Frois–Wittmann, J. (1930). The judgment of facial expression. *Journal of Experimental Psychology, 13*, 133–151.

Fromm–Reichman, F. (1950). *Psychoanalysis and psychotherapy.* Chicago: University of Chicago Press.

Fry, C. (1966). Training children to communicate to listeners. *Child Development, 37*, 675–685.

Fulcher, J. S. (1942). "Voluntary" facial expression in blind and seeing children. *Archives of Psychology, 38* (No. 272).

Gage, N. L. (1953). Explorations in the understanding of others. *Educational and Psychological Measurement, 13*, 14–26.

Gage, N. L., & Cronbach, L. J. (1955). Conceptual and methodological problems in interpersonal perception. *Psychological Review, 62*, 411–422.

Gage, N. L., & Suci, G. (1951). Social perception and teacher–pupil relationships. *Journal of Educational Psychology, 42*, 144–153.

Gagne, R. M., Baker, K. E., & Foster, H. (1950). On the relation between similarity and transfer of training in the learning of discriminative motor tasks. *Psychological Review, 57*, 67–79.

Gagne, R. M., & Foster, H. (1949). Transfer to a motor skill from practice on a pictured representation. *Journal of Experimental Psychology, 39*, 342–354.

Gandevia, S. C., & McCloskey, D. I. (1976). Joint sense, muscle sense, and their combination as position sense, measured at the distal interphalangeal joint of the middle finger. *Journal of Physiology, 260*, 387–407.

Gantt, S., Billingsley, D., & Giordano, J. A. (1980). Paraprofessional skill: Maintenance of empathic sensitivity after training. *Journal of Counseling Psychology, 27*, 374–379.

Garbarino, J. (1976). A preliminary study of some ecological correlates of child abuse: The impact of socioeconomic stress on mothers. *Child Development, 47*, 178–185.

Garfield, S. L., & Bergin, A. E. (1971). Therapeutic conditions and outcome. *Journal of Abnormal Psychology, 77*, 108–114.

Gates, G. S. (1923). An experimental study of the growth of social perception. *Journal of Educational Psychology, 14*, 449–462.

Gatewood, J. B., & Rosenwein, R. (1981). Interactional synchrony: Genuine or spurious? A critique of recent research. *Journal of Nonverbal Behavior, 6*, 12–29.

Geary, E. A. (1979). *A construct validity study of "developmental empathy" in counselor skills training programs.* Unpublished doctoral dissertation, Catholic University of America.

Gellen, M. I. (1970). Finger blood volume response of counselors, counselor trainees, and noncounselors to stimuli from an empathy test. *Counselor Education and Supervision, 10*, 64–74.

Gelles, R. J. (1973). Child abuse as psychopathology: A sociological critique and reformulation. *American Journal of Orthopsychiatry, 43*, 611–621.

Gellhorn, E. (1964). Motion and emotion: The role of proprioception in the physiology and pathology of the emotions. *Psychological Review, 71*, 457–472.

Gendlin, E. (1981). *Focusing* (2nd ed.). New York: Bantam Books.

Gendlin, E. (1984). The politics of giving therapy away: Listening and focusing. In D. Larson (Ed.), *Teaching psychological skills: Models for giving psychology away*. Monterey, CA: Brooks/Cole.

Getzels, J. W., & Jackson, P. W. (1964). The teacher's personality and characteristics. In N. L. Gage (Ed.), *Handbook of research on teaching* (pp. 306–582). Chicago: Rand McNally.

Gil, D. G. (1973).*Violence against children*. Cambridge, MA: Harvard University Press.

Gilstad, R. (1978). *Acquisition and generalization of empathic response through self-administered and leader-directed structured learning training and the interaction between training method and conceptual level*. Unpublished doctoral dissertation, Syracuse University.

Ginott, H. G. (1969). *Between parent and teenager*. New York: Macmillan.

Ginsberg, B. G. (1977). Parent–adolescent relationship program. In B. G. Guerney, Jr., *Relationship enhancement: Skill-training program for therapy, problem prevention and enrichment*. San Francisco: Jossey–Bass.

Gladding, S. T. (1978). Empathy, gender, and training as factors in the identification of normal infant cry signals. *Perceptual and Motor Skills, 47*, 267–270.

Gladstein, G. A. (1977a). Empathy and counseling outcome: An empirical and conceptual review. *The Counseling Psychologist, 6*, 70–79.

Galdstein, G. A. (1977b). Is empathy important in counseling? *Personnel and Guidance Journal, 48*, 823–827.

Glass, C. R., Gottman, J. M., & Shmurak, S. H. (1976). Response acquisition and cognitive self-statement modification approaches to dating-skills training. *Journal of Counseling Psychology, 23*, 520–526.

Goldbeck, R. A., Bernstein, B. B., Hellix, W. A., & Marx, M. H. (1957). Application of the half-split technique to problem-solving tasks. *Journal of Experimental Psychology, 53*, 330–338.

Goldberg, H. D. (1951). The role of "cutting" in the perception of motion picture. *Journal of Applied Psychology, 35*, 70–71.

Goldfried, M. R., & Davison, G. C. (1976). *Clinical behavior therapy*. New York: Holt, Rinehart, & Winston.

Goldman–Eisler, F. (1955). Speech-breathing activity: A measure of tension and affect during interviews. *British Journal of Psychology, 46*, 53–63.

Goldstein, A. P. (1971). *Psychotherapeutic attraction*. New York: Pergamon Press.

Goldstein, A. P. (1973). *Structured learning therapy: Toward a psychotherapy for the poor*. New York: Academic Press.

Goldstein, A. P. (1981). *Psychological skill training*. New York: Pergamon Press.

Goldstein, A. P., Cohen, R., Blake, G., & Walsh, W. (1971). The effects of modeling and social class structuring in paraprofessional psychotherapist training. *Journal of Nervous and Mental Diseases, 153*, 47–56.

Goldstein, A. P., & Goodhart, A. (1973). The use of structure learning for empathy enhancement in paraprofessional psychotherapist training. *Journal of Community Psychology, 3*, 168–173.

Goldstein, A. P., Heller, K., & Sechrest, L. B. (1966). *Psychotherapy and the psychology of behavior change*. New York: Wiley.

Goldstein, A. P., & Kanfer, F. H. (Eds.). (1979). *Maximizing treatment gains: Transfer enhancement in psychotherapy*. New York: Academic Press.

Goldstein, A. P., & Sorcher, M. (1974). *Changing supervisor behavior*. New York: Pergamon Press.

Goldstein, A. P., Sprafkin, R. P., & Gershaw, N. J. (1976). *Skill training for community living*. New York: Pergamon Press.

Goldstein, A. P., Sprafkin, R. P., Gershaw, N. J., & Klein, P. (1980). *Skillstreaming the adolescent*. Champaign, IL: Research Press.

Goldstein, A. P., Sprafkin, R. P., Gershaw, N. J., & Klein, P. (1983). Structured learning: A psychoeducational approach for teaching social competencies. *Behavior Disorders, 8,* 161–170.

Goldstein, A. P., & Stein, N. (1976). *Prescriptive psychotherapies.* New York: Pergamon Press.

Goldstein, I. B. (1964). Role of muscle tension in personality theory. *Psychological Bulletin, 61,* 413–425.

Goldstein, I. B. (1972). Electromyography: A measure of skeletal muscle responses. In N. S. Greenfield & R. A. Sternbach (Eds.), *Handbook of Psychophysiology.* New York: Holt, Rinehart, & Winston.

Goleman, D. (1977). *The varieties of the mediatative experience.* New York: E. P. Dutton.

Gombrich, E. H. (1972). The representation of things and people. In E. H. Gombrich, J. Hochberg, & M. Black, *Art, perception, and reality.* Baltimore, MD: Johns Hopkins University Press.

Goodenough, F. L. (1932). Expression of the emotions in a blind–deaf child. *Journal of Abnormal and Social Psychology, 27,* 328–333.

Goodwin, G. M., McCloskey, D. I., & Matthews, P. B. C. (1972). The contribution of muscle afferents to kinaesthesia shown by vibration induced illusions of movement and by the effects of paralysing joint afferents. *Brain, 95,* 705–748.

Goodyear, R. K. (1979). Inferences and intuition as components of empathy. *Counselor Education and Supervision, 18,* 214–223.

Gordon, G., & Jukes, M. G. M. (1964). Descending influences on the exteroceptive organizations of the cat's gracile nucleus. *Journal of Physiology, 173,* 291–319.

Gordon, T. (1970). *Parent effectiveness training.* New York: Wyden.

Gordon, T. (1976). *P.E.T. in action.* New York: Wyden.

Goud, N. H. (1975). Effects of empathy training on undergraduate education majors. *Student Personnel Association for Teacher Education Journal, 13,* 121–127.

Gove, F. L., & Keating, D. P. (1979). Empathic role-taking precursors. *Developmental Psychology, 15,* 594–600.

Grand, R., & Ginsberg, B. G. (1976). Communication in the father–son relationship: The Parent Adolescent Development Program (PARD). *Family Coordinator, 4,* 465–473.

Graves, J. R., & Robinson, J. D. (1976). Proxemic behavior as a function of inconsistent verbal and nonverbal messages. *Journal of Counseling Psychology, 23,* 333–338.

Gray, G. W. (1926). An experimental study of the vibrato in speech. *Quarterly Journal of Speech, 13,* 296–333.

Greenberg, S. L. (1981). *The effects of an interpersonal skills training course on interviewing skills, empathy, and assertion in fourth-year optometry students.* Unpublished doctoral dissertation, Loyola University of Chicago.

Greenleaf, D. O. (1977). *The use of structured learning therapy and transfer of training programming with disruptive adolescents in a school setting.* Unpublished masters thesis, Syracuse University.

Greenson, R. (1960). Empathy and its vicissitudes. *International Journal of Psychoanalysis, 41,* 418–424.

Greenspan, S., Barenboim, C., & Chandler, M. (1976). Empathy and pseudo-empathy: the affective judgments of first and third graders. *The Journal of Genetic Psychology, 129,* 77–88.

Gruber, R. P. (1971). Behavioral therapy: Problems in generalization. *Behavior Therapy 2,* 361–368.

Grusec, J. (1982). The socialization of altruism. In N. Eisenberg (Ed.),*The development of prosocial behavior* (pp. 139–166). New York: Academic Press.

Guenther, H. V. (1974). *Philosophy and psychology in the Abhidharma.* Berkeley: Shambala Press.

Guerney, B. G. (1964). Filial therapy: Description and rationale. *Journal of Consulting Psychology, 28,* 303–310.

Guerney, B. G. (1977). *Relationship enhancement: Skill-training programs for therapy, problem-prevention, and enrichment.* San Francisco, Jossey–Bass.

Guerney, B. Jr., Goufal, J., & Voeglsong, E. (1981). Relationship enhancement versus a traditional approach to therapeutic/preventive/enrichment parent–adolescent programs. *Journal of Consulting and Clinical Psychology, 49*(6), 927–939.

Guerney, B., Stover, L., & DeMeritt, S. (1968). A measurement of empathy in parent–child interaction. *The Journal of Genetic Psychology, 112,* 49–55.

Guilford, J. P. (1929). An experiment in learning to read facial expression. *Journal of Abnormal and Social Psychology, 24,* 191–202.

Gulanick, N., & Schmeck, R. R. (1977, June). Modeling, praise, and criticism in teaching empathic responding. *Counselor Education and Supervision,* 284–290.

Gunther, B. (1968). *Sense relaxation below your mind.* New York: Collier Books.

Gurman, A. S. (1973). Instability of therapeutic conditions in psychotherapy. *Journal of Counseling Psychology, 20,* 16–24.

Gurman, A. S. (1977). The patient's perception of the therapeutic relationship. In A. S. Gurman & A. M. Razin (Eds.), *Effective psychotherapy.* New York: Pergamon Press.

Gustafson, K. (1975). *An evaluation of enriching intimacy—a behavioral approach to the training of empathy, respect–warmth, and genuineness.* Unpublished doctoral dissertation, University of Massachusetts.

Gustafson, K., & Authier, J. (1976). *Marathon versus weekly enriching intimacy relationship skills training for physician assistants.* Unpublished manuscript, Omaha: University of Nebraska Medical Center.

Gutride, M., Goldstein, A., & Hunter, G. (1973). The use of modeling and role playing to increase social interaction among asocial psychiatric patients. *Journal of Consulting and Clinical Psychology, 40,* 408–415.

Guzzetta, R. A. (1974). *Acquisition and transfer of empathy by the parents of early adolescents through structured learning training.* Unpublished doctoral dissertation, Syracuse University.

Guzzetta, R. (1976). Acquisition and transfer of empathy by the parents of early adolescents through structured learning training. *Journal of Counseling Psychology, 23,* 449–453.

Haase, R. F., & Tepper, D. T. Jr. (1972). Nonverbal components of empathic communication. *Journal of Counseling Psychology, 19,* 417–424.

Hackney, P. (in press). Bartenieff Fundamentals. In S. J. Cohen (Ed.), *International encyclopaedia of dance.* New York: Scribner.

Hagbarth, K. E., & Kerr, D. I. B. (1954). Central influences on spinal afferent conduction. *Journal of Neurophysiology, 17,* 295–307.

Hager, J. C., & Ekman, P. (1981). Methodological problems in Tourangeau and Ellsworth's study of facial expression and experience of emotion. *Journal of Personality and Social Psychology, 40,* 358–362.

Haggard, E. A., & Isaacs, F. S. (1966). Micromomentary facial expressions as indicators of ego mechanisms in psychotherapy. In L. A. Gottschalk & A. H. Averback (Eds.), *Methods of research in psychotherapy.* New York: Appleton–Century–Crofts.

Halkides, G. (1958). *An investigation of therapeutic success as a function of four variables.* Unpublished doctoral dissertation, University of Chicago.

Hall, E. T. (1964). Silent assumptions in social communication. *Disorders of Communication, 42,* 41–55.

Hall, J. A. (1979). Gender, gender roles, and nonverbal communication skills. In R. Rosenthal (Ed.), *Skill in nonverbal communication.* Cambridge, MA: Oelgeschlager, Gunn, & Hain.

Ham, M. D. (1980). *The effects of the relationship between client behavior and counselors' predicted empathic ability upon counselors' in-session empathic performance: An analogue study.* Unpublished doctoral dissertation, University of Rochester.

Hammer, E. F. (1977, July). *Advances in projective drawing techniques.* Presented at Conference on Projective Drawings, New York, NY.

Hanawalt, N. G. (1944). The role of the upper and the lower parts of the face as the basis for judging facial expressions: II. In posed expressions and "Candid camera" picture. *Journal of General Psychology, 31,* 23–36.

Hargrove, D. S. (1974). Verbal interaction analysis of empathic and nonempathic responses of therapists. *Journal of Consulting and Clinical Psychology, 42,* 305.

Harman, J. P. (1978). *The relationship between a measure of empathy (RA–E) and an overall performance rating and empathy rating by cooperating classroom teachers across four groups of undergraduate pre-service teachers.* Unpublished doctoral dissertation, Kent State University.

Harootunian, B. (1978). Teacher training. In A. P. Goldstein (Ed.), *Prescriptions for child mental health and education.* New York: Pergamon Press.

Harrell, J., & Guerney, B. G. (1976). Training married couples in conflict negotiation skills. In D. Olson (Ed.), *Treating relationships.* Lake Mills, IA: Graphic Publishing.

Hasse, R. F., & Tepper, D. T. (1972). Nonverbal components of empathic communication. *Journal of Counseling Psychology, 19,* 417–424.

Hastorf, A. H., & Bender, J. E. (1952). A caution respecting the measurement of empathic ability. *Journal of Abnormal & Social Psychology, 47,* 574–576.

Hatch, E. J., & Guerney, B. G. (1975). A pupil relationship enhancement program. *Personnel and Guidance Journal, 54,* 103–105.

Hawks, C. F., & Egbert, R. L. (1954). Personal values and the empathic response: Their interrelationship. *Journal of Educational Psychology, 45,* 469–476.

Hayes, L. (1979). *A comparison of techniques for teaching empathic responding to counselor-directed hostility.* Unpublished doctoral dissertation, University of Tennessee.

Haynes, L., & Avery, A. (1979). Training adolescent in self-disclosure and empathy skills. *Journal of Counseling Psychology, 26,* 526–530.

Healy, J. A. (1975). *Training of hospital staff in accurate affective perception of anger from vocal cues in the context of varying social cues.* Unpublished doctoral dissertation, Syracuse University.

Hebb, D. O. (1955). Drives and the CNS (conceptual nervous system). *Psychological Review, 62,* 243–254.

Heck, E. J., & Davis, C. S. (1973). Differential expression of empathy in a counseling analogue. *Journal of Counseling Psychology, 20,* 101–104.

Hefferline, R. F. (1958). The role of proprioception in the control of behavior. *Transactions of the New York Academy of Sciences, 20,* 739–764.

Hefferline, R. F., & Bruno, L. J. J. (1971). The psychophysiology of private events. In A. Jacobs & L. B. Sachs (Eds.), *The psychology of private events: Perspectives on covert response systems.* New York: Academic Press.

Hefferline, R. F., & Perera, T. B. (1963). Proprioceptive discrimination of a covert operant without its observation by the subject. *Science, 139,* 834–835.

Helfand, I. (1955). Role-playing in schizophrenia: A study of empathy. *Dissertation Abstracts, 15,* 1117.

Heller, K. (1979). The effects of social support: Prevention and treatment implications. In A. P. Goldstein & F. H. Kanfer (Eds.), *Maximizing treatment gains: Transfer enhancement in psychotherapy.* New York: Academic Press.

Hellman, R. P., & Zwislocki, J. (1961). Some factors affecting the estimation of loudness. *Journal of the Acoustical Society of America, 33,* 687–694.

Hendrickson, G., & Schroeder, W. H. (1941). Transfer of training in learning to hit a submerged target. *Journal of Educational Psychology, 32,* 205–213.

Henley, N. M. (1977). *Body politics: Power, sex, and nonverbal communication.* Englewood Cliffs, NJ: Prentice–Hall.

Hess, E. H. (1975). *The tell-tale eye.* New York: Van Nostrand Reinhold.

Hiatt, S., Campos, J., & Emde, R. (1979). Facial patterning and infant emotional expression: Happiness, surprise, and fear. *Child Development, 50,* 1020–1035.

Hill, R. C. (1965). *Freedom's code: The historic American standards of character, conduct, and citizen responsibility.* San Antonio, TX: The Children's Fund.

Hirai, T. (1974). *Psychophysiology of Zen.* Tokyo: Igaku Shoin.

Hirakawa, A. (1973). *Index to the Abhidharmakosabhasya, P. Pradhan Edition Sanskrit–Tibetan–Chinese.* Tokyo: Daizo Shuppan Kabushikikaisha.

Hjortsjo, C. H. (1970). *Man's face and mimic language.* Lund, Sweden: Student–Litteratur.

Hodge, E. A. (1976). *Supervision of empathy training: Programmed versus individual and peer versus professional.* Unpublished doctoral dissertation, University of Cincinnati.

Hoffman, M. L. (1970). Conscience, personality, and socialization techniques. *Human Development, 13,* 90–126.

Hoffman, M. L. (1975). Sex differences in moral internalization. *Journal of Personality and Social Psychology, 32,* 720–729(b).

Hoffman, M. L. (1976). Empathy role-taking guilt and development of Altruistic motives. In T. Lickona (Ed.), *Moral development and behavior: Theory, research, and social issues.* New York: Holt, Rinehart, & Winston.

Hoffman, M. L. (1977a). Sex differences in empathy and related behaviors. *Psychological Bulletin, 84,* 712–722.

Hoffman, M. L. (1977b). Sex differences in empathy and related behaviors. *Psychological Bulletin, 84,* 712–722.

Hoffman, M. L. (1977c). Empathy, its development and prosocial implications. *Nebraska Symposium on Motivation* (Vol. 25, pp. 169–218). Lincoln: University of Nebraska.

Hoffman, M. L. (1980). Adolescent morality in developmental perspective. In J. Adelson (Ed.), *Handbook of adolescent psychology,* 295–344.

Hoffman, M. L. (1982). Development of prosocial motivation: Empathy and guilt. In N. Eisenberg (Ed.), *The development of prosocial behavior,* 281–313.

Hoffman, M. L., & Saltzstein, H. D. (1967). Parent discipline and the child's moral development. *Journal of Personality and Social Psychology, 5,* 45–57.

Hogan, R. (1969). Development of an empathy scale. *Journal of Consulting and Clinical Psychology, 33,* 307–316.

Hogan, R. (1975). Empathy: A conceptual and psychometric analysis. *The Counseling Psychologist, 5,* 14–18.

Hohmann, G. W. (1966). Some effects of spinal cord lesions on experienced emotional feelings. *Psychophysiology, 3,* 143–156.

Holt, R., & Havel, J. (1960). A method for assessing primary and secondary processes in the Rorschach. In M. Rickers–Orsiankina (Ed.), *Rorschach psychology.* New York: Wiley.

Hornberg, R. H. (1960). The projective effects of fear and sexual arousal on the ráting of pictures. *Journal of Clinical Psychology, 16,* 328–331.

Hornblow, A. R. (1980). The study of empathy. *New Zealand Psychologist, 9,* 19–28.

Housley, W. F., & Magnus, R. E. (1974, March). Increasing empathy for employment service counselors: A practicum. *Journal of Employment Counseling,* 28–31.

Houts, D. S., MacIntosh, S., & Moos, R. H. (1969). Patient–therapist interdependence: Cognitive and behavioral. *Journal of Consulting and Clinical Psychology, 33,* 40–45.

Howard, M. S. (1975). The effectiveness of an action training model (using roleplaying, doubling and role reversal) in improving the facilitative interpersonal functioning (empathy, respect and genuineness) of nursing students with dying patients. Unpublished doctoral dissertation, University of Maryland.

Howell, R. J., & Jorgenson, E. C. (1970). Accuracy of judging emotional behavior in a natural setting—A replication. *Journal of Social Psychology, 81,* 269–270.

Hughes, H. (1900). *Die mimik des mensehen.* Frankfurt: Johannes Alt.

Hughes, R., Tingle, B., & Sawin, D. (1981). Development of empathic understanding in children. *Child Development, 52,* 122–128.

Hull, C. L. (1943). *Principles of behavior.* New York: Appleton–Century–Crofts.

Hummel, J. W. (1977). *Teaching preadolescents alternatives to aggression using structured learning training under different stimulus conditions.* Unpublished doctoral dissertation, Syracuse University.

Hundleby, G., & Zingle, H. (1975). Communication of empathy. *Canadian Counsellor, 9,* 148–154.

Hunt, D. E. (1971). *Matching models in education: The coordination of teaching methods with student characteristics.* Toronto: Ontario Institute for Studies in Education.

Hunt, W. A. (1941). Recent developments in the field of emotion. *Psychological Bulletin, 38*(5), 249–276.

Huth, P. K. B. (1979). *The effects of therapist anxiety and cognitive differentiation on empathic understanding and responding.* Unpublished doctoral dissertation, University of Illinois at Chicago Circle.

Ianoti, R. (1975). The nature and measurement of empathy in children. *The Counseling Psychologist, 5*(2), 21–25.

Irving, S. G. (1965). Parental empathy and adolescent adjustment. *Dissertation Abstracts International.*

Isquick, M. F. (1978). *Empathy, self-exploration, and attitudes in older people following empathy training.* Unpublished doctoral dissertation, California School of Professional Psychology, San Diego.

Ivey, A. E., & Authier, J. (1971). *Microcounseling,* Springfield, IL: Charles C. Thomas.

Izard, C. E. (1971). *The face of emotion.* New York: Appleton–Century–Crofts.

Izard, C. E. (1977). *Human emotions.* New York: Plenum.

Izard, C. E. (1979). *The maximally discriminative facial movement coding system.* Newark, DE: University of Delaware Instructional Resources Center.

Izard, C. E. (1981). Differential emotions theory and the facial feedback hypothesis of emotion activation: Comments on Tourangeau and Ellsworth's "The role of facial reponse in the experience of emotion." *Journal of Personality and Social Psychology, 40,* 350–354.

Izard, C. E., Huebner, R., Risser, D., McGinnes, G., & Dougherty, L. (1980). The young infant's ability to produce discrete emotion expressions. *Developmental Psychology, 16,* 132–140.

Jacobsen, E. (1938). *Progressive relaxation: A physiological and clinical investigation of muscular states and their significance in psychology and medical practice* (2nd rev. ed.). Chicago: University of Chicago Press.

Jacoby, H. (1925). *Must there be unmusical people?* Zurich, Switzerland: Publisher unknown.

James, W. (1884). What is an emotion? *Mind, 9,* 188–204.

Janaka, C. H. (1977). *Twelve, twenty-four, and thirty-six hours of Carkhuff empathy training with federally incarcerated youth offenders.* Unpublished doctoral dissertation, New Mexico State University.

Jarden, E., & Fernberger, S. W. (1926). The effect of suggestion on the judgment of facial expression of emotion. *American Journal of Psychology, 37,* 565–570.

Jenness, A. F. (1930. *Experimental studies of response to social stimulation.* Unpublished doctoral dissertation, Syracuse University.

Jenness, A. F. (1932). The effect of coaching subjects in the recognition of facial expressions. *Journal of Genetic Psychology, 7,* 163–178.

Johnson, D. (1977). *The protean body: A Rolfer's view of human flexibility.* New York: Harper & Row.

Jones, P. Jr. (1975). *The relative effects of types of nonverbal cues and social class on effective empathic communication in counseling.* Unpublished doctoral dissertation, West Virginia University.

Jones, L. K. (1974). Toward more adequate selection criteria: Correlates of empathy, genuineness, and respect. *Counselor Education and Supervision, 13,* 13–21.

Jordan, J. V. (1983). Empathy and the mother–daughter relationship. *Work in Progress,* No. 82–02, 2–5, Stone Center, Wellesley College, Wellesley, MA.

Josephson, L. M. (1979). *The effect of modeling and interpersonal process recall on paraprofessional trainees.* Unpublished doctoral dissertation, University of Cincinnati.

Judd, C. H. (1902). The relation of special training to general intelligence. *Educational Review, 36,* 28–42.

Kagan, N. (1972). *Influencing human interaction.* East Lansing: Michigan State University.

Kagan, N., & Schauble, P. G. (1969). Affect simulation in interpersonal process recall. *Journal of Consulting Psychology, 16,* 309–313.

Kallman, J., & Stollak, G. (1974). Maternal behavior toward children in need arousing situations. Midwestern Psychological Association, Chicago.

Kanner, L. (1931). Judging emotions from facial expressions. *Psychological Monographs,* No. 3.

Kaplan, A. G. (1983). Empathic communication in the psychotherapy relationship. *Work in Progress, Stone Center.* Wellesley, MA: Wellesley College.

Kapleau, P. (1967). *The three pillars of Zen: Teaching, practice, and enlightenment.* Boston: Beacon Press.

Karoly, P. & Kanfer, F. H. (1982). *Self-management and behavior change.* New York: Pergamon Press.

Karoly, P., & Steffen, J. J. (Eds.). (1980). *Improving the long-term effects of psychotherapy.* New York: Gardner Press.

Karniol, R. (1982). Settings, scripts, and self-schemata: A cognitive analysis of the development of prosocial behavior. In N. Eisenberg (Ed.), *The development of prosocial behavior.*

Katz, R. L. (1963). *Empathy: Its nature and uses.* New York: Free Press.

Kazdin, A. E. (1975). *Behavior modification in applied settings.* Homewood, IL: Dorsey Press.

Kazdin, A. E. (1980).*Research design in clinical psychology.* New York: Harper & Row.

Keefe, T. (1976). Empathy: The critical skill. *Social Work, 21,* 10–14.

Keefe, T. (1979). The development of empathic skill. *Journal of Education for Social Work, 15,* 30–37.

Keele, S. W. (1973). *Attention and human performance.* Pacific Palisades, CA: Goodyear Publishing.

Keeley, S. M., Shemberg, K. M. & Carbonell, J. (1976). Operant clinical intervention: Behavior management or beyond? *Behavior Therapy, 7,* 292–305.

Keen, S. (1970, October). Sing the body electric. *Psychology Today,* 56–61.

Keenan, R. C. (1976). *An investigation of the effects of four training approaches on the empathic communication skill levels of selected career soldiers and their spouses.* Unpublished doctoral dissertation, American University.

Keleman, S. (1974). *Living your dying.* New York: Random House.

Kellogg, W. N., & Eagleson, B. M. (1931). The growth of social perception in different racial groups. *Journal of Educational Psychology, 22,* 367–375.

Kelly, E. (1962). The fully functioning self. In S. W. Combs (Ed.), *Perceiving, behaving, becoming.* Washington, DC: Association for Supervision and Curriculum Development.

Kendon, A. (1970). Movement coordination in social interaction: Some examples described. *Acta Psychologica, 32,* 101–125.

Kenny, D. A. (1973). Cross-lagged and synchronous common factors in panel data. In A. S. Goldberger & D. D. Duncan (Eds.), *Structural equation models in the social sciences.* New York: Seminar Press.

Kenny, D. A. (1975). Cross-lagged panel correlation: A test for spuriousness. *Psychological Bulletin, 82,* 887–903.

Kenshalo, D. R. (1977). Age changes in touch, vibration, temperature, kinesthesis, and pain sensitivity. In J. Birren & K. W. Schaie (Eds.), *Handbook of the psychology of aging*. New York: Van Nostrand Reinhold.

Kerckhoff, A. C. (1969). Early antecedants of role-taking and role-playing ability. *Merrill–Palmer Quarterly, 15*, 229–247.

Kerr, W., & Speroff, B. J. (1954). Validation and evaluation of the Empathy Test. *Journal of General Psychology, 50*, 269–276.

Kestenberg, J. S. (1965a). The role of movement patterns in development: I. Rythms of movement. *Psychoanalytic Quarterly, 34*, 1–36.

Kestenberg, J. S. (1965b). The role of movement patterns in development: II. Flow of tension and effort. *Psychoanalytic Quarterly, 34*, 517–563.

Kestenberg, J. S. (1967). The role of movement patterns in development: III. The Control of shape. *Psychoanalytic Quarterly, 36*, 356–409.

Kestenberg, J. S. (1977). Psychoanalytic observation of children. *International Review of Psychoanalysis, 4*, 393–407.

Kesterberg, J. S., & Buelte, A. (1977). Prevention, infant therapy, and the treatment of adults. 1: Toward understanding mutuality. *International Journal of Psychoanalytic Psychotherapy, 6*, 339–367.

Kieran, S. S. (1979). *The development of a tentative model for analyzing and describing empathic understanding in teachers of young children*. Unpublished doctoral dissertation, Columbia University Teachers College.

Kiesler, D. J. (1966). Some myths of psychotherapy research and the search for a paradigm. *Psychological Bulletin, 65*, 110–136.

Kiesler, D. J., Mathieu, P. L., & Klein, M. H. (1967a). A summary of issues and conclusions. In C. R. Rogers, E. T. Gendlin, D. J. Kiesler, & C. B. Truax (Eds.), *The therapeutic relationship and its impact*. Madison: University of Wisconsin Press.

Kiesler, D. J., Mathieu, P. L., & Klein, M. H. (1967b). Measurement of conditions and process variables. In C. R. Rogers, E. T. Gendlin, D. J. Kiesler & C. B. Truax (Eds.) *The therapeutic relationship and its impact*. Madison, Wisc.: University of Wisconsin Press.

Kimberlin, C., & Friesen, D. (1977). Effects of client ambivalence, trainee conceptual level, and empathy training condition on empathic responding. *Journal of Counseling Psychology, 24*, 354–358.

Kipper, D. A., & Ben–Ely, Z. (1979). The effectiveness of the psychodramatic double method, the reflection method, and lecturing in the training of empathy. *Journal of Clinical Psychology, 39*, 370–375.

Kline, L. W., & Kline, F. L. (1927). *Psychology by experiment*. Boston: Gin.

Klock, E. M. (1977). *The development and testing of a microtraining program to enhance empathic communication by parents of young children*.

Koestler, A. (1949). The novelist deals with character. *Saturday Review of Literature, 32*, 7–8.

Kohlberg, L. (1969). Stage and sequence: The cognitive-developmental approach to socialization. In D. A. Goslin (Ed.), *Handbook of socialization theory and research*. Chicago: Rand–McNally.

Kohlberg, L. (1970). Education for justice: A modern statement of the platonic view. In N. F. Sizer & T. R. Sizer (Eds.), *Moral education: Five lectures*. Cambridge, MA: Harvard University Press.

Kohlberg, L. (1972). A cognitive-developmental approach to moral education. *The Humanist, 32*, 13–16.

Kohlberg, L. (1976). Moral stages and moralization: The cognitive-developmental approach. In T. Lickona (Ed.), *Moral development and behavior: Theory, research, and social issues*. New York: Holt, Rinehart, & Winston.

Kohut, Heinz (1977). *The restoration of the self*. New York: International Universities Press.

Konia, C. (1975). Orgone therapy: A case presentation. *Psychotherapy: Theory Research and Practice, 12,* 192–197.

Kozel, N. J., & Gitter, A. G. (1968). *Perception of emotion: Differences in mode of presentation, sex of perceiver, and role of expressor* (Tech. Rep 18). Boston: Boston University.

Kozma, R. B. (1974, April). *Evaluation of a self-instructional minicourse on empathic responding.* Presented at American Educational Research Association, Chicago.

Krasner, L. (1962). The therapist as a social reinforcement machine. In H. H. Strupp & L. Luborsky (Eds.), *Research in psychotherapy* (Vol. 2). Washington, DC: American Psychological Association.

Krause, M. S., & Pilisuk, M. (1961). Anxiety in verbal behavior: A validation study. *Journal of Consulting Psychology, 25,* 414–419.

Kraut, R. E. (1982). Social presence, facial feedback and emotion. *Journal of Personality and Social Psychology, 42,* 853–863.

Kris, E. (1952). Psychoanalytic exploration in art. New York: International Universities Press.

Kuchenbecker, S., Feshbach, N., & Pletcher, G. (1974). *The effects of age, sex, and modality upon social comprehension and empathy.* San Francisco: Western Psychological Association.

Kurtz, R. R., & Grummon, D. L. (1972). Different approaches to the measurement of therapist empathy and their relationship to therapy outcomes. *Journal of Consulting and Clinical Psychology, 39,* 106–115.

Laban, R., & Lawrence, F. C. (1947). *Effort.* London: Macdonald & Evans.

Lack, D. Z. (1975). *The effects of problem solving, structured learning, and contingency management in training paraprofessional mental health personnel.* Unpublished doctoral dissertation, Syracuse University.

Lacroix, J. M. (1981). The acquisition of autonomic control through biofeedback: The case against an afferent process and a two-process alternative. *Psychophysiology, 18,* 573–587.

LaFrance, M. (1979). Nonverbal synchrony and rapport: Analysis by the cross-lag panel technique. *Social Psychology Quarterly, 42,* 66–70.

LaFrance, M. (1982). Posture mirroring and rapport. In M. Davis (Ed.), *Interaction rhythms: Periodicity in communicative behavior.* New York: Human Sciences Press.

LaFrance, M., & Broadbent, M. (1976). Group rapport: Posture sharing as a nonverbal indicator. *Group and Organizational Studies, 1,* 328–333.

LaFrance, M., & Ickes, W. (1981). Posture mirroring and interactional involvement: Sex and sex typing effects. *Journal of Nonverbal Behavior, 5,* 139–154.

Laird, J. D. (1974). Self-attribution of emotion: The effects of expressive behavior on the quality of emotional experience. *Journal of Personality and Social Psychology, 29,* 475–486.

Laird, J. D., Wagener, J. J., Halal, M., & Szegda, M. (1982). Remembering what you feel: Effects of emotion on memory. *Journal of Personality and Social Psychology 42,* 646–657.

Lamb, M. E., & Campos, J. J. (1982). *Development in Infancy,* New York: Random House.

Lambert, M. J., DeJulio, S. S., & Stein, D. M. (1978). Therapist interpersonal skills: Process, outcome, methodological considerations, and recommendations for future research. *Psychological Bulletin, 85,* 467–489.

LaMonica, E. L., Carew, D. K., Winder, A. E., Haase, A. B., & Blanchard, K. H. (1976). Empathy training as the major thrust of a staff development program. *Nursing Research, 25,* 447–451.

Landis, C. (1929). The interpretation of facial expression in emotion. *Journal of General Psychology, 2,* 59–72.

Landis, C., & Hunt, W. A. (1939). *The startle pattern.* New York: Farrar, Straus, & Giroux.

Lange, C. (1922). The emotions. In K. Dunlap (Ed.), *The emotions.* Baltimore, MD: Williams & Wilkins. (Original work published 1885, I. Haupt, Trans.)

Langfeld, H. S. (1918). The judgment of emotions from facial expressions. *Journal of Abnormal & Social Psychology, 13,* 172–184.

Lanzetta, J. T., Cartwright–Smith, J., & Kleck, R. E. (1976). Effects of nonverbal dissimulation on emotional experience and autonomic arousal. *Journal of Personality and Social Psychology, 33*, 354–370.

Lanzetta, J. T., & Kleck, R. (1970). Encoding and decoding of facial affect in humans. *Journal of Personality and Social Psychology, 16*(1), 12–19.

Larabee, D. H. (1980). Effects of a modified theme-centered-interactional method on raising empathy in psychiatric nurses and patient care assistants. Unpublished doctoral dissertation, University of Pittsburgh.

Laughlin, S. G. (1978). *Use of self-instruction in teaching empathic responding to social work students.* Unpublished doctoral dissertation, University of California at Berkeley.

Law, E. J. (1978). *Toward the teaching and measurement of empathy for staff nurses.* Unpublished doctoral dissertation, Brigham Young University.

Layton, J. M. (1978). *The use of modeling to teach empathy to nursing students.* Unpublished doctoral dissertation, Michigan State University.

Lazar, J. N. (1976). *The effects of varied accurate empathy levels, participant contexts and data forms on the perception of empathy.* Unpublished doctoral dissertation, Virginia Commonwealth University.

Lehman, J. D. (1972). *The effects of empathy training involving modeling, feedback, and reinforcement on the ability of high school students to respond empathically in a tutoring session.* Unpublished doctoral dissertation, University of Tennessee.

Lennon, R., Eisenberg, N. E., & Carroll, J. (1983). *The relation between nonverbal indices of empathy and preschooler's prosocial behavior.* Presented at Society for Research in Child Development, Detroit.

Lesh, T. V. (1970). Zen meditation and the development of empathy in counselors. *Journal of Humanistic Psychology, 10,* 3974.

Lesser, W. M. (1961). The relationship between counseling progress and empathic understanding. *Journal of Counseling Psychology, 8,* 330–336.

Letourneau, C. (1981). Empathy and stress: How they affect parental aggression. *Journal of Social Work, 26,* 383–389.

Leventhal, H., & Sharp, E. (1965). Facial expressions as indicators of distress. In S. S. Tomkins & C. E. Izard (Eds.), *Affect, cognition and personality, empirical studies* (pp 296–318). New York: Springer.

Levi, B. (1975). *The phenomenology of intercorporeal expression as exemplified in and through moving together in improvisational dance.* Unpublished doctoral dissertation, Duquesne University.

Levitt, E. A. (1964). *The relationships between abilities to express emotional meaning vocally and facially. In J. R. Davitz (Ed.), The communication of emotional meaning* (pp 43–55). New York: McGraw–Hill.

Lewis, W. A., Lovell, J. T., & Jessee, B. E. (1965). Interpersonal relationship and pupil progress. *Personnel and Guidance Journal, 44,* 396–401.

Lichtenberg, J. D. (1983). *Psychoanalysis and infant research, The Analytic Press,* Distributed by Hillsdale, NJ: Lawrence Erlbaum Associates.

Lifton, W. M. (1958). The role of empathy and aesthetic sensitivity in counseling. *Journal of Counseling Psychology, 5,* 267–275.

Lindgren, H. C., & Robinson, J. (1953). The evaluation of Dymond's test of insight and empathy. *Journal of Consulting Psychology, 17,* 172–176.

Lipps, T. (1907). Das Wissen von Fremden Ichen. *Psychologischen Untersuchungen, 1,* 694–722.

Lipps, T. (1926). *Psychological studies.* Baltimore: Williams & Wilkins.

Litwack, S. E. (1976). *The helper therapy principle as a therapeutic tool: Structured learning therapy with adolescents.* Unpublished doctoral dissertation, Syracuse University.

Livesley, W. J., & Bromley, D. B. (1973). *Person perception in childhood and adolescence.* London: Wiley.

Lopez, M. A. (1977). *The influence of vocal and facial cue training on the identification of affect communicated via paralinguistic cues.* Unpublished masters thesis, Syracuse University.

Lowen, A. (1958). *The physical dynamics of character structure.* New York: Grune & Stratton. (Republished in 1971 as *The language of the body.* New York: Macmillan)

Lowen, A. (1965). *Breathing movement and feeling.* (Available from Institute for Bioenergetic Analysis, 144 East 36th Street, New York, NY 10016)

Lowen, A. (1967). *The betrayal of the body.* New York: Macmillan.

Lowen, A. (1975). *Bioenergetics.* New York: Coward, McCann, & Geoghegan.

Lowen, A., & Lowen, L. (1977). *The way to vibrant health: A manual of bioenergetic exercises.* New York: Harper & Row.

Lubin, J. A. (1979). *Client–counselor complementarity and its effects on counselor confluent and predictive empathy.* Unpublished doctoral dissertation, New York University.

Luborsky, L., & Spence, P. (1978). Quantitative research on psychoanalytic therapy. In S. L. Garfield & A. E. Bergin (Eds.), *Handbook of psychotherapy and behavior change: An empirical analysis* (2nd ed.). New York: Wiley.

Luchins, A. S. (1957). A variational approach to empathy. *Journal of Social Psychology, 45,* 11–18.

Lynch, G. (1934). A phonophotographic study of trained and untrained voices reading factual and dramatic material. *Archives of Speech, 1,* 9–25.

Macarov, D. (1978). Empathy: The charismatic chimera. *Journal of Education for Social Work, 14,* 86–92.

Mahl, G. F. (1956). Disturbances and silences in the patient's speech in psychotherapy. *Journal of Abnormal and Social Psychology, 53,* 1–15.

Mahl, G. F. (1968). Gestures and body movements in interviews. In J. Shlien (Ed.), *Research in psychotherapy* (Vol. III). Washington, DC: American Psychological Association.

Malmo, R. B., Smith, A. A., & Kohlmeyer, W. A. (1956). Motor manifestations of conflict in interview: A case study. *Journal of Abnormal and Social Psychology, 52,* 268–271.

Mandler, G. (1954). Transfer of training as a function of degree of response overlearning. *Journal of Experimental Psychology, 47,* 411–417.

Mandler, G., & Heinemann, S. H. (1956). Effects of overlearning of a verbal response on transfer of training. *Journal of Experimental Psychology, 52,* 39–46.

Mantaro, C. A. (1971). *An investigation of the relationship between the interpersonal relationships perceived by a pupil to exist between himself and his reading teacher and (1) his reading achievement and (2) his self-concepts.* Unpublished doctoral dissertation, Syracuse University.

Marholin, D., & Touchette, P. E. (1979). The role of stimulus control and response consequences. In A. P. Goldstein & F. H. Kanfer (Eds.), *Maximizing treatment gains: Transfer enhancement in psychotherapy.* New York: Academic Press.

Markus, H. (1977). Self schemata and the processing of information about the self. *Journal of Personality and Social Psychology, 35,* 63–79.

Marshall, G. D., & Zimbardo, P. G. (1979). Affective consequences of inadequately explained physiological arousal. *Journal of Personality and Social Psychology, 37,* 970–988.

Maslach, C. (1979). Negative emotional biasing of unexplained arousal. *Journal of Personality and Social Psychology, 37,* 953–969.

Maslow, A. (1962). Some basic propositions of a growth and self-actualizing psychology. In A. W. Combs (Ed.), *Perceiving, behaving, becoming.* Washington, DC: Association for Supervision and Curriculum Development.

Maslow, A. (1971). *The farthest reaches for human nature.* New York: Viking Press.

Matarazzo, J. D., & Weins, A. N. (1977). Speech behavior as an objective correlate of empathy and outcome in interview and psychotherapy research. *Behavior Modification, 4,* 453–480.

Matas, L., Arend, R., & Sroufe, L. (1978). Continuity of adaptation in the second year: The relationship between quality of attachment and later competence. *Child Development, 49*, 547–556.

Matthews, P. B. C. (1982). Where does Sherrington's "Muscular sense" originate? Muscles, Joints, corollary discharges? *Annual Review of Neuroscience, 5*, 189–218.

Maupin, E. (1962). Zen Buddhism: A psychological review. *Journal of Consulting Psychology, 26*, 362–378.

Maupin, E. W. (1965). Individual differences in response to a Zen meditation exercise. *Journal of Consulting Psychology, 29*, 139–145.

Maupin, E. W. (1972). On meditation. In C. Tart (Ed.), *Altered states of consciousness.* New York: Doubleday.

May, R. (Ed.). (1969). *Existential psychology.* New York: W. W. Norton.

McCaul, K. D., Holmes, D. S. & Solomon, S. (1982). Voluntary expressive changes and emotion. *Journal of Personality and Social Psychology, 42*, 145–152.

McAuliffe, S. E. (1974). The differential effect of three training models upon the acquisition and transfer of enterpersonal communication skills. Unpublished doctoral dissertation, University of Minnesota.

McCloskey, D. I., & Gandevia, S. C. (1978). Role of inputs from skin, joints and muscles and of corollary discharges, in human discrimination tasks. In G. Gordon (Ed.), *Active touch: The mechanism of recognition of objects by manipulation.* New York: Pergamon Press.

McDougall, W. (1908). *Introduction to social psychology.* London: Methuen.

McDowall, J. J. (1978a). Interactional synchrony: A reappraisal. *Journal of Personality and Social Psychology, 36*, 963–975.

McDowall, J. J. (1978b). Microanalysis of filmed movement: The reliability of boundary detection by trained observers. *Environmental Psychology and Nonverbal Behavior, 3*, 77–88.

McKay, J. K. (1979). *The effect of rehabilitation counselor disability status on similarly disabled clients' perceptions of counselor social influence and empathy.* Unpublished doctoral dissertation, Florida State University, 1979.

McLean, M. M. (1979). *The differential effects of three training programs on attained levels of facilitative conditions: Empathy, warmth, and genuineness.* Unpublished doctoral dissertation, University of Toronto.

McV.Hunt, J., Cole, M., & Reis, E. (1958). Situational cues distinguishing anger, fear, and sorrow. *American Journal of Psychology, 71*, 136–151.

Mead, G. H. (1934).*Mind, self and society.* Chicago: University of Chicago Press.

Means, B. L. (1973). Levels of empathic response. *Personnel and Guidance Journal, 52*, 23–28.

Mehrabian, A. (1968). Relationship of attitude to seated posture, orientation, and distance. *Journal of Personality and Social Psychology, 10*, 26–30.

Mehrabian, A. (1969a). Some referents and measures of nonverbal behavior. *Behavior Research Methods and Instrumentation, 1*, 203–207.

Mehrabian, A. (1969b). Significance of posture and position in the communication of attitude and status relationships. *Psychological Bulletin, 71*, 359–372.

Mehrabian, A., & Epstein, W. A. (1972). A measure of emotional empathy. *Journal of Personality, 40*, 523–543.

Mehrabian, A., & Ferris, S. R. (1967). Inference of attitudes from nonverbal communication in two channels. *Journal of Consulting Psychology, 31*, 248–252.

Melton, C. (1965). The helping relationship in college reading clinics. *Personnel and Guidance Journal, 43*, 925–928.

Mendelsohn, G. A. (1966). Effect of client personality and client–counselor similarity on the duration of counseling. *Journal of Counseling Psychology, 13*, 228–234.

Messé, L. A., Stollak, G. E., Watts, P., Perlmutter, L., & Peshkess, I. (1982). *Person perception biases and caregiving behaviors of first-time parents.* Presented at American Psychological Association, Washington, DC.

Michaels, G. Y., Hoffman, M. L., & Goldberg, W. (1982). *Longitudinal investigation of value system changes at transition to parenthood.* Presented at American Psychological Association, Washington, DC.

Michaels, G. Y., Messe, L. A. & Stollak, G. E. (1983). Seeing parental behavior through different eyes. *Genetic Psychology Monographs, 107,* 3–60.

Miller, G. A., Heise, G. A., & Lichten, W. (1951). The intelligibility of speech as a function of the test materials. *Journal of Experimental Psychology, 41,* 329–335.

Miller, R. L. (1980). *The impact of training upon the level of affective sensitivity (empathy) in fifth- and sixth-grade children.* Unpublished doctoral dissertation, Michigan State University.

Miller, T. (1976). The effects of core facilitative conditions in mother on adolescent self-esteem. *Journal of Social Psychology, 100,* 147–148.

Minsel, W., Bommert, H., Bastine, R., Langer, I., Nickel, H., & Tausch, R. (1971). Weitere untersuchung der auswirkung und prozcse klienten-zentrieter gespraschs-psychotherapie zertsch R. G. *Klinische Psychologie, 1,* 232–250.

Mintz, J., Luborsky, L., & Auerbach, A. H. (1971). Dimensions of psychotherapy: A factor-analytic study of ratings of psychotherapy sessions. *Journal of Consulting and Clinical Psychology, 36,* 106–120.

Mitchell, K. M., Truax, C. B., Bozarth, J. D., & Krauft, C. C. (1973, March). Antecedants to psychotherapeutic outcome. Arkansas Rehabilitation Research and Training Center, Hot Springs, Arkansas.

Mitchell, K. M., Bozarth, J. D. & Krauft, C. C. (1977). A reappraisal of the therepeutic effectiveness of accurate empathy, nonpossessive warmth, and genuineness. In A. S. Gurman and A. M. Rezin (Eds.), *Effective psychotherapy: A handbook of research.* New York: Pergamon Press.

Modell, A. H. (1976). "The holding environment" and the therapeutic action of psychoanalysis. *Journal of the American Psychoanalytic Association, 24*(2), 285–307.

Montagu, A. (1971). *Touching: The human significance.* New York: Columbia University Press.

Moore, D. D. (1978). *The relationship of selected familial, personality, and participant characteristics to empathy in middle childhood.* Unpublished doctoral dissertation, University of Maine.

Moore, J. E. (1980). *Facilitating children's social understanding through cognitive conflict and role playing.* Unpublished doctoral dissertation, University of Toronto.

Moore, T. V. (1926). *Dynamic psychology.* Philadelphia: Lippincott.

Moos, R. H., & MacIntosh, S. (1970). Multivariate study of the patient–therapist system: A replication and extension. *Journal of Consulting and Clinical Psychology, 35,* 298–307.

Morgan, S. R. (1979). A model of the empathic process for teachers of emotionally disturbed children. *American Journal of Orthopsychiatry, 49,* 446–453.

Moritz, E. (1976). The acquisition of empathic communication skills through the active listening training in Thomas Gordon's Parent Effectiveness Training. *Dissertation Abstracts International,* 19441.

Morris, D. (1977). *Manwatching: A field guide to human behavior.* New York: Harry N. Abrams.

Morrison, J. L. (1974). *The effects of videotape focused feedback on levels of facilitative conditions.* Unpublished doctoral dissertation, University of North Dakota.

Moses, J., & Byham, W. (1978). *Applying the assessment center method.* New York: Pergamon Press.

Mosso, A. (1896). *Fear.* New York: Longmans, Green.

Moustakas, C. E. (1955). The frequency and intensity of negative attitudes expressed in play therapy: A comparison of well-adjusted and disturbed young children. *Journal of Genetic Psychology, 86,* 309–325.

Moyer, L. M. (1981). *The effects of empathy training on levels of self-actualization in senior citizens.* Unpublished doctoral dissertation, University of Toledo.

Muehlberg, N., Pierce, R., & Drasgow, J. (1969). A factor analysis of therapeutically facilitative conditions. *Journal of Clinical Psychology, 25,* 93–95.

Mullen, J., & Abeles, N. (1971). Relationship of liking, empathy, and therapist's experience to outcome of therapy. *Journal of Counseling Psychology, 18,* 39–43.

Mummenmsa, T. (1964). The language of the face. *Jyvaskyla studies in education psychology, and social research.* Jyvaskyla, Finland: Jyvaskylen Yllopistry hdistip.

Munig, G. R. (1979). *The effects of physical attractiveness and voice attractiveness on ratings of therapists' empathy, warmth, and genuineness.* Unpublished doctoral dissertation, California School of Professional Psychology, Berkeley.

Munn, N. L. (1940). The effect of knowledge of the situation upon judgment of emotion from facial expressions. *Journal of Abnormal and Social Psychology, 35,* 324–338.

Murphy, C. (1979). Increasing potential awareness of children's feelings in families of disabled children. *Dissertation Abstracts International,* 4765.

Murphy, L. (1932). *Social behavior and child personality: An exploratory study of some roots of sympathy.* New York: Columbia University Press.

Nehr, L. A., & Dickens, C. (1975). Empathy and the counselor's experience of the client's problem. *Psychotherapy: Theory, Research and Practice, 12,* 360–363.

Neisser, U. (1967). *Cognitive psychology.* New York: Appleton.

Nelson, C. A., Morse, P. A., & Leavitt, L. A. (1979). Recognition of facial expressions by seven-month old infants. *Child Development, 56,* 1239–1242.

Norman, R. D., & Ainsworth, P. (1954). The relationships among projection, empathy, reality, and adjustment, operationally defined. *Journal of Consulting Psychology, 18,* 53–58.

North, M. (1975). *Personality assessment through movement.* Boston: Plays, Inc.

Ober, R. W. (1980). Effects of reduction of physiological anxiety on counseling student's empathy and anxiety. *Dissertation Abstracts International, 40,* 6154–A.

O'Connor, R. M. (1974). Mother–child empathy and problem-solving skill training: Evaluation of a developmental model. *Dissertation Abstracts International,* Order No. 75–12, *137* (7657-A).

Olden, C. (1958). Notes on the development of empathy. *Psychoanlaytic Study of the Child, 13,* 505–518.

Olesker, W., & Balter, L. (1972). Sex and empathy. *Journal of Counseling Psychology, 19,* 559–562.

Ortleb, R. (1937). An objective study of emphasis in oral reading of emotional and unemotional material. *Speech Monographs, 4,* 56–74.

Osgood, C. E. (1949). The similarity paradox in human learning: A resolution. *Psychological Review, 56,* 132–143.

Osgood, C. E. (1953). *Method and theory in experimental psychology.* New York: Oxford University Press.

Osgood, C. E. (1966). Dimensionality of the semantic space for communication via facial expressions. *Scandinavian Journal of Psychology, 7,* 1–30.

Oster, H., & Ekman, P. (1978). Facial behavior in child development. In A. Collins (Ed.), *Minnesota symposium on child psychology* (Vol. 11). Hillsdale, NJ: Lawrence Erlbaum Associates.

Paivio, A. (1978). Mental comparisons involving abstract attributes. *Memory and Cognition, 6,* 199–208.

Parloff, M. B., Waskow, I. E., & Wolfe, B. E. (1978). Research on therapist variables in relation to process and outcome. In S. L. Garfield & A. E. Bergin (Eds.), *Handbook of psychotherapy and behavior change.* New York: Wiley.

Parsons, P. N. (1977). *The differential effects of counselor–client match in conceptual level upon perceived and predictive empathy.* Unpublished doctoral dissertation, SUNY at Buffalo.

Passons, W. R., & Olsen, L. C. (1969). Relationship of counselor characteristics and empathic sensitivity. *Journal of Counseling Psychology, 16,* 440–445.

Patterson, G. R. (1971). Behavioral intervention procedures in the classroom and in the home. In A. E. Bergin & S. L. Garfield (Eds.), *Handbook of psychotherapy and behavior change.* New York: Wiley.

Paul, N. L. (1970). Parental empathy. In E. J. Anthony & T. Benedek (Eds.), *Parenthood: Its psychology and psychopathology*. Boston: Little, Brown.

Peebles, M. (1980). Personal therapy and ability to display empathy, warmth, and genuineness in psychotherapy. *Psychotherapy: Theory, Research and Practice. 17,* 258–262.

Pengel, J. E. (1979). *The repression-sensitization scale as a predictive measure of certain client and counselor behavior in the initial interview.* Unpublished doctoral dissertation, University of Connecticut.

Pepinsky, H. B., & Karst, T. O. (1964). Convergence, a phenomenon in counseling and in psychotherapy. *American Psychologist, 19,* 333–338.

Pereira, G. J. (1978). *Teaching empathy through skill building versus interpersonal anxiety reduction methods.* Unpublished doctoral dissertation, Catholic University of American.

Perkins, E. R. (1971). *Relationships among empathy, genuineness, and nonpossessive warmth, and college teacher effectiveness and selected characteristics.* Unpublished doctoral dissertation, University of Kentucky.

Perls, F. S., Hefferline, R. F., & Goodman, P. (1951). *Gestalt therapy: Excitement and growth in the human personality.* New York: Julian Press.

Perry, M. A. (1970). *Didactic instructions for and modeling of empathy.* Unpublished doctoral dissertation, Syracuse University.

Perry, M. A. (1975). Modeling and instructions in training for counselor empathy. *Journal of Counseling Psychology, 22,* 173–179.

Perry, T. J. Jr. (1975). *The effect of racially similar/dissimilar client–counselor dyads upon black client perception of accurate empathy and general counselor effectiveness.* Unpublished doctoral dissertation, West Virginia University.

Pesso, A. (1969). *Movement in psychotherapy.* New York: New York University Press.

Petro, C. S., & Hansen, J. C. (1977). Counselor sex and empathic judgment. *Journal of counseling Psychology, 24,* 373–376.

Piderit, T. (1886). *Mimik und physiognomik.* Detmold: Meyer.

Pierce, R., Carkhuff, R. R., & Berenson, B. G. (1967). The differential effects of high and low functioning conselors upon counselors-in-training. *Journal of Clinical Psychology, 23,* 212–215.

Pitt, N. W. (1979). *The effects of therapist–patient similarity on the therapist's level of accurate empathy and selected psychotherapy process and outcome criteria.* Unpublished doctoral dissertation, Temple University.

Pittenger, R. E., & Smith, H. L. (1957). A basis for some contributions of linguistics to psychiatry. *Psychiatry, 20,* 61–78.

Plutchik, R. (1954). The role of muscular tension in maladjustment. *Journal of General Psychology, 50,* 45–62.

Plutchik, R. (1962). *The emotions: Facts, theories and a new model.* New York: Random House.

Plutchik, R., Wasserman, N., & Mayer, M. (1975). A comparison of muscle tension patterns in psychiatric patients and normals. *Journal of Clinical Psychology, 31,* 4–8.

Prager, R. A. (1970). *The relationship of certain client characteristics to therapist-offered conditions and therapeutic outcome.* Unpublished doctoral dissertation, Columbia University.

Preston, J. C., & Guerney, B. G. (1982). *Relationship enhancement skill training.* Unpublished manuscript, Pennsylvania State University.

Price, R. H. (1979). The social ecology of treatment gains. In A. P. Goldstein & F. H. Kanfer (Eds.), *Maximizing treatment gains: Transfer enhancement in psychotherapy*. New York: Academic Press.

Pruden, C. W. (1976). *The effects of role playing and trainee feedback in the development of selected facilitative skills.* Unpublished doctoral dissertation, University of Cincinnati.

Rachman, S. J. (1973). The effects of psychological treatment. In H. Eysenck (Ed.), *Handbook of abnormal psychology*. New York: Basic Books.

Rappaport, D. N. (1975). *Client behaviors effecting the therapist offerings of nonpossessive warmth, accurate empathy and geniuneness.* Unpublished doctoral dissertation, California School of Professional Psychology, Los Angeles.

Rappaport, J., & Chinsky, J. M. (1972). Accurate empathy: Confusion of a construct. *Psychological Bulletin, 77,* 400–404.

Raush, H. L., & Bordin, E. S. (1957). Warmth in personality development and in psychotherapy. *Psychiatry, 20,* 351–363.

Rector, R. (1953). Reciprocal empathy: A study of student–teacher interaction. *Oklahoma Academy of Science, 34,* 175–177.

Reich, W. (1949). *Character analysis* (3rd ed., T. P. Wolfe, Trans). New York: Farrar, Straus, & Giroux. (Original work published 1933)

Reichenbach, L., & Masters, J. C. (1983). Children's use of expressive and contextual cues in judgments of emotion. *Child Development, 54,* 993–1004.

Reik, T. (1949). *Listening with the third ear.* New York: Farrar, Straus.

Rimon, R., Stenback, A., & Huhmar, E. (1966). Electromyographic findings in depressive patients. *Journal of Psychosomatic Research, 10,* 159–170.

Relfalvy–Fodor, M. V. (1976). *Effects of supervisory style on the learning of empathy fro trainees with high/low levels of dogmatism.* Unpublished doctoral dissertation, West Virginia University.

Ringness, T. A. (1975). *The affective domain in education.* Boston: Little, Brown.

Rinn, W. E. (1984). The neuropsychology of facial expression: A review of the neurological and psychological mechanisms for producing facial expressions. *Psychological Bulletin, 95,* 52–77.

Rizzo, S. (1977). A comparison of the effects of variations in microcounseling training with groups of parents of the developmentally disabled. *Dissertation Abstracts* International, No. 77–13,584.

Roberts, W. E. (1977). *The assessment of anxiety with the counselor relationship skills of accurate empathy, nonpossessive warmth and genuineness.* Unpublished doctoral dissertation, Iowa State University.

Robinson, R. (1973). *Evaluation of a structured learning empathy training program for lower socioeconomic status home-aide trainees.* Unpublished masters thesis, Syracuse University.

Robinson, W. H., Wilson, E. S., & Robinson, S. L. (1978). The effects of perceived levels of warmth and empathy on student achievement. *Reading Improvement, 8,* 313–318.

Roche, M. A. (1974, Spring). Comment . . . *Bulletin of the Charlotte Selver Foundation 6,* 8. (Available from Charlotte Selver Foundation, 32 Cedars Rd., Caldwell, N.J. 07006)

Rocks, T. G., Baker, S. B., & Guerney, B. G. (1982). *Effects of counselor-directed relationship enhancement training on underachieving, poorly communicating students and their teachers.* Unpublished manuscript, Pennsylvania State University.

Roe, K. V. (1976). A cross-cultural study of empathy in young children. Los Angeles: (ERIC document production Service No. ED 141 671).

Roe, K. V. (1977). A study of empathy in young Greek and U.S. children. *Journal of Cross-Cultural Psychology, 8,* 493–501.

Roe, K. V. (1980). Toward a contingency hypothesis of empathy development. *Journal of Personality and Social Psychology, 39,* 991–994.

Rogers, C. R. (1949). The attitude and orientation of the counselor. *Journal of Consulting Psychology, 13,* 82–94.

Rogers, C. R. (1951). *Client-centered therapy: Its current practice, implications, and theory.* Boston: Houghton–Miffin.

Rogers, C. R. (1957). The necessary and sufficient conditions of therapeutic personality change. *Journal of Consulting Psychology, 21,* 95–103.

Rogers, C. R. (1975). Empathic: An unappreciated way of being. *The Counseling Psychologist, 5,* 2–10.

Rogers, C. (1983). *Freedom to learn.* Columbus, OH: Charles E. Merrill.

Rolf, I. (1977). *Rolfing: The integration of human structures.* Boulder, CO: The Rolf Institute.

Ronnestad, M. H. (1977, March). The effects of modeling, feedback and experiential methods on counselor empathy. *Counselor Education and Supervision,* 194–201.

Rose, J. E., & Mountcastle, V. B. (1959). Touch and Kinaesthesis. In J. Field (Ed.), *Handbook of physiology* (Vol. 1, Sec. I). Washington, DC: American Physiological Society.

Rosen, J. (1978). *The efficacy of modeling and instructional techniques for counselor acquisition of nonverbal empathy skills.* Unpublished doctoral dissertation, Indiana University.

Rosenberg, J. L. (1973). *Total Orgasm.* Clinton MA: Colonial Press.

Rosenfeld, H. M. (1981). Whither interactional synchrony? In K. Bloom (Ed.), *Prospective issues in infancy research.* Hillsdale, NJ: Lawrence Erlbaum Associates.

Rosenthal, R. (1966). *Experimenter effects in behavioral research.* New York: Appleton–Century–Crofts.

Rosenthal, R. (Ed.). (1979). *Skill in nonverbal communication.* Cambridge, MA: Oelgeschlager, Gunn, & Hain.

Rosenthal, R. (1982). Conducting judgment studies. In K. R. Scherer & P. Ekman (Eds.), *Handbook of methods in nonverbal behavior research.* Cambridge, MA: Cambridge University Press.

Rosenthal, R., & DePaulo, B. M. (1979). Sex differences in accommodation in nonverbal communication. In R. Rosenthal (Ed.), *Skill in nonverbal communication* (pp. 68–103). Cambridge, MA: Oelgeschlager, Gunn, & Hain.

Rosenthal, R., Hall, J. A., DiMatteo, M. R., Rogers, P. L., & Archer, D. (1979). *Sensitivity to nonverbal communication: The PONS test.* Baltimore: Johns Hopkins University Press.

Ross, A., & Brener, J. (1981). Two procedures for training cardiac discrimination: A comparison of solution strategies and their relationship to heart rate control. *Psychophysiology, 18,* 62–70.

Rothbart, M. K., & Meccoby, E. (1966). Parents' differential reactions to sons and daughters. *Journal of Personality and Social Psychology, 24,* 237–243.

Rothenberg, B. (1970). Children's social sensitivity and the relationship to interpersonal competence, intrapersonal comfort, and intellectual level. *Developmental Psychology, 2,* 335–350.

Rubenstein, L. (1969). Facial expressions: An objective method in the qualitative evaluation of emotional change. *Behavior Research Methods and Instruments, 1,* 305–306.

Ruckmick, C. A. (1926). *Directions for demonstrating emotional expression.* Chicago: Stoelting.

Rudolph, H. (1903). *Der ausdruck der gemutsbewegungen des menschen.* Dresden: Kuhtmann.

Saarni, C. (1979). Children's understanding of display rules for expressive behavior. *Developmental Psychology, 15,* 424–429.

Saarni, C. (1983, April). Suggestion and expectancy in emotional socialization. *Society For Research in Child Development,* Detroit.

Sackett, G. P. (1966). Monkeys reared in visual isolation with pictures as visual input: Evidence for an innate releasing mechanism. *Science, 154,* 1468–1472.

Sagi, A., & Hoffman, M. L. (1976). *Developmental Psychology, 12,* 175–176.

Salomon, G. (1972). Heuristic models for the generation of aptitude-treatment interaction hypotheses. *Review of Educational Research, 42,* 327–343.

Saltmarsh, R. E. (1973). Development of empathic interview skills through programmed instruction. *Journal of Counseling Psychology, 20,* 375–377.

Schacter, S. (1975). Cognition and peripheralist-centralist controversies in motivation and emotion. In M. S. Gazzaniga & C. Blakemore (Eds.), *Handbook of Psychobiology.* New York: Academic Press.

Schacter, S., & Singer, J. E. (1962). Cognitive, social, and physiological determinants of emotional state. *Psychological Review, 69,* 379–399.

Schantz, C. V. (1983). Social cognition. In P. H. Mussen (Ed.), *Carmichael's manual of child psychology* (4th ed. New York: Wiley.

Scheflen, A. (1964). The significance of posture in communication systems. *Psychiatry, 27,* 316–331.

Scheflen, A. E. (1972). *Body language and social order: Communication as behavioral control.* Englewood Cliffs, NJ: Prentice–Hall.

Scheler, M. (1954). *The nature of sympathy.* New Haven: Yale University Press.

Scheuer, A. L. (1971). The relationship between personal attributes and effectiveness in teachers of the emotionally disturbed. *Exceptional Children, 37,* 723–731.

Schiffenbauer, A. (1974). Effects of observer's emotional state on judgments of the emotional state of others. *Journal of Personality and Social Psychology, 30,* 31–35.

Schmidt, R. F. (1973). Control of the access of afferent activity to somotosensory pathways. In A. Iggo (Ed.), *Handbook of sensory physiology:* (Vol. 2) *Somatosensory system.* Berlin: Springer–Verlag.

Schultz, J. H., & Luthe, W. (1959). *Autogenic Training: A psychophysiologic approach in psychotherapy.* New York: Grune & Stratton.

Schultze, R. (1912). *Experimental psychology and pedagogy.* New York: Macmillan.

Schwartz, G. E., Fair, P. L., Salt, P. S., Mandel, M. R., & Klerman, J. L. (1976). Facial muscle patterning to affective imagery in depressed and nondepressed subjects. *Science, 192,* 489–491.

Schwartz, G. E., Weinberger, D. A., & Singer, J. A. (1981). Cardiovascular diffentiation of happiness, sadness, anger, and fear following imagery and exercise. *Psychosomatic Medicine, 43,* 343–364.

Seay, T. A., & Altebruse, M. K. (1979). Verbal and nonverbal behavior in judgments of facilitative conditions. *Journal of Counseling Psychology, 26,* 108–119.

Selman, R. (1980). *The growth of interpersonal understanding.* New York: Academic Press.

Selan, R. L., & Bryne, D. F. (1974). A structural-developmental analysis of levels of role-taking in middle childhood. *Child Development, 45,* 803–806.

Selver, C. (1957). Sensory awareness and total functioning. *General Semantics Bulletin, 20–21,* 5–17.

Shagass, L., & Malmo, R. B. (1954). Psychodynamic themes and localized muscular tension in psychotherapy. *Psychosomatic Medicine, 16,* 295–313.

Shapiro, D. A. (1969). Empathy, warmth, and genuineness in psychotherapy. *British Journal of Social and Clinical Psychology, 8,* 350–361.

Sensue, M. E. (1981). Filial therapy follow-up study. Effects of parental acceptance and child adjustment. Unpublished doctoral dissertation, Pennsylvania State University.

Shapiro, J. G., Foster, C. P., & Powell, T. (1968). Facial and bodily cues of genuineness, empathy, and warmth. *Journal of Clinical Psychology, 24,* 233–236.

Shaw, L. W. (1978). *A study of empathy training effectiveness: Comparing computer assisted instruction, structured learning training and encounter training exercises.* Unpublished doctoral dissertation, Syracuse University.

Shelton, J. L. (1979). Instigation therapy: Using therapeutic homework to promote treatment gains. In A. P. Goldstein & F. H. Kanfer (Eds.), *Maximizing treatment gains: Transfer enhancement in psychotherapy.* New York: Academic Press.

Shipman, W. G., Oken, D., Goldstein, I. B., Grinker, R. R., & Heath, H. A. (1964). Study in psychophysiology of muscle tension II: Personality factors. *Archives of General Psychiatry, 11,* 330–345.

Shore, E., & Sechrest, L. (1961). Concept attainment as a function of number of positive instances presented. *Journal of Educational Psychology, 52,* 303–307.

Silverman, J., Rappaport, M., Hopkins, H. K., Ellman, G., Hubbard, R., & Kling, R. (1973). Stress, stimulus intensity control, and the structural integration technique. *Confinia Psychiatrica, 16,* 201–219.

Sime, W. E., & DeGood, D. E. (1977). Effect of EMG biofeedback and progressive muscle relaxation training on awareness of frontalis muscle tension. *Psychophysiology, 14,* 522–530.

Simmer, J. A. (1977). *Bodhidharma's eyelids: Sensory awareness in the Buddhist meditative tradition.* Unpublished doctoral dissertation, Walden University.

Simner, M. L. (1971). Newborn's response to the cry of another infant. *Developmental Psychology, 5,* 136–150.

Sloane, R. B., Staples, F. R., Cristol, A. H., Yorkston, N. J., & Whipple, K. (1975). *Short-term analytically oriented psychotherapy vs. behavior therapy.* Cambridge, MA: Harvard University Press.

Sloman, L., Berridge, M., Homatidis, S., Hunter, D., & Duck, T. (1982). Gait patterns of depressed patients and normal subjects. *American Journal of Psychiatry, 139,* 94–97.

Smith, H. C. (1966). *Sensitivity to people.* New York: McGraw–Hill.

Smith, H. C. (1973). *Sensitivity training.* New York: McGraw–Hill.

Smith–Hanen, S. S. (1977). Effects of nonverbal behaviors on judged levels of counselor warmth and empathy. *Journal of Counseling Psychology, 24,* 87–91.

Smith, J. L. (1979). *The role of empathy in the treatment of high school students with public speaking anxiety.* Unpublished doctoral dissertation, Catholic University.

Smith, P. B., & Pederson, D. R. (1983). *Maternal sensitivity and patterns of infant–mother attachment.* Paper presented at the Biennial Meeting of the Society for Research in Child Development, Detroit.

Smither, S. (1977). A reconsideration of the developmental study of empathy. *Human Development, 20,* 253–276.

Solomon, E. J. (1978). *Structured learning therapy with abusive parents: Training in self-control.* Unpublished doctoral dissertation, Syracuse University.

Sommer, R. (1967). Small group ecology. *Psychological Bulletin, 67,* 145–151.

Soskin, W. F., & Kauffman, P. E. (1961). Judgment of emotion in word-free voice samples. *Journal of Communication, 11,* 73–80.

Spadone, A. L. (1974). *An investigation of rated levels of accurate empathy as a function of training method.* Unpublished doctoral dissertation, University of Southern California.

Spencer, H. (1910). *Principles of psychology.* New York: Appleton.

Spielberger, C. D., Gorsuch, R. L., & Lushene, R. L. (1970). *STAI: Manual for the State-Trait Anxiety Inventory.* Palo Alto: Consulting Psychologist's Press.

Sriram, C. M. (1978). The relationship between self-actualization and the levels of facilitative conditions in parent–adolescent communication. *Dissertation Abstracts International,* Order No. 7901206 (3492B).

Sroute, L. A. (1982). Infant–caregiver attachment and patterns of adaptation in preschool: The roots of maladaption and competence. In M. Perlmutter (Ed.), *Minnesota symposium in child psychology* (Vol. 16). Hillsdale, NJ: Lawrence Erlbaum Associates.

Steinitz, H. S. (1976). *Perspectives on psychotherapy process and empathy.* Unpublished doctoral dissertation, Michigan State University.

Stern, G. G. (1970). *People in context.* New York: Wiley.

Stevens, S. S. (1951). Mathematics, measurement, and psychophysics. In S. S. Stevens (Ed.), *Handbook of experimental psychology.* New York: Wiley.

Stevens, S. S. (1975). *Psychophysics* (2nd ed.). New York: Wiley.

Stilson, D. W., Matus, I., & Ball, G. (1980). Relaxation and subjective estimates of muscle tension: Implications for a central efferent theory of muscle control. *Biofeedback and Self-Regulation, 5,* 19–36.

Stoffer, D. L. (1970). Investigation of positive behavioral change as a function of genuineness, nonpossessive warmth, and empathic understanding. *Journal of Educational Research, 63,* 225–228.

Stollak, G. E. (1973). Undergraduates and children: An integrated undergraduate program in the assessment, treatment and prevention of child psychopathology. *Professional Psychology, 4,* 158–169.

Stollak, G. E. (1974). Education for early childhood consultation. *Journal of Clinical Child Psychology, 3,* 20–24.

Stollak, G. E. (1978). *Until we are six: Toward the actualization of human potential.* Englewood Cliffs, NJ: Prentice–Hall.

Stollak, G. E., Messe, L. A., Michaels, G. Y., Buldain, R., Catlin, T., & Paritee, F. (1982). Parental interpersonal perceptual style, child adjustment, and parent–child interactions. *Journal of Abnormal Child Psychology, 10,* 61–76.

Stollak, G. E., Scholom, A., Kallman, J., & Suturnasky, C. (1973). Insensitivity to children: Responses of undergraduates to children in problem situations. *Journal of Abnormal Child Psychology, 1,* 169–180.

Stotland, E. (1969). Exploratory investigations of empathy. In L. Berkowitz (Ed.), *Advances in experimental social psychology* (pp. 271–314). New York: Academic Press.

Stotland, E., & Walsh, J. (1963). Birth order in an experimental study of empathy. *Journal of Abnormal and Social Psychology, 66,* 610–614.

Stotland, E., Sherman, S. E., & Shover, K. G. (1971). *Empathy and birth order.* Lincoln: University of Nebraska Press.

Stover, L., & Guerney, B. G. (1967). Efficacy of training procedures for mothers in filial therapy. *Psychotherapy: Theory, Research and Practice, 4,* 110–115.

Straker, G., & Jacobson, R. S. (1981). Aggression, emotional maladjustment, and empathy in the abused child. *Developmental Psychology, 17,* 762–765.

Strayer, J. (1980). A naturalistic study of empathic behaviors and their relation to affective states and perspective-taking skills in preschool children. *Child Development, 51,* 815–822.

Strunk, O. (1957). Empathy: A review of theory and research. *Psychological Newsletter, 9,* 47–57.

Strunk, O., & Reed, K. (1960). The learning of empathy: A pilot study. *Journal of Pastoral Care, 14,* 44–48.

Sullivan, H. S. (1945). *Conceptions of modern psychiatry.* Washington, DC: W. A. White Psychiatric Foundation.

Sullivan, H. S. (1953). *The interpersonal theory of psychiatry,* New York: W. W. Norton.

Sutton, K. (1970). *Effects of modeled empathy and structured social class upon level of therapist displayed empathy.* Unpublished masters thesis, Syracuse University.

Sweeney, M. A., & Cottle, W. C. (1976). Nonverbal acuity: A comparison of counselors and noncounselors. *Journal of Counseling Psychology, 23,* 394–397.

Sweet, L. (1929). *The measurement of personal attitudes in younger boys.* New York: Association Press.

Symonds, P. (1946). *The dynamics of human adjustment.* New York: Appleton Century.

Symonds, P. M., & Dudek, S. (1956). Use of the Rorschach in the diagnosis of teacher effectiveness. *Journal of Projective Techniques and Personality Assessment 20,* 227–234.

Sywulak, A. E. (1977). The effect of filial therapy on parental acceptance and child adjustment. *Dissertation Abstracts International,* Order No. 7808432.

Taft, R. (1950). *Some correlates of the ability to make accurate social judgments.* Unpublished doctoral dissertation, University of California.

Taft, R. (1955). The ability to judge people. *Psychological Bulletin, 52,* 1–23.

Taguiri, R. (1969). Person perception. In G. Lindzey & E. Aronson (Eds.), *The handbook of social psychology* (Vol. 3, pp. 395–449). Reading, MA: Addison–Wesley.

Tausch, A., Kettner, U., Steinbach, I., & Tonnies, S. E. (1973). Effekte kindzentrierter Einzel-und Gruppengesprache mit unter-privileglierten Kindergarten und Grundschulkindern. *Psychol. in Erz. U. Unterricht, 20,* 77–88.

Tausch, A., Witters, O., & Albus, J. (1976). Erzieher-Kind-Interaktionen in einer Vorschul-Lernsituation im Kindergarten, *Psycho. in Erz. u. Unterricht, 23,* 1–10.

Tausch, R., & Tausch, A. (1980). *Verifying the facilitative dimensions in German schools, families, and with German clients.* Unpublished manuscript, West Germany.

Taylor, C. E. (1972). *Counselor's level of empathic understanding as a function of counselor sex and client sex.* Unpublished doctoral dissertation, University of South Carolina.

Taylor, R. H. (1975). *A comparison of conceptual and behavioral formats for interpersonal training.* Unpublished doctoral dissertation, University of California.

Tepper, D. T. Jr., & Haase, R. F. (1978). Verbal and nonverbal communication of facilitative conditions. *Journal of Counseling Psychology, 25,* 35–44.

Tharp, R. G., & Wetzel, R. J. (1969). *Behavior modification in the natural environment.* New York: Academic Press.

Thomas, D. L., Franks, D. D., & Calonico, J. M. (1972). Role-taking and power in social psychology. *American Sociological Review, 37,* 605–614.

Thompson, J. (1941). Development of facial expression of emotion in blind and seeing children. *Archives of Psychology, 37,* No. 264.

Thorndike, E. L., & Woodworth, R. S. (1901). The influence of improvement in one mental function upon the efficiency of other functions. *Psychological Review, 8,* 247–261.

Tinbergen, N. (1974). Ethology and stress disorders. *Science, 185,* 20–27.

Titchner, E. B. (1910). *Textbook of psychology.* New York: Macmillan.

Tomkins, S. S. (1962). *Affect, imagery, consciousness* (Vol. 1). *The positive affects.* New York: Springer.

Tomkins, S. S. (1963). *Affect, imagery, consciousness* (Vol. 2). *The negative affects.* New York: Springer.

Tomkins, S. S. (1981). The role of facial response in the experience of emotion: A reply to Tourangeau and Ellsworth. *Journal of Personality and Social Psychology, 40,* 355–357.

Tosi, D. J. (1970). Dogmatism within the counselor–client dyad. *Journal of Counseling Psychology, 17,* 284–288.

Tourangeau R., & Ellsworth, P. C. (1979). The role of facial response in the experience of emotion. *Journal of Personality and Social Psychology, 37,* 1519–1531.

Towe, A. L. (1973). Somatosensory cortex: Descending influence on ascending systems. In A. Iggo (Ed.), *Handbook of sensory physiology:* (Vol. 2) *Somatosensory system.* Berlin: Springer Verlag.

Towe, A. L., & Jabbur, S. J. (1961). Cortical inhibition of neurons in dorsal column nuclei of act. *Journal of Neurophysiology, 24,* 488–498.

Trevitt, V. (1964). *The American heritage: Design for national character.* Santa Barbara, CA: McNally & Loftin.

Trief, P. M. (1977). *The reduction of egocentrism in emotionally disturbed adolescents: Practical and theoretical aspects.* Unpublished doctoral dissertation, Syracuse University.

Traemeo–Ploetz, S. (1980). ''I'd come to you for therapy'': Interpretation, redefinition and paradox in Rogerian therapy. *Psychotherapy: Theory, Research and Practice, 17,* 246–257.

Trotter, R. (1983). Baby Face. *Psychology Today, 17,* 14–20.

Trout, D. L., & Rosenfeld, H. M. (1980). The effect of postural lean and body congruence on the judgment of psychotherapeutic rapport. *Journal of Nonverbal Behavior, 4,* 176–190.

Truax, C. B. (1963). Effective ingredients in psychotherapy: An approach to unravelling the patient–therapist interaction. *Journal of Counseling Psychology, 10,* 256–263.

Truax, C. B. (1966). Therapist empathy, warmth, and genuineness and patient personality change in group psychotherapy. *Journal of Clinical Psychology, 22,* 225–229.

Truax, C. B. (1970). Length of therapist response, accurate empathy and patient improvement. *Journal of Clinical Psychology, 26,* 539–541.

Truax, C. B., & Carkhuff, R. R. (1967). *Toward effective counseling and psychotherapy.* Chicago: Aldine.

Truax, C. B., Carkhuff, R. R., & Douds, J. (1964). Toward an integration of the didactic and experiential approaches to training in counseling and psychotherapy. *Journal of Counseling Psychology, 11,* 240–247.

Truax, C. B., Carkhuff, R. R., & Kodman, F. (1965). Relationships between therapist-offered conditions and patient change in group psychotherapy. *Journal of Clinical Psychology, 21,* 327–329.

Truax, C. B., & Mitchell, K. M. (1971). Research on certain therapist skills in relation to process and outcome. In A. E. Bergin & S. E. Garfield (Eds.), *Handbook of psychotherapy and behavioral change*. New York: Wiley.

Truax, C. B., & Tatum, C. D. (1966). An extension from the effective psychotherapeutic model to constructive personality change in preschool children. *Childhood Education, 42*, 456–462.

Truax, C. B., & Wargo, D. G. (1966). Psychotherapeutic encounters that change behavior: For better or for worse. *American Journal of Psychotherapy, 22*, 499–520.

Truax, C. B., Wargo, D. G., & Silber, L. D. (1966). Effects of group psychotherapy with high accurate empathy and nonpossessive warmth upon female institutionalized delinquents. *Journal of Abnormal Psychology, 71*, 267–274.

Truax, C. B., & Wittmer, J. (1971). The effects of therapist focus on patient anxiety source and the interaction with therapist level of accurate empathy. *Journal of Clinical Psychology, 27*, 297–299.

Truax, C. B., Wittmer, J., & Wargo, D. G. (1971). Effects of therapeutic conditions of accurate empathy, nonpossessive warmth, and genuineness of hospitalized mental patients during group psychotherapy. *Journal of Clinical Psychology, 27*, 137–142.

Trujillo, N. P., & Wartkin, T. A. (1968). The frowning sign multiple forehead furrows in peptic ulcer. *Journal of the American Medical Association, 205*, 218.

Trungpa, C. (1976). *The myth of freedom*. Berkeley: Shambala Press.

Tully, B. L. (1974). *The relationship of counselor and client feeling states to client self-exploration and counselor empathy*. Unpublished doctoral dissertation, East Texas State University.

Uhlemann, M. R., Lea, G. W., & Stone, G. L. (1976). Effect of instructions and modeling on trainees low in interpersonal-communication skills. *Journal of Counseling Psychology, 23*, 509–513.

Ulmer, G. (1939). Teaching geometry to cultivate reflective thinking: An experimental study with 1239 high school pupils. *Journal of Experimental Education, 8*, 18–25.

Underwood, B. E., & Moore, B. (1982). Perspective-taking and altruism. *Psychological Bulletin, 91*, 143–173.

Underwood, B. J. (1951). Associative transfer in verbal learning as a function of response similarity and first-list learning. *Journal of Experimental Psychology, 42*, 44–53.

Underwood, B. J., & Schulz, R. W. (1960). *Meaningfulness and verbal behavior*. New York: Lippincott.

Urberg, K. A., & Docherty, E. M. (1976). Development of role-taking skills in young children. *Developmental Psychology, 12*, 198–203.

Vallbo, A. B. (1974). Human muscle spindle discharge during isometric voluntary contractions. Amplitude relations between spindle frequency and torque. *Acta Physiologica Scandinavia, 90*, 19–36.

Vanderpool, J. P., & Barratt, E. S. (1970). Empathy: Towards a psychophysiological definition. *Diseases of the Nervous System, 31*, 464–467.

VanderVeen, F. (1965). Effects of the therapist and the patient on each other's therapeutic behavior. *Journal of Consulting Psychology, 29*, 19–26.

VanZeldt, R. H. (1952). Empathy test scores of union leaders. *Journal of Applied Psychology, 36*, 293–295.

Vernon, P. E. (1933). Some characteristics of the good judge of personality. *Journal of Social Psychology, 4*, 42–57.

Vesprani, G. J. (1969). Personality correlates of accurate empathy in a college companion program. *Journal of Consulting and Clinical Psychology, 33*, 722–727.

Vinacke, W. E. (1949). The judgment of facial expressions by three national–racial groups in Hawaii: I. Caucasian faces. *Journal of Personality, 17*, 407–429.

Vogelsong, E. L. (1974). *Empathy training for preadolescents in public schools*. Unpublished manuscript, Pennsylvania State University.

Vogelsong, E. L. (1975). *Preventive therapeutic programs for mothers and adolescent daughters:*

A follow-up of relationship enhancement versus discussion and booster versus no-booster methods. Unpublished doctoral dissertation, Pennsylvania State University.

Vogelsong, E. (1978). Relationship enhancement training for children *Elementary School Guidance and Counseling, 272–279.*

von Baeyer, C. L., & Wyant, G. M. (1982, March). *The "spring reflex" and psychological disturbance in chronic pain patients.* Paper presented at Symposium on Professional Psychology: Pain and pain management, University of Saskatchewan, Saskatoon.

Wagner, H. M. (1969). *A measurement of instructors' and students' perception of empathy, warmth, and genuineness in the instructors compared with the students' final examination scores.* Unpublished doctoral dissertation, University of Arkansas.

Wallbott, H. G. (1982). Contributions of the German "expression psychology" to nonverbal communication research (Part III): Gait, gestures, and body movement. *Journal of Nonverbal Behavior, 7,* 20–32.

Walstedt, J. J. (1968). Teaching empathy. *Mental Hygiene, 52,* 600–611.

Walter, G. H. (1977). *The relationship of teacher-offered empathy, genuineness, and respect to pupil classroom behavior.* Unpublished doctoral dissertation, University of Florida.

Walters, E. D. (1978). Skin temperature biofeedback training for empathic sensitivity in counseling students. *Dissertation Abstracts International, 38,* 5261-A.

Ware, L. (1977). Parent training in empathy. *The Psychiatric Forum, 7,* 33–38.

Wasz–Hocket, O., Partanen, T. J., Vuorenkoski, V., Valanne, E., & Michelson, K. (1964). Effects of training and ability to identify preverbal vocalizations. *Developmental Medicine and Child Neurology, 6,* 393–398.

Waters, E., Wippman, J., & Srowfe, L. A. (1978). Attachment, positive affect and competence in the peer group: Two studies in construct validation. *Child Development, 50,* 821–829.

Watts, A. W. (1961). *Psychotherapy East and West.* New York: Pantheon.

Watts, A. W. (1974, Fall). On the work of Charlotte Selver. *Bulletin of the Charlotte Selver Foundation, 8,* 2–7. (Available from Charlotte Selver Foundation, 32 Cedars Rd., Caldwell, NJ 07006)

Wedeck, J. (1947). The relationship between personality and "psychological ability." *British Journal of Psychology, 37,* 133–151.

Weinstein, E. A. (1969). The development of interpersonal competence. In D. A. Goslin (Ed.), *Handbook of socialization theory and research.* Chicago: Rand McNally.

Weinstein, G., & Fantini, M. D. (1970). *Toward humanistic education.* New York: Praeger.

Weinstein, L. (1980). Parent empathy, child empathy, and student performance. *Dissertation Abstracts International,* (7A)2946.

Weits, E. (1980). The effect of progressive relaxation training on empathy. *Dissertation Abstracts International, 40,* 5738-A.

Weitz, S. (Ed.). (1974). *Nonverbal communication: Readings with commentary.* New York: Oxford University Press.

Welkowitz, J., Cohen, J., & Ortmeyer, D. (1967). Value system similarity: Investigation of patient–therapist dyads. *Journal of Consulting Psychology, 31,* 48–55.

Wenegrat, A. (1974). A factor analytic study of the Truax accurate empathy scale. *Psychotherapy: Theory, Research and Practice, 11,* 48–51.

Wentink, E. (1975). *The effect of social perspective-taking training on role-taking ability and social interaction in preschool and elementary school children.* Presented at International Study for the Study of Behavioral Development, Guildford, Great Britain.

Whatmore, G. B. (1966). Some neurophysiologic differences between schizophrenia and depression. *American Journal of Psychiatry, 123,* 712–716.

Whatmore, G. B., & Ellis, R. M., Jr. (1959). Some neurophysiologic aspects of depressed states: An electromyographic study. *Archives of General Psychiatry, 1,* 70–80.

Whatmore, G. B., & Ellis, R. M., Jr. (1962). Further neurophysiologic aspects of depressed states: An electromyographic study. *Archives of General Psychiatry, 6,* 243–253.

Whatmore, G. B., & Kohli, D. R. (1974). *The physiopathology and treatment of functional disorders*. New York: Grune & Stratton.

Whitehorn, J. C., & Betz, B. J. (1954). A study of psychotherapeutic relationships between physicians and schizophrenic patients. *American Journal of Psychiatry, 3,* 321–331.

Wieman, R. J. (1973). *Conjugal relationship modification and reciprocal reinforcement: A comparison of treatments for marital discord.* Unpublished doctoral dissertation, Pennsylvania State University.

Wienpahl, P. (1964). *The matter of Zen: A brief account of Zazen.* New York: New York University Press.

Winnicott, D. W. (1965). *The maturational processes and the facilitating environment.* New York: International Universities Press.

Winnicott, D. W. (1970). The mother–infant experience of mutuality. In E. J. Anthony & T. Bewedek (Eds.), *Parenthood: Its psychology and psychopathology,* Boston: Little, Brown.

Wisdom, S. S. (1978). *The relationship of teacher offered empathy to behaviors described by a system of interaction analysis in classes for the handicapped.* Unpublished doctoral dissertation, University of Alabama.

Withall, J., & Lewis, W. W. (1963). Social interaction in the classroom. In N. L. Gage (Ed.), *Handbook of research on teaching.* Chicago: Rand McNally.

Wolf, S., & Wolff, H. G. (1947). *Human gastric function* (2nd ed.). New York: Oxford University Press.

Woo, S. L. Y., Matthews, J. V., Akeson, W. H., Amiel, D., & Convery, F. R. (1975). Connective tissue response to immobility. *Arthritis and Rheumatism, 18,* 257–264.

Wood, M. A. (1977). *Acquisition and transfer of assertiveness in passive and aggressive adolescents through the use of structured learning therapy.* Unpublished doctoral dissertation, Syracuse University.

Woodbury, J. W., Gordon, A. M., & Conrad, J. T. (1965). Muscle. In T. C. Ruch, H. D. Patton, J. W. Woodbury, & A. L. Towe (Eds.), *Neurophysiology.* Philadelphia: W. B. Saunders.

Woodrow, H. (1927). The effect of type of training upon transference. *Journal of Educational Psychology, 18,* 159–172.

Woodworth, R. S. (1938). *Experimental psychology.* New York: Henry Holt.

Wundt, W. (1911). *Grundzuge der physiologischen psychologie.* Leipzig: Engelmann.

Wylie, L., & Stafford, R. (1977). *Beaux gestes: A guide to French body talk.* New York: Dutton.

Yarrow, L. J., Rubenstein, J. L., Pederson, F. A. & Jenkowski, J. J. (1972). Dimensions of early stimulation and their differential effects on infant development. *Merrill Palmer Quarterly of Behavior Development, 18,* 205–218.

Yergensen, D. C. (1978). *The effects of dyadic and patient variables upon therapists' empathic ability: A multivariate study.* Unpublished doctoral dissertation, California School of Professional Psychology, Fresno.

Young–Browne, G., Rosenfield, H., & Horowitz, F. D. (1977). Infant discrimination of facial expressions. *Child Development, 48,* 55–562.

Young, R. K., & Underwood, B. J. (1954). Transfer in verbal materials with dissimilar stimuli and response similarity varied. *Journal of Experimental Psychology, 47,* 153–159.

Youniss, J. (1975). Another perspective on social cognition. In A. Pich (Ed.), *Minnesota symposium on child psychology* (Vol. 9). Minneapolis: University of Minnesota Press.

Zahn–Waxler, C., Cummings E. M., McKnew, D. H., & Radke–Tanner, M. (1984). Altruism, aggression, and social interactions in young children with a manic depressive parent. Child Development, 54, 1522–1528.

Zahn–Waxler, C., & Radke–Yarrow, M. (1982). The development of altruism: Alternative research strategies. In N. Eisenberg, *The development of prosocial behavior* (pp. 109–137). New York: Academic Press.

Zahn–Waxler, C., Radke–Yarrow, M., & King, R. (1979). Child rearing and children's prosocial initiations toward victims of distress. *Child Development, 50,* 319–330.

Zaidel, S. F. & Mehrabian (1969). The ability to communicate and infer positive and negative attitudes facially and vocally. *Journal of Experimental Research in Personality, 3,* 233–241.

Zajonc, R. B. (1980). Feeling and thinking: Preferences need no inferences. *American Psychologist, 35,* 151–175.

Zuckerman, M., DeFrank, R. S., Hall, J. A., Larrance, D. T., & Rosenthal, R. (1979). Facial and vocal cues of deception and honesty. *Journal of Experimental and Social Psychology, 15,* 378–396.

Zuckerman, M., Hall, J. A., DeFrank, R. S. & Rosenthal, R. (1976). Encoding and decoding of spontaneous and posed facial expressions. *Journal of Personality and Social Psychology, 34,* 966–977.

Zuckerman, M., Klorman, R., Larrance, D. T. & Spiegel, N. H. (1981). Facial autonomic and subjective components of emotion: The facial feedback hypothesis versus the externalizer-internalizer distinction. *Journal of Personality and Social Psychology, 41,* 929–944.

Zuckerman, M., Lysets, M. S., Koivermaki, J. H. & Rosenthal, R. (1975). Encoding and decoding nonverbal cues of emotion. *Journal of Personality and Social Psychology, 32,* 1068–1076.

Zwislocki, J. J., & Goodman, D. A. (1980). Absolute scaling of sensory magnitudes: A validation. *Perception and Psychophysics, 28,* 28–38.

Author Index

Subject Index

A

aestetics, 4
affective component, 18–20, 33–45
affective discrimination, 18
affective reverberation, Alexander technique, 96–97
  by Bioenergetics, 96–96
  by biofeedback, 98–100
  by dance therapy, 98
  by Feldenkrais training, 97
  by focusing, 104–105
  by meditation, 100–103
  by Reichian therapy, 95–96
  by Rolfing, 94–95
  by sensory awareness, 103–104
  by Structural Integration, 94–95
affective reverberation component, 62–63
affective reverberation, Laban/Bartenieff method, 105–107
affective reverberation training, 228–229
affective sensitivity, 5
Alexander technique, 96–97
altruism, 33
altruistic motivation, 13

B

Bioenergetics, 95–96
biofeedback, 80–93, 98–100

C

Character Analysis, 79–85
classical conditioning, 14
cognitive analysis component, 109–130
cognitive analysis training, 229
cognitive component, 16–18, 20–31
communication component, 45–51
communication training, 229–230

D

dance therapy, 98
decentration, 20–21
Didactic-Experiential training, 196–201
display rules, 116–117

E

egocentric empathy, 16
emotion, facial components of, 121–127
emotional communication, nonverbal, 127–130
emotional responsiveness, 18
empathic arousal, classical conditioning, 14
empathic arousal, motor mimicry, 15
  observed discomfort, 15
  reactive newborn cry, 14
  role taking, 15
  symbolic association, 15
empathic distress, 14